Critical Legal Studies

CRITICAL LEGAL STUDIES

EDITED BY
Allan C. Hutchinson

Osgoode Hall Law School
York University, Toronto

ROWMAN & LITTLEFIELD PUBLISHERS, INC.

ROWMAN & LITTLEFIELD PUBLISHERS, INC.

Published in the United States of America in 1989
by Rowman & Littlefield Publishers, Inc.
81 Adams Drive, Totowa, New Jersey 07512

Library of Congress Cataloging-in-Publication Data

Critical legal studies.

  "December 1986."
  Includes index.
  1. Law—Philosophy. 2. Sociological jurisprudence.
I. Hutchinson, Allan C., 1951-   .
K235.C754   1989   340'.1   87-9627
ISBN 0-8476-7532-1
ISBN 0-8476-7533-5 (pbk.)

Printed in the United States of America

Contents

vi   *Contents*

Preface

Little needs to be said about the reasons for an anthology of CLS work. The problem arises in selecting a small number of pieces from a continually expanding body of excellent work and in editing them sensitively and sensibly to meet the space constraints that a commercial project inevitably imposes. I have made the selections and done the editing in a way that tries to reflect and accommodate many people's view of the best/most representative/significant/helpful/etc., work in CLS. The end result reveals some of my own prejudices and preferences, but I hope that they are not too idiosyncratic or jarring. I am very conscious of the fact that any effort to organize the material has imposed a particular structure and order on it. While I believe it to be defensible and illuminating, I know that my structuring will inevitably point the reader to certain understandings and conclusions about CLS. Accordingly, I urge all readers to remember that this is only a sample and assortment of Critical offerings: there is no substitute for reading CLS work in its original, growing, and unedited form.

The choice of material and the wielding of editorial scissors have to a large extent been dictated by the overall mix. The editing of individual pieces will, I hope, be understandable in the context of the accompanying selections and general organization. Most pieces have been heavily edited. I have left in the original footnote numbers to indicate that supporting documentation and arguments have been omitted. Also time moves on: some of the selections form part of a continuing dialogue, but others have been qualified or restated in response to developing circumstances. Nonetheless, even though ferment continues apace, this book comprises an up-to-date and representative distillation of CLS work and thinking.

I believe that the dangers and risks in an edited collection of work are more than compensated for by the benefits and gains of such a project. I hope that the book will make CLS work more available and more accessible to an even broader range of readers and enhance discussion of it both inside and outside the United States and inside and outside the law schools. Further, as editor, I have tried not to betray the confidence and trust that the contributors have placed in me.

In putting together this anthology, I have relied on the industry and initiative of many people. I am especially grateful to Jane Hutchinson, Gail Kenny, Jenny Neil, and Marcus Pratt. Also, I would like to thank Patrick Monahan for his intellectual support and friendship; in a real sense, this collection flows from our joint efforts to appreciate and benefit from CLS work. After beginning as a "sympathetic critic" or "critical sympathizer," I now see myself as an enthusiastic member of CLS; my own work is profoundly influenced by the insights and ideas of CLS.

Throughout the preparation of this book, the problem has been not what to include, but what to leave out from the rich body of Critical literature. It is fitting that this book should be dedicated to all Critical scholars everywhere, past and future, who have combined to make CLS the exciting and important force that it is and will continue to be.

ALLAN C. HUTCHINSON

Critical Legal Studies

1

Introduction

"Do you know who made you?"
"Nobody, as I knows on," said the child, with a short laugh . . .
"I 'spect I grow'd."
                    Harriet Beecher Stowe, *Uncle Tom's Cabin*

Something of a precocious child, Critical Legal Studies is ten years old. In its short but hectic life, it has already made a significant contribution to modern legal thought and practice. Measured quantitatively, its presence is strong and incontestable: around 700 articles and books in print can be grouped loosely under the rubric of CLS. Its qualitative impact is more controversial: its intellectual reception runs from enthusiastic acceptance to vehement rejection. Indeed, the intensity and heat generated by CLS writers, both collectively and individually, testifies to its growing significance in jurisprudential debate and practice. Many have chastised CLS for its irreverence, and a few have gone so far as to demand its ejection from the law schools.[1] Yet most would agree that CLS is the most challenging and exciting genre of legal criticism to force its way onto the jurisprudential scene for many a decade.

As CLS faces the awkward rites of adolescent passage—a certain crisis of identity, a keener appreciation of gender and race differences, and a relative loss of social innocence—the time is ripe to take stock of the movement's development and to explain the nature and thrust of its central ideas and ambitions. Like any legal scholarship, CLS deserves to be treated on its merits and to speak on its own behalf. Any evaluation or assessment ought to be based on an informed and genuine understanding; caricature has no place. As the body of CLS work grows apace, such an undertaking is a daunting prospect. This book is offered as a basic primer on CLS. It is intended to be an accessible and representative sample of the CLS genre that will satisfy the needs of the initiated and uninitiated alike. In a similar vein, this introduction provides some general contextual material and observations on the sources and sweep of CLS.[2]

* * *

1

Modern jurisprudence is an intellectual battleground in which internecine struggle is commonplace and seems to represent its natural condition. Vast intellectual energies are spent in hair-splitting exercises, and minor disagreements are allowed (or encouraged) to mushroom into full-blown intellectual wars. But the divergence of opinion is more apparent than real. Behind the theoretical clamor and personal antagonism is a not-so-surprising homogeneity of philosophical interest and political affiliation. There exists a tacitly shared agenda of issues to be confronted, and their attempted resolution proceeds on the basis of joint assumptions about the availability and acceptability of certain methods and answers. The vast bulk of this mainstream scholarship is devoted to describing and justifying the role of the judiciary within a liberal democracy: how do extant legal materials and practices constrain judges so as to satisfy the democratic demand for judicial objectivity and the popular demand for social justice? The nature and siting of those constraints consumes legal academics' attention; that some constraints exist is taken for granted.

Over the past decade, the vigorous challenge of CLS to jurisprudential orthodoxy has gained momentum and force. CLS has mounted a major offensive on the whole edifice of modern jurispudence. In the face of this determined defiance, the warring factions of traditional jurisprudence have closed ranks to resist better the Critical challenge to the terms and conditions of traditional jurisprudential warfare. It is one thing to fight over the meaning and enforcement of "the entrenched clauses of the constitution of the republic of [legal] knowledge,"[3] but it is considered entirely another thing to call for root-and-branch reform of that constitution or, even more threatening still, to decry the need for any constitution at all.

Put crudely, the central thrust of the CLS attack has been to follow through on and go beyond the realist project by allying it to a program of "left" politics. Many CLS conclusions are far from novel or surprising, but they do comprise the most sustained and serious attempt to date by leftist lawyers to expose the political dimensions of the adjudicative and legal process. Not simply an intellectual tendency, it exists as a membership organization. Many of the founding CLS members were students during the civil rights movement and the anti-Vietnam campaign of the 1960s. As such, CLS recognizes these activist roots as the energy source of much of its theoretical endeavor—nothing is as practical as a good theory. Practical commitment and group solidarity remain crucial values in the CLS ethos. In the early 1970s, the closest place to a haven for legal radicals was the Law and Society Association. But there was already disenchantment with its "empirico-behaviorist" alignment.[4] After some discussion, CLS was officially born in the spring of 1977 at a conference at the University of Wisconsin at Madison.[5] Its membership includes law teachers, lawyers, social theorists, and law students. As well as being an intellectual focus and clearinghouse for left writers, it represents a collaborative network to support and reinforce the professional lives of like-minded people.

There are many different strands to CLS, and its members run from the disaffected liberal through the radical feminist to the utopian anarchist. Much of its organizational strength and intellectual integrity reside in this diversity and eclecticism. But the members unite in their common opposition to the intellectual and political dominance of the liberal establishment. Although liberalism once contributed to the improvement of the social lot, it has now outlived its usefulness and has become a dangerous political anachronism. Offended by the hierarchical structures of domination that characterize modern society, CLS people work toward a world that is more just and egalitarian. They do not wish to embroider still further the patchwork quilt of liberal politics, but strive to cast it aside and reveal the vested interests that thrive under its snug cover. Their ambition is to make a bigger social bed with more popular bedding. It is not surprising that CLS's particular contribution to this social struggle has concentrated on the leading part that law has played in maintaining the status quo and stymieing efforts to effect fundamental change.

For CLS, critique must begin and proceed with the operation of law as ideology. This is not to trivialize the coercive functioning of much law, but to supplement and strengthen the radical critique. For CLS, the Rule of Law is a mask that lends to existing social structures the appearance of legitimacy and inevitability; it transforms the contingency of social history into a fixed set of structural arrangements and ideological commitments (see Chapter 8). CLS's demonstration that the status quo and its intellectual footings, far from being built on the hard rock of historical necessity, are actually sited on the shifting sands of social contingency, is both critical and constructive. Not only does it expose the illusory and fraudulent claims of traditional writers, but it also clears the ground for different and transformative ways of thinking about law and society (see Chapter 11). By laying bare the rhetorical status of law, it becomes possible to subvert law's philosophical and political authority. In a world in which law plays such an important role and in which it is almost impossible to appreciate social life without utilizing, often implicitly, the framework of legal relations, the need to understand the historicity and ideology of the lawyer's way of thinking about and acting in the world is extremely important (see Chapter 5). From abstract theory to thick descriptions of legal doctrine (see Chapters 7 and 14), CLS writers have explored the intimate relation between law and the routine practices of social life.

In mounting its uncompromising offensive on law and legal theory, CLS has operated on two major and mutually supportive fronts. Although they function in harness, they can be treated separately for the purposes of explication as operating "internally" and "externally." The internal critique takes seriously conventional writing, both scholarly and judicial. CLS engages jurists and judges on their own turf and shows how they fail to live up to their vaunted standards of rationality and coherence: they cannot withstand the debilitating force of their own critical apparatus (see Chapter 9). The main target of CLS has been the crucial distinction between law and politics or, to be more precise, the alleged contrast between the open ideological nature of political debate and the bounded objectivity of legal reasoning. CLS rejects this axiomatic premise of traditional lawyering (Chapter 10). Beneath the patina of legalistic jargon, law and judicial decisionmaking are neither separate nor separable from disputes about the kind of world we want to live in. Legal reasoning consists of an endless and contradictory process of making, refining, reworking, collapsing, and rejecting doctrinal categories and distinctions. Doctrinal patterns can never be objectively justified and consist of a haphazard cluster of ad hoc and fragile compromises; legal doctrine is a small and unrepresentative sample of conflictual problems and their contingent solution (Chapter 3).

The esoteric and convoluted nature of legal doctrine is an accommodating screen to obscure its indeterminacy and the inescapable element of judicial choice. In the cold light of CLS day, traditional lawyering is reduced to a clumsy and repetitive series of bootstrap arguments, and legal discourse becomes only a stylized version of political discourse (Chapter 15). Yet, and most important, this revelation of indeterminacy is not tantamount to a dismissal of legal doctrine as incoherent or unintelligible; its purpose is to clarify rather than to cloud our understanding of doctrinal operations (Chapter 12). Nor is it tantamount to a suggestion that doctrinal development is autonomous from the status quo–oriented prejudices of ideological debate: there is a deep logic and structure to law that broadly reflects the contradictory relations of modern hierarchical society (Chapter 18). There exists doctrinal indeterminacy with an ideological slant. The judicial emperor, clothed and coifed in appropriately legitimate and voguish garb by the scholarly rag trade, chooses and acts to protect and preserve the propertied interest of vested white and male power (Chapters 6 and 15).

The CLS claims of indeterminacy and contradiction do not simply penetrate legal doctrine and theorizing; they go to the very heart of liberal democratic politics. Doctrinal indeterminacy is a localized illustration of the bankruptcy of liberal theory and practice. The ailing corpus of black-letter legal theory cannot be made good by injecting a dose of black-letter political theory. Liberalism embraces a host of dualities, such as subjective/objective, male/female, public/private, self/other, individual/community, or whatever, as devices for providing a plausible description of the world and a convenient prescription for action. As in the legal sphere, political debate is open-ended and unclosable. It exhausts itself in an agonized struggle for the ever elusive Archimedean point outside history and society from which to mediate the dualities and sustain a position of normative equilibrium. Liberalism is pervaded by contradictory principles with no metatheory to reconcile them. Political decisions and social arrangements can never be justified objectively and amount to contingent choices. But while they are arbitrary in a theoretical sense, these decisions are not arbitrary in any practical sense, for they follow the general pattern of established interests (Chapter 16).

Although most CLS work is seen to work along the "internal" front, it draws much of its theoretical resources and supplies from the simultaneous campaign being waged on the "external" front. While the internal critique is powerful and productive, its success is necessarily limited. A demonstration of rational incoherence and internal contradiction is fatal only within a liberal tradition of rationalist epistemology.[6] This concession far from trivializes the internal critique, for the established and irrepressible presence of incoherence and contradiction delegitimates and demystifies the authority of law in constructing and maintaining social reality. To be fully convincing and successful, the whole liberal tradition of rationalist epistemology must be discredited and dismantled. This is exactly what the "external" critique of CLS takes aim at (Chapter 4). CLS does not simply contest the practical policies yielded by traditional legal theorizing; it rejects the very basis of contemporary legal theorizing. As in the celebrated dispute between Galileo and the Italian establishment, it is not merely the truth of nature that is at stake, but the nature of truth itself. CLS seeks to reformulate the ground rules by revising the epistemological and political criteria for valid legal theory. Drawing on the work of radical philosophers and social theorists, CLS is attempting to provide a fresh touchstone for distinguishing good knowledge from bad. Although traditional scholars pride themselves on being engaged in "a continuing dialogue with reality,"[7] CLS rejects the structure of that dialogue and the substance of that reality (Chapter 13).

Despite its pluralist protestations, mainstream lawyering and legal thought remain in thrall to an ideal of legal/political rationality. CLS writers have ruthlessly attacked this "foundational" thinking; no privileged ground exists for legal/political argument to stand or build on (Chapter 1). Doctrinal understanding is more a matter of professional familiarity and political partiality than moral insight and technical correctness. Legal/political rationality is no less constructed than the courts of law themselves. For CLS, there is no position of theoretical innocence or political neutrality. Any act of interpretation or judgment, in both its practical and theoretical performance, has indissociable political and historical dimensions. The question of what amounts to valid knowledge is itself a socio-political matter. Legal epistemology is ideological warfare fought by other, more esoteric means.

*   *   *

By operating along these two fronts, CLS has waged an increasing campaign against the privileged citadel of traditional lawyering. Yet no matter how well CLS is presented in its own positive terms, there will inevitably arise the need to locate it in relation to other radical trends in law and politics. While this can be a useful and productive exercise, it can easily slip into an obsessive and sterile witchhunt. Some critics use such inquiries as a weak excuse to sidetrack the debate and dismiss CLS solely on the basis of the company it keeps; others use it as an occasion to indulge in the most counterproductive and unnecessary form of family feuding. Nevertheless, as already stated, CLS proudly draws much of its intellectual inspiration and radical energy from legal realism and marxism: its originality lies in its particular borrowing from and combining of these fertile sources. At its best CLS is a self-conscious blending and baking of neo-realist and neo-marxist ingredients in such a way as to produce a singular and fruity jurisprudential cake that, it is hoped, appeals to and nurtures the popular appetite.

At this point, it should be noted that CLS is an American phenomenon. Although it derives much of its intellectual inspiration from European sources and is beginning to establish itself outside the United States, CLS's political and legal project is firmly anchored in concrete American conditions. Its very shape and life history, short as it is, can be fully comprehended only in terms of the history and practice of the American legal, academic, and political establishments. That history is, of course, complex and itself the basis for interpretive controversy. The most pertinent factors include the lack of any established or sizable left tradition in popular politics; the isolation and victimization of left intellectuals in the universities; the male monopoly on legal and political power; the legacy of institutional racism; the thoroughly professional orientation of legal education; the neo-formalists' domestication of realism's radical message; and the centrality of the Supreme Court in the American constitutional scheme and national psyche. To ignore its American identity is not only to run the considerable risk of misunderstanding the substantive thrust of CLS, but also to undermine its commitment to comprehending action and thinking as largely constituted by their socio-political and historical context.[8]

Is CLS realism rewarmed or realism rejected?[9] It is both and neither. As CLS views it, in the 1920s and 1930s realism toppled the regnant formalism, not as a prelude to overthrowing liberalism but as a way of making good on the liberal promise. Realism's attacks were never intended to be more than a palace revolution.[10] The realists were ideologically and practically wedded to the reform program of New Deal liberalism. They effected a pragmatic shift of institutional focus rather than a thoroughgoing rejection of liberal politics: they wanted to replace judge-dominated legal science with bureaucracy-wielded policy science. Indeed, the fact that most lawyers today can chant, with considerable credibility, that "we are all realists now"[11] says much about the traditional view of realism. In contrast, CLS has pushed through on the realist assault on formalism and extended it to political as well as legal claims of scientific rationality. Like the neo-formalists, such as Hart and Sacks, who followed them, the realists smothered the truly radical insights and implications of its critique. CLS has salvaged these powerful insights and insists that no objectively correct results exist, regardless of whether presented in terms of legal doctrine or policy analysis and no matter how skilled the advocate or judge. The taking of political sides is inescapable.

Although CLS offers a thoroughgoing and ideological critique of law and liberalism, it has not stepped back into the welcoming arms of an orthodox marxism. CLS has no truck with the belief that there is a direct causal and substantive nexus between material conditions and the legal superstructure; it denies the possibility of discovering intelligible and settled laws of historical/social/economic/etc., change. While recognizing that law often does act as a weapon and shield for the "capitalistic" organization of society, CLS argues that law functions as much as a legitimating force as a deterministic instrument; law and society are not separate spheres, but are mutually constitutive and interpenetrative. In this sense, CLS builds on the more *Critical* part of the marxist canon.[12] Like liberalism, marxism glimpsed the corrosive power of social relativity and historical contingency, but suffered a final lack of nerve in completing the modern rebellion against the view that there is any natural or inevitable form of social organization. CLS has refused to shrink back from the subversive implications of this imperative (Chapter 19).

* * *

As with all fledgling radical movements, CLS has experienced the predictable series of critical reactions to its development and growth. Although often following a bare chronology, these reactions tend to overlap and occur simultaneously. In the first few years, the best response was thought to be no response: to acknowledge CLS's existence, let alone its possible merit, would have provided unnecessary publicity and legitimacy for a dangerous group of scholars and ideas. When CLS expanded in numbers and literature, the reaction was ridicule and condescension: CLS was a tasteless joke, a petulant phase from which its more perceptive members would soon turn and move on to more mature and professional concerns: "Let's face it, who could take seriously such absurd claims?" Not simply surviving but thriving on such patronizing attitudes came the most evasive, yet cunning reply to CLS: "What's new? We've heard all this before. Now tell us something we don't already know." Although this jurisprudential form of confession-and-avoidance has some force (for example, CLS's relation to realism and marxism), it offers little succor to non-CLS writers, for the best of those other and earlier ideas have been studiously and steadfastly ignored. Moreover, this response signals a certain lack of traditional confidence and opens the way, if successfully negotiated, to the next reactive stage. This is the serious or, at least, pseudo-serious intellectual engagement in which traditional scholars claim to face and undermine the theoretical claims and radical arguments. In one sense, we are entering that phase now. The resilience and visibility of CLS have obliged traditional scholars, like Ronald Dworkin, at least to acknowledge it and to make some cursory response.[13]

Although this book and this introduction do not cover the vast secondary and critical literature that is growing up around CLS, some recurring and related criticisms are worth mentioning. For instance, it is often remarked that, despite its sharp critical edge, CLS does not offer any constructive alternatives to liberalism and that, when it does, they are hopelessly utopian. First, the claim that constructive proposals are lacking is wildly inaccurate in simple descriptive terms. CLS is full of suggestions on what a just society might look like and, what is more important, how it might be achieved (see Chapters 17 and 18). The fact that traditional theorizing has no need to provide an account of "how to get from here to there" underlies the proximity of its own reform proposals to the status quo. This is not to deny that criticism alone can be a liberating and creative form of therapy. By unfreezing the world as it now appears, new possibilities for meaningful self-development and innovative social interaction can be imagined and grasped. Indeed, the elaboration of grand schemes for future societies runs the danger of simply imposing one more form of "alien" social consciousness; "one must step outside the liberal paradigm, into a realm where truth may be experiential, where knowledge resides in world views that are themselves situated in history, where power and ideas do not exist separately."[14] Only when each individual victim becomes the means of his or her emancipation will social liberation be possible.

Of course, at this point, the charge of utopianism is leveled at CLS. Yet, since these suggestions make good only on some of the supposed virtues and aspirations of liberal democracy, such criticism reveals the establishment's fearful lack of vision and the extent of its enslavement to the status quo. CLS should wear the badge of utopianism with pride, for more, not less, not-status-quo-oriented thinking is needed.

Moreover, the inhabitants of traditional glass houses should be wary about throwing such critical brickbats. For instance, the ostensibly hard-headed practitioners of law and economics view life as a perfect market, populated by rational, risk-neutral, perfectly informed egoists who voluntarily maximize their stable preferences in conditions of relative scarcity. Not only is this objectionable as utopian speculation, but it is used as *the* basis for explaining and organizing our *present* society.

Of course, many hazards, hidden and otherwise, emerge at this stage of reaction when traditional theorists begin to engage CLS. Apart from the obvious danger (CLS might be wrong!), a real likelihood is that there will be only a sham locking of academic horns. Insofar as CLS attacks the very nature and status of traditional theorizing, the siting of this confrontation in traditional scholarship's own theoretical backyard tends to beg the question. Although CLS maintains that "the entrenched clauses of the constitution of the republic of legal knowledge" are, like the law itself, confused and indeterminate, its fundamental challenge is to the whole constitutional structure and its political ethos. The problem and disagreement are ideological, not philosophical: theory is a part of, and not apart from, an ideological position.

Also, while this stage of engaged reaction indicates the attainment of institutional respectability and legitimacy, it is a dangerous occasion for that very reason. It represents the incipient signs of cooptation; subtle strategies are designed and implemented to avert and neutralize CLS's destabilizing influence by absorbing its major radical insights. CLS must resist at all costs—for its very existence is at stake—the urge to turn it into one more exotic delicacy on the smorgasbord of liberal pluralism. Beneath the superficial color and enticing aroma of these liberal offerings lie the oppressive blandness and uniformity of political taste. Traditional scholars embrace Critical colleagues only to better smother and suffocate their radical threat.[15] In struggling to avoid conventional approval, it must not define itself out of critical contention. CLS must strive to dwell on the threshold; it must decline any invitation to step inside as well as resist the temptation to withdraw to the political wilderness of resigned irrelevance.

The next few years will be crucial for CLS. Like any child passing through its teenage years, CLS will have to struggle to retain its radical sense of self and to remain true to its Critical ideals in the face of the pervasive socializing pressures of liberal maturity. As it almost inevitably becomes an institution in its own right, it must be on guard against hierarchy and inertia in its own ranks; solidarity is valuable only as a support for risk and not as a cushion for complacency. The future is open, but dangerous. But, as Duncan Kennedy puts it, "it was hardly probable that in late '70s and early '80s America there would arise anything like the critical legal studies movement. And if we've been lucky in the past, why shouldn't we be lucky in the next stage? *Pessimism of the intellect, optimism of the will.*"[16]

NOTES

1. See John Carrington, "Of Law and The River," *Journal of Legal Education* 34 (1984): 227; "Exchange," *Journal of Legal Education* 35 (1985): 1.

2. This introduction draws on a few, but by no means all, of the ideas and insights developed in Allan Hutchinson and Patrick Monahan, "Law, Politics, and the Critical Legal Scholars: The Unfolding Drama of American Legal Thought," *Stanford Law Review* 36 (1984): 199. I am grateful to Patrick Monahan for allowing me to use this material.

3. Bryan Magee, "Sandcastles and the Search for Certainty," *The Listener* 99 (1978): 570, an interview with Ernest Gellner.

4. On the relation between CLS and Law and Society, see David Trubek, "Where the Action Is: Critical Legal Studies and Empiricism," *Stanford Law Review* 36 (1984): 575.

5. For an interesting and more personalized account of the early years of CLS, see Henry Schlegel, "Notes Towards an Intimate, Opinionated, and Affectionate History of the Conference on Critical Legal Studies," *Stanford Law Review* 36 (1984): 391.

6. See Alan Hunt, "The Theory of Critical Legal Studies," *Oxford Journal of Legal Studies* 6 (1986): 33.

7. Ellen Peters, "Reality and the Language of the Law," *Yale Law Journal* 90 (1981): 1193.

8. This is not to suggest that CLS has to remain a purely American phenomenon; CLS already has an international network and strong presence in other countries. Its insights might need some adjustment however, when applied in those other jurisdictions. For my own attempt to offer a CLS analysis of Anglo-Canadian, as well as American, law and legal thought, see Allan Hutchinson, *Dwelling on the Threshold* (Toronto: Carswell Publishing, 1987).

9. This question is generally posed by non–CLS writers. Whereas many in CLS, like Alan Freeman and Mark Tushnet, are content to see it as a continuation of the realist project, it is critics/observers who seem to be drawn into this issue. This fact alone is reason for suspicion about the motives of a few of these writers. See, for example, Debra Livingston, " 'Round and 'Round the Bramble Bush: From Legal Realism to Critical Legal Scholarship," *Harvard Law Review* 95 (1982): 1669; Boliek, "The Two Worlds of The Trashers and the Lotus-Eaters: Flushing CLS from Out of the Bramble Bush," *Alabama Law Review* 37 (1985): 89; and Jeffrey A. Standen, "Critical Legal Studies as an Anti-Positivist Phenomenon," *Virginia Law Review* 72 (1986): 983.

10. See G. Gilmore, *The Ages of American Law* (New Haven: Yale Univ. Press, 1977), p. 87.

11. W. Twining, *Karl Llewellyn and the Realist Movement* (London: Weidenfeld & Nicolson, 1973), p. 382.

12. See. A. Gouldner, *The Two Marxisms* (New York: Seabury Press, 1980). Although the influence of the Frankfurt School, consisting of scholars like Adorno, Horkheimer, and Marcuse, was very strong at the beginning, the insights of other continental writers, like Foucault, Derrida, and Habermas, have been incorporated into more recent CLS work.

13. See R. Dworkin, *Law's Empire* (Cambridge: Harvard University Press, 1986), pp. 271–75.

14. Alan Freeman, "Truth and Mystification in Legal Scholarship," *Yale Law Journal* 90 (1981): 1237.

15. See G. Edward White, "The Inevitability of Critical Legal Studies," *Stanford Law Review* 36 (1984): 672: "If history is any guide, liberalism will absorb and convert Critical theory, thus producing a new synthesis. Or, possibly, liberalism may collapse . . .

and, over time, a new orthodoxy may emerge, perhaps containing some of the presuppositions of CLS. But, either way, very little will have changed, and nothing will have progressed, let alone of being transformed. Change is neither transformation nor progress; it is just a series of inevitabilities."

16. "Psycho-Social CLS: A Comment on the Cardozo Symposium," *Cardozo Law Review* 6 (1985): 1031.

PART I

Toward Critical Theory

In these opening pieces, the most important themes and motifs of Critical thinking are introduced. The attempt is to push deep into the intellectual territory of the prevailing social and political theories, to seek out their most basic commitments and assumptions, and to hold them up for a thoroughgoing critical scrutiny. As the leading theories on offer, liberalism and marxism are found wanting. Each seizes upon a significant, but limited, dimension of human experience and treats it as the basis for a total explanation and critique or justification of that experience. Moreover, as the reigning theory in traditional circles, liberalism informs political and legal practice, justifies its continued authority, and limits the possibilities of change. The Critical challenge is to expose the inadequacy of these theoretical constructs and to identify the particular values and interests that lurk within and behind them. While each critic adopts a slightly different perspective and target, they combine to assemble the basic building blocks of CLS—the contingency of history, the poverty of individualism, the politics of knowledge, the hierarchical basis of modern life, the contradictions of social relations, the role of legal consciousness, the existence of indeterminacy, the limits of instrumentalism, the hegemony of legal thinking, and the like.

In a chapter from an early book, Roberto Unger tackles the deep antagonisms in the individualistic account of society. At the heart of the liberal account is the attempt to resolve the competing problems of order and freedom through a set of public rules. His aim is to demonstrate that liberal theory cannot generate an adequate or coherent account of legislation or adjudication; it founders on the reefs of subjective value and objectivity. The implications of his critique lead him to suggest a nonliberal theory of politics that looks to a common form of social life and shared values.

In a similar vein, but with a slightly different agenda and focus of

13

inquiry, Duncan Kennedy travels deep into the belly of the legal beast. He brings out for inspection and criticism the contradictions that constitute and confound legal doctrine and thinking. In particular, he relates an evolving tale of disintegration within legal consciousness. The modern lawyer manages to embrace the radically incompatible visions of individualism and altruism and, in the process, highlights the irrepressible political nature of the lawyering task. Kennedy concludes by showing how this precarious state of affairs opens up opportunities for radical and transformative action.

Catherine MacKinnon indicts both liberalism and marxism. She insists that the approximation of a scientific or nonsituated viewpoint, or lack of one, is plausible only because a particular point of view is so widespread and pervasive. For her, the objective way of thinking is inscribed with a male point of view and results in the objectification of women. Knowledge and gender are not mutually exclusive categories: the metaphysical commitments of male-stream scholarship operate to conceal the man-made and man-serving construction of reality by making women's experience and standpoint invisible or trivial. Advocating the development of a strictly feminist jurisprudence, she connects up her philosophical reflections with its practical manifestations in the state's treatment of rape.

2

Liberal Political Theory

Roberto Mangabeira Unger

The individual is made up of reason and will. Will directs reason, but does not control the content of knowledge. Society is the plurality of individuals with understanding and desire.

As desiring beings, men are blind creatures of appetite. Nevertheless, with the important qualification suggested by the antinomy of theory and fact, they are capable of an objective understanding of the world. Different men, each by the use of his own mind, can come ever closer to the same truth about reality. On the other hand, the things men want, and therefore the purposes they make their minds serve, are infinitely diverse.

Amidst this abundance of ends, there are some goals almost everyone pursues. Men want comfort and honor, and avoid the opposite of these. Above all, they try to keep life, for desire wants to be satisfied, not annihilated. Comfort is the satisfaction of material wants by material things. Honor is the satisfaction of the wish to be the object of other men's obedience or admiration.

A society of individuals who seek to achieve their particular objectives and to satisfy their needs for comfort and honor must be characterized by mutual hostility and mutual dependence. Both hostility and dependence are based on the nature of human ends and on the scarcity of means to satisfy them.

The first source of hostility, given the scarcity of material resources, is the desire for comfort. There are not enough of the goods people want in order to be comfortable. They must therefore scramble.

Power is the second cause of antagonism in society. The power of some is the powerlessness of others. The more one man's desire for power is satisfied, the more will his fellows' wish for it remain

An earlier version of this chapter appeared in *Knowledge and Politics* (New York: The Free Press, 1975). Reprinted by permission of author and publisher.

15

frustrated. The fight for power must be as unceasing as the struggle for things.

The same goals that make men enemies also make them indispensable allies. To satisfy their hunger for comfort, they depend on each other's labor. In a sense, the necessary reliance on other people's work is a consequence of the scarcity of time. No man has enough time to satisfy his desire for material things through his own efforts, for death comes soon. Hence, individuals must find ways to buy and sell one another's time. There must be a labor market and the institution of contract for services.

The wants of comfort and honor, together with the circumstance of scarcity, which is implied in them, make reciprocal antagonism and reciprocal need the everlasting conditions of society. To promote their interests in hostility and collaboration, men are constantly making alliances by forming groups. But these groups are always precarious. Left to themselves, they would last only as long as the common convenience that brought them into being. The two fundamental problems of politics, order and freedom, are the consequences of the conditions of mutual antagonism and need, and of the drives that underlie those conditions.

The first task of society is to place the restraints on mutual antagonism necessary to satisfy mutual need. The struggle for comfort, power, and glory can be moderated so that everyone may be assured that he will not be threatened by the worst of discomfort, enslavement, and disrespect, or by violent death. But how is the control of hostility to be achieved? This is the problem of order.

As soon as men seek to place limits on their antagonism they confront a second difficulty. For each person, the good is the satisfaction of his own desires; no other good exists. Freedom, to rephrase the earlier definition, is the power to choose arbitrarily the ends and means of one's striving. In principle, nothing makes one man's goals worthier of success than another's. Yet it seems that whatever restraints are established to ensure order will benefit the purposes of some individuals more than those of their fellows. Any such preference would be arbitrary, in the sense that it could not be justified. How then can order be instituted in such a way that no one's liberty is unjustifiably preferred or downgraded and that everyone has the largest amount of liberty compatible with the absence of such arbitrariness? This is the problem of freedom.

The common solution to the problems of order and freedom is the making and applying of impersonal rules or laws.

THE PRINCIPLE OF RULES AND VALUES

The distinction between rules and values, as the two basic elements of social order, is the first principle of liberal political thought. It may be called simply the principle of rules and values. It articulates the conception, embraced by the unreflective view of society, that the eternal hostility of men to one another requires that order and freedom be maintained by government under law. . . .

Value and Rule

The satisfaction of an individual's wants is his good. The sole measure of good is the wants of an individual or some combination of the wants of different individuals revealed by the choices they make. The good has no existence outside the will.

The need for rules arises from the undying enmity and the demands of collaboration that mark social life. Because there are no conceptions of the good that stand above the conflict and impose limits on it, artificial limits must be created. Otherwise, the natural hostility men have for one another will run its course relentlessly to the prejudice of their interdependence.

Self-interest, the generalized search for comfort and glory, and any sharing of common values will all be insufficient to keep the peace. It is in the individual's self-interest to benefit from a system of laws established by others but not to obey or establish that system himself. As long as most persons are not robbers, robbery can be a profitable business. Furthermore, though everyone has similar interests in comfort and glory, they are interests that, because of the scarcity of their objects, throw men against one another as much as they bring men together. Finally, every other sharing of values is bound to be both precarious and morally indifferent. It is precarious because the individual will is the true and only seat of value, forever changing direction as the dangers and opportunities of the struggle for comfort and glory shift. The sharing of values is also without ethical significance. We are not entitled to pass from the fact that we happen to agree upon our ends to the claim that someone else ought to agree to them, or at least should do nothing to stop us from attaining them.

Peace must therefore be established by rules. By its significance to society, by its origin, and by its form, a rule differs from a value. A good way to develop the point is to make the concept of rule used in liberal political thought more precise.

Rules are general and they bear on conduct. Beyond this, however, little can be said before we have distinguished three sorts of rules. . . . Constitutive rules define a form of conduct in such a way that the distinction between the rule and the ruled activity disappears. It has been said that the rules of games and the rules of logic are of this sort. Technical or instrumental rules are guides for the choice of the most effective means to an end. They take the form, do *x* if you want *y*. Prescriptive rules are imperatives that state what some category of persons may do, ought to do, or ought not to do. Accordingly, they are permissions, general commands, and prohibitions. Prescriptive rules differ from constitutive rules because they are clearly distinguishable from the conduct they govern and from instrumental rules because they are not hypothetical.

The rules to which the first principle of liberal political doctrine refers must be prescriptive. The war of men against one another lacks the voluntary or unthinking stability of conduct presupposed by constitutive rules. Moreover, the same antagonism precludes the constant and general agreement about ends that would be necessary for instrumental rules to serve effectively as a basis for the ordering of social relations.

The prescriptive rules established by government are usually called laws. They place limits on the pursuit of private ends, thereby ensuring that natural egoism will not turn into a free-for-all in which everyone and everything is endangered. They also facilitate mutual collaboration. The two tasks are connected because a peaceful social order in which we know what to expect from others is a condition for the accomplishment of any of our goals. More specifically, it is the job of the laws to guarantee the supreme goods of social life, order, and freedom.

Positivism and Natural Right

The two basic manners in which the political doctrine of liberalism defines the opposition of rules and values correspond to two ideas about the source of the laws and to two conceptions of how freedom and order may be established. To establish order and freedom the laws must be impersonal. They must embody more than the values of an individual or of a group. Rules whose source is the interest of a single person or class of persons destroy the good of freedom because, by definition, they constitute a dominion of some wills over the wills of others. Furthermore, they leave order without any support except the terror by which it is imposed, for the oppressed will not love the laws. . . .

For these reasons, there arises within liberal thought a second family of attempts to define the relationship between rules and values. It consists in trying to formulate standards or procedures that will establish in a general fashion which laws are impersonal and therefore capable of securing order and freedom in society. The more familiar liberal theories of legislation fall into this category.

Among such views, there is one that calls for separate and immediate treatment because of its direct bearing on the relationship between rules and values. It starts from the premise that the circumstances of reciprocal hostility and need, and the universal interest in comfort and glory, carry implications of their own for how society ought to be arranged. Intelligence can spell out the implications and then take them as a basis for impersonal legislation. Thus, the solution to problems of order and freedom pre-exists the making of the laws and can be used as a standard with which to judge them. It is this pre-existing solution that settles the entitlements of individuals; rights precede rules. Here you have the core of the modern theory of natural right, under whose star the liberal state was born.

There is in most statements of the natural rights conception an ambiguity that obscures a fatal dilemma. If we treat the rights as somehow derived from the circumstances of social life, we are forced to explain how evaluative standards can be inferred from facts. If, on the contrary, we present the rights as simply prudent means to achieve agreed-upon ends, like peace and prosperity, we have to explain how we go about judging divergence from these ends and what happens when, in a particular case, the purpose seems to be better served by disrespecting the right. . . .

Despite their divergence, the positivist and natural right interpretations of the principle of rules and values have in common the insistence that it is on the whole better for men to live under laws than to be without them. The two doctrines agree that the absence of coercively enforced public rules would deny us the blessings of collaboration and security in the search for comfort and glory.

To will intelligently and consequentially is to will that others respect our objectives. We wish to be entitled to the objects of our choices. Entitlements, however, are possible only when there is a system of general rules that limits the wants of each man in comparison to those of his fellows so that each may be safe in the enjoyment of what is his. In short, will implies the will to be entitled, which in turn implies the acceptance of a system of rules either to distribute or to confirm and enforce the entitlements.

At a still more basic level, positivism and natural rights theory may be viewed as expressions in political thought of opposing yet complementary views of the dualism of the universal and the particular.

To the positivist, society has no inherent order of its own. He sees rules as the impositions of a will, even though of an enlightened one, on the chaos of social life. The universal laws are simply conventions that set the boundaries among particular interests so that these interests will not destroy each other.

The natural rights theorist, on the contrary, claims to discover an intrinsic order in social relations, an order it is his purpose to make explicit and to develop. For him the universals that describe this order—rights, rules, and institutional categories—have an existence and a worth quite independent of the particular interests that may take advantage of them. Thus, the natural rights thinker treats the system of private law concepts of contract and property or the doctrine of separation of powers in public law as if they had an autonomous logic that survived in all their transmutations.

Though they differ in the priorities they assign to the universal and the particular, positivism and natural rights doctrine are at one in accepting a radical distinction between universals and particulars and in identifying the former with the abstract and the latter with the concrete.

The Legal Mentality

For liberal political thought, the laws must be general, uniform, public, and capable of coercive enforcement. . . . These foundations of the idea of law are aspects of the peculiar legal mentality that animates liberal political thought.

Generality is associated with the political ideal of formal equality and with the moral ideal of universalism. Formal equality means that as citizens of the state and legal persons men are viewed and treated by the law as fundamentally equal. Social circumstances must therefore be clearly distinguished from legal-political status. By disregarding or accepting the inequality of the former in order to emphasize all the more intensely the equality of the latter, we commit ourselves to general laws. To equalize men's social circumstances with respect to even a few of the divergences among those circumstances, we would have to treat each man or each group differently and thus to move away from the attribute of generality. The language of formal equality is a language of rights as abstract opportunities to enjoy certain advantages rather than a language of the concrete and actual experience of social life.

The ethical analogue to formal equality is universalism. It is the belief that moral judgment, like political order, is primarily a matter of rights and duties. The rights and duties are established by principles whose formulation becomes more general and therefore more perfect the less their applicability turns on who and where one is. The morality of reason is a classic form of the universalist ethic.

Formal equality and moral universalism both include the conception of universals and particulars encountered before. The legal person and the moral agent are constructed, as abstract and formal universals, out of individual lives, and then treated as if they were real and independent beings. Particular interests, experiences, or circumstances are viewed as a contingent substance of the forms, or as concrete examples of the abstract propositions. Thus, one can define a right independently of the interests an individual may use it to promote.

The basis of uniformity is the formal conception of reason. Reason cannot establish the ends of action, nor does it suffice to determine the concrete implications of general values on which we may happen to agree. That is why rules are so important in the first place. Nevertheless, if the laws are to be uniformly applied, we need a technique of rule application. This technique must rely on the powers that reason possesses because it is a machine for analysis and combination: the capacity to deduce conclusions from premises and the ability to choose efficient means to accepted ends. Consequently, the major liberal theories of adjudication view the task of applying law either as one of making deductions from the rules or as one of choosing the best means to advance the ends the rules themselves are designed to foster.

The public character of law has its immediate ground in the distinction between state and society and in the more inclusive dichotomy of public and private life. The state appears in a double light, as the providential alternative to the blindness of private cupidity and as the supreme weapon of some men in their self-interested struggle against others. The separation of the public and the private alternates with the destruction of the latter by the former. In either event, the conflict between the two is never resolved.

The assumption of the belief that the laws must be capable of coercive enforcement is the artificial view of society. According to this view, even though society may have an implicit order, as the natural rights theorist claims, it is not a self-regulating or self-enforcing one. Because individuals and individual interests are the primary elements of social life, and because they are locked in a perpetual struggle with one another, social order must be established by acts of will and protected against the ravages of self-interest.

The ideas that there is no natural community of common ends and that group life is a creature of will help explain the importance of rules and of their coercive enforcement. But the same factors may also account for the fascination of terror, the systematic use of violence unlimited by law, as a device of social organization. The less one's ability to rely on participation in common ends, the greater the importance of force as a bond among individuals. Punishment and fear take the place of community.

Moreover, when they view everything in the social world as a creation of the will, men come to believe there is nothing in society a will sufficiently violent cannot preserve or destroy. Thus, legalism and terrorism, the commitment to rules and the seduction of violence, are rival brothers, but brothers nonetheless.

THE PRINCIPLE OF SUBJECTIVE VALUE

There is an aspect of the principle of rules and values so important that it deserves to be distinguished and developed in its own right. It is the proposition that all values are individual and subjective, the principle of subjective value.

Ends are viewed by liberal theory as individual in the sense that they are always the objectives of particular individuals. By contrast, values are called communal when they are understood as the aims of groups, and of individuals only to the extent that the individuals are members of those groups. The political doctrine of liberalism does not acknowledge communal values. To recognize their existence, it would be necessary to begin with a vision of the basic circumstances of social life that took groups rather than individuals as the intelligible and primary units of social life. The individuality of values is the very basis of personal identity in liberal thought, a basis the communal conception of value destroys.

Values are subjective in the sense that they are determined by choice. Subjectivity emphasizes that an end is an end simply because someone holds it, whereas individuality means that there must always be a particular person whose end it is. The opposing conception is the idea of objective value, a major theme of the philosophy of the ancients. Objective values are standards and goals of conduct that exist independently of human choice. Men may embrace or reject objective values, but they cannot establish or undo their authority.

From the start, liberal political thought has been in revolt against the conception of objective value. If we were able to perceive such values, they would become the true foundation of the social order. Public rules would be relegated to a subsidiary role, as devices for the specification of the objective standards, when those standards were imprecise, or for their enforcement, when they were disobeyed. The problems of order and freedom would be cast in a different light if we could think of these norms of conduct as ends whose fulfillment would bring our worthiest capacities to their richest development rather than as constraints imposed by an external will.

Granted that the doctrine of objective value is incompatible with the premises of liberalism and that its political implications are unclear, might it nevertheless be true?

First, the theory of objective value presupposes that the mind can grasp and establish moral essences or goods. But this has never been shown, and the conception of reason on which it rests has been discredited in nonmoral areas of thought.

Second, the doctrine denies any significance to choice other than the passive acceptance or rejection of independent truths. Our experience of moral judgment, however, seems to be one of at least contributing to shape the ends we pursue. A conception that puts this fact aside disregards the significance of choice as an expression of personality.

Third, the inability of the theory of objective value to determine how we should act in particular situations is no remediable mishap. To make the doctrine plausible in the absence of divinely revealed moral truth, its proponents rely on references to moral opinions shared by men of many different ages and societies. The more concrete the allusions to this allegedly timeless moral agreement, the less convincing they become. Therefore, to make their case the proponents of objective value must restrict themselves to a few abstract ideals whose vagueness allows almost any interpretation.

The doctrine that there are no intelligible essences is the ultimate basis of the principle of subjective value. The theory of intelligible essences states that there are a limited number of classes of things in the world, that each thing has characteristics that determine the class to which it belongs, and that these characteristics can be known directly by the mind.

Were we to make any concessions to the doctrine of intelligible essences in our view of natural facts, there seems to be no way we could keep the doctrine from penetrating into the sphere of language, conduct, and values. This is an obvious conclusion in a philosophy that denies the separation of values from facts. For such a philosophy our notions of right and wrong, good and bad, have to be taken as interpretations of objective standards of value just as our capacity to distinguish tables from chairs is a consequence of our ability to perceive the respective essences of each.

But even a doctrine like the liberal one that contrasts facts and values cannot ultimately uphold the ontological distinction between them. Values may be experienced as subjective, and desires as arbitrary, but there is still an important sense in which they are facts like all other facts. The arbitrariness of desires and the subjectivity of values have to do with the significance of ends as bases for the criticism or justification of conduct. The fundamental point remains: precisely because ends are denied an objective existence, they must be conceived as psychic events going on in the heads of particular men. If events in general had intelligible essences, so would these psychic events. The battle against objective values would be lost. Thus, to maintain the principle of subjective value, we must reject the doctrine of intelligible essences completely.

Now, however, a difficulty arises. If there are no intelligible essences, how do we go about classifying facts and situations, especially social facts and social situations? Because facts have no intrinsic identity, everything depends on the names we give them. The conventions of naming rather than any perceived quality of "tableness" will determine whether an object is to count as a table. In the same way, convention rather than nature will dictate whether a particular bargain is to be treated as a contract.

It is not surprising, then, that language should become an obsession of the liberal thinker, for he worships it as the demiurge of the world. But the real sovereigns that stand behind the demiurge are the interests that lead men to classify things as they do. He who has the power to decide what a thing will be called has the power to decide what it is. This is as true of persons as of things.

Properly understood, the system of public rules is itself a language. Every rule is addressed to a category of persons and acts, and marks its addresses off from others. To mark off is to name. To apply the rules to particular cases is to subsume individual persons and acts under the general names of which the rules consist. Hence, the theory of law is a special branch of the general theory of naming.

At last, I can state the great political problem toward which I have been winding my way. The resort to a set of public rules as the foundation of order and freedom is a consequence of the subjective conception of value. The subjective conception of value in turn presupposes the abandonment of the doctrine of intelligible essences. In the absence of intelligible essences, however, there are no obvious criteria for defining general categories of acts and persons when we make the rules. (The making of rules is legislation.) Nor are there clear standards by which to classify the particular instances under rules when we come to the stage of applying the rules we have made. (The application of rules is adjudication.)

THE PRINCIPLE OF INDIVIDUALISM

The interplay of rules and values in society, described by the first two principles of liberal political thought, does not exhaust the basic features of the unreflective view described.

There is still the problem of the relation of individuals to groups. Thus, the need for a third principle: a group is simply a collection of individuals; in other words, the attributes of a group are the sum of the attributes of its individual members. It is the principle of individualism, or simply individualism. If we take the group as the whole and the members as parts, the principle of individualism affirms that the whole is just the sum of its parts.

When I say that the group is viewed as a collection of individuals, or that all the attributes of the group can be explained as a combination of the attributes of its members, I have both a methodological and a moral idea in mind. The methodological idea is that by summing up all we know about the individual members taken separately we can find out all there is to know about the group. But what is summed up in this operation? Clearly, we must count in the addition characteristics the individuals have because they are members of the group. Otherwise, the principle of individualism would be trivial and without importance for our ideas about society. But once these characteristics are included and their causes elucidated, there is nothing more about the group left to explain. If group behavior is governed by scientific laws, these laws derive from the more general laws that govern individual conduct. Psychology is more basic than sociology.

The moral side of individualism follows as a result of its methodological aspect. The group must never be viewed as a source of values in its own right. Within the group there will be a greater or lesser degree of sharing of values. But this sharing will be contingent and subjective. . . . Typically, there will be no single set of shared ends, but only varying coalitions of interests among particular members. Suppose we admit the possibility of values held by the group as an entity, and by individuals only partially and insofar as they are absorbed into the group. The consequence would be that an important feature of group life could not be either described or explained through a study of its members. The postulate of individualism is meant to avoid this.

Individualism is so deeply rooted in our thought that it is hard to understand. A great part of the difficulty lies in imagining a different principle that might help define it by contrast. Yet such a polar view has been a staple of social thought in the West since the Romantic movement and the birth of sociology as a discipline. It is the principle of collectivism, exemplified by romantic, organicist conceptions of the group. These conceptions view the group as an entity with independent existence irreducible to the lives of its members, with group values that stand apart from the individual and subjective ends of its membership, even with its own "personality." Collectivism is one of the most influential partial critiques of the liberal doctrine.

The antagonism between the liberal and the collectivist view of the relation of individuals to groups is illustrated by their divergent conceptions of the state. For liberal thinkers the state is an artifact of the laws; indeed, for some it is the legal order itself. Rules, procedures, and sanctions are what hold the state together. The state has a vicarious existence; its true life is the life of its citizens. For the organicist, however, the core of the state is the "nation." The unity of the nation is based on the tradition of collective values to which countless individuals have contributed as streams flowing into a great sea. . . . The core of the collectivist view is the idea of the spontaneity of social bonds and of their priority over individual striving.

Individualism and the first two postulates of liberal political theory depend on each other. Groups are artificial because all values are individual and subjective. If the group had an autonomous existence and was a source of value in its own right, we could no longer maintain that all ends were individual. If we went further, with some of the collectivists, and claimed an objective moral worth for the values of the community or the nation, we would also have to abandon the idea of subjectivity. Finally, the liberal doctrine of groups is connected with the principle of rules and values. Because community is always precarious and depends on the convergence of private interests, fixed rules are needed as the guarantees of peaceful and free association.

ORDER, FREEDOM, AND LAW: THE PROBLEM OF LEGISLATION

The problems of order and freedom collapse into each other. If one knew to what standards the laws would have to conform so as not to prefer arbitrarily one man's advantage to another's (freedom), one would also be able to determine how best to restrain antagonism in society in the interest of collaboration (order). Put in different words, to be effective as a means of order, the laws must deserve and win the allegiance of the citizenry, and to do that they must be capable of being justified. The justification of the laws would consist in showing that the restraints put on men's struggle for comfort, power, and glory are fair because no man's freedom is set without reason above another's and each man is allowed the maximum freedom compatible with the prohibition of arbitrary preference. A study of the theory of legislation can therefore rest content with an inquiry into the foundations of freedom. . . . There are three main ways in which modern political philosophy conceives of the establishment of freedom through legislation. . . .

The first type of solution to the problem of freedom attempts to derive the laws solely from the idea of freedom itself. Consequently, it denies that legislation has to choose among competing individual and subjective values, and to give preference to some over others. This is the formal theory of freedom. . . .

The theory of formal freedom suffers from the same dilemma as the morality of reason, of which it is the political equivalent. Take Kant's universal principle of right, "Every action is right that in itself or in its maxim is such that the freedom of the will of each can coexist together with the freedom of the will of everyone according to a universal law." When this proposition is left in its abstract form, it seems impossible to derive from it definite conclusions about what precisely the laws should command, prohibit, or permit. . . . But, as soon as we try to reach the level of concrete regulation of conduct, we are forced to prefer some values to others. This, however, is just what the formal theory of freedom was meant to avoid. Like the morality of reason, the formal doctrine of freedom has to choose between being unworkable and being incoherent.

The second main response to the question of freedom in liberal thought is the claim that there exists some procedure for lawmaking on the basis of the combination of private ends, to which procedure all individuals might subscribe in self-interest. Self-interest means the intelligent understanding of what we need in order to achieve our own individual and subjective goals. . . .

This doctrine, the substantive theory of freedom, has three main forms. According to the first, the method directly determines the aggregation of interests to be protected by the state and, therefore, the content of the laws. Classical utilitarianism is an example of this view. According to the second form, we subscribe in self-interest to procedures for making laws and settling disputes rather than to a concrete plan of social organization. The doctrine of the social contract, as formulated by Locke and Rousseau, represents this position.

The utilitarian and social contract versions of the substantive theory of freedom can be collapsed into a third. It appeals to the conception of an ideal system of procedures for lawmaking that all men might accept in self-interest and the operation of which can be shown to lead to certain specific conclusions about the distribution of wealth and power. The work of J. Rawls, the American moralist, illustrates this view.

The main deficiencies of the substantive doctrine of freedom turn out to be similar to those of the formal doctrine. The substantive theory of freedom breaks down because it does not succeed in finding a neutral way to combine individual, subjective values.

In the utilitarian variant of the theory, the problem is to find a standpoint outside the subjective purposes of individuals from which to decide which combination of those values should be favored by the laws. Which of the infinite number of ends will be added up and what weight will be given to each? Such a neutral, Archimedean point, however, would be precisely the objective good whose nonexistence drove us into the attempt to devise a liberal doctrine of legislation.

Similarly, the social contract version of the substantive theory of freedom presupposes the possibility of finding a procedure for lawmaking to which any man, no matter what his values, would have reason to agree. The more indeterminate the procedure in specifying particular laws, the less would anyone have reason to object to it. But, then, the problem of legislation would simply be postponed. On the other hand, the more concrete the procedure, the less would it be likely to benefit equally everyone's wants. . . .

The third subcategory of the substantive theory of freedom resembles the social contract doctrine because it proposes a procedure for lawmaking, and utilitarianism because it seeks to prove that this procedure would result in specific laws governing power and wealth. It tries to escape from the traps of both the social contract and utilitarian doctrines by imagining a hypothetical ideal situation in which men would be able to legislate without knowing their positions in society, and thus without knowing what their particular values as real individuals would be. The difficulty with this is analogous to the objections against the earlier types of the substantive theory of freedom. The less concreteness we allow to the persons in the ideal position, the less will they have standards by which to legislate specific laws, leaving the problem of legislation unsolved. But the more they become like actual human beings, with their own preferences, the more will they be forced to choose among individual, subjective values in the ideal situation itself. . . .

The third solution to the conundrum of freedom denies the assumption upon which the conundrum rests, the subjectivity of values. It appeals to the idea of shared values as the basis for lawmaking. In each well-organized society there is a core of widely agreed upon purposes on which either lawmaking itself or the choice of procedures for lawmaking can be based. Laws or procedures with such a foundation are not arbitrary preferences for certain ends; they are the embodiment of the common ends. The shared values do more than serve as a source of legislation. They also work beyond the limits of formal rules as a fundamental tie among men. . . .

THE ANTINOMY OF RULES AND VALUES: THE PROBLEM OF ADJUDICATION

It is no help to have a doctrine for the justification of rulemaking unless we also have one for the application of rules. . . . Unless we can justify one interpretation of the rules over another, the claim of legislative generality will quite rightly be rejected as a sham. The theory of adjudication is therefore a continuation of the theory of legislation. Its main question is, by what standards, or in what manner, can the laws be applied without violating the requirements of freedom? If the law applier cannot justify his decisions, because they appear to rest on his own individual and subjective values, liberty will suffer. Those to whom the law is applied will have surrendered their freedom to the judge, the person authorized to apply the rules. . . .

To understand the nature of adjudication one must distinguish two different ways of ordering human relations. One way is to establish rules to govern general categories of acts and persons, and then to decide particular disputes among persons on the basis of the established rules. This is legal justice. The other way is to determine goals and then, quite independently of rules, to decide particular cases by a judgment of what decision is most likely to contribute to the predetermined goals, a judgment of instrumental rationality. This is substantive justice.

In the situation of legal justice, the laws are made against the background of the ends they are designed to promote, even if the sole permissible end is liberty itself. Only after the rules have been formulated do decisions "under the rules" become possible. Hence, the possibility of some sort of distinction between legislation and adjudication is precisely what defines legal justice. The main task of the theory of adjudication is to say when a decision can truly be said to stand "under a rule," if the rule we have in mind is the law of the state, applied by a judge. Only decisions "under a rule" are consistent with freedom; others constitute arbitrary exercises of judicial power.

Decisions made under rules must be capable of a kind of justification different from the justification for the rules themselves. The task of judging is distinct from that of lawmaking.

In substantive justice each decision is justified because it is the one best calculated to advance some accepted objective. The relation between a particular decision and the objective is that of a means to an end. . . .

The distinctive feature of substantive justice is the nonexistence of any line between legislation and adjudication. In the pure case of substantive justice, there is neither rulemaking nor rule applying, because rather than prescriptive rules there are only choices as to what should be accomplished and judgments of instrumental rationality about how to get it done. . . .

The central thesis of this section is that neither the regime of formal nor that of substantive justice is able to solve the problem of freedom. Nevertheless, formal and substantive justice cannot be reconciled. Thus, there is no coherent solution to the problem of adjudication as it is defined by liberal thought; we cannot dispose of the difficulties with which that problem confronts liberal political doctrine by embracing either substantive or formal justice. A system of laws or rules (legal justice) can neither dispense with a consideration of values in the process of adjudication, nor be made consistent with such a consideration. Moreover, judgments about how to further general values in particular situations (substantive justice) can neither do without rules, nor be made compatible with them. This is the antinomy of rules and values. . . .

The simplest and most familiar account of legal justice goes in the literature of jurisprudence under the name of formalism. . . . In its strictest version, the formalist theory of adjudication states that the legal system will dictate a single, correct solution in every case. It is as if it were possible to deduce correct judgments from the laws by an automatic process. The regime of legal justice can therefore be established through a technique of adjudication that can disregard the 'policies' or 'purposes' of the law.

Those who dismiss formalism as a naive illusion, mistaken in its claims and pernicious in its effect, do not know what they are in for. Their contempt is shallower than the doctrine they ridicule, for they fail to understand what the classic liberal thinkers saw earlier: the destruction of formalism brings in its wake the ruin of all other liberal doctrines of adjudication. The first step toward understanding this is to discover that the argument against formalism rests on a basis altogether broader than has been thought necessary. Once this broader basis is described, it will become clear that the formalist position is incoherent because it is inconsistent with the premises of liberal political theory, which it also presupposes.

The formalist believes that words usually have clear meanings. . . . If, to recall Puffendorf's example, the law prohibits the spilling of blood in the streets, it is clear that it refers to fighting, not to the emergency assistance given by a surgeon. Rules consist of strings of names, the words that describe the categories of persons and acts to which the rules apply. To the extent that words have plain meanings, it will be clear to what fact situations they apply. The judge who applies the laws to the persons and acts they denote is, by definition, applying the laws uniformly. He exercises no arbitrary power. . . .

The view of rules and therefore of naming implicit in the formalist thesis depends on the preliberal conception of intelligible essences. To subsume situations under rules, and things under words, the mind must be able to perceive the essential qualities that mark each fact or situation as a member of a particular category. As soon as it is necessary to engage in a discussion of purpose to determine whether the surgeon's emergency assistance falls in the class of acts prohibited by the law, formalism has been abandoned.

The sole possible alternative to the belief in intelligible essences as a basis of formalism would be the notion that in the great majority of cases, common values and common understandings of the world fostered by a shared mode of social life will make perfectly clear to what category something belongs. Social practice will take the place of both intelligible essences and explicit consideration of purpose.

The basic objection to formalism is that the doctrine of intelligible essences, whose truth the formalist's confidence in plain meanings assumes, is incompatible with the view of social life to whose consequences it responds. The aim of theories of legislation and adjudication in liberal thought is precisely to show how freedom is possible despite the individuality and subjectivity of values. If objective values were available to us, if we knew the true good with certainty, and understood all its implications and requirements perfectly, we would not need a method of impartial adjudication. . . . The problem of adjudication, as presented in modern jurisprudence, is therefore inextricably linked with the conception that values are subjective and individual. . . .

The chief vice of formalism is its dependence on a view of language that cannot be reconciled with the modern ideas of science, nature, and language that formalists themselves take for granted. Formalism is a doctrine of adjudication that relies on two sets of premises, premises about language and premises about value, that contradict one another.

The history of modern jurisprudence may be characterized as a continuing attempt to find an adequate alternative to formalism as a basis for legal justice. If the true nature of the formalist fallacy had been understood, the attempt might have been less enthusiastically undertaken. For the very considerations that defeat formalism vitiate the main doctrine of adjudication that has taken its place, the purposive theory.

The purposive theory states that to apply the laws correctly and uniformly, the judge must consider the purposes or policies the laws serve. Thus, the decision not to punish the surgeon turns on the determination that the objective of the law is to guarantee safety in the streets and that this objective would be more hindered than helped by the punishment of the surgeon. The purposes or policies are the ends; the laws themselves are the means.

Whatever values or combinations of values are accepted by the theory of legislation as adequate justification of the laws will also be used as standards for distinguishing good interpretations from bad ones. Thus, the same value of public safety that justifies the law determines who ought to be punished under its provisions. Lawmaker and law applier are viewed as participants in a collaborative endeavor. . . .

The purposive theory leaves the regime of legal justice hanging in the air. Notice first that the purposive doctrine needs some way of defining the values, policies, or purposes that are to guide the judge's work. In general, a rule will be thought to serve many purposes. Moreover, a judge deals with a whole system of rules, from which he must select the rule appropriate to the case before him. When he applies one of these rules to the case, he must weigh the policy of the rule he is choosing against the policies of all other rules he might have applied to the case with a different result. Thus, the purposive theory of adjudication requires not only a criterion for the definition of controlling policies, but also a method of balancing them off one against another. In the absence of a procedure for policy decision, the judge will inescapably impose his own subjective preferences, or someone else's, on the litigants.

But in fact no such method for the choice and arrangement of values exists, nor can it exist within liberal thought. Even devices like majority rule or the market, used to deal with the problems of freedom at the legislative level, are of little help in adjudication. Adjudication presupposes the separation of functions; the judge cannot pretend to base his decision directly on the "political" forces that the market or the electoral process pit against one another. He must be the master of some independent mechanism for the combination and weighing of policies. For this mechanism to be created, however, the principle of subjective value would have to be abandoned and, together with it, all the related postulates of liberal political thought that set the stage for the problem of adjudication. . . .

A second major objection to the purposive doctrine is the impossibility of reconciling the prescriptive view of rules with the implications of judgments of purpose or policy. For the purposive theory, the decision about when to apply a given rule to a case depends on the responses to a prior question: Will the ends of this law and of the legal order as a whole best be served by its application to the case? The interpretation of the law turns on a calculus of instrumental rationality. . . .

A judgment of instrumental rationality, however, cannot pretend to have any generality or stability. It is always possible to discover a more efficient means, either because circumstances have changed or because knowledge has improved. Thus, the only kind of rule consistent with the standpoint of means and ends is an instrumental rule. If the scope of every rule has to be determined in the end by a judgment of instrumental rationality, the whole law is reduced to a body of instrumental rules. The consequences for a regime of legal justice are fatal.

First, it is no longer sensible in such a situation to speak of fixed entitlements and duties. If the policy of the law of contract is to promote national wealth, and if the scope of the rules of contract law has to be determined by the analysis of purpose, a bargain that harms the objective more than it helps it will not be considered an enforceable contract. We would be neither under an obligation to keep promises as private citizens, nor justified in enforcing contractual arrangements as officials whenever a refusal to comply or to enforce was authorized by an appropriate judgment of instrumental rationality.

Another consequence of the purposive theory is to undermine the separation of functions and powers. The judges will be called upon to engage in the same kinds of assessments of instrumental rationality that characterize legislation and administration. Moreover, the rules that allocate authority among different agencies of government will themselves have to be applied in the light of their policies. One can never exclude in principle the possibility that in a particular case the benefit done to the policies underlying the jurisdictional rules by disobeying those rules may outweigh the disadvantages, proximate or remote, of violating the rules. In such a case the apparent usurpation will be permitted, indeed commanded. . . .

The problem of purposive adjudication is the chief preoccupation of every system of judge-made law. When the cases that make the law are the same ones that apply it, and the influence of views about what the law should be on views about what it is are constantly before one's eyes, the distinction between legislation and adjudication hangs by a slender thread. If the thread is only as strong as the purposive theory, it will break. . . .

It remains to consider briefly whether the problem of freedom can be solved by a regime of substantive justice that, unlike both the formalist and purposive theories of legal justice, does not pretend to be committed to rules at all.

The first prerequisite of substantive justice is a set of values so firmly established that they can be taken for granted when decisions about individual cases are made. Particular choices may then be viewed either as means to the accepted values conceived as ends, or as ways of giving concreteness or substance to the formal or abstract values. For example, a decison not to enforce bargains between husband and wife may be considered either as a means to the end of marital trust, or as a specification of the general value of marital trust. In the first case, the method of substantive justice is one of instrumental rationality; in the second case, it is a method of practical or prudential reason, which mediates between the abstract and the concrete. Because such an idea of practical reason is unknown to liberal thought and inconsistent with its premises, my discussion will be confined to the form of substantive justice that relies on instrumental rationality. . . .

To begin with, the principles of subjective value and of individualism preclude the possibility of any stable set of common ends. Moreover, the values or goals taken for granted are always indeterminate. They still leave us to determine the means we should prefer to further the ends we have chosen, or what substantive content we should give an abstract value. Thus, one cannot base a social order on judgments about how to advance given goals without relying on rules that establish what counts as an available means, and what does not. These boundary rules can do their job only if they function prescriptively rather than instrumentally. . . .

The area of free play surrendered to instrumental rationality may vary enormously, but in any ordered social situation there must be boundary conditions set by prescriptive rules whose scope is not in turn subject to the calculus of instrumental rationality. . . . However, once prescriptive rules are introduced to rescue substantive justice, we are back with all the difficulties of legal justice and of the theory of adjudication, difficulties from which substantive justice seemed to promise an escape. Because the prescriptive rules that establish the boundary conditions must be interpreted, we are again caught in the quicksand of the theory of adjudication. . . .

An especially important conclusion is that no coherent theory of adjudication is possible within liberal political thought. This means that even if the liberal doctrine of politics could establish an adequate theory of legislation, it would be unable to solve its own central problems of order and freedom. What a nonliberal theory of adjudication might look like we can hardly say, for our very notions of the making and applying of law have been shaped by liberal principles. . . .

THE SHARING OF VALUES

Of all the devices used to deal with the difficulties of liberal political theory, there is one that surpasses the others in the richness of its implications. It is the view that order and freedom can be achieved because in every society men share a core of common beliefs and values. The thesis is of interest here as a metaphysical doctrine about the conditions of order and freedom instead of as a description of society.

At its most modest, it is a commentary on the possibilities of understanding. Men who participate in a common form of social life have a similar experience. It might be said that this allows them to comprehend each other and to assign conventional meanings to words and hence to rules, independently of the ends they hold. Thus, individuals who disagree about the good might nevertheless be able to agree about how fact situations ought to be distinguished and rules applied. Formalism would be saved as a doctrine of plain meanings based upon a social situation rather than as a theory of self-evident meanings founded on intelligible essences. . . .

Shared values might be the basis for a regime of substantive justice; every decision would be judged according to its capacity to promote the common ends. Similarly, the shared values would be the neutral source of the policy judgments which purposive theories of adjudication must bring into play.

Most remarkable of all, the idea of shared values might even make it possible to recast the formalist theory of adjudication in a version much more powerful than the familiar one, and free from the need to rely on the doctrine of intelligible essences. The modern, conventionalist view of language teaches that every distinction among facts must be justified by an interest. We prefer those classifications of things most useful in furthering our purposes. If we suppose that in any community certain ends are broadly shared, men will tend to classify things in the same manner without ever having to consider purposes explicitly. For example, the value of life may be so universally respected and preferred to that of cleanliness of the cobblestones that it would never occur to anyone to suggest that the surgeon should be punished under the law that prohibits bloodletting in the streets.

In most cases, rules will have plain meanings not because men believe in intelligible essences, but because their common interests lead them to categorize the world, and to subsume facts under the categories, in similar ways. Rules and the acts by which they are applied to particular situations can then be viewed as the working out of a common vision of the world, based on agreed-upon values. The convergence of values might in turn be explained, though it could not be justified, as the product of a particular form of social organization. As a possible solution to the problems of legislation and adjudication, this view is a special case of the more general idea of the sharing of values and beliefs in society.

There are two distinct ways to conceive of a sharing of values. On one view, it is a coincidence of individual preferences, which, even when combined, retain the characteristics of individuality and subjectivity. On another view, it refers to group values that are neither individual nor subjective. If we start from the premises of liberal political thought, we must treat every sharing of values as a precarious alliance of ends that simply reveals the subjective preferences of the allies. There is no reason in such a system of thought to expect that these convergences of interest will be stable, nor to bestow upon them an authority any greater than that of the individual choices that produced them. In these circumstances, the sharing of values will not be able to resolve the problems of the theories of legislation and adjudication. It will not constitute the stable, authoritative Archimedean point from which the laws can be assessed and on which criteria of naming can be based.

To achieve a different result, we would have to abandon the system of liberal political thought, and the ideas about knowledge and human nature connected with it. Only by rejecting the principles of subjective values and of individualism could we allow for the possibility of communal values. And only by repudiating the distinction between fact and value could we go from the mere description of these communal values to their use as standards of evaluation.

It would be a dangerous illusion indeed to suppose that a mere revision of our philosophical ideas could suffice to accomplish the objective of giving force to the idea of shared values. The seriousness of the political premises of liberalism is a consequence of the accuracy with which they describe a form of social experience that theory alone cannot abolish. It is the experience of the precariousness and contingency of all shared values in society. This experience arises from the sense that shared values reflect the prejudices and interests of dominant groups rather than a common perception of the good. Thus, individuality remains an assertion of the private will against the conventions and traditions of the public life.

Two things are necessary for the conception of shared values to solve the problems of freedom and order, a theoretical advance and a political event.

The theoretical advance consists in the development of a system of thought that would enable us to deny the contrast of description and evaluation by taking the ends men share in their groups as indications of the good or right. The intuitive idea from which one might start is that a man's choices express his nature; that common choices maintained over time and capable of winning ever greater adherence reflect a common human nature; and that the flourishing of human nature is the true basis of moral and political judgment. . . . The political event would be the transformation of the conditions of social life, particularly the circumstances of domination, that produce the experience of the contingency and arbitrariness of values.

3

Form and Substance in Private Law Adjudication

Duncan Kennedy

This article is an inquiry into the nature and interconnection of the different rhetorical modes found in American private law opinions, articles and treatises. I argue that there are two opposed rhetorical modes for dealing with substantive issues, which I will call individualism and altruism. There are also two opposed modes for dealing with questions of the form in which legal solutions to the substantive problems should be cast. One formal mode favors the use of clearly defined, highly administrable, general rules; the other supports the use of equitable standards producing ad hoc decisions with relatively little precedential value.

My purpose is the rational vindication of two common intuitions about these arguments as they apply to private law disputes in which the validity of legislation is not in question. The first is that altruist views on substantive private law issues lead to willingness to resort to standards in administration, while individualism seems to harmonize with an insistence on rigid rules rigidly applied. The second is that substantive and formal conflict in private law cannot be reduced to disagreement about how to apply some neutral calculus that will "maximize the total satisfactions of valid human wants."[1] The opposed rhetorical modes lawyers use reflect a deeper level of contradiction. At this deeper level, we are divided, among ourselves and also within ourselves, between irreconcilable visions of humanity and society, and between radically different aspirations for our common future. . . .

Excerpted from its original publication in *Harvard Law Review* 89, 1976. Reprinted by permission of the author and the Harvard Law Review Association.

II. TYPES OF RELATIONSHIP BETWEEN FORM AND SUBSTANCE

B. Form as Substance

The choice of form is seldom purely instrumental or tactical. As they appear in real life, the arguments pro and con the use of rules have powerful overtones of substantive debates about what values and what visions of the universe we should adopt. In picking a form through which to achieve some goal, we are almost always making a statement that is independent or at least distinguishable from the statement we make in choosing the goal itself. What we need is a way to relate the values intrinsic *to* form to the values we try to achieve *through* form.

The different values that people commonly associate with the formal modes of rule and standard are conveyed by the emotive or judgmental words that the advocates of the two positions use in the course of debate about a particular issue. Here is a suggestive list drawn from the vast data bank of casual conversation. Imagine, for the items in each row, an exchange: "Rules are A." "No, they are B." "But standards are C." "On the contrary, they are D."

RULES		STANDARDS	
Good	*Bad*	*Bad*	*Good*
Neutrality	Rigidity	Bias	Flexibility
Uniformity	Conformity	Favoritism	Individualization
Precision	Anality	Sloppiness	Creativity
Certainty	Compulsiveness	Uncertainty	Spontaneity
Autonomy	Alienation	Totalitarianism	Participation
Rights	Vested Interests	Tyranny	Community
Privacy	Isolation	Intrusiveness	Concern
Efficiency	Indifference	Sentimentality	Equity
Order	Reaction	Chaos	Evolution
Exactingness	Punitiveness	Permissiveness	Tolerance
Self-reliance	Stinginess	Romanticism	Generosity
Boundaries	Walls	Invasion	Empathy
Stability	Sclerosis	Disintegration	Progress
Security	Threatenedness	Dependence	Trust

This list suggests something that we all know: that the preference for rules or standards is an aspect of opposed substantive positions in family life, art, psychotherapy, education, ethics, politics, and economics. It is also true that everyone is to some degree ambivalent in his feelings about these substantive conflicts. There are only a few who are confident either that one side is right or that they have a set of metacategories that allow one to choose the right side for any particular situation. Indeed, most of the ideas that might serve to dissolve the conflict and make rational choice possible are claimed vociferously by both sides:

RULES		STANDARDS	
Good	*Bad*	*Bad*	*Good*
Morality	Moralism	Moralism	Morality
(playing by the	(self-righteous	(self-righteous-	(openness to the
rul:s)	strictness)	ness about own	situation)
		intuitions)	
Freedom			Freedom
Fairness	Mechanical	Arbitrariness	Fairness
	arbitrariness	of subjectivity	
Equality	of right to	of subjection	Equality
(of opportunity)	sleep under the	to other people's	(in fact)
	bridges of Paris	value judgments	
Realism	Cynicism	Romanticism	Realism

So long as we regard the debate about form as a debate only about means, it is a debate about facts, and reality can be conceived as an ultimate arbiter to whose final decision we must submit if we are rational. But if the question is whether "real" equality is equality of opportunity or equality of enjoyment of the good things of life, then the situation is different. Likewise if the question is whether human nature "is" good or bad, or whether people "do" act as rational maximizers of their interests. For this kind of question, whether phrased in terms of what is or what ought to be, we accept that there is no arbiter (or that he is silent, or that the arbiter is history, which will have nothing to say until we are all long dead). Thus the pro-rules and pro-standards positions are more than an invitation to a positivist investigation of reality. They are also an invitation to choose between sets of values and visions of the universe.

The method I have adopted might be called, in a loose sense, dialetical or structuralist or historicist or the method of contradictions.[73] One of its premises is that the experience of unresolvable conflict among our *own* values and ways of understanding the world is here to stay. In this sense it is pessimistic, one might even say defeatist. But another of its premises is that there is order and meaning to be discovered even within the sense of contradiction. Further, the process of discovering this order and this meaning is both good in itself and enormously useful. In this sense, the method of contradiction represents an attitude that is optimistic and even utopian. None of which is to say that any particular attempt will be worth the paper it is printed on.

III. ALTRUISM AND INDIVIDUALISM

These are two opposed attitudes that manifest themselves in debates about the content of private law rules. My assertion is that the arguments lawyers use are relatively few in number and highly stereotyped, although they are applied in an infinite diversity of factual situations. What I have done is to abstract these typical forms or rhetorical set pieces and attempt to analyze them. . . .

A. The Content of the Ideal of Individualism

The essence of individualism is the making of a sharp distinction between one's interests and those of others, combined with the belief that a preference in conduct for one's own interests is legitimate, but that one should be willing to respect the rules that make it possible to coexist with others similarly self-interested. The form of conduct associated with individualism is self-reliance. This means an insistence on defining and achieving objectives without help from others (i.e., without being dependent on them or asking sacrifices of them). It means accepting that they will neither share their gains nor one's own losses. And it means a firm conviction that I am entitled to enjoy the benefits of my efforts without an obligation to share or sacrifice them to the interests of others.

It is important to be clear from the outset that individualism is sharply distinct from pure egotism, or the view that it is impossible and undesirable to set any limits at all to the pursuit of self-interest. The notion of self-reliance has a strong affirmative moral content, the demand for respect for the rights of others. This means that the individualist ethic is as demanding in its way as the counterethic of altruism. It involves the renunciation of the use of both private and public force in the struggle for satisfaction, and acquiescence in the refusal of others to behave in a communal fashion.

Individualism provides a justification for the fundamental legal institutions of criminal law, property, tort, and contract. The function of law is the definition and enforcement of rights, of those limits on the pursuit of self-interest that distinguish an individualist from a purely egotistical regime. The great preoccupation of individualist legal philosophy is to justify these restrictions, in the face of appetites that are both boundless and postulated to be legitimate.

A pure egotist defends the laws against force on the sole ground that they are necessary to prevent civil war. For the individualist, the rules against the use of force have intrinsic rightness, because they are identified with the ideal of self-reliance, the economic objective of security for individual effort, and the political rhetoric of free will, autonomy, and natural rights.[77] Rules against violence provide a space within which to realize this program, rather than a mere bulwark against chaos. . . .

Beyond these fundamental legal institutions, the individualist program is much less clear. Moreover, it has varied greatly even within the two-hundred-year history of individualism as an organizing element in American public discourse. . . .

Just as there are a multitude of implications that legal thinkers of different periods have drawn from individualism, there are a number of more abstract ideas that are possible bases for adopting it as an attitude and as a guide in formulating legal rules. What this means is that the idea of the "legitimacy" of the pursuit of self-interest within a framework of rights is ambiguous, and different thinkers have given it different contents. . . .

[One justification] is the notion of the invisible hand transforming apparent selfishness into public benefit. In this view, the moral problem presented by the law's failure to interfere with unsavory instances of individualism is apparent rather than real. If we are concerned with the ultimate good of the citizenry, then individualists are pursuing it *and will achieve it,* even when they are most convinced that they care only about themselves.

A much more common justification for individualism in law might be called the "clenched teeth" idea. It is that the refusal to consult the interests of others is an evil, and an evil not redeemed by any long-term good effects. But for the *state* to attempt to suppress this evil would lead to a greater one. As soon as the state attempts to legislate an ethic more demanding than that of individualism, it runs up against two insuperable problems: the relative inability of the legal system to alter human nature, and the tendency of officials to impose tyranny behind a smokescreen of morality. The immorality of law is therefore the necessary price for avoiding the greater immoralities that would result from trying to make law moral. . . .

B. The Content of the Ideal of Altruism

The rhetoric of individualism so thoroughly dominates legal discourse at present that it is difficult even to identify a counterethic. Nonetheless, I think there is a coherent, pervasive notion that constantly competes with individualism, and I will call it altruism. The essence of altruism is the belief that one ought *not* to indulge a sharp preference for one's own interest over those of others. Altruism enjoins us to make sacrifices, to share, and to be merciful. It has roots in culture, in religion, ethics and art, that are as deep as those of individualism. (Love thy neighbor as thyself.)

The simplest of the practices that represent altruism are sharing and sacrifice. Sharing is a static concept, suggesting an existing distribution of goods which the sharers rearrange. It means giving up to another gains or wealth that one has produced oneself or that have come to one through some good fortune. It is motivated by a sense of duty or by a sense that the other's satisfaction is a reward at least comparable to the satisfaction one might have derived from consuming the thing oneself. Sharing may also involve participation in another's losses: a spontaneous decision to shift to oneself a part of the ill fortune, deserved or fortuitous, that has befallen someone else. Sacrifice is the dynamic notion of taking action that will change an ongoing course of events, at some expense to oneself, to minimize another's loss or maximize his gain.

The polar opposite concept for sharing and sacrifice is exchange (a crucial individualist notion). The difference is that sharing and sacrifice involve a vulnerability to non-reciprocity. Further, this vulnerability is undergone out of a sense of solidarity: with the hope of a return but with a willingness to accept the possibility that there will be none. Exchange, on the contrary, signifies a transfer of resources in which equivalents are defined, and the structure of the situation, legal or social, is designed in order to make it unlikely that either party will disappoint the other. If there is some chance of disappointment, then this is experienced as a risk one must run, a cost that is unavoidable if one is to obtain what one wants from the other. The difference is one of degree, and it is easy to imagine arrangements that are such a thorough mixture, or so ambiguous, that they defy characterization one way or the other.

Individualism is to pure egotism as altruism is to total selflessness or saintliness. Thus the altruist is unwilling to carry his premise of solidarity to the extreme of making everyone responsible for the welfare of everyone else. The altruist believes in the necessity and desirability of a sphere of autonomy or liberty or freedom or privacy within which one is free to ignore both the plights of others and the consequences of one's own acts for their welfare.

Just as the individualist must find a justification for those minimal restraints on self-interest that distinguish him from the pure egotist, the altruist must justify stopping short of saintliness. The basic notion is that altruistic duties are the product of the interaction of three main aspects of a situation. First, there is the degree of communal involvement or solidarity or intimacy that has grown up between the parties. Second, there is the issue of moral fault or moral virtue in the conduct by A and B that gives rise to the duty. Third, there is the intensity of the deprivation that can be averted, or of the benefit that can be secured in relation to the size of the sacrifice demanded by altruism. Thus we can define a continuum. At one extreme, there is the duty to make a small effort to save a best friend from a terrible disaster that is no fault of his own. At the other, there are remote strangers suffering small injuries induced by their own folly and remediable only at great expense.

At first glance the usefulness of the concept of altruism in describing the legal system is highly problematic. A very common view alike in the lay world and within the legal profession is that law is unequivocally the domain of individualism, and that this is true most clearly of the private law of property, torts, and contract. Private legal justice supposedly consists in the respect for rights, never in the performance of altruistic duty. The state acts through private law only to protect rights, not to enforce morality.

Nonetheless, it is easy enough to fit fundamental legal institutions into the altruist mold. . . .

The rules of tort law can [for example] be seen as enforcing some degree of altruism. Compensation for injuries means that the interests of the injured party must be taken into account by the tortfeasor. In deciding what to do, he is no longer free to consult only his own gains and losses, since these are no longer the only gains and losses for which he is legally responsible. Likewise in contract, when I want to breach because I have found a better deal with a new partner, the law makes me incorporate into my calculation the losses I will cause to the promisee. If my breach is without fault because wholly involuntary, I may be excused for mistake or impossibility.

C. Methodological Problems

Given that individualism and altruism are sets of stereotyped pro and con arguments, it is hard to see how either of them can ever be "responsible" for a decision. First, each argument is applied, in almost identical form, to hundreds or thousands of fact situations. When the shoe fits, it is obviously not because it was designed for the wearer. Second, for each pro argument there is a con twin. Like Llewellyn's famous set of contradictory "canons on statutes," the opposing positions seem to cancel each other out.[86] Yet somehow this is not *always* the case in practice. Although each argument has an absolutist, imperialist ring to it, we find that we are able to distinguish particular fact situations in which one side is much more plausible than the other. The difficulty, the mystery, is that there are no available metaprinciples to explain just what it is about these particular situations that make them ripe for resolution. And there are many, many cases in which confidence in intuition turns out to be misplaced. . . .

Most contemporary students of legal thought agree that an account of adjudication limited to the three dimensions of authoritative premises, facts, and analysis is incomplete. One way to express this is to say that "policy" plays a large though generally unacknowledged part in decisionmaking. The problem is to find a way to describe this part. My hope is that the substantive and formal categories I describe can help in rendering the contribution of "policy" intelligible. Although individualism and altruism can be reduced neither to facts nor to logic, although they cannot be used with any degree of consistency to characterize personalities or opinions or the outcomes of lawsuits, they may nonetheless be helpful in this enterprise.

The ultimate goal is to break down the sense that legal argument is autonomous from moral, economic, and political discourse in general. There is nothing innovative about this. Indeed, it has been a premise of legal scholars for several generations that it is impossible to construct an autonomous logic of legal rules. What is new is the attempt to show an orderliness to the debates about "policy" with which we are left after abandonment of the claim of neutrality.

IV. THREE PHASES OF THE CONFLICT OF INDIVIDUALISM AND ALTRUISM

C. Modern Legal Thought (1900 to the present): The Sense of Contradiction

In private law modern legal thought begins with the rejection of Classical individualism. Its premise is that Classical theory failed to show either that the genius of our institutions is individualist or that it is possible to deduce concrete legal rules from concepts like liberty, property, or bodily security. For this reason, morality and policy reappear in modern discussions, in place of first principles and logic. The problem is that morality is no longer unequivocally altruist— there is a conflict of moralities. Nor is policy any longer unequivocally individualist—there are arguments for collectivism, regulation, the welfare state, along with the theory of economic development through laissez-faire. This conflict of morality with morality and of policy with policy pervades every important issue of private law. . . .

In private law, this modern phase of conflict occurs over three main issues, which I will call, somewhat arbitrarily, community vs. autonomy, regulation vs. facilitation, and paternalism vs. self-determination. Each particular debate has a stalemated quality that reflects the inability of either individualism or altruism to generate a new set of principles or metaprinciples to replace the late lamented concepts.

(a) Community vs. Autonomy.—The issue here is the extent to which one person should have to share or make sacrifices in the interest of another in the absence of agreement or other manifestation of intention. At first sight this issue may seem largely confined to torts and quasi-contract, but it arises in identical form in many other areas as well. The law must define the reciprocal right of neighboring landholders through the law of easements, and the rights of third-party beneficiaries and assignees against obligors. Within consensual arrangements, it must decide how to dispose of the multitude of possible controversies not covered or ambiguously covered by the parties themselves. There is the issue of the scope and intensity of the duties of fiduciaries to beneficiaries, including duties of directors and officers of corporations to shareholders. There is the whole apparatus of interpretation, excuses, and damage measures in the law of contracts. And there is the borderline area of pre- or extra-contractual liability represented by the doctrine of promissory estoppel.

The conflict of community and autonomy is the modern form of the early nineteenth-century debate about the impact on economic growth of extending or contracting nonconsensual altruistic duties. The legal institutions involved are those intermediate between pure formalities (where the law is indifferent as to which of a number of courses of action the parties undertake) and rules designed to deter wrongdoing. This category could be regarded either as designed to deter tort and breach of contract as wrongful in themselves, or, in the more common mode, as designed to offer a choice between no injury and injury *cum* compensation.

The adoption of the second view represents a decision to place *general* limits on the ability of the legal system to enforce altruistic duty. If damages are a tariff, the "wrongdoer" is authorized to consult his own interest exclusively, so long as he is willing to make the payment that secures the other party's rights. This may well involve two distinct breaches of altruistic duty.

First, even if compensation is perfect, the injuring party is forcing the injured party to take compensation, rather than specific performance or freedom from tortious interference. Second, the injuring party is under no obligation to share the excess over the compensation payment that he may derive from inflicting the injury. Once I have paid the expectation damage measure, *all* the windfall profits from breach of contract go to me.

Given the decision to regard contract and tort law as compensatory rather than punitive, the altruist and individualist have disagreements at three levels:

> *Scope of obligation:* Given a particular relationship or situation, is there any duty at all to look out for the interests of the other?
>
> *Intensity of obligation:* Given duty, how great is the duty on the scale from mere abstention from violence to the highest fiduciary obligation?
>
> *Extent of liability for consequences:* Given breach of duty, how far down the chain of causation should we extend liability?

The individualist position is the restriction of obligations of sharing and sacrifice. This means being opposed to the broadening, intensifying, and extension of liabilty *and* opposed to the liberalization of excuses once duty is established. This position is only superficially paradoxical. The contraction of initial liability leaves greater areas for people to behave in a self-interested fashion. Liberal rules of excuse have the opposite effect: they oblige the beneficiary of a duty to share the losses of the obligor when for some reason he is unable to perform. The altruist position is the expansion of the network of liability and also the liberalization of excuses.

(b) Regulation vs. Facilitation.—The issue here is the use of bargaining power as the determinant of the distribution of desired objects and the allocation of resources to different uses. It arises whenever two parties with conflicting claims or interests reach an accommodation through bargaining, and the stronger party attempts to enforce it through the legal system. The judge must then decide whether the stronger party has pressed her advantage further in her own interests than is acceptable to the legal system. If she has not, then the

agreement will be enforced; if she has, a sanction will be applied, ranging from the voiding of the agreement to criminal punishment of the abuse of bargaining power.

There are many approaches to the control of bargaining power, including:

Incapacitation of classes of people deemed particularly likely to lack adequate bargaining power (children, lunatics, etc.) with the effect that they can void their contracts if they want to.

Outlawing particular tactics, such as the use of physical violence, duress of goods, threats to inflict malicious harm, fraudulent statements, "bargaining in bad faith," etc.

Outlawing particular transactions that are thought to involve great dangers of overreaching, such as the settlement of debts for less than the full amount or the making of unilaterally beneficial modifications in the course of performance of contracts.

Control of the competitive structure of markets, either by atomizing concentrated economic power or by creating countervailing centers strong enough to bargain equally.

Direct policing of the substantive fairness of bargains, whether by direct price fixing or quality specification, by setting maxima or minima, or by announcing a standard such as "reasonableness" or "unconscionability."

The individualist position is that judges ought not to conceive of themselves as regulators of the use of economic power. This means conceiving of the legal system as a limited set of existing restraints imposed on the state of nature, and then refusing to extend those constraints to new situations. The altruist position is that existing restraints represent an attempt to achieve distributive justice which the judges should carry forward rather than impede.

(c) Paternalism vs. Self-Determination.—This issue is distinct from that of regulation vs. facilitation because it arises in situations not of conflict but of error. A party to an agreement or one who has unilaterally incurred a legal obligation seeks to void it on the grounds that he acted against his "real" interests. The beneficiary of the agreement or duty refuses to let the obligor back out. An issue of altruistic duty arises because the obligee ought to take the asserted "real" interests into account, both at the bargaining stage, if he is aware of them, and at the enforcement stage, if he only becomes aware of them then. On the other hand, he may have innocently relied on the obligor's own definition of his objectives, so that he will have to sacrifice something of his own if he behaves mercifully.

No issue of bargaining power is necessarily involved in such situations. For example:

Liquidated damage clauses freely agreed to by both parties are often voided on grounds of unreasonableness.

Express conditions unequivocal on their face are excused on grounds of forfeiture or interpreted out of existence.

Merger clauses that would waive liability for fraudulent misrepresentations are struck down or reinterpreted.

No oral modification clauses are held to be waived by actions of the beneficiary or disallowed altogether.

Modifications of contract remedy such as disclaimers of warranty or of liability for negligence, limitations of venue, waiver of defenses, and limitations on time for complaints are policed under various standards, even where they apparently result from conscious risk allocation rather than from mere superior power.

Persons lacking in capacity are allowed to void contracts that are uncoerced and substantively fair.

Consideration doctrine sometimes renders promises unenforceable because there was no "real" exchange, as in the cases of the promissory note of a widow given in exchange for a discharge of her husband's worthless debts, or that of a contract for "conjuring."

Fraud and Unconscionability doctrine protect against "unfair surprise" in situations where a party is a victim of his own foolishness rather than of the exercise of power.

The individualist position is that the parties themselves are the best and only legitimate judges of their own interests, subject to a limited number of exceptions, such as incapacity. People should be allowed to behave foolishly, do themselves harm, and otherwise refuse to accept any other person's view of what is best for them. Other people should respect this freedom; they should also be able to rely on those who exercise it to accept the consequences of their folly. The altruist response is that the paternalist rules are not exceptions, but the representatives of a developed counterpolicy of forcing people to look to the "real" interests of those they deal with. This policy is as legitimate as that of self-determination and should be extended as circumstances permit or require.

*   *   *

One way of conceiving of the transition from Classical to modern legal thought is through the imagery of core and periphery. Classical individualism dealt with the issues of community vs. autonomy, regulation vs. facilitation, and paternalism vs. self-determination by affirming the existence of a core of legal freedom that was equated with firm adherence to autonomy, facilitation, and self-determination. The existence of countertendencies was acknowledged, but in a backhanded way. By its "very nature," freedom must have limits; these could be derived as implications *from* that nature; and they would then constitute a periphery of exceptions to the core doctrines.

What distinguishes the modern situation is the breakdown of the conceptual boundary between the core and the periphery, so that all the conflicting positions are at least potentially relevant to all issues. The Classical concepts oriented us to one ethos or the other—to core or periphery—and then permitted consistent argument within that point of view, with a few hard cases occurring at the borderline. Now, each of the conflicting visions claims universal relevance, but is unable to establish hegemony anywhere. . . .

V. THE CORRESPONDENCE BETWEEN FORMAL AND SUBSTANTIVE MORAL ARGUMENTS

One might attempt to link the substantive and formal dimensions at the level of social reality. This would involve investigating, from the points of view of individualism and altruism, the actual influence of private law decisions on economic, social, and political life. One could then ask how the form in which the judge chooses to cast his decision contributes to these effects, being careful to determine the *actual* degree of formal realizability and generality of the rule or standard in question. This method is hopelessly difficult, given the current limited state of the art of assessing either actual effects of decisions or their actual formal properties. *Theories* of the practical importance of deciding private law disputes in one way or another abound, but ways to test those theories do not. This gives most legal argument a distinctly unreal, even fantastic quality that this essay will do nothing to dispel. Rather, my subject is that often unreal and fantastic rhetoric itself. This is no more than a first step, but it may be an important one.

There is a strong analogy between the arguments that lawyers make when they are defending a "strict" interpretation of a rule and those they put forward when they are asking a judge to make a rule that is substantively individualist. Likewise, there is a rhetorical analogy between the arguments lawyers make for "relaxing the rigor" of a regime of rules and those they offer in support of substantively altruist lawmaking. The simplest of these analogies is at the level of moral argument. Individualist rhetoric in general emphasizes self-reliance as a cardinal virtue. In the substantive debate with altruism, this means claiming that people *ought* to be willing to accept the consequences of their own actions. They ought not to rely on their fellows or on government when things turn out badly for them. They should recognize that they must look to their own efforts to attain their objectives. It is implicit in this idea that they are entitled to put others at arms length—to refuse to participate in their losses or make sacrifices for them.

In the formal dispute about rules and standards, this argument has a prominent role in assessing the seriousness of the over- and under-inclusiveness of rules. Everyone agrees that this imprecision is a liability, but the proponent of rules is likely to argue that we should not feel too badly about it, because those who suffer have no one to blame but themselves. Formally realizable general rules are, by definition, knowable in advance. A person who finds that he is included in liability to a sanction that was designed for someone else has little basis for complaint. Conversely, a person who gains by the victim's miscalculation is under no obligation to forego those gains.

This argument is strongest with respect to formalities. Here the meaning of underinclusion is that because of a failure to follow the prescribed form, the law refuses to carry out a party's intention to create some special set of legal relationships (e.g., voiding a will for failure to sign it). Overinclusion means that a party is treated as having an intention (e.g., to enter a contract) when he actually intended the opposite. The advocate of rules is likely to present each of these adverse results as in some sense deserved, since there is no good reason why the victim should not have engaged in competent advance planning to avoid what has happened to him.

The same argument applies to rules that are designed to enforce substantive policies rather than merely to facilitate choice between equally acceptable alternatives. Like formalities, these rules are concerned with intentional behavior in situations defined in advance. When one enters a perfectly fair contract with an infant, one has no right to complain when the infant voids it for reasons having nothing to do with the law's desire to protect him from his own folly or from overreaching.

The position of the advocate of rule enforcement is umistakably individualist. It is the sibling if not the twin of the general argument that those who fare ill in the struggle for economic or any other kind of success should shoulder the responsibility, recognize that they deserved what they got, and refrain from demanding state intervention to bail them out. The difference is that the formal argument is interstitial. It presupposes that the state has already intervened to some extent (e.g., by enforcing contracts rather than leaving them to business honor and nonlegal sanctions). It asserts that *within* this context, it is up to the parties to look out for themselves. The fact of altruistic substantive state intervention does not ipso facto wipe out the individual's duty to take care of herself.

The argument of the advocate of "relaxation," of converting the rigid rule into a standard, will include an enumeration of all the particular factors in the situation that mitigate the failure to avoid over- or underinclusion. There will be reference to the substantive purpose of the rule in order to show the arbitrariness of the result. But the ultimate point will be that there is a moral duty on the part of the private beneficiary of the over- or underinclusion to forego an advantage that is a result of the other's harmless folly. Those who take an inheritance by course of law because the testator failed to sign his will should hand the property over to those the testator wanted to receive it. A contracting party *ought not* to employ the statute of frauds to void a contract honestly made but become onerous because of a price break.

This argument smacks as unmistakably of altruism as the argument for rules smacks of individualism. The essential idea is that of mercy, here concretized as sharing or sacrifice. The ethic of self-reliance is rejected in both its branches: the altruist will neither punish the incompetent nor respect the "right" of the other party to cleave to her own interests. Again, the difference between the substantive and the formal arguments is the area of their application. It may well be that the structure of rules falls far short of requiring the level of altruistic behavior that the altruist would prefer. But within that structure, whatever it may be, there are still duties of sharing and sacrifice evoked by the very operation of the rules.

It is important to note that the altruist demand for mercy will be equally strong whether we are dealing with formalities, or with rules designed to deter substantively undesirable behavior (crimes, unconscionable contracts). The party who tries to get out of a losing contract because of failure to comply with a formality is betraying a contractual partner, someone toward whom he has assumed special duties. The infant who voids the same contract although it was neither foolish nor coerced is behaving equally reprehensibly. . . .

VIII. FUNDAMENTAL PREMISES OF INDIVIDUALISM AND ALTRUISM

Whatever their status may have been at different points over the last hundred years, individualism and altruism are now strikingly parallel in their conflicting claims. The individualist attempt at a comprehensive rational theory of the form and content of private law was a failure. But altruism has not emerged as a comprehensive rational countertheory able to accomplish the task that has defeated its adversary.

Nonetheless, the two positions live on and even flourish. The individualist who accepts the (at least temporary) impossibility of constructing a truly neutral judicial role still insists that there is a rational basis for a presumption of non-intervention or judicial passivity. The altruist, who can do no better with the problem of neutrality, is an activist all the same, arguing that the judge should accept the responsibility of enforcing communitarian, paternalist, and regulatory standards wherever possible.

The persistence of these attitudes as organizing principles of legal discourse is derived from the fact that they reflect not only practical and moral dispute, but also conflict about the nature of humanity, economy, and society. There are two sets of conflicting fundamental premises that are available when we attempt to reason abstractly about the world, and these are linked with the positions that are available to us on the more mundane level of substantive and formal issues in the legal system.

The importance of adding this theoretical dimension to the moral and practical is that it leads to a new kind of understanding of the conflict of individualism and altruism. In particular, it helps to explain the sticking points of the two sides—the moments at which the individualist, in his movement towards the state of nature, suddenly reverses himself and becomes an altruist, and the symmetrical moment at which the altruist becomes an advocate of rules and self-reliance rather than slide all the way to total collectivism or anarchism.

A. Fundamental Premises of Individualism

The characteristic structure of individualist social order consists of two elements. First, there are areas within which actors (groups or individuals) have total arbitrary discretion (often referred to as total freedom) to pursue their ends (purposes, values, desires, goals, interests) without regard to the impact of their actions on others. Second, there are rules, of two kinds: those defining the spheres of freedom or arbitrary discretion, and those governing the cooperative activities of actors—that is, their activity outside their spheres of arbitrariness. A full individualist order is the combination of (a) property rules that establish, with respect to everything valued, a legal owner with arbitrary control within fixed limits, and (b) contract rules—part supplied by the parties acting privately and part by the group as a whole acting legislatively—determining how the parties shall interact when they choose to do so. . . .

The creation of an order within which there are no occasions on which it is necessary for group members to achieve a consensus about the ends they are to pursue, or indeed for group members to make the slightest effort toward the achievement of other ends than their own, makes perfect sense if one operates on the premise that values, as opposed to facts, are inherently arbitrary and subjective.

The *subjectivity* of values means that it is, by postulate, impossible to verify directly another person's statement about his experience of ends. That is, when *A* asserts that for him a particular state of affairs involves particular values in particular ways, *B* must choose between accepting the statement or challenging the good faith of the report. *B* knows about the actual state of affairs only through the medium of *A*'s words and actions. She cannot engage *A* in an argument about *A*'s values except on the basis of that information.

The postulate of the *arbitrariness* of values means that there is little basis for discussing them. Even supposing that values were objective, so that we could all agree which ones were involved in a particular situation, and how they were involved, it would still be impossible to show by any rational process how one ought to change that objective situation. Our understanding of the existence of values, according to the postulate, is not founded on rational deductive or inductive processes. Values are simply *there* in the psyche as the springs of all action. And since we cannot explain—except by appeal to behavioristic notions like those of learning theory—why or how they *are* there, we cannot expect to converse intelligently about what they ought to be or become.

Given these conditions, it seems likely that mechanisms of social order dependent on consensus about ends will run into terrible trouble. If, by providential arrangement (or perhaps by conditioning) everyone's values turn out to be identical (or to produce identical effects), then all is well; if there is disagreement, chaos ensues. This expectation is reinforced by the other major postulate of liberal theory: that people enter groups in order to achieve ends that pre-exist the group, so that the group is a means or instrument of its members considered as individuals.

Once again, this idea is *logically* connected neither with the postulate of the arbitrariness of values nor with the characteristic rule/discretion structure of an individualist social order. It merely "resonates" these allied conceptions. Thus, if the state is only an instrument each party adopts to achieve his individual purposes, it is hard to see how it would ever make sense to set up state processes founded on the notions of changing or developing values. If the state is truly only a means to values, and all values are inherently arbitrary and subjective, the only legitimate state institutions are *facilitative*. The instant the state adopts change or development of values as a purpose, we will suspect that it does so in opposition to certain members whose values other members desire to change. The state then becomes not a means to the ends of all, but an instrument of some in their struggle with others, supposing that those others desire to retain and pursue their disfavored purposes.

The individualist theory of the judicial role follows directly from these premises. In its pure form, that theory makes the judge a simple rule applier, and rules are defined as directives whose predicates are always facts and never values. So long as the judge refers only to facts in deciding the question of liability, and the remedial consequences, he is in the realm of the objective. Since facts are objective rather than subjective, they can be determined, and one can assert that the judge is right or wrong in what he does. The result is both the certainty necessary for private maximization and the exclusion of arbitrary use of state power to further some ends (values) at the expense of others.

Modern individualism accepts that this enterprise was a failure, but it does not follow that the judge is totally at large. There is still a rational presumption in favor of nonintervention, based on the fundamental liberal premises. . . . He may not be able to frame a coherent theory of what it means to be neutral, and in this sense the legitimacy of everything he does is problematic. All reason can offer him in this dilemma is the injunction to respect autonomy, to facilitate rather than to regulate, to avoid paternalism, and to favor formal realizability and generality in his decisions. If nothing else, his action should be relatively predictable, and subject to democratic review through the alteration or prospective legislative overruling of his decisions.

B. Fundamental Premises of Altruism

The utopian counterprogram of altruist justice is collectivism. It asserts that justice consists of order according to shared ends. Everything else is rampant or residual injustice. The state, and with it the judge, are destined to disappear as people come to feel their brotherhood: it will be unnecessary to make them act "as if." The direct application of moral norms through judicial standards is therefore far preferable to a regime of rules based on moral agnosticism. But it still leaves us far from anything worthy of the name of altruistic order. The judge, after all, is there because we feel that force is necessary. Arbitrators are an improvement; mediators even better. But we attain the goal only when we surmount our alienation from one another and share ends to such an extent that contingency provides occasions for ingenuity but never for dispute.

Altruism denies the arbitrariness of values. It asserts that we understand our own goals and purposes and those of others to be at all times in a state of evolution, progress, or retrogression, in terms of a universal ideal of human brotherhood. The laws of this evolution are reducible neither to rules of cause and effect, nor to a logic, nor to arbitrary impulses of the actor. We do not control our own moral development in the sense that the mechanic controls his machine or legal rules control the citizen, but we do participate in it rather than simply undergoing it.

Altruism also denies the subjectivity of values. My neighbor's experience is anything but a closed book to me. Economists make the simplifying assumption of the "independence of utility functions," by which they suppose that A's welfare is unaffected by B's welfare. This notion is at *two* removes from reality: A's utility function is not only dependent on B's, it cannot truthfully be distinguished from B's. Quite true that we suffer *for* the suffering of others; more important that we suffer directly the suffering of others.

For the altruist, it is simply wrong to imagine the state as a means to the pre-existing ends of the citizens. Ends are collective and in process of development. It follows that the purposes that form a basis for moral decision are those of man-in-society rather than those of individuals. The administration of justice is more than a means to the ends of this whole. It is a part of it. In other words, judging is not something we have to *tolerate;* it is not a *cost* unavoidable if we are to achieve the various individual benefits of living together in groups.

Good judging, in this view, means, the creation and development of values, not just the more efficient attainment of whatever we may already want. The parties and the judge are bound together, because their disputes derive an integral part of their meaning from his participation, first imagined, later real.

Altruism offers its own definitions of legal certainty, efficiency, and freedom. The certainty of individualism is perfectly embodied in the calculations of Holmes's "bad man," who is concerned with law only as a means of an obstacle to accomplishment of his antisocial ends. The essence of individualist certainty-through-rules is that because it identifies for the bad man the precise limits of toleration for his badness, it authorizes him to hew as close as he can to those limits. To the altruist this is a kind of collective insanity by which we traduce our values while pretending to define them. Of what possible benefit can it be that the bad man calculates with certainty the contours within which vice is unrestrained? Altruism proposes an altogether different standard: the law is certain when not the bad but the *good* man is secure in the expectation that if he goes forward in good faith, with due regard for his neighbor's interest as well as his own, and a suspicious eye to the temptations of greed, then the law will not turn up as a dagger in his back. As for the bad man, let him beware; the good man's security and his own are incompatible.

"Efficiency" in the resolution of disputes is a pernicious objective unless it includes in the calculus of benefits set against the costs of administering justice the moral development of society through deliberation on the problem of our apparently disparate ends. Indeed, attempts to achieve the efficiency celebrated by individualism are likely to make these true benefits of judging unattainable, and end in a cheaper production of injustice and social disintegration.

The "freedom" of individualism is negative, alienated, and arbitrary. It consists in the absence of restraint on the individual's choice of ends, and has no moral content whatever. The altruist asserts that the staccato alternation of mechanical control and obliviousness is destructive of every value that makes freedom a thing to be desired. We can achieve real freedom only collectively through *group* self-determination. We are simply too weak to realize ourselves in isolation. True, collective self-determination, short of utopia, implies the use of force against the individual. But we experience and accept the use of physical and psychic coercion every day, in family life, education, and culture. We experience it indirectly, often unconsciously, in political and economic life. The problem is the conversion of force into moral force, in the fact of the experience of moral indeterminacy. A definition of freedom that ignores this problem is no more than a rationalization of indifference, or the velvet glove for the hand of domination through rules.

C. The Implications of Contradictions
Within Consciousness

The explanation of the sticking points of the modern individualist and altruist is that both believe quite firmly in both of these sets of premises, in spite of the fact that they are radically contradictory. The altruist critique of liberalism rings true for the individualist who no longer believes in the possibility of generating concepts that will in turn generate rules defining a just social order. The liberal critique of anarchy or collectivism rings true for the altruist, who acknowledges that after all we have not overcome the fundamental dichotomy of subject and object. So long as others are, to some degree, independent and unknowable beings, the slogan of shared values carries a real threat of tyranny more oppressive than alienation in an at least somewhat altruistic liberal state.

The acknowledgment of contradiction does not abate the moral and practical conflict, but it does permit us to make some progress in characterizing it. At an elementary level, it makes it clear that it is futile to imagine that moral and practical conflict will yield to analysis in terms of higher level concepts. The meaning of contradiction at the level of abstraction is that there is no metasystem that would, if only we could find it, key us into one mode or the other as circumstances "required."

Second, the acknowledgment of contradiction means that we cannot "balance" individualist and altruist values or rules against equitable standards, except in the tautological sense that we can, as a matter of fact, decide if we have to. The imagery of balancing presupposes exactly the kind of more abstract unit of measurement that the sense of contradiction excludes. The only kind of imagery that conveys the process by which we act and act and act in one direction, but then reach the sticking point, is that of existentialist philosphy. We make commitments, and pursue them. The moment of abandonment is no more rational than that of beginning, and equally a moment of terror.

Third, the recognition that both participants in the rhetorical struggle of individualism and altruism operate from premises that they accept only in this problematic fashion weakens the individualist argument that result orientation is dynamically unstable. Given contradiction at the level of pure theory, the open recognition of the altruist element in the legal system does not mean an irrevocable slide down the slope to totalitarianism, any more that it would lead to the definitive establishment of substantive justice in the teeth of the individualist rule structure.

Individualism, whether in the social form of private property or in that of rules, is *not* an heroically won, always precariously held symbol of man's fingernail grip on civilized behavior. That is a liberal myth. In any developed legal system, individualist attitudes, and especially the advocacy of rules, respond to a host of concrete interests having everything to lose by their erosion. Lawyers are necessary because of rules; the prestige of the judge is professional and technical, as well as charismatic and arcane, because of them; litigants who have mastered the language of form can dominate and oppress others, or perhaps simply prosper because of it; academics without number hitch their wagonloads of words to the star of technicality. Individualism is the structure of the status quo.

But there is more to it even than that. In elites, it responds to fear of the masses. In the masses, it responds to fear of the caprice of rulers. In small groups, it responds to fear of intimacy. In the psyche, it responds to the ego's primordial fear of being overwhelmed by the id. Its roots are deep enough so that one suspects an element of the paranoid in the refusal to recognize its contradictory sibling within consciousness.

Finally, the acknowledgment of contradiction makes it easier to understand judicial behavior that offends the ideal of the judge as a supremely rational being. The judge cannot, any more than the analyst, avoid the moment of truth in which one simply shifts modes. In place of the apparatus of rule making and rule application, with its attendant premises and attitudes, we come suddenly on a gap, a balancing test, a good faith standard, a fake or incoherent rule, or the enthusiastic adoption of a train of reasoning all know will be ignored in the next case. In terms of individualism, the judge has suddenly begun to act in bad faith. In terms of altruism *she has found herself.* The only thing that counts is this change in attitude, but it is hard to imagine anything more elusive of analysis.

NOTES

1. H. Hart and A. Sacks, *The Legal Process* 113 (tentative ed. 1958).
73. Some important works in the tradition I am referring to are G. Hegel, *Philosophy of Right* (Oxford: Clarendon Press, Knox trans. 1952); K. Marx, "On the Jewish Question," in *Early Writings* (Benton trans. 1975; Harmondsworth: Penguin); Lukacs, "Reification and the Consciousness of the Proletariat," in *History and Class-Consciousness: Studies in Marxist Dialectics* (Livingstone trans. 1971, M.I.T. Press: Cambridge, Mass.); K. Mannheim, *Ideology and Utopia: An Introduction to the Sociology of Knowledge* (San Diego: Harcourt, Brace, Jovanovitch, 1936); H. Marcuse, *Reason and Revolution: Hegel and the Rise of Social Theory*, Boston: Beacon Press (1941); C. Levi-Strauss, *The Savage Mind* (1966) Chicago: U. of Chic. Press: R. Unger, *Knowledge and Politics* (1975) New York: Free Press.
80. *See* K. Llewellyn, *The Common Law Tradition: Deciding Appeals* (1960), pp. 521–35. (Boston: Little, Brown).

Feminism, Marxism, Method, and the State: Toward Feminist Jurisprudence

Catharine A. MacKinnon

Feminism has no theory of the state. It has a theory of power: sexuality is gendered as gender is sexualized. Male and female are created through the erotization of dominance and submission. The man/woman difference and the dominance/submission dynamic define each other. This is the social meaning of sex and the distinctively feminist account of gender inequality.[1] Sexual objectification, the central process within this dynamic, is at once epistemological and political. The feminist theory of knowledge is inextricable from the feminist critique of power because the male point of view forces itself upon the world as its way of apprehending it. . . .

The perspective from the male standpoint[3] enforces woman's definition, encircles her body, circumlocutes her speech, and describes her life. The male perspective is systemic and hegemonic. The content of the signification "woman" is the content of women's lives. Each sex has its role, but their stakes and power are not equal. If the sexes are unequal, and perspective participates in situation, there is no ungendered reality or ungendered perspective. And they are connected. In this context, objectivity—the nonsituated, universal standpoint, whether claimed or aspired to—is a denial of the existence or potency of sex inequality that tacitly participates in constructing reality from the dominant point of view. Objectivity, as the epistemological stance of which objectification is the social process, creates the reality it apprehends by defining as knowledge the reality it creates through its way of apprehending it. Sexual metaphors for

Excerpted from its original publication in *Signs: Journal of Women in Culture and Society* 7, 1983. Reprinted by permission of author and University of Chicago Press.

knowing are no coincidence. The solipsism of this approach does not undercut its sincerity, but it is interest that precedes method.

Feminism criticizes this male totality without an account of our capacity to do so or to imagine or realize a more whole truth. Feminism affirms women's point of view by revealing, criticizing, and explaining its impossibility. This is not a dialectical paradox. It is a methodological expression of women's situation, in which the struggle for consciousness is a struggle for world: for a sexuality, a history, a culture, a community, a form of power, an experience of the sacred. If women had consciousness or world, sex inequality would be harmless, or all women would be feminist. Yet we have something of both, or there would be no such thing as feminism. Why can women know that this—life as we have known it—is not all, not enough, not ours, not just? Now, why don't all women?[5]

The practice of a politics of all women in the face of its theoretical impossibility is creating a new process of theorizing and a new form of theory. Although feminism emerges from women's particular experience, it is not subjective or partial, for no interior ground and few if any aspects of life are free of male power. Nor is feminism objective, abstract, or universal. It claims no external ground or unsexed sphere of generalization nor abstraction beyond male power, nor transcendence of the specificity of each of its manifestations. How is it possible to have an engaged truth that does not simply reiterate its determinations? *Dis*engaged truth only reiterates *its* determinations. Choice of method is choice of determinants—a choice which, for women as such, has been unavailable because of the subordination of women. Feminism does not begin with the premise that it is unpremised. It does not aspire to persuade an unpremised audience, because there is no such audience. Its project is to uncover and claim as valid the experience of women, the major content of which is the devalidation of women's experience.

This defines our task not only because male dominance is perhaps the most pervasive and tenacious system of power in history, but because it is metaphysically nearly perfect. Its point of view is the standard for point-of-viewlessness, its particularity the meaning of universality. Its force is exercised as consent, its authority as participation, its supremacy as the paradigm of order, its control as the definition of legitimacy. Feminism claims the voice of women's silence, the sexuality of our eroticized desexualization, the fullness of "lack," the centrality of our marginality and exclusion, the public nature of privacy, the presence of our absence. This approach is more complex than transgression, more transformative than transvaluation, deeper than mirror-imaged resistance, more affirmative than the negation of our negativity. It is neither materialist nor idealist; it is feminist. Neither the transcendence of liberalism nor the determination of materialism works for us. Idealism is too unreal; women's inequality is enforced, so it cannot simply be thought out of existence, certainly not by us. Materialism is too real; women's inequality has never not existed, so women's equality never has. That is, the equality of women to men will not be scientifically provable until it is no longer necessary to do so. Women's situation offers no outside to stand on or gaze at, no inside to escape to, too much urgency to wait, no place else to go, and nothing to use but the twisted tools that have been shoved down our throats. If feminism is revolutionary, this is why.

Feminism has been widely thought to contain tendencies of liberal feminism, radical feminism, and socialist feminism. But just as socialist feminism has often amounted to marxism applied to women, liberal feminism has often amounted to liberalism applied to women. Radical feminism is feminism. Radical feminism—after this, feminism unmodified—is methodologically post-Marxist.[8] It moves to resolve the Marxist-feminist problematic on the level of method. Because its method emerges from the concrete conditions of all women as a sex, it dissolves the individualist, naturalist, idealist, moralist structure of liberalism, the politics of which science is the epistemology. Where liberal feminism sees sexism primarily as an illusion or myth to be dispelled, an inaccuracy to be corrected, true feminism sees the male point of view as fundamental to the male power to create the world in its own image, the image of its desires, not just as its delusory end product. Feminism distinctively as such comprehends that what counts as truth is produced in the interest of those with power to shape reality, and that this process is as pervasive as it is necessary as it is changeable. Unlike the scientific strain in Marxism or the Kantian imperative in liberalism, which in this context share most salient features, feminism neither claims universality nor, failing that, reduces to relativity. It does not seek a generality that subsumes its particulars or an abstract theory or a science of sexism. It rejects the approach of control over nature (including us) analogized to control over society (also including us) which has grounded the "science of society" project as the paradigm for political knowledge since (at least) Descartes. Both liberalism and Marxism have been subversive on women's behalf. Neither is enough. To grasp the inadequacies for women of liberalism on one side and Marxism on the other is to begin to comprehend the role of the liberal state and liberal legalism[9] within a post-Marxist feminism of social transformation.

As feminism has a theory of power but lacks a theory of the state, so Marxism has a theory of value which (through the organization of work in production) becomes class analysis, but a problematic theory of the state. Marx did not address the state much more explicitly than he did women. Women were substratum, the state epiphenomenon. Engels, who frontally analyzed both, and together, presumed the subordination of women in every attempt to reveal its roots, just as he presupposed something like the state, or state-like social conditions, in every attempt to expose its origins. Marx tended to use the term "political" narrowly to refer to the state or its laws, criticizing as exclusively political interpretations of the state's organization or behavior which took them as sui generis. Accordingly, until recently, most Marxism has tended to consider political that which occurs between classes, that is, to interpret as "the political" instances of the Marxist concept of inequality. In this broad sense, the Marxist theory of social inequality has been its theory of politics. This has not so much collapsed the state into society (although it goes far in that direction) as conceived the state as determined by the totality of social relations of which the state is one determined and determining part— without specifying which, or how much, is which.

In this context, recent Marxist work has tried to grasp the specificity of the institutional state: how it wields class power, or transforms class society, or responds to approach by a left aspiring to rulership or other changes. While liberal theory has seen the state as emanating power, and traditional Marxism has seen the state as expressing power constituted elsewhere, recent Marxism, much of it structuralist, has tried to analyze state power as specific to the state as a form, yet integral to a determinate social whole understood in class terms. This state is found "relatively autonomous". This means that the state, expressed through its functionaries, has a definite class character, is definitely capitalist or socialist, but also has its own interests which are to some degree independent of those of the ruling class and even of the class structure. The state as such, in this view, has a specific power and interest, termed "the political," such that class power, class interest expressed by and in the state, and state behavior, although inconceivable in isolation from one another, are nevertheless not linearly or causally linked or strictly coextensive. Such work locates "the specificity of the political" in a mediate "region" between the state as its own ground of power (which alone, as in the liberal conception, would set the state above or apart from class) and the state as possessing no special supremacy or priority in terms of power, as in the more orthodox Marxist view.

The idea that the state is relatively autonomous, a kind of first among equals of social institutions, has the genius of appearing to take a stand on the issue of reciprocal constitution of state and society while straddling it. Is the state essentially autonomous of class but partly determined by it, or is it essentially determined by class but not exclusively so? Is it relatively constrained within a context of freedom or relatively free within a context of constraint? As to who or what fundamentally moves and shapes the realities and instrumentalities of domination, and where to go to do something about it, what qualifies what is as ambiguous as it is crucial. Whatever it has not accomplished, however, this literature has at least relieved the compulsion to find all law—directly or convolutedly, nakedly or clothed in unconscious or devious rationalia—to be simply bourgeois, without undercutting the notion that it is determinately driven by interest.

A methodologically post-Marxist feminism must confront, on our own terms, the issue of the relation between the state and society, within a theory of social determination adequate to the specificity of sex. Lacking even a tacit theory of the state of its own, feminist practice has instead oscillated between a liberal theory of the state on the one hand and a left theory of the state on the other. Both treat law as the mind of society: disembodied reason in liberal theory, reflection of material interest in left theory. In liberal moments the state is accepted on its own terms as a neutral arbiter among conflicting interests. The law is actually or potentially principled, meaning predisposed to no substantive outcome, thus available as a tool that is not fatally twisted. Women implicitly become an interest group within pluralism, with specific problems of mobilization and representation, exit and voice, sustaining incremental gains and losses. In left moments, the state becomes a tool of dominance and repression, the law legitimizing ideology, use of the legal system a form of utopian idealism or gradualist reform, each apparent gain deceptive or cooptive, and each loss inevitable.

Applied to women, liberalism has supported state intervention on behalf of women as abstract persons with abstract rights, without scrutinizing the content of these notions in gendered terms. Marxism applied to women is always on the edge of counseling abdication of the state as an arena altogether—and with it those women whom the state does not ignore or who are, as yet, in no position to ignore it. Feminism has so far accepted these constraints upon its alternatives: either the state, as primary tool of women's betterment and status transformation, without analysis (hence strategy) for it as male; or civil society, which for women has more closely resembled a state of nature. The state, with it the law, has been either omnipotent or impotent: everything or nothing.

The feminist posture toward the state has therefore been schizoid on issues central to women's survival: rape, battery, pornography, prostitution, sexual harassment, sex discrimination, abortion, the Equal Rights Amendment, to name a few. Attempts to reform and enforce rape laws, for example, have tended to build on the model of the deviant perpetrator and the violent act, as if the fact that rape is a crime means that the society is against it, so law enforcement would reduce or delegitimize it. Initiatives are accordingly directed toward making the police more sensitive, prosecutors more responsive, judges more receptive, and the law, in words, less sexist. This may be progressive in the liberal or the left senses, but how is it empowering in the feminist sense? Even if it were effective in jailing men who do little different from what nondeviant men do regularly, how would such an approach alter women's rapability? Unconfronted are *why* women are raped and the role of the state in that. Similarly, applying laws against battery to husbands, although it can mean life itself, has largely failed to address, as part of the strategy for state intervention, the conditions that produce men who systematically express themselves violently toward women, women whose resistance is disabled, and the role of the state in this dynamic. Criminal enforcement in these areas, while suggesting that rape and battery are deviant, punishes men for expressing the images of masculinity that mean their identity, for which they are otherwise trained, elevated, venerated, and paid. These men must be stopped. But how does that change them or reduce the chances that there will be more like them? Liberal strategies entrust women to the state. Left theory abandons us to the rapists and batterers. The question for feminism is not only whether there is a meaningful difference between the two, but whether either is adequate to the feminist critique of rape and battery as systemic and to the role of the state and the law within that system.

Feminism has descriptions of the state's treatment of the gender difference, but no analysis of the state as gender hierarchy. We need to know. What, in gender terms, are the state's norms of accountability, sources of power, real constituency? Is the state to some degree autonomous of the interests of men, or an integral expression of them? Does the state embody and serve male interests in its form, dynamics, relation to society, and specific policies? Is the state constructed upon the subordination of women? If so, how does male power become state power? Can such a state be made to serve the interests of those upon whose powerlessness its power is erected? Would a different relation between state and society, such as may pertain under socialism, make a difference? If not, is masculinity inherent in the state form as such, or is some other form of state, or some other way of governing, distinguishable or imaginable? In the absence of answers to such questions, feminism has been caught between giving more power to the state in each attempt to claim it for women and leaving unchecked power in the society to men. Undisturbed, meanwhile, like the assumption that women generally consent to sex, is the assumption that we consent to this government. The question for feminism, for the first time on its own terms, is: what is this state, from women's point of view?

As a beginning, I propose that the state is male in the feminist sense. The law sees and treats women the way men see and treat women. The liberal state coercively and authoritatively constitutes the social order in the interest of men as a gender, through its legitimizing norms, relation to society, and substantive policies. It achieves this through embodying and ensuring male control over women's sexuality at every level, occasionally cushioning, qualifying, or de jure prohibiting its excesses when necessary to its normalization. Substantively, the way the male point of view frames an experience is the way it is framed by state policy. To the extent possession is the point of sex, rape is sex with a woman who is not yours, unless the act is so as to make her yours. If part of the kick of pornography involves eroticizing the putatively prohibited, obscenity law will putatively prohibit pornography enough to maintain its desirability without ever making it unavailable or truly illegitimate. The same with prostitution. As male is the implicit reference for human, maleness will be the measure of equality in sex discrimination law. To the extent that the point of abortion is to control the reproductive sequelae of intercourse, so as to facilitate male sexual access to women, access to abortion will be controlled by "a man or The Man."[16] Gender, elaborated and sustained by behavioral patterns of application and administration, is maintained as a division of power.

Formally, the state is male in that objectivity is its norm. Objectivity is liberal legalism's conception of itself. It legitimizes itself by reflecting its view of existing society, a society it made and makes by so seeing it, and calling that view, and that relation, practical rationality. If rationality is measured by point-of-viewlessness, what counts as reason will be that which corresponds to the way things are. Practical will mean that which can be done without changing anything. In this framework, the task of legal interpretation becomes "to perfect the state as mirror of the society."[17] Objectivist epistemology is the law of law. It ensures that the law will most reinforce existing distributions of power when it most closely adheres to its own highest ideal of fairness. Like the science it emulates, this epistemological stance cannot see the social specificity of reflection as method or its choice to embrace that which it reflects. Such law not only reflects a society in which men rule women; it rules in a male way: "The phallus means everything that sets itself up as a mirror."[18] The rule form, which unites scientific knowledge with state control in its conception of what law is, institutionalizes the objective stance as jurisprudence. . . .

II

Feminists have reconceived rape as central to women's condition in two ways. Some see rape as an act of violence, not sexuality, the threat of which intimidates all women.[20] Others see rape, including its violence, as an expression of male sexuality, the social imperatives of which define all women. The first, formally in the liberal tradition, comprehends rape as a displacement of power based on physical force onto sexuality, a pre-existing natural sphere to which domination is alien. Thus, Susan Brownmiller examines rape in riots, wars, pogroms, and revolutions; rape by police, parents, prison guards; and rape motivated by racism—seldom rape in normal circumstances, in everyday life, in ordinary relationships, by men as men. Women are raped by guns, age, white supremacy, the state—only derivatively by the penis. The more feminist view to me, one which derives from victims' experiences, sees sexuality as a social sphere of male power of which forced sex is paradigmatic. Rape is not less sexual for being violent; to the extent that coercion has become integral to male sexuality, rape may be sexual to the degree that, and because, it is violent.

The point of defining rape as "violence not sex" or "violence against women" has been to separate sexuality from gender in order to affirm sex (heterosexuality) while rejecting violence (rape). The problem remains what it has always been: telling the difference. The convergence of sexuality with violence, long used at law to deny the reality of women's violation, is recognized by rape survivors, with a difference: where the legal system has seen the intercourse in rape, victims see the rape in intercourse. The uncoerced context for sexual expression becomes as elusive as the physical acts come to feel indistinguishable.[23] Instead of asking what is the violation of rape, what if we ask what is the nonviolation of intercourse? To tell what is wrong with rape, explain what is right about sex. If this, in turn, is difficult, the difficulty is as instructive as the difficulty men have in telling the difference when women see one. Perhaps the wrong of rape has proven so difficult to articulate because the unquestionable starting point has been that rape is definable as distinct from intercourse, when for women it is difficult to distinguish them under conditions of male dominance.

Like heterosexuality, the crime of rape centers on penetration.[26] The law to protect women's sexuality from forcible violation/expropriation defines the protected in male genital terms. Women do resent forced penetration. But penile invasion of the vagina may be less pivotal to women's sexuality, pleasure or violation, than it is to male sexuality. This definitive element of rape centers upon a male-defined loss, not coincidentally also upon the way men define loss of exclusive access. In this light, rape, as legally defined, appears more a crime against female monogamy than against female sexuality. Property concepts fail fully to comprehend this,[27] however, not because women's sexuality is not, finally, a thing, but because it is never ours. The moment we "have" it—"have sex" in the dual sexuality/gender sense—it is lost as ours. This may explain the male incomprehension that, once a woman has had sex, she loses anything when raped. To them we *have nothing* to lose. Dignitary harms, because nonmaterial, are remote to the legal mind. But women's loss through rape is not only less tangible, it is less existent. It is difficult to avoid the conclusion that penetration itself is known to be a violation and that women's sexuality, our gender definition, is itself stigmatic. If this is so, the pressing question for explanation is not why some of us accept rape, but why any of us resent it.

The law of rape divides the world of women into spheres of consent according to how much say we are legally presumed to have over sexual access to us by various categories of men. Little girls may not consent; wives must. If rape laws existed to enforce women's control over our own sexuality, as the consent defense implies, marital rape would not be a widespread exception, nor would statutory rape proscribe all sexual intercourse with underage girls regardless of their wishes. The rest of us fall into parallel provinces: good girls, like children, are unconsenting, virginal, rapable; bad girls, like wives, are consenting, whores, unrapable. The age line under which girls are presumed disabled from withholding consent to sex rationalizes a condition of sexual coercion women never outgrow. As with protective labor laws for women only, dividing and protecting the most vulnerable becomes a device for not protecting everyone. Risking loss of even so little cannot be afforded. Yet the protection is denigrating and limiting (girls may not choose to be sexual) as well as perverse (girls are eroticized as untouchable; now reconsider the data on incest).

If the accused knows us, consent is inferred. The exemption for rape in marriage is consistent with the assumption underlying most adjudications of forcible rape: to the extent the parties relate, it was not really rape, it was personal.[29] As the marital exemptions erode, preclusions for cohabitants and voluntary social companions may expand. In this light, the partial erosion of the marital rape exemption looks less like a change in the equation between women's experience of sexual violation and men's experience of intimacy, and more like a legal adjustment to the social fact that acceptable heterosexual sex is increasingly not limited to the legal family. So although the rape law may not now always assume that the woman consented simply because the parties are legally one, indices of closeness, of relationship ranging from nodding acquaintance to living together, still contraindicate rape. Perhaps this reflects men's experience that women they know meaningfully consent to sex with them. That cannot be rape; rape must be by someone else, someone unknown. But *women* experience rape most often by men we know. Men believe that it is less awful to be raped by someone one is close to: "the emotional trauma suffered by a person victimized by an individual with whom sexual intimacy is shared as a normal part of an ongoing marital relationship is not nearly as severe as that suffered by a person who is victimized by one with whom that intimacy is not shared."[31] But women feel as much, if not more, traumatized by being raped by someone we have known or trusted, someone we have shared at least an illusion of mutuality with, than by some stranger. In whose interest is it to believe that it is not so bad to be raped by someone who has fucked you before as by someone who has not? Disallowing charges of rape in marriage may also "remove a substantial obstacle to the resumption of normal marital relations;"[32] depending upon your view of normal. Note that the obstacle to normalcy here is not the rape but the law against it. Apparently someone besides feminists finds sexual victimization and sexual intimacy not all that contradictory. Sometimes I think women and men live in different cultures.

Having defined rape in male sexual terms, the law's problem, which becomes the victim's problem, is distinguishing rape from sex in specific cases. The law does this by adjudicating the level of acceptable force starting just above the level set by what is seen as normal male sexual behavior, rather than at the victim's, or women's, point of violation. Rape cases finding insufficient force reveal that acceptable sex, in the legal perspective, can entail a lot of force. This is not only because of the way specific facts are perceived and interpreted, but because of the way the injury itself is defined as illegal. Rape is a sex crime that is a not a crime when it looks like sex. To seek to define rape as violent, not sexual, is understandable in this context, and often seems strategic. But assault that is consented to is still assault; rape consented to is intercourse. The substantive reference point implicit in existing legal standards is the sexually normative level of force. Until this norm is confronted as such, no distinction between violence and sexuality will prohibit more instances of women's experienced violation than does the existing definition. The question is what is *seen as* force, hence as violence, in the sexual arena. Most rapes, as women live them, will not be seen to violate women until sex and violence are confronted as mutually definitive. It is not only men convicted of rape who believe that the only thing they did different from what men do all the time is get caught.

The line between rape and intercourse commonly centers on some measure of the woman's "will." But from what should the law know woman's will? Like much existing law, Brownmiller tends to treat will as a question of consent and consent as a factual issue of the presence of force.[33] Proof problems aside, force and desire are not mutually exclusive. So long as dominance is eroticized, they never will be. Women are socialized to passive receptivity; may have or perceive no alternative to acquiescence; may prefer it to the escalated risk of injury and the humiliation of a lost fight; submit to survive. Some eroticize dominance and submission; it beats feeling forced. Sexual intercourse may be deeply unwanted—the woman would never have initiated it—yet no force may be present. Too, force may be used, yet the woman may want the sex—to avoid more force or because she, too, eroticizes dominance. Women and men know this. Calling rape violence, not sex, thus evades, at the moment it most seems to confront, the issue of who controls women's sexuality and the dominance/submission dynamic that has defined it. When sex is violent, women may have lost control over what is done to us, but absence of force does not ensure the presence of that control. Nor, under conditions of male dominance, does the presence of force make an interaction nonsexual. If sex is normally something men do to women, the issue is less whether there was force and more whether consent is a meaningful concept.

To explain women's gender status as a function of rape, Brownmiller argues that the threat of rape benefits all men.[35] She does not specify in what way. Perhaps it benefits them sexually, hence as a gender: male initiatives toward women carry the fear of rape as support for persuading compliance, the resulting appearance of which has been called consent. Here the victims' perspective grasps what liberalism applied to women denies: that forced sex as sexuality is not exceptional in relations between the sexes but constitutes the social meaning of gender: "Rape is a man's act, whether it is male or a female man and whether it is a man relatively permanently or relatively temporarily; and being raped is a woman's experience, whether it is a female or a male women and whether it is a woman relatively permanently or relatively temporarily."[36] To be rap*able*, a position which is social, not biological, defines what a woman *is*.

Most women get the message that the law against rape is virtually unenforceable as applied to them. Our own experience is more often delegitimized by this than the law is. Women radically distinguish between rape and experiences of sexual violation, concluding that we have not "really" been raped if we have ever seen or dated or slept with or been married to the man, if we were fashionably dressed or are not provably virgin, if we are prostitutes, if we put up with it or tried to get it over with, if we were force-fucked over a period of years. If we probably couldn't prove it in court, it wasn't rape. The distance between most sexual violations of women and the legally perfect rape measures the imposition of someone else's definition upon women's experience. Rape, from women's point of view, is not prohibited; it is regulated. Even women who know we have been raped do not believe that the legal system will see it the way we do. We are often not wrong. Rather than deterring or avenging rape, the state, in many victims' experiences, perpetuates it. Women who charge rape say they were raped twice, the second time in court. If the state is male, this is more than a figure of speech.

The law distinguishes rape from intercourse by the woman's lack of consent coupled with a man's (usually) knowing disregard of it. A feminist distinction between rape and intercourse, to hazard a beginning approach, lies instead in the *meaning* of the act from women's point of view. What is wrong with rape is that it is an act of the subordination of women to men. Seen this way, the issue is not so much what rape "is" as the way its social conception is shaped to interpret particular encounters. Under conditions of sex inequality, with perspective bound up with situation, whether a contested interaction is rape comes down to whose meaning wins. If sexuality is relational, specifically if it is a power relation of gender, consent is a

communication under conditions of inequality. It transpires somewhere between what the woman actually wanted and what the man
comprehended she wanted. Instead of capturing this dynamic, the
law gives us linear statics face to face. Nonconsent in law becomes a
question of the man's force or the woman's resistance, or both.[37] Rape,
like many crimes and torts, requires that the accused possess a
criminal mind (mens rea) for his acts to be criminal. The man's mental
state refers to what he actually understood at the time or to what a
reasonable man should have understood under the circumstances.
The problem is this: the injury of rape lies in the meaning of the act to
its victims, but the standard for its criminality lies in the meaning of
the same act to the assailants. Rape is an injury only from women's
point of view. It is a crime only from the male point of view, explicitly
including that of the accused.

Thus is the crime of rape defined and adjudicated from the male
standpoint, that is, presuming that (what feminists see as) forced sex is
sex. Under male supremacy, of course, it is. What this means doctrinally is that the man's perceptions of the woman's desires often
determine whether she is deemed violated. This might be like other
crimes of subjective intent if rape were like other crimes. But with
rape, because sexuality defines gender, the only difference between
assault and (what is socially considered) noninjury is the meaning of
the encounter to the woman. Interpreted this way, the legal problem
has been to determine whose view of that meaning constitutes what
really happened, as if what happened objectively exists to be objectively determined, thus as if this task of determination is separable
from the gender of the participants and the gendered nature of their
exchange. Thus, even though the rape law oscillates between subjective tests and more objective standards invoking social reasonableness,
it uniformly presumes a single underlying reality, not a reality split by
divergent meanings, such as those inequality produces. Many women
are raped by men who know the meaning of their acts to women and
proceed anyway.[38] But women are also violated every day by men who
have no idea of the meaning of their acts to women. To them, it is sex.
Therefore, to the law, it is sex. That is the single reality of what
happened. When a rape prosecution is lost on a consent defense, the
woman has not only failed to prove lack of consent, she is not
considered to have been injured at all. Hermeneutically unpacked,
read: because he did not perceive she did not want him, she was not
violated. She had sex. Sex itself cannot be an injury. Women consent
to sex every day. Sex makes a woman a woman. Sex is what women
are *for*.

To a feminist analysis, men set sexual mores ideologically and
behaviorally, define rape as they imagine the sexual violation of
women through distinguishing it from their image of what they
normally do, and sit in judgment in most accusations of sex crimes. So

rape comes to mean a strange (read "black") man knowing a woman does not want sex and going ahead anyway. But men are systematically conditioned not even to notice what women want. They may have not a glimmer of women's indifference or revulsion. Rapists typically believe the woman loved it. Women, as a survival strategy, must ignore or devalue or mute our desires (particularly lack of them) to convey the impression that the man will get what he wants regardless of what we want. In this context, consider measuring the genuineness of consent from the individual assailant's (or even the socially reasonable, i.e., objective, man's) point of view.

Men's pervasive belief that women fabricate rape charges after consenting to sex makes sense in this light. To them, the accusations *are* false because, to them, the facts describe sex. To interpret such events as rapes distorts their experience. Since they seldom consider that their experience of the real is anything other than reality, they can only explain the woman's version as maliciously invented. Similarly, the male anxiety that rape is easy to charge and difficult to disprove (also widely believed in the face of overwhelming evidence to the contrary) arises because rape accusations express one thing men cannot seem to control: the meaning to women of sexual encounters.

Thus do legal doctrines, incoherent or puzzling as syllogistic logic, become coherent as ideology. For example, when an accused wrongly but sincerely believes that a woman he sexually forced consented, he may have a defense of mistaken belief or fail to satisfy the mental requirement of knowingly proceeding against her will.[40] One commentator notes, discussing the conceptually similar issue of revocation of prior consent (i.e., on the issue of the conditions under which women are allowed to control access to their sexuality from one time to the next): "Even where a woman revokes prior consent, such is the male ego that, seized of an exaggerated assessment of his sexual prowess, a man might genuinely believe her still to be consenting; resistance may be misinterpreted as enthusiastic cooperation; protestations of pain or disinclination, a spur to more sophisticated or more ardent love-making; a clear statement to stop, taken as referring to a particular intimacy rather than the entire performance."[41] This equally vividly captures common male readings of women's indications of disinclination under all kinds of circumstances.[42] Now reconsider to what extent the man's perceptions should determine whether a rape occurred. From whose standpoint, and in whose interest, is a law that allows one person's conditioned unconsciousness to contraindicate another's experienced violation? This aspect of the rape law reflects the sex inequality of the society not only in conceiving a cognizable injury from the viewpoint of the reasonable rapist, but in affirmatively rewarding men with acquittals for not comprehending women's point of view on sexual encounters.

Whether the law calls this coerced consent or mistake of fact, the more the sexual violation of women is routine, the more beliefs equating sexuality with violation become reasonable, and the more honestly women can be defined in terms of our fuckability. It would be comparatively simple if the legal problem were limited to avoiding retroactive falsification of the accused's state of mind. Surely there are incentives to lie. But the deeper problem is the rape law's assumption that a single, objective state of affairs existed, one that merely needs to be determined by evidence, when many (maybe even most) rapes involve honest men and violated women. When the reality is split—a woman is raped but not by a rapist?—the law tends to conclude that a rape *did not happen*. To attempt to solve this by adopting the standard of reasonable belief without asking, on a substantive social basis, to whom the belief is reasonable and why—meaning, what conditions make it reasonable—is one-sided: male-sided. What is it reasonable for a man to believe concerning a woman's desire for sex when heterosexuality is compulsory? Whose subjectivity becomes the objectivity of "what happened" is a matter of social meaning, that is, it has been a matter of sexual politics. One-sidedly erasing women's violation or dissolving the presumptions into the subjectivity of either side are alternatives dictated by the terms of the object/subject split, respectively. These are alternatives that will only retrace that split until its terms are confronted as gendered to the ground.

Desirability to men is commonly supposed to be a woman's form of power. This echoes the view that consent is women's form of control over intercourse, different but equal to the custom of male initiative. Look at it: man initiates, woman chooses. Even the ideal is not mutual. Apart from the disparate consequences of refusal, or openness of original options, this model does not envision a situation the woman controls being placed in, or choices she frames, yet the consequences are attributed to her as if the sexes began at arm's length, on equal terrain, as in the contract fiction. Ambiguous cases of consent are often archetypically referred to as "half-won arguments in parked cars."[43] Why not half lost? Why isn't half enough? Why is it an argument? Why do men still want "it," feel entitled to "it," when women don't want them? That sexual expression is even framed as a matter of woman's consent, without exposing these presuppositions, is integral to gender inequality. Woman's so-called power presupposes her more fundamental powerlessness.

III

The state's formal norms recapitulate the male point of view on the level of design. In Anglo-American jurisprudence, morals (value judgments) are deemed separable and separated from politics (power contests), and both from adjudication (interpretation). Neutrality, including judicial decisionmaking that is dispassionate, impersonal, disinterested, and precedential, is considered desirable and descriptive. Courts, forums without predisposition among parties and with no interest of their own, reflect society back to itself resolved. Government of laws, not men, limits partiality with written constraints and tempers force with reasonable rule following. This law aspires to science: to the immanent generalization subsuming the emergent particularity, to prediction and control of social regularities and regulations, preferably codified. The formulaic "tests" of "doctrine" aspire to mechanism, classification to taxonomy. Courts intervene only in properly factualized disputes, cognizing social conflicts as if collecting empirical data. But the demarcations between morals and politics, the personality of the judge and the judicial role, bare coercion and the rule of law,[46] tend to merge in women's experience. Relatively seamlessly they promote the dominance of men as a social group through privileging the form of power—the perspective on social life—feminist consciousness reveals as socially male. The separation of form from substance, process from policy, role from theory and practice, echoes and reechoes at each level of the regime its basic norm: objectivity.

Consider a central example. The separation of public from private is as crucial to the liberal state's claim to objectivity as its inseparability is to women's claim to subordination. Legally, it has both formal and substantive dimensions. The state considers formal, not substantive, the allocation of public matters to itself to be treated objectively, of private matters to civil society to be treated subjectively. Substantively, the private is defined as a right to "an inviolable personality,"[47] which is guaranteed by ensuring "autonomy or control over the intimacies of personal identity."[48] It is hermetic. It means that which is inaccessible to, unaccountable to, and unconstructed by anything beyond itself. Intimacy occurs in private; this is supposed to guarantee original symmetry of power. Injuries arise in violating the private sphere, not within and by and because of it. Private means consent can be presumed unless disproven. To contain a systematic inequality contradicts the notion itself. But feminist consciousness has exploded the private. For women, the measure of the intimacy has been the measure of the oppression. To see the personal as political means to see the private as public. On this level, women have no privacy to lose or to guarantee. We are not inviolable. Our sexuality, meaning gender identity, is not only violable, it *is* (hence we are) our violation. Privacy is everything women as women have never been allowed to be or to have; at the same time the private is everything women have been equated with and defined in terms of *men's* ability to have. To confront the fact that we have no privacy is to confront our private degradation as the public order. To fail to recognize this place of the private in women's subordination by seeking protection behind a right to that privacy is thus to be cut off from collective verification and state support in the same act.[49] The very place (home, body), relations (sexual), activities (intercourse and reproduction), and feelings (intimacy, selfhood) that feminism finds central to women's subjection form the core of privacy doctrine. But when women are segregated in private, one at a time, a law of privacy will tend to protect the right of men "to be let alone,"[50] to oppress us one at a time. A law of the private, in a state that mirrors such a society, will translate the traditional values of the private sphere into individual women's right to privacy, subordinating women's collective needs to the imperatives of male supremacy. It will keep some men out of the bedrooms of other men.

Liberalism converges with the left at this edge of the feminist critique of male power. Herbert Marcuse speaks of "philosophies which are 'political' in the widest sense—affecting society as a whole, demonstrably transcending the sphere of privacy."[52] This does and does not describe the feminist political: "Women both have and have not had a common world."[53] Isolation in the home and intimate degradation, women share. The private sphere, which confines and separates us, is therefore a political sphere, a common ground of our inequality. In feminist translation, the private is a sphere of battery, marital rape, and women's exploited labor; of the central social institutions whereby women are deprived of (as men are granted) identity, autonomy, control, and self-determination; and of the primary activity through which male supremacy is expressed and enforced. Rather than transcending the private as a predicate to politics, feminism politicizes it. For women, the private necessarily transcends the private. If the most private also most "affects society as a whole," the separation between public and private collapses as anything other than potent ideology. The failure of Marxism adequately to address intimacy on the one hand, government on the other, is the same failure as the indistinguishability between Marxism and liberalism on questions of sexual politics.

Interpreting further areas of law, a feminist theory of the state will reveal that the idealism of liberalism and the materialism of the left have come to much the same for women. Liberal jurisprudence that the law should reflect society and left jurisprudence that all law does or can do is reflect existing social relations will emerge as two guises of objectivist epistemology. If objectivity is the epistemological stance of which women's sexual objectification is the social process, its imposition the paradigm of power in the male form, then the state will appear most relentless in imposing the male point of view when it comes closest to achieving its highest formal criterion of distanced aperspectivity. When it is most ruthlessly neutral, it will be most male; when it is most sex-blind, it will be most blind to the sex of the standard being applied. When it most closely conforms to precedent, to "facts," to legislative intent, it will most closely enforce socially male norms and most thoroughly preclude questioning their content as having a point of view at all. Abstract rights will authoritize the male experience of the world. The liberal view that law is society's text, its rational mind, expresses this in a normative mode; the traditional left view that the state, and with it the law, is superstructural or epiphenomenal expresses it in an empirical mode. Both rationalize male power by presuming that it does not exist, that equality between the sexes (room for marginal corrections conceded) is society's basic norm and fundamental description. Only feminism grasps the extent to which the opposite is true: that anti-feminism is as normative as it is empirical. Once masculinity appears as a specific position, not just as the way things are, its judgments will be revealed in process and procedure, as well as adjudication and legislation. Perhaps the objectivity of the liberal state has made it appear "autonomous of class." Including, but beyond, the bourgeois in liberal legalism, lies what is male about it. However autonomous of class the liberal state may appear, it is not autonomous of sex. Justice will require change, not reflection—a new jurisprudence, a new relation between life and law.

NOTES

1. Much has been made of the distinction between sex and gender. Sex is thought the more biological, gender the more social. The relation of each to sexuality varies. Since I believe sexuality is fundamental to gender and fundamentally social, and that biology is its social meaning in the system of sex inequality, which is a social and political system that does not rest independently on biological differences in any respect, the sex/gender distinction looks like a nature/culture distinction. I use sex and gender relatively interchangeably.

3. Male is a social and political concept, not a biological attribute. As I use it, it has nothing whatever to do with inherency, pre-existence, nature, inevitability, or body as such. It is more epistemological than ontological, undercutting the distinction itself, given male power to conform being with perspective. The perspective from the male standpoint is not always each man's opinion, although most men adhere to it, nonconsciously and without considering it a point of view, as much because it makes sense of their experience (the male experience) as because it is in their interest. It is rational for them. A few men reject it; they pay. Because it is the dominant point of view and defines rationality, women are pushed to see reality in its terms, although this denies their vantage point as women in that it contradicts (at least some of) their lived experience. Women who adopt the male standpoint are passing, epistemologically speaking. This is not uncommon and is rewarded. The intractability of maleness as a form of dominance suggests that social constructs, although they flow from human agency, can be less plastic than nature has proven to be. If experience trying to do so is any guide, it may be easier to change biology than society.

5. Feminism aspires to represent the experience of all women as women see it, yet criticizes antifeminism and misogyny, including when it appears in female form. This tension is compressed in the epistemic term of art "the standpoint of all women." We are barely beginning to unpack it. Not all women agree with the feminist account of women's situation, nor do all feminists agree with any single rendition of feminism. Authority of interpretation—the claim to speak as a woman—thus becomes methodologically complex and politically crucial for the same reasons. Consider the accounts of

their own experience given by right-wing women and lesbian sadoma
patriarchy be diminishing to women when women embrace and del
it? How can dominance and submission be violating to women when
Now what is the point of view of the experience of all women? Mo
name of feminism, stated in terms of method, either (1) simply rega.. --
views as "false consciousness," or (2) embrace any version of women's experience that a
biological female claims as her own. The first approach treats some women's views as
unconscious conditioned reflections of their oppression, complicitous in it. Just as
science devalues experience in the process of uncovering its roots, this approach
criticizes the substance of a view because it can be accounted for by its determinants.
But if both feminism and antifeminism are responses to the condition of women, how is
feminism exempt from devalidation by the same account? That feminism is critical, and
antifeminism is not, is not enough, because the question is the basis on which we know
something is one or the other when women, all of whom share the condition of women,
disagree. The false consciousness approach begs this question by taking women's self-
reflections as evidence of their stake in their own oppression, when the women whose
self-reflections are at issue question whether their condition is oppressed at all. The
second response proceeds as if women are free. Or, at least, as if we have considerable
latitude to make, or to choose, the meanings if not the determinants of our situation.
Or that the least feminism can do, since it claims to see the world through women's eyes,
is to validate the interpretations women choose. Both responses arise because of the
unwillingness, central to feminism, to dismiss some women as simply deluded while
granting other women the ability to see the truth. These two resolutions echo the
object/subject split: objectivity (my consciousness is true, yours false, never mind why)
or subjectivity (I know I am right because it feels right to me, never mind why). Thus is
determinism answered with transcendence, traditional marxism with traditional liberalism, dogmatism with tolerance. The first approach claims authority on the basis of its
lack of involvement, asserting its view independent of whether the described concurs—
sometimes because it does not. It also has no account, other than its alleged lack of
involvement, of its own ability to provide such an account. How can some women see
the truth and other women not? The second approach claims authority on the basis of
its involvement. It has no account for different interpretations of the same experience
or any way of choosing among conflicting ones, including those between women and
men. It tends to assume that women, as we are, have power and are free in exactly the
ways feminism, substantively, has found we are not. Thus, the first approach is one-
sidedly outside when there is no outside, the second one-sidedly inside when someone
(probably a woman) is inside everything, including every facet of sexism, racism, and so
on. So our problem is this: the false consciousness approach cannot explain experience
as it is experienced by those who experience it. The alternative can only reiterate the
terms of that experience. This is only one way in which the object/subject split is fatal to
the feminist enterprise. The feminist criticism is not that the objective stance fails to be
truly objective because it has social content, all the better to exorcise that content in the
pursuit of the more truly point-of-viewless viewpoint. The criticism is that objectivity is
largely accurate to its/the/a world, which world is criticized; and that it becomes more
accurate as the power it represents and extends becomes more total.

8. This feminism seeks to define and pursue women's interest as the fate of all
women bound together. It seeks to extract the truth of women's commonalities out of
the lie that all women are the same. If whatever a given society defines as sexual defines
gender, and if gender means the subordination of women to men, "woman" means—is
not qualified or undercut by—the uniqueness of each woman and the specificity of race,
class, time, and place. In this sense, lesbian feminism, the feminism of women of color,
and socialist feminism are converging in a feminist politics of sexuality, race, and class,
with a left-to-right spectrum of its own. This politics is struggling for a practice of unity
that does not depend upon sameness without dissolving into empty tolerance, including
tolerance of all it exists to change whenever that appears embodied in one of us. A new
community begins here. As critique, women's communality describes a fact of male
supremacy, of sex "in itself": no woman escapes the meaning of being a woman within a
gendered social system, and sex inequality is not only pervasive but may be universal (in

the sense of never having not been in some form) although "intelligible only in . . . locally specific forms" (M. Z. Rosaldo, "The Use and Abuse of Anthropology: Reflections on Feminism and Cross-cultural Understanding," *Signs: Journal of Women in Culture and Society* 5, no. 3 [Spring 1980]: 389–417, 417). For women to become a sex "for ourselves" moves community to the level of vision.

9. See Karl Klare, "Law-Making as Praxis," *Telos* 12, no. 2 (Summer 1979): 123–35.

16. Johnnie Tillmon, "Welfare Is a Women's Issue," *Liberation News Service* (February 26, 1972), in *America's Working Women: A Documentary History, 1600 to the Present*, ed. Rosalyn Baxandall, Linda Gordon, and Susan Reverby (New York: Vintage Books, 1976), pp. 357–58.

17. Laurence Tribe, "Constitution as Point of View" (Harvard Law School, Cambridge, Mass., 1982, mimeographed), p. 13.

18. Madeleine Gagnon, "Body I," in *New French Feminisms*, ed. Elaine Marks and Isabelle de Courtivron (Amherst: University of Massachusetts Press, 1980), p. 180.

20. Susan Brownmiller, *Against Our Will: Men, Women and Rape* (New York: Simon & Schuster, 1976), p. 15.

23. "Like other victims, I had problems with sex, after the rape. There was no way that Arthur could touch me that it didn't remind me of having been raped by this guy I never saw" (Carolyn Craven, "No More Victims: Carolyn Craven Talks about Rape, and about What Women and Men Can Do to Stop It," ed. Alison Wells [Berkeley, Calif., 1978, mimeographed[), p. 2.

26. Sec. 213.0 of the *Model Penal Code* (Official Draft and Revised Comments 1980), like most states, defines rape as sexual intercourse with a female who is not the wife of the perpetrator "with some penetration however slight." Impotency is sometimes a defense. Michigan's gender-neutral sexual assault statute includes penetration by objects (sec. 520a[h]; 520[b]). See *Model Penal Code*, annotation to sec. 213.1(d) (Official Draft and Revised Comments 1980).

27. Although it is true that men possess women and that women's bodies are, socially, men's things, I have not analyzed rape as men treating women like property. In the manner of many socialist-feminist adaptations of Marxian categories to women's situation, that analysis short-circuits analysis of rape as male sexuality and presumes rather than develops links between sex and class. We need to rethink sexual dimensions of property as well as property dimensions of sexuality.

29. On "social interaction as an element of consent," in a voluntary social companion context, see *Model Penal Code*, sec. 213.1. "The prior social interaction is an indicator of consent in addition to actor's and victim's behavioral interaction during the commission of the offense" (Wallace Loh, "Q: What Has Reform of Rape Legislation Wrought? A: Truth in Criminal Labeling," *Journal of Social Issues* 37, no. 4 [1981]: 28–52, 47). Perhaps consent should be an affirmative defense, pleased and proven by the defendant.

31. Answer Brief for Plaintiff-Appellee at 10, People v. Brown, 632 P.2d 1025 (Colo. 1981).

32. Brown, 632 P.2d at 1027 (citing Comment, "Rape and Battery between Husband and Wife," *Stanford Law Review* 6 [1954]: 719–28, 719, 725).

33. Brownmiller, *Against Our Will*, pp. 8, 196, 400–407, 427–36.

35. Ibid., p. 5.

36. Carolyn M. Shafer and Marilyn Frye, "Rape and Respect" in *Feminism and Philosophy*, ed. Mary Vetterling-Braggin, Frederick A. Elliston and Jane English (Towota, N.J.: Littlefield, Adams & Co., 1977), pp. 334. Battery of wives has been legally separated from marital rape not because assault by a man's fist is so different from assault by a penis. Both seem clearly violent. I am suggesting that both are also sexual. Assaults are often precipitated by women's noncompliance with gender requirements. See R. Emerson Dobash and Russell Dobash, *Violence Against Wives: A Case Against the Patriarchy* (New York: Free Press, 1979), pp. 14–20. Nearly all incidents occur in the home, most in the kitchen or bedroom. Most murdered women are killed by their husbands, most in the bedroom. The battery cycle accords with the rhythm of heterosexual sex (see Leonore Walker, *The Battered Woman* [New York: Harper & Row, 1979], pp. 19–20). The rhythm of lesbian S/M appears similar (Samois, ed., *Coming to*

Power [Palo Alto, Calif.: Up Press, 1981]). Perhaps most interchange between genders, but especially violent ones, make sense in sexual terms. However, the larger issue for the relation between sexuality and gender, hence sexuality and violence generally, including both war and violence against women, is: what is heterosexuality? If it is the erotization of dominance and submission, altering the participants' gender is comparatively incidental. If it is males over females, gender matters independently. Since I see heterosexuality as the fusion of the two, but with gender a social outcome (such that the acted upon is feminized, is the "girl" regardless of sex, the actor correspondingly masculinized), battery appears sexual on a deeper level. In baldest terms, sexuality is violent, so violence is sexual, violence against women doubly so. If this is so, wives are beaten, as well as raped, as women—as the acted upon, as gender, meaning sexual, objects. It further follows that all acts by anyone that treat a woman according to her object label "woman" are sexual acts. The extent to which sexual acts are acts of objectification remains a question of our account of our freedom to make our own meanings. It is clear, at least, that it is centering sexuality upon genitality that distinguishes battery from rape at exactly the juncture that both the law, and seeing rape as violence not sex, does.

37. Even when nonconsent is not a legal element of the offense (as in Michigan), juries tend to infer rape from evidence of force or resistance.

38. This is apparently true of undetected as well as convicted rapists. Samuel David Smithyman's sample, composed largely of the former, contained self-selected respondents to his ad, which read: "Are you a rapist? Researchers Interviewing Anonymously by Phone to Protect Your Identity. Call . . ." Presumably those who chose to call defined their acts as rapes, at least at the time of responding ("The Undetected Rapist" [Ph.D. diss., Claremont Graduate School, 1978], pp. 54–60, 63–76, 80–90, 97–107).

40. See Director of Public Prosecutions v. Morgan, [1976] A.C. 182; Pappajohn v. The Queen, 11 D.L.R. (3d) 1 (1980); People v. Mayberry, 15 Cal. 3d 143, 542 P.2d 1337 (1975).

41. Richard H. S. Tur, "Rape: Reasonableness and Time," *Oxford Journal of Legal Studies* 3 (Winter 1981): 432–41, 441. Tur, in the context of the Morgan and Pappajohn cases, says the "law ought not to be astute to equate wickedness and wishful, albeit mistaken, thinking" (p. 437). In feminist analysis, a rape is not an isolated or individual or moral transgression but a terrorist act within a systematic context of group subjection, like lynching.

42. See Silke Vogelmann-Sine et al., "Sex Differences in Feelings Attributed to a Woman in Situations Involving Coercion and Sexual Advances," *Journal of Personality* 47, no. 3 (September 1979): 420–31, esp. 429–30.

43. Note, "Forcible and Statutory Rape: An Exploration of the Operation and Objectives of the Consent Standard," *Yale Law Journal* 62 (1952): 55–56.

46. Rawls's "original position," for instance, is a version of my objective standpoint (John Rawls, *A Theory of Justice* [Cambridge: Harvard University Press, 1971]). Not only apologists for the liberal state, but also some of its most trenchant critics, see a real distinction between the rule of law and absolute arbitrary force. E. P. Thompson, *Whigs and Hunters: The Origin of the Black Act* (New York: Pantheon Books, 1975), pp. 258–69. Douglas Hay argues that making and enforcing certain acts as illegal reinforces a structure of subordination ("Property, Authority, and the Criminal Law," in *Albion's Fatal Tree: Crime and Society in Eighteenth Century England*, D. Hay et al., eds. [New York: Pantheon Books, 1975], pp. 17–31). Michael D. A. Freeman ("Violence against Women: Does the Legal System Provide Solutions or Itself Constitute the Problem?" [Madison, Wis., 1980, mimeographed], p. 12, n. 161) applies this argument to domestic battery of women. Here I extend it to women's situation as a whole, without suggesting that the analysis can end there.

47. S. D. Warren and L. D. Brandeis, "The Right to Privacy," *Harvard Law Review* 4 (1890):193–205.

48. Tom Gerety, "Redefining Privacy," *Harvard Civil Right–Civil Liberties Law Review* 12, no. 2 (Spring 1977): 236.

49. Harris v. McRae, 448 U.S. 287 (1980), which holds that withholding public funds for abortions does not violate the federal constitutional right to privacy, illustrates.

50. Robeson v. Rochester Folding Box Co., 171 NY 538 (1902); W. Cooley, *Torts*, sec. 135, 4th ed. (Chicago: Callaghan & Co., 1932).

51. Herbert Marcuse, "Repressive Tolerance," in *A Critique of Pure Tolerance*, ed. Robert Paul Wolff, Barrington Moore, Jr., and Herbert Marcuse (Boston: Beacon Press, 1965), pp. 81–117, esp. p. 91.

53. Adrienne Rich, "Conditions for Work: The Common World of Women," in *Working It Out: Twenty-three Women Writers, Artists, Scientists, and Scholars Talk About Their Lives and Work*, ed. Sara Ruddick and Pamela Daniels (New York: Pantheon Books, 1977), pp. xiv–xxiv, esp. p. xiv.

PART II

Tracking History

History has always been at the heart of the legal enterprise. Lawyers are taught to use the past to shape future solutions out of present problems. Long the orphan of the academic community, legal history has recently become its favored child. Indeed, one scholar has gone so far as to say that the study of legal history has become the study of law *tout court*. Yet, oblivious to Maitland's warning, traditional writers have infected the study of legal history with a distinctly legal mind-set; they have not sought to understand the past through the force of evidence, but to utilize that past through the logic of authority. In charting the relation between law and historical change, they have tended to muffle and suppress the subversive threat of history rather than to open up legal study to its destabilizing influence. Critical histories demonstrate that law, and the legal theory that rationalizes it, is historically contingent.

The challenge to Critical scholars has been to keep sharp the radical edge of history in the face of traditional attempts to blunt it. Always a crucial dimension of the Critical genre, various historiographical essays and histories have been written as a challenge to the traditional stories and their narrative commitments. In a wide-ranging piece, Robert Gordon tackles the assumed inevitability of law's tendency to evolve to the benefit and for the enhancement of an advanced form of Western capitalism. He rejects the dominant functionalism and any attempt to objectify the contingent character of history. Explaining the contribution Critical legal history has made to our understanding of law, he notes some of its strengths and, in the spirit of critical seriousness, possible weaknesses. He ends by looking to the challenges ahead. The other two selections provide richly textured examples of the Critical method of historical scholarship at work.

As part of a major study on how 19th-century legal doctrine developed to subsidize economic development and promote class interests, Morton Horwitz offers an account of contract law that challenges the benign orthodoxy. He demonstrates how the massive changes in contract doctrine related to the rise of the modern market economy. Alan Freeman looks at how the courts neutralized the revolutionary potential of antidiscrimination doctrine. By posing the problem in terms of individual action and not systemic conditions, the courts managed to avoid confronting the pervasive and entrenched nature of racism and taking steps toward its eradication. For Freeman, law projects an image that it is responsive to and remedying racial practices, when it is actually perpetuating their deep effects and causes.

5

Critical Legal Histories

Robert W. Gordon

THE DOMINANT VISION:
EVOLUTIONARY FUNCTIONALISM

A. Common Threads

Over the last 150 years or so, enlightened American legal opinion has adhered with remarkable fidelity to what, in broad conception, looks like a single set of notions about historical change and the relation of law to such change. Stated baldly, these notions are that the natural and proper evolution of a society (or at least of a "progressive" society, to use Maine's qualification) is towards the type of liberal capitalism seen in the advanced Western nations (especially the United States), and that the natural and proper function of a legal system is to facilitate such an evolution. . . .

"Law" and "society" are separate social categories, each describable independently from the other but related to each other through various mechanisms of causal linkage.

Writers in the dominant tradition make an important, though usually silent, move even before they start saying anything substantive about law-in-history: they divide the world into two spheres, one social and one legal. "Society" is the primary realm of social experience. It is "real life": what's immediately and truly important to people, like desire and its fulfillment or frustration, goes on there. This realm is the realm of production, commerce, the market, the family. "Law" or "the legal system," on the other hand, is a distinctly secondary body of phenomena. It is a specialized realm of state and professional activity that is called into being by the primary social

Excerpted from its original publication in *Stanford Law Review* 36, 1984. Reprinted by permission of the author and the Stanford Law Review.

world in order to serve that world's needs. Law is auxiliary—an excrescence on social life, even if sometimes a useful excrescence.

Though law and society are separate, they are related. And the big theoretical problem for writers who see the world this way is to work out the secret of that relationship. Thus, they ask questions such as, "Is law a dependent or independent variable?" "Is everything about law—norms, rules, processes, and institutions—determined by society, or does law have 'autonomous' internal structures or logic? If it has internal structures, do they enable it to have an independent causal effect—to act as a positive feedback loop—on social life?" Writers in the liberal tradition (like those in the Marxist tradition) have resolved these questions in wildly different ways and reached wildly different conclusions, but they all assume that these *are* the vital questions.

Societies have needs.

This proposition is the functionalist heart of the dominant vision. Social needs may be universal—needs such as survival, stability, maintenance of social order, conflict management, organization of production, security against foreign enemies, allocation of scarce resources, or preservation of continuity in the midst of change—or they may be specific to a given stage of social or economic development. One key need is the *need to develop* along the appropriate social evolutionary path.

Needs operate both as pressures and as constraints. They are the motors driving the society to find means for their fulfillment, and they set the limits on the possibilities of social experimentation—limits beyond which lie dysfunction, futility, failure, and chaos.

There is an objective, determined, progressive social evolutionary path.

The general idea here is that the causal responsibility for change lies with impersonal forces of historical "becoming." More specifically, the histories of certain advanced Western societies, most notably the United States, describe an evolutionary development that is both natural (in the sense that some version of it will happen in every society unless "artificial" constraints force a deviation) and, on the whole, progressive.

Different generations have described this evolutionary process somewhat differently, but the contemporary United States almost always ends up sitting at the developmental summit.

What all these histories have in common is their determinist teleologies, whose elemental parts—the "extension of the market," the "breakdown of traditional communities and status hierarchies," the "shift from ascribed to achieved social status," the "triumph of the middle class," the "revolution of production in the factory system," the "rise of the administrative state," and the "development of the multi-divisional form of corporate organization"—are all linked together in a master *process* of social evolution. . . .

Legal systems should be described and explained in terms of their functional responsiveness to social needs.

Functionalist sociological legal history has an exceedingly distinguished lineage, beginning with Montesquieu and Adam Smith, continuing through Karl Marx, Max Weber, and Rudolph von Jhering, and virtually all lesser nineteenth-century writers on law, and including among twentieth-century lawyers such figures as Oliver Wendell Holmes, Roscoe Pound, Karl Llewellyn, Franz Neumann, and Willard Hurst. The general functionalist method is to construct (or, as is rather more common, to assume without much discussion) a typology of stages of social development and then to show how legal forms and institutions have satisfied, or failed to satisfy, the functional requirements of each stage. Obviously, an enormous gap in sophistication and conceptual power separates the best and worst examples of this method. At its best, as in Weber's work, complex bundles of rules are tied through explicit theorizing to elaborate accounts of social development. At its comically vulgar worst, the method produces wholly speculative functional rationales for legal rules in underlying social changes—vacuously described rationales such as "the evolution of the right of privacy was a response to the increasing complexity and interdependence of modern society." . . .

The legal system adapts to changing social needs.

This concept expresses the confidence that, in the advanced Western nations and especially in the United States, the legal system *has in fact* responded to evolving social needs. Save for egregiously Panglossian writers (Blackstone in some moods is one of these), the proponents of this notion do not feel a need to attribute a social function to every piece of law in the system; most writers will concede that even major legal forms and processes can be dysfunctional for short periods. But a committed functionalist will maintain that, despite undeniable instances of lag and reaction, adaptation is the normal course. The perspective thus tends to produce statements such as the following: . . .

- Tort law rules such as the negligence standard and the fellow-servant rule were adopted to meet the needs of early industrial development. (They allowed employers and transportation entrepreneurs to externalize a portion of their costs.) But as technological change increased the risks of accidents stemming from employment and from the use of consumer goods, the law responded with rules of strict liability.
- Warranty rules such as "caveat emptor" reflected a society in which most commercial trading was face-to-face. But with the rise of mass

consumer transactions between remote sellers and purchasers and with increasing ignorance about the risks of defects, the law implied warranties of merchantability.
- The corporate form developed in order to fulfill the need for capital accumulation during the period of industrial take-off. . . .
- Courts and legislatures were competent to handle the problems of regulating the early nineteenth-century economy of competitive individuals. By the late nineteenth century, however, the concentration of corporate enterprise was raising problems of such complexity that administrative agencies were required to handle them.
- Professionalism of the bar—the development of bar associations, law schools, formalized training and entry requirements, the large urban law office, etc.—was necessary to enable lawyers to take on the complex specialized tasks of law in a modern economy.

This perspective also produces some very large claims indeed. The first two examples listed below were commonplace in legal rhetoric through the end of the last century; the third is asserted by some lawyer-economists in our own time:

- The common law over time tends to work itself pure.
- Progressive improvements in legal science have tended to clarify legal doctrine, making it ever more certain and predictable, as well as more adaptable to social needs.
- Common law rules have tended to become more and more efficient.

Divisions Within Functionalism

By now it will be evident that my "dominant tradition" is a very broad umbrella, covering legal writers whose views on many issues differ radically, some of whom would be appalled to find themselves sharing even a limited-purpose category with the others. In particular, I mean to group under the common shelter of "evolutionary functionalism" both of the great antagonistic parties of modern American legal thought, labeled here for simplicity's sake "Formalism" and "Realism."

The Formalist side has a very restrictive notion of law as judgemade law: "The legal system is the domain of the legal specialist; the legislature is in general not part of the legal system but a source of the goals that the legal system is to carry out." Legislation and usually administration as well are thus relegated to the "social" sphere of the great law/society dichotomy. On the Realist side, however, law is "what officials do about disputes," or even more broadly, the work of anyone, including the private bar, whose task is the administration of public policy.

Formalists and Realists also divide over the issue of the "autonomy" of legal decision-making processes in relation to political, social, and economic decisonmaking. Formalists think that it is both usual and desirable for legal decisions to follow an internal professional agenda such as "a taught legal tradition" of the common law. The idea is that such decisions will best perform their social/functional task of adaptation if lawyers and judges are not thinking about society at all but only about perfecting their own craft, because a logic of liberty or efficiency is inherent in the practice of that craft. Realists think that this proposition is nonsense, that policymaking can't be socially functional unless it is self-consciously directed towards the satisfaction of social needs. Realists do, however, have their own notion of legal "autonomy": policymakers ought to be, and sometimes actually are, insulated from the immediate pressures of short-term political or economic interests so they can concentrate on their society's long-run needs.

These differences lead to differing Formalist and Realist approaches to legal history. Formalist legal history focuses exclusively on the development of legal doctrine, while Realist legal history considers doctrine as one component of a general, if not always well-coordinated, policy-making enterprise. Further, Formalist legal history considers phenomena outside the legal craft as distorting judicial decisionmaking or as simply irrelevant to the important story to be told: the Formalist hero is the judge or treatise-writer who best clarifies doctrinal categories. Realist history, on the other hand, takes as its main subject the relations of function or dysfunction between law and major trends of social development; the Realist hero is the social engineer who masterfully wields law as an instrument of policy.

Naturally these differences lead to fundamental disagreements about the course of recent history. For many Formalists, the high point of legal development was reached around the end of the nineteenth century when the ideal of the rule of law as primarily enforced by judges through an autonomous legal order was at its peak of influence. But the Formalists' high is the Realists' low: at that time, abstraction from concrete social forces had put the legal system badly out of sync with evolving requirements of society, and we climbed out of this trough of dysfunction only through the implementation of the policies of Progressivism and the New Deal.

INTERLUDE FOR QUESTIONS ABOUT THE POINT OF THIS PROJECT

Before going on to say something about the attacks that have been eating away at the evolutionary-functionalist vision of legal history, it is worth pausing a moment to ask why anyone should bother to attack the vision at all. Social scientists who have heard previous versions of this piece wonder why I worry so much about evolutionism . . . and functionalism . . . the mainstays of the liberal sociology of the 1950s; these views have been so thoroughly discredited in modern social theory, they argue, as to be left almost without serious defenders. On the other hand, some of my legal colleagues, who have spent their working lives trying to slay the Formalist hydra that is still powerfully present in legal-academic and professional thought generally, think it perverse and ungrateful to attack the Realist versions of functionalism, for these versions have proved to be the most reliable weapons against the dogma that legal forms can be understood apart from their social context. If the weapons are broken, won't the hydra stalk the law schools unafraid?

To the first question, the second is itself a partial answer. Evolutionary functionalism, in both the Formalist and Realist versions, has been kept going much longer in legal thought than in social thought generally. This isn't only because the law schools tend to pick up mainstream intellectual opinion ten to fifteen years late. The notion that law always is, or at least ought to be, functionally adapting to evolving social needs is so deeply embedded in standard legal speech that one isn't likely to make a legal argument of any length without at least mentioning it. This notion presumably persists because of its serviceability to the liberal idea of law as the neutral arbiter of social conflict: it tells the managers of the legal system that their basic instructions are specified by a social process outside the legal system and that they have no responsibility for that process except to solve the technical problems of devising functional responses that will help rather than hinder it. Hence, the inevitable ambiguities of legislative command, prior case law, custom, or constitutional text need never force a legal system to the pain of political choice because its managers can always claim to be serving the logic of an historical process or immanent social consensus that exists beyond and prior to politics.

What's more, not only is evolutionary functionalism still a living force in traditional legal argument, it has in recent years received a terrific hormone boost from some of the fanciest and most interesting *new* work coming out of the law schools: the Chicago law and economics movement. Williamson's "transaction cost" approach to legal institutions,[29] Bob Clark's explicitly evolutionary approach to the history of the modern corporation,[30] and Selznick and Nonet's theory of "responsive law."[31]

Perhaps by now the second question, "Why knock functionalism when it's been so good to you?," is on its way to being answered. Realist functionalism has unquestionably been a politically progressive and intellectually liberating force; it has moved us away from the occasionally useful but ultimately sterile studies of technical forms evolving in a cultural vacuum and from the idea that lawyers and judges will always and automatically do the most possible good through complacent inattention to the society in which they live. Its empirical investigations of the law "in action" have exploded forever the Formalist fantasy that a universal scheme of neutral, general rules controls equally and impersonally the discretion of every class and faction of civil society. We owe to the Realist tradition of scholarship most of our understanding of variations in the effectiveness of law according to the power and wealth of the people it touches or who seek to use it, of "legal pluralism" (the fact that real social life is prodigal of sovereigns—different governments, officials at different levels of government, "private" associations—each making its own brand of law in cooperation or competition with the others), and of the complexity and perversity of legal/social relations (how it so often happens that a legal form seemingly designed to strengthen A's at the expense of B's ends up wiping out A's and entrenching B's more immovably than ever). So much indeed have the Realist functionalists accomplished that it's hard not to sympathize with their resentment of Critics who seem to be trying to displace them.

The Critics can give this *cri de coeur* a straightforward answer: any intelligent Critical approach will make use of the insights and empirical findings of Realist functionalism, but there are apologetic aspects even to the Realist versions of the dominant vision that the Critics feel compelled to resist. For example, by emphasizing law as policy, Realist functionalism almost unconsciously reserves even what it believes to be the very marginal opportunities for legal influence on the direction of social change to an elite of policymakers: mass movements and local struggles are not ordinarily thought of as makers of legal change. Because it assumes a natural harmony of interests in the fulfillment of social needs, it has trouble seeing conflict as other than dysfunctional disturbance of equilibrium. And, with all regard for its heroic contributions, I believe its essential working assumptions misleadingly objectify history, making highly contingent developments appear to have been necessary. . . . Surely there are other ways of thinking about history that don't trap us into supposing we're permanently stuck with what we happen to be used to, with only the tiniest margins for maneuvering. The hope of getting out of that trap and of exploring the alternatives is what fuels the enterprise of criticizing the dominant vision.

PARTIAL CRITIQUES: VARIATIONS ON THE DOMINANT THEME

I call the sample of views that follow partial critiques because they remain faithful to many elements of the dominant vision while rejecting others. These critiques come from all colors of the political spectrum.

A. Variation #1: Collapse "Needs" into Interests

This move is so common that it could be called a subtheme rather than a variation of the dominant view. It consists simply of breaking down the universal category of societal needs into the particular conflicting desires or interests of society's members. The function of law then becomes that of responding to some balance of those interests. . . . There are several different ways of characterizing the interests that law tries to satisfy. Right-wing economism says that interests are just the arbitrary desires of individual subjects, revealed through crude behavioral proxies such as "willingness to pay" or votes. This school has no theory at all of how such desires originate, except perhaps a vague notion that people in a given occupational or institutional role will want to maximize the interest the theorist casually attributes to that role. Centrist-liberal pluralism discovers what interests are by looking at the programs of organized groups and largely explains legal enactments as compromises among those interests. While this view is certainly a big advance over the view of society as isolated individuals or roles, its mainstream forms have been famously vulnerable to the charge of lacking any plausible account of power or social structure that would help explain why some groups get their way more than others or why some groups never get to be "interests" at all because they can't organize. Finally, various economisms, not all on the left, do pay attention to power and social structure and explain law as the instrument of ruling groups. These last merit their own subheading and are treated under Variation #2.

B. Variation #2: Transpose "Needs" into "Domination"

In other words, every time a mainstream writer says a legal rule or process or institution serves the needs of society, show instead how it serves to maintain the power of a dominant class or group. Opponents of this variation are inclined to call it "Marxist," although the classical Marxist theory of law is just one highly specific subset of this variation. In reality, this general proposition would be adopted as well by many non-Marxists. . . . On the other hand, modern *Marxisant* theorists of law and the state, as well as most Critical Legal Studies people, have become so disenchanted with the project of trying to explain law as nothing more than the tool of the ruling class that their ideas can't be adequately treated under this subheading.

The great contribution of this variation has been to put social structure, class, and power—whose very existence much liberal legal writing seems so astonishingly to deny—back into our accounts of law. Histories of legal oppressions—of slavery, Indian Removal laws, Black Codes, labor injunctions—are indispensable reminders that there's often nothing subtle about the way the powerful deploy the legal system to keep themselves organized and their victims disorganized and scared. But the crude versions of the law-as-an-elite-tool theory are as vulnerable as mainstream functionalism to the critique which points out how incredibly difficult it is to relate events in the realm of "law" in any straightforward causal way to those in the realm of "society."

C. Variation #3: Weaken the Instrumental Links Between Law and Society

Instrumentalist theories of law—which here include mainstream functionalism as well as the right-wing economics of Variation #1 and the orthodox Marxism of Variation #2—generally aspire to a positivist style of explanation. The idea is that someday (that jubilee when all the data have been gathered in) we will be able to generalize convincingly and fairly abstractly about what social conditions will produce what legal responses and what effects upon society those responses will have in their turn. Yet I think it's fair to say that on the whole such statements of regularity in legal-social relations don't stand up very well to historical criticism. These statements keep running up against (a) comparative studies showing that social and economic conditions that are apparently similar in relevant respects have actually produced radically different legal responses, and (b) demonstrations that the social effects of adopting a legal form are *never* predictable from the form itself, because the interpretation of a form, its enforcement by lower-level officials, and the response it's likely to elicit (enthusiasm, indifference, resistance) may all vary with the minutest particulars of context.

Take, for example, the once familiar proposition that the negligence principle was a functional response to the social needs of industrialization in its earlier phases (because it protected infant industry by externalizing its costs onto farmers, worker, city resident, etc.). The problems with this proposition are that (a) lots of societies industrialized without the negligence principle or after the principle had been around so long that it could hardly be a "response" to industrialization, and (b) the fact that there was a "negligence principle" doesn't by itself imply *any* determinate set of social consequences because the principle can be interpreted (or ignored) by judges, administrators, jurors, or employers so as to produce any imaginable combination of liability and damages (including none of either). These signs of indeterminacy naturally do not daunt the committed functionalist; they only spur him on to more refined hypotheses that will account for most of the variations. But in practice the progressive refinement of general statements about causal relationships between legal and social forms tends rapidly to decompose such statements into the detailed histories of particular societies. One's brave and sweeping original hypothesis of the necessary relation between industrialization and a negligence standard of liability gets boiled down to something like this: "In those places where the negligence principle was recognized and routinely applied in a certain way, it may have helped somewhat to facilitate capital accumulation; in other places, where there seems to have been lots of capital accumulation under different legal conditions, (a) some other form served the same function as the negligence principle, or (b) for various special reasons it wasn't necessary to the accumulation process to have that function served, or (c) perhaps there would have been still more accumulation if there had been a negligence principle." There's nothing wrong with this modest sort of proposition; it's the common stuff of historical writing. But it is an awfully long distance from demonstrating that economic requirements *produced* the form and that it duly performed its functional services to those requirements. . . .

D. Variation #4: Turn Background Social Necessity into Contingency

The preceding discussion pointed out the perils of matching legal responses to social needs: You end up having either to concede that the law has responded differently to the same needs or to multiply the number of needs in order to account for the differences. The first move calls into question the "functional" nature of the legal responses, the second whether it's useful to attribute "needs" to societies at all, especially needs emerging from the "logic" of some stage of historical development. . . .

E. Variation #5: Fill the Vacuum Left by the Collapse of Functionalism with Disengagement, Legitimating Ideologies, or Symbolic Ritualism

Now that historical experience has turned out to be too prodigal of multiple developmental paths and of multiple legal adaptations to those paths for the comfort of traditional functionalist explanations, where can one turn in the hope of finding some coherent explanation of law-in-history? One possibility I've mentioned already: Explain anything that happens in the legal system by referring to someone's interest (Variation #1). This method, subtly employed, yields narratives that are both subtle and exciting, but sooner or later, as every legal change is attributed in turn to a different set of bargains among interests, as a form of explanation it's going to seem discouragingly ad hoc. Moreover, one must at some point deal with what's known as the "autonomy" problem—the fact that legal norms and practices aren't completely plastic and don't alter every time another set of interests gets its paws on them because they do have some resilience, some long- or medium-term continuity of inner structure. Indeed, one of the properties that *makes* them legal norms and practices is that they at least appear to stand aloof from the everyday conflicts of civil society and to provide stable structures for the mediation of those conflicts. The classic preoccupation of legal sociology has been to try to pin down what's in this "autonomous" realm and theorize about its relation to the rest of society. I present three theories that are especially relevant to the background of the Critical approaches to legal history.

DISENGAGEMENT

By "disengagement" I mean beating a retreat to the position that although law is something that happens within societies, it doesn't have *any* important relations with the rest of society. Law is a realm of its own with its own history and categories and professional habits, and the only other thing you can compare it to is another legal system. You can't hope to explain anything that goes on in it except by reference to its own peculiar internal details or to its borrowings from the details of *other* legal systems.

There are grave problems with this approach. For one thing, as legal sociologists like Friedman and Macaulay point out, these writers, writing about the insular lawyer's law of cases, seem to be talking about awfully tiny corners of the law in any age (compared to legislation, administration, decrees, local law and custom, etc.) and especially in the current age of statutes and regulations.[79] If this is the only "law" that legal intellectuals are going to write about, they will weirdly and incomprehensibly restrict their field to topics that, at least by their own hypothesis, aren't very important to anyone, including lawyers themselves, who actually spend most of their time dealing with statues and regulations.

More seriously, I believe that disengagement is an obscurantist approach to the autonomy problem. First, autonomy in my original sense of long-run structural characteristics that make legal practices outlast short-term swings in political pressure is hardly unique to lawyer's law. Entire subdisciplines are committed to studying the autonomous characteristics of state structures such as bureaucracies and armies to show how constraints of organizational forms, ingrown traditions, professional ideologies, etc., affect how political agendas are formed, options perceived, urged, or suppressed, and so forth. Just as Realism taught us that judging, like legislation and administration, was political policymaking, it ought to have taught us that legislation and administration were, like judging, relatively autonomous. Thus, focusing on the autonomy of *law* to deny its relevance seems somehow unsupportable.

Second, I find it very hard to believe that autonomous legal forms are best understood as the product of a culturally isolated tribe of beings. Would any society tolerate lawyers as mediators of disputes, practical problem-solvers, or instruments of legitimate rule if the lawyers' practices didn't resonate *at all* with anyone else's? It seems much more probable that the specific legal practices of a culture are simply dialects of a parent social speech and that studying the speech helps you understand the dialect, and vice versa. Even a legal system clotted with arcane technicalities is unlikely to depart drastically from the common stock of understanding in the surrounding culture in the methods it uses to categorize social realities, the arguments about facts and values that it recognizes as relevant and persuasive, and the justifications it gives for its exercises of power.

The position of the disengaged seems to me to rest on two confusions. One is the confusion of a possibly valid methodological precept with a wholly invalid social theory. The *precept* is that when you want to account for a legal form, you should start your search for explanations in legal materials. This precept makes sense because the form is bound to be embedded in a whole contextual structure. For example, if you want to know what Cicero meant by "the public good" it's a good idea to look for other uses he makes of the phrase, what he contrasts it with, and how other lawyers use it. The *theory* is that discourse that is autonomous in this sense must therefore be peripheral or irrelevant to everything else going on in the society. But this theory doesn't follow from the precept at all. It's like saying that because Cicero has a specialized usage of the "public good" his usage must not have anything to do with contemporary Roman political controversies.

The other confusion is between law as particular enactments or events and law as clusters of practices and packages of enactments, processes repeated not once but many times over. Law in the sense of isolated enactments, decisions in a single case, or one proposition on page 351 of a hornbook, if rarely of any immediate instrumental significance. . . .

But the whole complex of contract, tort, and property rules? The whole apparatus of debt collection? Slave codes and fugitive slave laws? One might suppose, without falling back into the functionalist position that all this law *had* to exist in order to serve the needs of basic economic or evolutionary processes, that it was pretty important inconstituting social life as actually experienced, and that removing any of these big pieces might well have drastically altered that experience. . . .

LAW AS (LEGITIMATING) IDEOLOGY

Like the theory that law serves the interest of dominant groups, this one has come to be associated with the left, but again there's no necessary connection. Mainstream liberal functionalism has its own Durkheimian version of the legitimating role of law: legal norms are primary expressions of and means of reproducing the "shared values" that function as the integrating glue in liberal societies, orienting everyone's highly differentiated tasks towards a set of common social purposes. But concededly it has been the left-wing theories, theories that have emerged to deal with the difficulties posed by the "autonomy" problem for any account of law as the direct instrument of class oppression, that have attracted the most attention. Let me, for convenience's sake, try to arrange some of these theories on a spectrum, starting with those closest to straight instrumental theories, and ending with those emphasizing the most diffuse and indirect ways in which law makes up the elements of a culture:

1. "All law is pig law dressed up in judges' robes." That is, law is a means for organizing the ruling class and for coercing, cheating, and disorganizing the working class. Thus, law allows capital freely to collectivize but sets limits on labor combinations; it allows "capital strikes" (disinvestment) but restricts labor strikes; it confirms capitalist control over the organization of work; it criminalizes "vagrancy" as a means of keeping docile the urban unemployed; and it provides that employment is "at will" so that the unorganized workforce has no job security.

2. "The ruling class induces consent and demobilizes opposition by masking its rule in widely shared utopian norms and fair procedures, which it then distorts to its own purposes." For example, the classical bourgeois legal norms of "private property," "free contract," "free speech," and "due process" express universal longings for security, privacy, autonomy, free choice about what to buy and sell and whom to work for, the right to speak one's mind freely, and the universal desire for protection against arbitrary coercion. But in a class society these supposedly universal norms are deployed for the benefit of a particular class. Private property, free contract, (complex and expensive) due process, (well-heeled and organized-interest-group-responsive) democratic procedures, and even (expensive-and-technology-dependent) free speech operate de facto to reinforce the advantages of wealth and power. The victims of these outcomes feel powerless to complain because the outcomes seem to have been produced by legitimate rules and procedures.

3. "The ruling class confirms its rule by actually making good on enough of its utopian promises to convince potential opposition that the system is tolerably fair and capable of improvement, even with all its faults." This proposition is essentially Machiavellian. The ruling class periodically sets up demonstrations to convince people that it really does rule in the universal interest.

4. "The ruling class itself is taken in by legal ideology; it believes that it's acting justly when it acts according to law, that everyone *is* getting approximately the best possible deal, and that change would make everyone worse off." This formulation is getting closer to the meaning of ideology in classical social theory: a partial vision of the world that appears to its proponents as well as to its victims as a universal vision. (In fact, in the case of the ideology of the "rule of law," middle-class people are rather *more* sold on it than working or lower-class people.)

5. "Law isn't just an instrument of class domination, it's an arena of class struggle." The content of legal rules and practices is ideologically

tilted in favor of class rule (or, more generally, the production of current modes of hierarchical domination, class-based or otherwise), but ruling classes don't have everything their own way when it comes to specifying that content. The concessions that cause legal systems to respond to the interests and ideal aspirations of the dominated result from bargains struck after hard struggle. The norms embodied in legal rules therefore are always double-edged: the underdogs who have won them can also be coopted by them; the overdogs who concede them in order to coopt are always vulnerable to being undermined by their radical potential.

6. "The discourse of law—its categories, arguments, reasoning modes, rhetorical tropes, and procedural rituals—fits into a complex of discursive practices that together structure how people perceive and that therefore act to reproduce or to try to change people's social reality." Because this assertion goes well beyond partial critique, and is one of the core views of many of the Critics, I'll postpone elaboration of it until the next section.

LAW AS SYMBOLS AND RITUALS

This is a catch-all heading for those writers who see much of what goes on in the legal system as theatrical or religious public spectacles and story-telling sessions that infuse ordinary social life with dramatic meanings and messages: the triumph of Virtue over Corruption, the marking off of a "sacred" sphere of ideals from the "profane" world of fallen self-interest, the purification of society of polluting deviance, the proclamations that most economic transactions are fair and decent implicit in the stigmatizing of a few deals as exceptionally rotten, the instruction that life is a game to be played according to rules, and the trappings that tell you that authority is authority. . . .

F. Variation #6: Drawing upon Different Story-Lines

I have argued that the dominant vision of the meaning of modern history is an optimistic liberal vision. Its principal story-line is one of the gradual recession of error before the advance of commerce, liberty, and science—an advance modestly but invaluably assisted by ever more efficiently adaptive technologies of law. There have been failures and setbacks, and work remains to be done; but we have triumphed over the major obstacles, and the remaining work is remedial reform of the details. To be sure, opposing schools within optimistic liberalism have developed somewhat conflicting stories. One sees the late nineteenth-century common law as the summit of legal enlightenment and the regulatory welfare state as a (presumably temporary) slide into Serfdom and Inefficiency; the other sees the regulatory welfare state not only as a useful corrective but as a *continuation* of the true American tradition of positive state interventions in the interest of the commonwealth.

Such sharply conflicting views even within mainstream functionalism had already shattered the tranquil complacency possible only to those in possession of uncontested mythic-historical ground. . . .

The reason all this matters is that the new availability of major deviant story-lines about the main action in modern social/legal history has the effect of *relativizing* the old story-lines, of making them look not like uncontroversial assumptions but like what they are: some among many possible interpretive frameworks in which to stick historical evidence.

G. Variation #7: Historicize Consciousness

The final twist on the dominant tradition that I'd like to mention here, one that ends up playing a central role in Critical thought, is simply the "Kuhnian" or "Collingwoodian" idea that the most basic ways in which people conceive of the natural and social universes in which they live, the most elementary categories that people use to organize everyday life, are culturally and historically contingent; that is, they are specific to given places and times. Pure functionalism, as we've seen, objectifies both social needs and adaptive responses, claiming that these are universal categories of real life. . . . The historicist perspective, on the other hand, teaches that even conceptual language in which the functionalist advances her claim of universal needs and adaptations is a time- and culture-bound language with a history. . . .

There are two basic ways of pursuing the historicist approach. One is simply to write the history of our own modes of thought, to try to identify when our categories for organizing how we speak about law solidified into something like their present shape. When, for example, did we separate a private realm of "market" activity from a public realm of "state" activity and come to think of the latter as "intervening" in the former? When does the term "regulation" begin to be used in its modern sense? When did tort separate from contract, "corporation" come to mean mostly "private business enterprise," and "efficiency" achieve its present significance for antitrust lawyers? When did lawyers start speaking of the need to "balance" a multiplicity of "interests" in order to decide hard cases?

The other technique is the reconstruction of historical or cross-cultural modes of thought in such detail as to illustrate (a) that other societies have not shared the ways of thinking that we believe to be essential and obvious (they just don't have a counterpart conception to our idea of a "market" or of a "free individual," they don't think a "corporation" is legally any different from a family or a city, and either they don't distinguish between a "public" and a "private" realm or they mean something completely different by the distinction); and (b) that these views were completely plausible for the people who held them. Such work can have a real political edge to it. . . . It tells us that the difficulties we have in imagining forms of social life different from and better than those we are accustomed to may be due to the limits on our conceptions of reality rather than to limits inherent in reality itself. After all, perfectly smart and forward-looking Americans of about a century ago habitually believed such things as that social order and economic prosperity depended absolutely on the maintenance of permanent class divisions or slavery; that it was absurd utopianism to suppose that blacks and whites could ever associate on terms of social intimacy or equality (or if they did, the results would be biological degradation of the species); that the physical constitution of women unfitted them for attendance at colleges; that unemployment insurance would take all the discipline and will to work out of the labor force; and that judicial failure to enforce harsh bargains to their rigorously formal letter would bring on the imminent collapse of capitalism.

Such historicism is not, in its weaker versions, actually incompatible with functionalism. One could continue to suppose that universal processes generate needs for ideally adaptive responses while conceding that both needs and responses will be perceived at different times and places through different colored, and more-or-less distorting, conceptual lenses and filters. The strong position, on the whole that adopted by Critical writers, is that both needs and responses, and indeed the idea of needs-and-responses itself, must be seen as the cultural products of contingent modes of thought.

GENERALIZING AND DEEPENING THE CRITIQUES

Having at last completed the catalogue of variations, let me restate in summary form those that have done the most to inform the varieties of Critical historiography:

1. The conditions of social life and the course of historical development are radically underdetermined, or at least not determined by any uniform evolutionary path.

2. The causal relations between changes in legal and social forms are likewise radically underdetermined: comparable social conditions (both within the same and across different societies) have generated contrary legal responses, and comparable legal forms have produced contrary social effects.

3. If a society's law can't be understood as an objective response to objective historical processes, neither can it be understood as a neutral technology adapted to the needs of that particular society. Legal forms and practices are political products that arise from the struggles of conflicting social groups who possess very disparate resources of wealth, power, status, knowledge, access to armed force, and organizational capability.

4. Although they are the product of political conflict, legal forms

and practices don't shift with every realignment of the balance of political forces. They tend to become embedded in "relatively autonomous" structures that transcend and, to some extent, help to shape the content of the immediate self-interest of social groups.

5. This relative autonomy means that they can't be explained completely by reference to external political/social/economic factors. To some extent they are independent variables in social experience, and therefore they require study elaborating their peculiar internal structures with the aim of finding out how those structures feed back upon social life.

6. Our accustomed ways of thinking about law and history are as culturally and historically contingent as "society" and "law" themselves. Though we can never completely escape from the limitations of our environment, we can to some extent protect against the risk of simply projecting our parochial categories onto the past with a self-conscious effort to relativize our own consciousness, by trying to write the story of its formative context and development, and by trying to reconstruct as faithfully as possible the different mentalities of past societies before translating them into our own.

7. It will also help us to relativize our understanding of the past's relation to the present if we see that our conventional views of that relation are mediated by familiar narrative story-lines, that are so deeply entrenched in our consciousness that we are often unaware of their rule over our conception of reality. These story-lines, like other mentalities, have a history filled with ideological purposes, and there always exist—and so we always may draw upon—competing stories that impress the same historical experience with radically divergent meanings.

Taken *en bloc* rather than separately, this set of partial critiques adds up to a position that most people who see themselves as doing Critical legal historiography would probably accept.[102] Many, though by no means all, would want to push the critique still further.

A. Blurring the "Law/Society" Distinction

You might think that after the ravages of partial critique there would not be much left of the dominant tradition. But there is. Its skeletal frame, its division of the world into social and legal spheres, tends to endure. Thus, even the more severe of the partial critics continue to assume—although conceding that all over the landscape of social life we can see the imprints, some deep and others almost imperceptible, of feedback reactions from the "autonomous" outputs of the legal system—that at bottom the really basic terms of community life are set by conditions and relations we can, and should, describe independently of law: family ties, personal affections, power struggles, technology, consumption preferences, association in interest groups, and the organization of production. These conditions and relations—the realm of "material life" in some formulations; of "basic needs" of all societies or of particular evolutionary stages in evolutionary functionalism; of "the forces of production" in some Marxisms; of the "interests" of individuals or groups in liberal pluralist theory; and finally of the "preferences" of self-constituting individual subjects in the ultimate reduction of classical and neoclassical economics—comprise the "real world" which law may serve or disserve or even partially twist out of shape but to which law is ancillary. The *fundamental* operations of this world originate before law and go forward independently of it; they fashion in general outline (if not in tiny detail) the agendas and limits of legal systems and are beyond the power of law to alter.

Yet, in practice, it is just about impossible to describe any set of "basic" social practices without describing the legal relations among the people involved—legal relations that don't simply condition how the people relate to each other, but to an important extent define the constitutive terms of the relationship, relations such as lord and peasant, master and slave, employer and employee, ratepayer and utility, and taxpayer and municipality. For instance, among the first words one might use to identify the various people in an office would likely be words connoting legal status: "That's the owner over there." "She's a partner; he's a senior associate; that means an associate with tenure." "That's a contractor who's come in to do repairs." "That's a temp they sent over from Manpower." This seems an obvious point, but if it's correct how can one square it with the standard view of law as peripheral to "real" social relations? . . .

I would guess that the notion of the fundamentally constitutive character of legal relations in social life is probably a lot easier to understand when made about slave or feudal societies than about liberal societies. After all, in liberal societies, differences of legal status are not supposed to define social relationships, but merely to channel and facilitate them. . . .

Again, since it all seems so incredibly obvious once it's said, what explains the persistent view of law's marginality in social life? Partly, it comes from the view of generations of disillusioned reformers—liberal reformers mostly, I suspect—who have come to doubt whether more than marginal social change can be achieved through deliberate promotion by those in control of the mechanisms of the liberal state. But this proposition is not really about the limits of law; it is about the limits of selective types of attempts to reorient, usually from the top down, selective formal institutions. Most legal change takes place all through civil society, in thousands of small interactions usually with no official visibly present at all. . . .

The view that law is marginal in social life probably also registers an overreaction to the preceding generation of Formalists, who often behaved as if once you described the legal form of an institution or practice, you had described the *whole* thing. A "corporation" or a "city" appeared as nothing more than a shell of legal rights and powers. The Realist successors to these Formalists yearned to break through the formal shell to (as they often expressed it) the "living" reality beneath it: the "realities" of trade practices, power politics, emotional ties, "behavior" and, of course, social needs. But there is no way to detach essences from their forms: the law (in the catholic sense that I've been using) was all along a part of the reality. If the program of Realists was to lift the veil of legal form to reveal living essences of power and need, the program of the Critics is to lift the veil of power and need to expose the legal elements in their composition.

B. Law as Constitutive of Consciousness

Many Critical writers would, I think, claim not only that law figures as a factor in the power relationships of individuals and social classes, but also that it is omnipresent in the very marrow of society—that law-making and law-interpreting institutions have been among the primary sources of the pictures of order and disorder, virtue and vice, reasonableness and craziness, Realism and visionary naiveté, and of some of the most commonplace aspects of social reality that ordinary people carry around with them and use in ordering their lives. To put this another way, the power exerted by a legal regime consists less in the force that it can bring to bear against violators of its rules than in its capacity to persuade people that the world described in its images and categories is the only attainable world in which a sane person would want to live. "Either this world," legal actions are always implicitly asserting, "some slightly amended version of this world, or the Deluge." . . .

Another way of looking at what seems to be the key difference of approach between functionalists and their Critical opponents is that the functionalist examines what has actually happened and explains how it all "works," how each development fits into the pattern created by all the others; while the Critic takes each event as situated not on a single developmental path but on multiple trajectories of possibility, the path actually chosen being chosen not because it had to be but because the people pushing for alternatives were weaker and lost out in their struggle or because both winners and losers shared a common consciousness that set the agenda for all of them, highlighting some possibilities and suppressing others completely. How can one identify the counterfactual trajectories, the roads not taken? From the experience of other societies, from the hopes of those who lost the struggle, from routine practices that the same society has tried in other spheres of life without ever dreaming they might be applied to the situation at hand, and from imagination disciplined, as one hopes, by the knowledge of past failures. . . .

C. Indeterminacy Located in Contradiction

The partial critiques attack the twin determinisms of functionalism and evolutionism. . . . Taken together, these partial critiques add up to the proposition that when you situate law in social context, it varies with variations in that context. Some of the most original and powerful recent Critical writing, however, carries the claim of law's indeterminate relation to social life a significant step further. The same body of law, in the same context, can always lead to contrary results because law is indeterminate at its core, in its inception, not just in its applications. This indeterminacy exists because legal rules derive from structures of thought, the collective constructs of many minds, that are fundamentally contradictory.[125]

The common thread of these histories is the observation that the contradiction makes available for the decision of every case matched pairs of arguments that are perfectly plausible within the logic of the system but that cut in exactly opposite directions. The managers of the legal system preserve their sense that law is actually relatively orderly and predictable by assembling a bunch of devices to keep these oppositions from becoming too starkly obvious (even to themselves). They classify some of the oppositions as "anomalies and exceptions." They stick others in separate categories (e.g., law/equity). They rule out still others (the capitalist wage-bargain is invalid, at least in times of high unemployment, because concluded under duress; the equal protection clause prohibits rationing scarce social goods by ability to pay) by a separation between law and politics or simply by arbitrary ideological fiat (interpretations of rules that would too much alter the status quo are wrong per se). Nonetheless, these fudging devices are subject to strains that eventually crack them apart. Enemies of the status quo expose obviously ideological contrivances for what they are and develop arguments based on utopian counterpossibilities of the system. ("Freedom of contract" as administered is just the rule of the stronger; contracts can't be really free unless entered into by parties with "equal bargaining power"; hence, "freedom of contract" norms require regulatory schemes equalizing bargaining power.) Ordinary lawyers and judges with no wish whatever to destroy the system lay bare its contradictions in adversary arguments or dissents. And jurists whose main ambition is to *justify* the system by showing how clear and orderly it is at its core end up expounding it so well that its faults appear in plain view. . . .

CRITICIZING THE CRITICS: SOME POINTS OF CONTROVERSY

One of the melancholy truths about Critical Legal Studies generally seems to be that its students, although many of them try hard to write free of jargon for wide audiences, have for the most part not succeeded in communicating their ideas clearly enough to attract much relevant criticism from outside opponents. Most of the interesting controversies that I've become aware of have taken place within CLS, among people who consider themselves part of the movement. I will devote the space remaining here to a brief account of some of these controversies and will scatter remarks here and there to indicate where I stand on them. These controversies tend to swirl around the validity of the approach described in the last section: legal historiography as the intellectual history of the rise and fall of paradigm structures of thought designed to mediate contradictions. This special kind of doctrinal history is surely the most distinctive Critical contribution, as well as the one that has caused most of the arguments.

A. Argument #1: *"The history of DOCTRINE? This is the big liberating move? You've got to be kidding!"*

This argument is more complex than first appears and usually turns out to consist of several different points.

1. "You're just doing the history of legal ideas; what we need is the history of the law's effects on actual behavior in the real world." This point I think has been sufficiently addressed already: it's another version of the false law/society dichotomy. "The economy" is no more "real" than "legal ideas." It's an assemblage of conventions of which "legal ideas" such as property, contract, promissory and fiduciary obligation, not to mention money itself, are indispensable elements and propagators.

2. "But assuming that you're right, that the Material is inextricably mixed up with the Ideal, isn't all this doctrinal history still excessively Idealist? For one thing, it seems so abstract and bloodless, so far removed from the world of concrete social experience. For another, the method makes it look as if the history of these legal/intellectual structures were somehow self-determining—as if the structures rose and fell because of some objective inner dynamic unrelated to the world of social struggle or, for that matter, to real people of any kind. Doesn't this just substitute another set of evolutionary determinisms for the social evolutionism that it rejects?" This point is troubling, though it is perhaps more about appearance than about substance. It's true, I think, that the kind of structuralist historiography that some of the Critics have written sometimes reads as if these impersonal structures had a life of their own and human beings were enslaved to the needs of that life-cycle, building or demolishing as the World-Spirit might dictate. This appearance is quite unfortunate because I don't believe that these Critics want to divorce the life-cycle of their structures from human agency. On the contrary, their point is that people build these systems to satisfy their needs for cooperation with, while protecting against their terror of, one another. As people build, they reify, attributing to their own creations an impersonal

determining force ("the logic of freedom of contract requires that legal lines be drawn strictly limiting the state's power to affect the substantive terms of the bargain"). But the Critics, far from believing that these structures determine everything, spend all their time showing how indeterminate they are—how they always lead to contra-dictory consequences. What the structures "determine" is not any particular set of social consequences, but the categories of thought and discourse wherein political conflict will be carried out. . . .

3. "All right then, I can see why you want to write legal history as the history of legal consciousness, and I can even understand why you think that, although that history is made by real people in social life, it can be told without reference to pressures of immediate interest. But what I can't understand is why you chose to write about these particular forms of legal consciousness—case law and treatise litera-ture produced by the high mandarins of the legal system—in the first place. After all, isn't part of your theory that everyone in society—not just lawyers and certainly not just jurists and appellate judges—produces, applies, and interprets law? And isn't it therefore perverse of you to stick with the mandarin materials beloved of the most reactionary of Formalists?"

This is not an easy criticism to answer, but as a start I might say that I've never heard any Critic argue (as some traditional legal historians have been known to do) that Critical histories ought to focus *exclusively* on mandarin materials. But for an historiographical practice just setting off on its travels, the choice of these materials does make a certain amount of sense for several reasons. First, case law and treatises are relatively accessible. Thus you don't have to do a lot of digging to get materials to practice the method on, and newcomers, your students for example, can learn the method and produce finished pieces of research in a reasonable time. (In a field like law, which doesn't give people a long dissertation period to do research and develop their ideas, this is a real advantage.)

Second, the mandarin materials are among the richest artifacts of a society's legal consciousness. Because they are the most rationalized and elaborated legal products, you'll find in them an exceptionally refined and concentrated version of legal consciousness. Moreover, if you can crack the codes of these mandarin texts, you'll often have tapped into a structure that isn't at all peculiar to lawyers but that is the prototype speech behind many different dialect discourses in the society. For one example, the elite legal thought of the late nineteenth century ("classical" legal thought, as it's sometimes called) is strikingly parallel in its basic structure to classical political economy. For an-other, the transformations in the structure of legal thought which eventually led to Realism and the legal ideology of the administrative state have very close analogues in the rise of institutional economics. But the crucial question is whether studying elite legal thought will equip you only to study other elite dialects or whether it will also help you understand the vernacular, the common forms of legal discourse. It would take a lot of nerve to answer this with much confidence, because I know of very few attempts so far to apply the structuralist method to legal discourse at the field levels of lower-order officials, practitioners, or private lawmakers, but it seems plausible to suppose that the method would work at that level also. . . .

Third, in the particular context of the law schools, it has made good strategic sense for Critics to focus their energies on the deconstruction of mandarin materials, because their method gives each other and their students alternative ways of thinking about the very materials that law teachers have traditionally cared about: the core doctrinal subjects of the first-year curriculum. Although the Law-and-Society movement tried for years to convince traditional law teachers that these core subjects were "irrelevant" because they didn't "have anything to do with the real world," it had very little effect on the teaching and writing that went on in law schools. The Critics, by contrast, have engaged traditional doctrinalists on their own turf and have in the process stirred up a fabulous ruckus. . . .

B. Argument #2: *The Critics who do intellectual-history-of-doctrinal-structures haven't got any theory of the causal relations between legal/doctrinal change and other social change, except their claim that the contradictions within legal structures make such relations completely indeterminate. But this claim of indeterminacy is surely exaggerated—there are lots of regularities in legal/social relations.*

This argument has to be broken down a bit to be responded to. I think that, at this stage, the response can be very short because much of it has been answered already. It's true that, for example, the Critics have not produced an analysis along the lines of the traditionalist functionalist histories or of instrumental Marxism that relates changes in the legal system to changes in the economy. The whole point, recall, of the Critics' critique is that the "economy" isn't something separate from the "law," which reacts on law and is in turn reacted upon by it; the idea of their separation is a hallucinatory effect of the liberal reification of "state" and "market" (or "public" and "private") into separate entities. Because the economy is partially composed of legal relations, legal and economic histories are not histories of distinct and interacting entities, but simply different cross-cutting slices out of the same organic tissue. Again, if the Critics want to make this point convincingly, they will have to start slicing their narratives out of field-level uses of law.

The other argument rests, I think, on a misunderstanding of what the Critics mean by indeterminacy. They don't mean—although

sometimes they sound as if they do—that there are never any predictable causal relations between legal forms and anything else. As
argued earlier in this essay, there are plenty of short- and medium-
run stable regularities in social life, including regularities in the
interpretation and application, in given contexts, of legal rules. Lawyers, in fact, are constantly making predictions for their clients on the
basis of these regularities. The Critical claim of indeterminacy is
simply that none of these regularities are *necessary* consequences of
the adoption of a given regime of rules. The rule-system could also
have generated a different set of stabilizing conventions leading to
exactly the opposite results and may, upon a shift in the direction of
political winds, switch to those opposing conventions at any time.

CONCLUSION

As this guided tour comes to an end, what shall we say about the
contribution of the Critical historians? Perhaps this: that they have
added powerfully to the critique of the functionalist-evolutionary
vision that has so long dominated legal studies and that they have
produced their own distinctive and exciting brand of doctrinal historiography and successfully taught others how to apply their method.
The Critics are still a long way from being able to deliver the brightest
promises of their Critical program: thickly described accounts of how
law has been imbricated in and has helped to structure the most
routine practices of social life. But they are trying; they are getting
there.

NOTES

29. See O. Williamson, *Markets and Hierarchies: Analysis and Antitrust Implications*
(New York: Free Press, 1975).
30. See Robert Clark, "The Four Stages of Capitalism: Reflections on Investment
Management Treatises," *Harvard Law Review* 94 (1981): 561; Clark, "The Interdiscipli-
nary Study of Legal Evolution," *Yale Law Journal* 90 (1981): 1238.
31. See, e.g., P. Selznick and P. Nonet, *Law and Society in Transition: Toward
Responsive Law* (New York: Octagon Press, 1978).
79. See, e.g., L. Friedman and S. Macaulay, "Contract Law and Contract Teaching:
Past, Present, and Future," *Wisconsin Law Review* (1967): 805.
102. I want to be clear that I am not making the absurd claim that particular people
affiliated with the Critical Legal Studies movement have *originated* these critiques. On
the contrary, those critiques are virtually all of long historical standing, to be found in
Hegel or Marx if not before; incorporated into the normal working assumptions of
many social theorists (e.g., Weber, Durkheim, Gramsci, Foucault, Giddens, Offe);
historians of political and economic thought (e.g., Maitland, McIlwain, Ernst Kantoro-
wicz, Pocock, Quentin Skinner, Karl Polanyi, Hirschman); social historians (e.g., Bloch,
Genovese, E. P. Thompson, M. I. Finley); virtually any modern intellectual historian;
philosophers of science (e.g. Kuhn); and cultural anthropologists (e.g., Geertz, Turner,
Sahlins); as well as many legal intellectuals, specifically among Legal Realists, sociolo-

gists, and historians. (This is my own, doubtless idiosyncratic list: others might well put together a different one.)

What some CLS people *have* done, I think, is (a) to *combine* these critiques in an interesting way; (b) to attempt to go somewhat beyond them, as specified in the next section; and (c) to apply the results to the historiography of American legal doctrine and institutions.

125. D. Kennedy, "The Structure of Blackstone's Commentaries," *Buffalo Law Review* 28 (1979): 205, the pioneer venture in this mode, may be said to have founded an entire school. See, e.g., James L. Kainen, "From Vested to Substantive Rights," *Buffalo Law Review* 31 (1982); F. Olsen, "The Family and the Market: A Study of Ideology and Legal Reform," *Harvard Law Review* 96 (1983): 1497; J. Singer, "The Legal Rights Debate in Analytical Jurisprudence from Bentham to Hohfeld," *Wisconsin Law Review* (1982): 975; Kenneth J. Vendevelde, "The New Property of the Nineteenth Century: The Development of the Modern Concept of Property," *Buffalo Law Review* 29 (1980): 325; Note, "Tortious Interference with Contractual Relations in the Nineteenth Century: The Transformation of Property, Contract, and Tort," *Harvard Law Review* 93 (1983): 1510.

6

The Triumph of Contract

Morton Horwitz

THE EQUITABLE CONCEPTION OF CONTRACT IN THE EIGHTEENTH CENTURY

The development of contract, it often has been observed, can be divided into three stages, which correspond to the history of economic and legal institutions of exchange. In the first stage, all exchange is instantaneous and therefore "involves nothing corresponding to 'contract' in the Anglo-American sense of the term. Each party becomes the owner of a new thing, and his rights rest, not on a promise, but on property." In a second stage, "exchange first assumes a contractual aspect when it is left half-completed, so that [only] an obligation on one side remains." The "third and final stage in the development occurs when the executory exchange becomes enforceable."[5] According to orthodox legal history, when English judges declare at the end of the sixteenth century that "every contract executory is an assumpsit in itself," and that "a promise against a promise will maintain an action upon the case," the conception of contract as mutual promises has triumphed and, according to Plucknett, "the process is complete and the result clear."[6]

It is my purpose to demonstrate that, contrary to the orthodox view, the process was not complete at the end of the sixteenth century. Instead, one finds that as late as the eighteenth century contract law was still dominated by a title theory of exchange, and damages were set under equitable doctrines that ultimately were to be rejected by modern contract law.

The original version of this chapter appeared in Morton Horwitz, *The Transformation of American Law, 1780–1860* (Cambridge: Harvard University Press, 1977). Reprinted by permission of author and publisher.

As a result of the subordination of contract to property, eighteenth-century jurists endorsed a title theory of contractual exchange according to which a contract functioned to transfer title to the specific thing contracted for.

The title theory of exchange was suited to an eighteenth-century society in which no extensive markets existed, and goods, therefore, were usually not thought of as being fungible. Exchange was not conceived of in terms of future monetary return, and as a result one finds that expectation damages were not recognized by eighteenth-century courts. . . .

To appreciate the radical difference between eighteenth-century and modern contract law, consider a case decided during a period in which the demise of the title theory was becoming plain. *Sands* v. *Taylor*[20] was an 1810 New York suit against a buyer who had received a part-shipment of wheat but had refused to receive the remainder contracted for. Under the old title theory, sellers were apparently required to hold the goods until they received the contract price from the buyer. But in *Sands* v. *Taylor* the sellers immediately "covered" by selling the wheat in the market and thereafter suing the buyer for the difference between market and contract price. While acknowledging that there were "no adjudications in the books, which either establish or deny the rule adopted in this case," the court ratified the seller's decision to "cover" and allowed him to sue for the difference. "It is a much fitter rule," it declared, "than to require [the seller] to suffer the property to perish, as a condition on which his right to damages is to depend." In reaching this result the court was forced to fundamentally transform the title theory. The sellers, it said "were, by necessity . . . thus constituted trustees or agents, for the defendants." The trust theory was thus created in order to overcome a result which, though inherent in eighteenth-century contract conceptions, was becoming increasingly anomalous in a nineteenth-century market economy. Under an economic system in which contract was becoming regularly employed for the purpose of speculating on the price of fungible goods, the old title theory of contract, conceived of as creating a property interest in specific goods, had outlived its usefulness. The demise of the title theory roughly corresponded to the beginnings of organized markets and the transformation of an economic system that had used contract as simply one means of transferring specific property.

The most important aspect of the eighteenth-century conception of exchange is an equitable limitation on contractual obligation. Under the modern will theory, the extent of contractual obligation depends upon the convergence of individual desires. The equitable theory, by contrast, limited and sometimes denied contractual obligation by reference to the fairness of the underlying exchange.

The most direct expression of the eighteenth-century theory was the well-established doctrine that equity courts would refuse specific enforcement of any contract in which they determined that the consideration was inadequate.[21] The rule was stated by South Carolina's Chancellor Desaussure as late as 1817: "It would be a great mischief to the community, and a reproach to the justice of the country, if contracts of very great inequality, obtained by fraud, or surprise, or the skillful management of intelligent men, from weakness, or inexperience, or necessity could not be examined into, and set aside."[22] Seven years later, the Chief Justice of New York noted the still widespread opinion of American judges that equity courts would refuse to enforce a contract where the consideration was inadequate.[23]

Contract law was essentially antagonistic to the interests of commercial classes. The law did not assure a businessman the express value of his bargain, but at most its specific performance. Courts and juries did not honor business agreements on their face, but scrutinized them for the substantive equality of the exchange.

For our purposes, the most important consequence of this hostility was that contract law was insulated from the purposes of commercial transactions. Businessmen settled disputes informally among themselves when they could, referred them to a more formal process of arbitration when they could not, and relied on merchant juries to ameliorate common law rules.

THE RISE OF A MARKET ECONOMY AND THE DEVELOPMENT OF THE WILL THEORY OF CONTRACT

Early Attacks on Eighteenth-Century Contract Doctrine

For a variety of reasons, it is appropriate to correlate the emergence of the modern law of contract with the first recognition of expectation damages. Executory sales contracts assume a central place in the economic system only when they begin to be used as instruments for "futures" agreements; to accommodate the market function of such agreements the law must grant the contracting parties their expected return. Thus, the recognition of expectation damages marks the rise of the executory contract as an important part of English and American law. Furthermore, the moment at which courts focus on expectation damages rather than restitution or specific performance to give a remedy for nondelivery is precisely the time at which contract law begins to separate itself from property. It is at this point that contract begins to be understood not as transferring the title of particular property, but as creating an expected return. Contract then becomes an instrument for protecting against changes in supply and price in a market economy.

The first recognition of expectation damages appeared after 1790 in both England and America in cases involving speculation in stock. Jurists initially attempted to encompass these cases within traditional legal categories. Thus, Lord Mansfield in 1770 referred to a speculative interest in stock as "a new species of property, arisen within the compass of a few years."[74] In 1789 the Connecticut Supreme Court of Errors held that recovery of expectation damages on a contract of stock speculation would be usurious.[75]

These efforts to encompass contracts of stock speculation within the old title theory were soon to be abandoned, however. Between 1799 and 1810 a number of English cases applied the rule of expectation damages for failure to deliver stock on a rising market.[77] In America the transformation occurred a decade earlier, in response to an active "futures" market for speculation in state securities which rapidly developed after the Revolutionary War in anticipation of the assumption of state debts by the new national government.

In Virginia, in *Groves* v. *Graves* (1790),[82] the rule of expectation damages arose in connection with a buyer's actions for securities. After a jury had awarded the plaintiff expectation damages, however, Chancellor Wythe, still reflecting eighteenth-century moral and legal conceptions, enjoined the enforcement of the judgment on the grounds that the transaction "appeared to have been designed to secure unconscionable profit . . . and to have been obtained from one whom he had cause to believe at that time to be needy." He allowed damages only to the extent of the original value plus interest. But the Virginia Court of Appeals reversed his decree, holding that "the contract was neither usurious, or so unconscionable as to be set aside." And, in marked contrast to the earlier practice of not reviewing jury damage awards, the court held that the jury erred in measuring damages as of the time of trial and not as of the time of delivery.[83] The case thus suggests that judicial supervision of juries' damage awards may have arisen simultaneously with the recognition of expectation damages. . . .

In America the application of expectation damages to commodities contracts correlates with the development of extensive internal commodities markets around 1815. The leading case is *Shepherd* v. *Hampton* (1818),[91] in which the Supreme Court held that the measure of damages for failure to deliver cotton was the difference between the contract price and the market price at the time of delivery. Within the next decade a number of courts worked out the problems of computing expectation damages for commodities contracts,[92] one of them noting that "most of the [prior] cases in which this principle has been adopted, have grown out of contracts for the delivery and replacing of stock."[93]

The absorption of commodities transactions into contract law is a major step in the development of a modern law of contracts. As a result of the growth of extensive markets, "futures" contracts became a normal device either to insure against fluctuations in supply and price or simply to speculate. And as a consequence, judges and jurists began to reject eighteenth-century legal rules that reflected an underlying conception of contract as fair exchange. Not surprisingly, the first direct assault upon the equitable conception of contract appeared in adjudications involving one of these forms, the negotiable instrument.

During the second half of the eighteenth century, a movement developed to eliminate the substantive significance of the doctrine of consideration in cases involving negotiable instruments. In 1767 the Massachusetts Superior Court held by a 3 to 2 vote that even in an action between the original parties to a promissory note, the promisor could not offer evidence of inadequate consideration in mitigation of damages.[94] "People," Chief Justice Hutchinson declared, "think themselves quite safe in taking a Note for the Sum due, and reasonably suppose all Necessity of keeping the Evidence of the Consideration at an End; it would be big with Mischief to oblige People to stand always prepared to contest Evidence that might be offered to the Sufficiency of the Consideration. This would be doubly strong in Favour of an Indorsee."

It was one thing to argue that in order to make notes negotiable a subsequent endorsee would be allowed to recover on a note regardless of the consideration between the original parties. This argument, of course, itself entailed a sacrifice of judicial control over bargains that commercial convenience was beginning to demand. It was, however, quite a different matter to exclude evidence of consideration between the original parties to the note, as the Massachusetts court decided. With this decision, it became possible for merchants to exclude the question of the equality of a bargain by transacting their business through promissory notes.

The nineteenth-century departure from the equitable conception of contract is particularly obvious in the rapid adoption of the doctrine of caveat emptor. It was only after Lord Mansfield declared in 1778, in one of those casual asides that seem to have been so influential in forging the history of the common law, that the only basis for an action for breach of warranty was an express contract,[106] that the foundation was laid for reconsidering whether an action for breach of an implied warranty would lie. In 1802 the English courts finally considered the policies behind such an action, deciding that no suit on an implied warranty would be allowed.[107] Two years later, in the leading American case of *Seixas* v. *Woods*,[108] the New York Supreme Court, relying on a doubtfully reported seventeenth-century English case, also held that there could be no recovery against a merchant who could not be proved knowingly to have sold defective goods. Other American jurisdictions quickly fell into line.[110]

While the rule of caveat emptor established in *Seixas* v. *Woods* seems to be the result of one of those frequent accidents of historical misunderstanding, this is hardly sufficient to account for the widespread acceptance of the doctrine of caveat emptor elsewhere in America. Nor are the demands of a market economy a sufficient cause. Although the sound price doctrine was attacked on the ground that there "is no standard to determine whether the vendee has paid a *sound* price,"[111] the most consistent legal theorist of the market economy, Gulian Verplanck, devoted his impressive analytical talents to an elaborate critique of the doctrine of caveat emptor. The sudden and complete substitution of caveat emptor in place of the sound price doctrine must therefore be understood as a dramatic overthrow of an important element of the eighteenth century's equitable conception of contract.

The Synthesis of the Will Theory of Contract

The development of extensive markets at the turn of the century contributed to a substantial erosion of belief in theories of objective value and just price. Markets for future delivery of goods were difficult to explain within a theory of exchange based on giving and receiving equivalents in value. Futures contracts for fungible commodities could be understood only in terms of a fluctuating conception of expected value radically different from the static notion that lay behind contracts for specific goods; a regime of markets and speculation was simply incompatible with a socially imposed standard of value. The rise of a modern law of contract, then, was an outgrowth of an essentially procommercial attack on the theory of objective value which lay at the foundation of the eighteenth century's equitable idea of contract.

It was not until after 1820 that attacks on the equitable conception began to be generalized to include all aspects of contract law. If value is subjective, nineteenth-century contract theorists reasoned, the function of exchange is to maximize the conflicting and otherwise incommensurable desires of individuals. The role of contract law was not to assure the equity of agreements, but simply to enforce only those willed transactions that parties to a contract believed to be to their mutual advantage. The result was a major tendency toward submerging the dominant equitable theory of contract in a conception of contractual obligation based exclusively on express bargains. In his *Essay on the Law of Contracts* (1822), for example, Daniel Chipman criticized the Vermont system of assigning customary values to goods that were used to pay contract debts. Only the market could establish a fair basis for exchange, Chipman urged. "Let money be the sole standard in making all contracts, [for] if, therefore, it were possible for courts in the administration of justice, to take this ideal high price as a standard of valuation, every consideration of policy, and a regard for the good of the people would forbid it."

Nathan Dane's *Abridgment* (1823) and Joseph Story's *Equity Jurisprudence* (1836) also contributed to the demise of the old equitable conceptions. But nowhere were the underlying bases of contract law more brilliantly and systematically rethought than in Gulian C. Verplanck's *An Essay on the Doctrine of Contracts* (1825).

Verplanck was the first English or American writer to see in the "different parts of the system" of contract law "clashing and wholly incongruous" doctrines. He emphasized "the singular incongruity" of a legal system that "obstinately refuses redress in so many, and such marked instances of unfairly obtained advantages [yet] occasionally permit[s] contracts to be set aside upon the ground of inadequacy of price." There were, he asserted, many "difficulties and contradictions" to be found in existing legal doctrine over "the question of the nature and degree of equality required in contracts of mutual interest," as well as over the standards of "inadequacy of price" and "inequality of knowledge." "Where," he asked, "shall we draw the line of fair and unfair, of equal and unequal contracts?"

The Application of the Will Theory of Contract to Labor Contracts

Thus far, we have seen the changes in contract law that were necessary to meet the needs of the newly emerging market economies in England and America. There is evidence, however, that the change from the eighteenth to the nineteenth century also involved a pervasive shift in the sympathies of the courts. In the eighteenth century the subjection of individual bargains to the extensive supervisory powers of courts and juries expressed the legal and ethical culture of the small town, of the farmer, and of the small trader. In the nineteenth century, the will theory of contract was part of a more general process whereby courts came to reflect commercial interests. The changing alliances are painfully obvious in nineteenth-century courts' discriminatory application of the recently discovered chasm between express and implied contracts.

The most important class of cases to which this distinction applied was labor contracts in which the employee had agreed to work for a period of time—often a year—for wages that he would receive at the end of his term. If he left his employment before the end of the term, jurists reasoned, the employee could receive nothing for the labor he had already expended. The contract, they maintained, was an "entire" one, and therefore it could not be conceived of as a series of smaller agreements. Since the breach of any part was therefore a breach of the whole, there was no basis for allowing the employee to recover "on the contract." Finally, citing the new orthodoxy proclaimed by the treatise writers, judges were led to pronounce the inevitable result: where there was an express agreement between the parties, it would be an act of usurpation to "rewrite" the contract and allow the employee to recover in quantum meruit for the "reasonable" value of his labor.[144]

Courts in fact seemed driven to resolve all ambiguity in contracts in favor of the employer's contention that they were "entire." It made no "difference . . . whether the wages are estimated at a gross sum, or are to be calculated according to a certain rate per week or month, or are payable at certain stipulated times, provided the servant agree for a definite and whole term." Under these circumstances, it should be emphasized, the assumption that the agreement was "for a definite and whole term" was simply a judicial construction not required by the terms of the agreement. Moreover, it did not "make any difference, that the plaintiff ceased laboring for his employer, under the belief that, according to the legal method of computing time, under similar contracts, he had continued laboring as long as could be required of him." Nor did it matter that the "employer, during the term, has from time to time made payments to the plaintiff for his labor."[145] The result of the cases was that any employee not shrewd or independent enough to demand immediate payment for his work risked losing everything if he should leave before the end of the contract period. The employer, in turn, had every inducement to create conditions near the end of the term that would encourage the laborer to quit.

The disposition of courts ruthlessly to follow conceptualism in the labor cases was not, however, quite matched in cases involving building contracts. Building contracts are similar to labor agreements in that there is no way of restoring the status quo after partial performance. Nevertheless, nineteenth-century courts allowed builders to recover "off the contract" when they had committed some breach of their express obligation. The leading case is *Hayward* v. *Leonard* (1828),[146] in which the Supreme Judicial Court of Massachusetts held that a builder could recover in quantum meruit "where the contract is performed, but, without intention, some of the particulars of the contract are deviated from." If there was "an honest intention to go by the contract, and a substantive execution of it," the court held, it would not decree a forfeiture. It should be noted that the Massachusetts court in *Hayward* v. *Leonard* expressly rejected Dane's view that the existence of an express contract barred recovery in quantum meruit. There was, Chief Justice Parker declared, "a great array of authorities on both sides, from which it appears very clearly that different judges and different courts have held different doctrines and sometimes the same court at different times."[147] The result was that in Massachusetts and in most other states two separate lines of cases were developed, one dealing with service contracts, for which recovery in quantum meruit was barred, and another applying to building contracts, for which recovery "off the contract" of the reasonable value of the performance was permitted.

Few courts attempted to rationalize what Theophilus Parsons was later to call these "very conflicting" decisions.[148] The leading explanation came from *Hayward* v. *Leonard* itself. In the labor cases the employee usually broke his contract "voluntarily" and "without fault" of his employer. Breach of building contracts was often "without intention" and compatible with an "honest intention" to fulfil the contract.[149] Thus, it was not that courts had abandoned an underlying moral conception of contracts, but that the morality had fundamentally changed. The focus had shifted from an emphasis on the role of quantum meruit in preventing "unjust enrichment." The express contract had become paramount; denial of quantum meruit recovery was now employed to enforce the contract system. It was now regarded as just for the employer to retain the unpaid benefits of his employee's labor as a deterrent to voluntary breach of contract. But it was still unjust for the beneficiary of a building contract to enrich himself because of an honest mistake in performing the contract.

While the judges who adhered to the distinction between labor and building contracts never acknowledged an economic or social policy behind the distinction, it seems to be an important example of class bias. A penal conception of contractual obligation could have deterred economic growth by limiting investment in high risk enterprise. Just as the building trade was beginning to require major capital investment during the second quarter of the nineteenth century, courts were prepared to bestow upon it that special solicitude which American courts have reserved for infant industry. Penal provisions in labor contracts, by contrast, have only redistributional consequences, since they can hardly be expected to deter the laboring classes from selling their services in a subsistence economy.

Although nineteenth-century courts and doctrinal writers did not succeed in entirely destroying the ancient connection between contracts and natural justice, they were able to elaborate a system that allowed judges to pick and choose among those groups in the population that would be its beneficiaries. And, above all, they succeeded in creating a great intellectual divide between a system of formal rules— which they managed to identify exclusively with the "rule of law"— and those ancient precepts of morality and equity, which they were able to render suspect as subversive of "the rule of law" itself.

CUSTOM AND CONTRACT

The growth of commerce and industry confronted American courts in the nineteenth century with the fundamentally new question of how to account for the legal significance of recently established commercial customs and trade practices too varied and diverse to be incorporated into general rules of law. . . .

Most courts at the turn of the nineteenth century were still unwill-

ing to yield to a conception of mercantile law that allowed commercial
interests to define entirely the scope and substance of the rules by
which they would be governed. For example, at a 1784 trial in
Massachusetts "evidence of eminent merchants in Boston" was offered to the jury of "a *mercantile usage there*" which involved the rules
governing nonpayment of bills of exchange. "But the Court directed
the jury" that "a clear rule of law" already existed and that it should
therefore ignore evidence of mercantile usage.[162] Yet in an 1813
insurance case, the Massachusetts Supreme Court, still citing Mansfield's view that evidence of custom would not be admitted where "the
law . . . is plain, well settled, and generally understood," had begun
nevertheless to reinterpret Mansfield in light of the new economic
relationships that were beginning to emerge. "The usage of no class of
citizens," the court continued to declare, "can be sustained in opposition to principles of law." Yet, anticipating the newly emerging "will"
theory of contract, the judges acknowledged that "evidence of custom
and usage is useful in many cases to explain the intent of parties to a
contract." While the court was thus unwilling simply to convert
commercial custom into law, it was prepared to bring about a similar
result through an interpretation of the parties' intent.[163]

By disguising the problem of class legislation, this effort to conceive
of custom simply as evidence of contractual intent relieved courts of
the embarrassing task of bestowing on commercial usage the dignity
of law. That such a problem was at the forefront of legal controversy
over the proper scope of mercantile custom can be seen in the great
case of *Gordon* v. *Little*,[165] decided by the Pennsylvania Supreme Court
in 1822. The case involved the economically crucial question of
whether the common law rule of strict liability for common carriers
would be applied to boats carrying freight on the Ohio and Mississippi rivers. The plaintiff sued for the value of goods destroyed when
the defendant's boat sank. Maintaining that he should be liable only
for negligence, the defendant offered evidence "of a general usage or
custom in relation to the liability of carriers on the western waters,"
which amounted to "an implied contract." The trial court rejected the
evidence, except so far as such usage served to explain "the common
and commercial meaning of the words 'the unavoidable dangers of
the river' " in the bill of lading. The question for the Supreme Court
was whether the trial court had correctly rejected the defendant's
offer of evidence of custom and usage.

Writing for the majority, Chief Justice Tilghman managed to strad-
dle between the old conception of a general commercial custom and a
still latent view of custom as merely establishing the intention of
contracting parties. He first affirmed the trial court's ruling that the
proper construction of the words of the contract did not support the
defendant's position. "If the case had rested solely on the written
contract, there would have been much to say in favour of the decision

of the [trial] Court, because, be the common law what it may, the parties have a right to alter or modify it by special contract, and when they have done so, the question is, what is the construction of the contract?"

Having thus acknowledged that the parties were free to alter legal rules by contract—an important and new conception of the relationship between legal rules and contractual powers—Tilghman nevertheless felt bound to abide by the trial court ruling that the parties had not actually agreed to contract out of common law liability. He was thus thrown back on the central argument that commercial custom itself was the source of general legal rules. And he concluded that it should have been open to the defendant to prove that a local custom existed on the Ohio and Mississippi rivers that suspended the common law rule and limited carrier liability only to damages arising from negligence.

As Judge John Gibson observed in a powerful dissent, Tilghman was prepared to bestow on local customary usage "the dignity of a law of local obligation . . . superseding the common law within the district where it is supposed to prevail." "What is the custom relied on here?" Gibson asked.

> Not a general one, pervading the State; for such would be part of the common law, and determinable by the Judges. . . . With us, particular customs have no force. I know not a greater or a more embarrassing evil than a law of merely local obligation. The rule of the carrying business of the Ohio ought to be that of the Juniata, the Susquehanna, the Delaware, and their tributary streams. Suppose a different usage to exist in respect to each—is there to be different law in respect to each? . . . It is impossible to get away from the conclusion, that by giving the usage any further effect than that of a convenient subject of reference, to explain a latent ambiguity in the expressions of the parties, where their meaning would be otherwise doubtful, we repeal an established principle of the common law, a matter which I apprehend is not open to us.

Gibson saw another problem in permitting customs of particular trades to vary the general rules of law. "If we go by the common law," he wrote,

> we shall have a definite, known rule; which, applied to the facts by the Court, will produce as much certainty of result, as legal proceedings are susceptible of; if we go by usage, the whole matter will have to be determined by the jury, on evidence of the common practice and understanding on the subject; which would be to go by no rule at all. So that the right to compensation will, in every instance, depend on what the jury may think the proper degree of diligence. We should be perpetually inquiring by a jury as to what is the law of the land; and the degree of diligence required of the carrier, would be as fluctuating as the opinions of the witnesses called to establish it.

Without an insulated and homogeneous commercial class from which . . . [to] draw merchant jurors, a law allowing proof of local usage, Gibson saw, would give lay jurors power to control commercial rules. But even beyond his fear that anticommercial juries might ultimately come to determine the substantive rules of commercial law, Gibson believed that such a system could not provide "a definite, known rule, which . . . will produce as much certainty of result as legal proceedings are susceptible of." The "embarrassing evil" of "a law of merely local obligation" seemed inevitable if the majority's view of custom were allowed to prevail. As each special interest sought to endow its own particular custom with "the dignity of . . . law," the claims of the legal system to impartiality were drawn into question. Commercial custom thus threatened not only to establish various "laws of local obligation" which fragmented the economy; it also enabled powerful interests to impose their usage on those outsiders with whom they dealt.

In a society in which commercial interests were becoming both increasingly powerful and diverse, any overt attempt to give commercial custom the force of law was both impolitic and impractical. It exposed the judiciary to the charge of class legislation, while it endowed lay jurors with the discretionary authority to decide which customs were binding. Indeed, by 1836 David Hoffman was prepared to acknowledge in his *Course of Legal Study* "the numerous legal doubts" that beset every attempt to absorb the law of merchants into the general law. Yet, in *Gordon* v. *Little* we see that a newer conception has already come to the fore. If there is disagreement about whether custom can change the general law, all agree that contract can. If the established common law rule "be not the most convenient," even Justice Gibson agreed, "the parties have, in every case, power to establish a particular measure of responsibility for themselves." The result was that by the time Theron Metcalf delivered his lectures on contract in 1828, judges had begun to move away from the late eighteenth-century notion that courts could convert mercantile custom into law. Their only function, Metcalf maintained, was simply to determine "if there be a usage which the parties must be supposed to have had in view, when their contracts were made." While both sides in *Gordon* v. *Little* still conceived of usage as performing the very limited function of "explain[ing] words of doubtful import," by 1844 W. W. Story could declare that in the interpretation of a contract, usage or custom should be resorted to, not only to explain the meaning of technical or ambiguous terms "but also to supply evidence of the intentions of the party in respect to matters, with regard to which the contract itself affords a doubtful indication, *or perhaps no indication at all.*"

Whatever their misgivings about mercantile usage as an appropriate source of law, most judges in the first half of the nineteenth century were eager to yield their objections before the new contractarian rationale. If the contracting parties were free to change or modify legal rules, as the court in *Gordon* v. *Little* acknowledged, they could surely be permitted to incorporate commercial custom into their agreement. Thus, under the guise of enforcing the party's intentions, courts by the middle of the century had begun, in fact, to follow W. W. Story's view that they were free to turn to custom "to supply evidence of . . . intentions . . . with respect to which the contract itself affords . . . no indication at all."

This unacknowledged shift back to a theory of preexisting custom under the guise of construing the parties' intentions would shortly shade into an explicit assertion of an "objective" theory of contract itself. If a "subjective" theory of contract served its historic function of destroying all remnants of an objective theory of value, it had the drastic limitation of making legal certainty and predictability impossible. Once contractual obligation was founded entirely on an arbitrary "meeting of minds," it endowed the parties with the power totally to remake law. Though it once had the important advantage of disguising judicial lawmaking, the contractarian justification for custom created an even more individualized and random "law of local obligation" deriving only from the parties' will. To the extent that it was seriously followed, it made every contract a unique event depending only on the momentary intention of the parties. Once the subjective theory of contract had performed the function of enabling judges and jurists to destroy the connection between contract law and a conception of objective value, they felt free once again to revive an objective theory of contract and to reintroduce its intellectual companion, a conception of general mercantile custom.

It was Joseph Story who first saw the disintegrating effects of a subjective theory of contract on commercial law. "I own myself no friend to the almost indiscriminate habit, of late years," he wrote in a case decided in 1837, only five years before his decision in *Swift* v. *Tyson*, "of setting up particular usages or customs in almost all kinds of business and trade, to control, vary, or annul the general liabilities of parties under the common law as well as under the commercial law."

> It has long appeared to me, that there is no small danger in admitting such loose and inconclusive usages and customs, often unknown to particular parties, and always liable to great misunderstandings and misinterpretations and abuses, to outweigh the well-known and well-settled principles of law. And I rejoice to find, that, of late years, the courts of law, both in England and America, have been disposed to narrow the limits of the operation of such usages and customs, and to discountenance any further extension of them.[176]

The connection between a subjective theory of contract and its corrosive effects on predictability in commercial law was first elaborated in Theophilus Parsons's *Law of Contracts* (1855). In order for the court and not the jury to have the power of construction, it was necessary to dispense with the subjective theory of intention. Thus, Parsons moved on to articulate the objective theory that would thereafter dominate American law. "The rule of law," he declared, "is not that the court will always construe a contract to mean that which the parties to it meant; but rather that the court will give to the contract the construction which will bring it as near to the actual meaning of the parties as the words they saw fit to employ, when properly construed, and the rules of law, will permit." "So," he concluded, "the rules of law, as well as the rules of language, may interfere to prevent a construction in accordance with the intent of the parties." Thus, in the interest of "rectitude, consistency and uniformity," Parsons was prepared to overthrow the orthodox view, propounded earlier by Chancellor Kent in his *Commentaries* (1832), that "the plain intent" of the parties to a contract should prevail even "over the strict letter of the contract."

Parsons's "objective" theory of contracts develops at roughly the same time as the social significance of the market was once more undergoing a major transformation. Between 1790 and 1850, the overwhelming emphasis in legal and economic thought was on the random and fluctuating nature of value that had been introduced by a market economy. . . .

As markets became more "mature" by becoming more extensive and uniform, due largely to improved transportation, the social experience of price stability tended to reintroduce, though in substantially diluted form, the power of a conception of objective value. During the 1850s, for example, courts no longer defended the rule of caveat emptor in terms of the subjectivity of value, but rather in the entirely different terms of whether the contracting parties had an equal opportunity to learn the objective market price of a commodity.[185] The need for a uniform and consistent set of essentially impersonal commercial rules had begun to overwhelm legal doctrines such as caveat emptor, which still presupposed an economy based on face-to-face dealings. . . .

By the time Samuel Williston published his treatise on *Contracts* in 1920, American jurists, still under the influence of Parson's treatise, were bent on establishing the historical validity of the objective theory of contractual obligation. "In the formation of contracts," Williston wrote, "it was long ago settled that secret intent was immaterial, only overt acts being considered in the determination of such mutual assent as that branch of the law requires." Though driven to establish the historical *bona fides* of the objective theory, Williston was nevertheless compelled to acknowledge that "during the first half of the nineteenth century there were many expressions which seem to indicate the contrary, chief of which was the familiar rubric, still re-echoing in judicial dicta, that a contract requires the meeting of the minds of the parties."

Williston's followers spared no effort in their attempt to discredit the earlier subjective theory. "The historical fallacy which has misled some American courts," one of them wrote, "was borrowing from . . . civil law doctrine . . . which was alien to Anglo-American theories of contract. . . . Of the channels through which this infusion of alien doctrine took place, the writings of Story and Kent had the widest influence."[193]

But what in fact accounted for the initial triumph of the "will" or "subjective" theory? Far from representing any "alien" infusion of legal ideas, it arose from the basic structure of legal change in the early nineteenth century. The earlier contract doctrine, which posited objective standards of value, was hostile to a market economy. The leading intellectual weapon employed to destroy this theory depended on the view that all value was subjective and that the only basis of legal obligation was an arbitrary convergence of individual wills or "meetings of the minds." Rules for construction of contracts, Chancellor Kent had thus maintained, existed solely to ascertain "the mutual intention of the parties. . . . To reach and carry that intention into effect, the law, when it becomes necessary, will control even the literal terms of the contract, if they manifestly contravene the purpose."

Radical subjectivism thus became the banner under which modern contract law triumphed during the first half of the nineteenth century. Yet, it soon became apparent that the new ideology had succeeded only too well. If a subjective theory of contract served its historical function of destroying all remnants of an objective theory of value, it had the drastic limitation of making legal certainty and predictability impossible. Once contractual obligation was founded entirely on an arbitrary "meeting of minds," it endowed the parties with a complete power to remake law. To the extent that it was seriously followed it made every contract a unique event depending only on the momentary intention of the parties. National markets, however, required uniformity and standardization, which inevitably entailed a sacrifice, at least in theory, of the individual's power to contract.

The emergence of the objective theory, then, is another measure of the influence of commercial interests in the shaping of American law. No longer finding it necessary to enter into battle against eighteenth-century just price doctrines, they could devote their energies to establishing in the second half of the nineteenth century a system of objective rules necessary to assure legal certainty and predictability. And having destroyed most substantive grounds for evaluating the justice of exchange, they could elaborate a legal ideology of formalism, of which Williston was a leading exemplar, that could not only disguise gross disparities of bargaining power under a facade of neutral and formal rules of contract law, but could also enforce commercial customs under the comforting technical rubric of "contract interpretation."

NOTES

5. See, e.g., F. Fuller and M. Eisenberg, *Basic Contract Law* (St. Paul: West Publishing Co., 1972), pp. 121–22; T. Plucknett, *A Concise History of the Common Law*, 5th ed. (London: Butterworth, 1956), pp. 643–44.

6. T. Plucknett, ibid., pp. 643–44.

20. 5 Johns. 395 (N.Y. 1810).

21. See, e.g., *Carberry* v. *Tannehill*, 1 Har. and J. 224 (Md. 1801); *Campbell* v. *Spencer*, 2 Binn. 129, 133 (Pa. 1809); *Clitherall* v. *Ogilvie*, 1 Des. 250, 257 (S.C. Eq. 1792); *Ward* v. *Webber*, 1 Va. (1 Wash.) 354 (1794).

22. Desaussure made this remark as an unnumbered footnote to his report of a case, *Clitherall* v. *Ogilvie*, 1 Des. 250, 259 n. (S.C. Eq. 1792).

23. *Seymour* v. *Delanc[e]y*, 3 Cow. 445, 447 (N.Y. 1824) (Savage C.J.).

74. *Nightingal* v. *Devisme*, 5 Burr. 2589, 2592, 98 Eng. Rep. 361, 363 (K.B. 1770).

75. *Fitch* v. *Hamlin* (Conn. Sup. Ct. Err. 1789), reported in Z. Swift, *A System of the Laws of the State of Connecticut* 410–12 (1795).

77. The leading case is *Shepherd* v. *Johnson*, 2 East. 211, 102 Eng. Rep. 349 (K.B. 1802).

82. 1 Va. (1 Wash.) 1 (1790).

83. 1 Va. (1 Wash.) at 4.

91. 16 U.S. (3 Wheat.) 200 (1818).

92. See, e.g., *West* v. *Wentworth*, 3 Cow. 82 (N.Y. Sup. Ct. 1824) (salt); *Merryman* v. *Criddle*, 18 Va. (4 Munf.) 542 (1815) (corn).

93. *Clark* v. *Pinney*, 7 Cow. 681, 687 (N.Y. Sup. Ct. 1827).

94. *Noble* v. *Smith*, Quincy 254 (Mass. 1767).

106. *Stuart* v. *Wilkins*, 1 Doug. 18, 20, 99 Eng. Rep. 15, 16 (K.B. 1778).

107. *Parkinson* v. *Lee*, 2 East. 314, 102 Eng. Rep. 389 (K.B. 1802).

108. 2 Cai. R. 48 (N.Y. Sup. Ct. 1804).

110. See, e.g., *The Monte Allegre*, 22 U.S. (9 Wheat.) 616 (1824); *Dean* v. *Mason*, 4 Conn. 428 (1822); *Bradford* v. *Manly*, 13 Mass. 139 (1816); *Curcier* v. *Pennock*, 14 S. & R. 51 (Pa. 1826); *Wilson* v. *Shackleford*, 25 Va. (4 Rand.) 5 (1826).

111. *Dean* v. *Mason*. 4 Conn. 428, 434–35 (1822) (Chapman J.).

144. See Annot., 19 *Am. Dec.* 268, 272 (1880).

145. T. Parsons, *The Law of Contracts* Vol. 7, 1st ed. 1853, p. 522, n. 1.

146. 24 Mass. (7 Pick.) 181 (1828), annotated, 19 *Am. Dec.* 268 (1880).

147. 24 Mass. (7 Pick.) at 184, 186, 187.

148. Parsons, *The Law of Contracts*, vol 2., 1st ed. 1855, p. 35 & n.(d).

149. 24 Mass. (7 Pick.) at 185.

162. *Clark* v. *Langdon* (Mass. 1784) in W. Cushing, "Notes on Cases Received in the Superior and Supreme Judicial Courts of Massachusetts from 1772 to 1789" (ms., Treasure Room, Harvard Law School), p. 47.

163. *Homer* v. *Dorr*, 10 Mass. 26, 28–29 (1813).

165. 8 S. & R. 533 (Pa. 1822).

176. *The Reeside*, 20 F. Cas. 458, 459 (No. 11,657), 2 Sumn. 567, 569 (1st Cir. 1837).

185. See, e.g., *Cronk* v. *Cole*, 10 Ind. 485, 489 (1858); *Kertz* v. *Dunlop*, 13 Ind. 277, 280–81 (1859).

193. E. Patterson, "Equitable Relief for Unilateral Mistake," *Columbia Law Review* 28 (1928): 859, 889–90.

7

Legitimizing Racial Discrimination Through Antidiscrimination Law: A Critical Review of Supreme Court Doctrine

Alan Freeman

I. The Perpetrator Perspective

The concept of racial discrimination may be approached from the perspective of either its victim or its perpetrator. From the victim's perspective, racial discrimination describes those conditions of actual social existence as a member of a perpetual underclass. This perspective includes both the objective conditions of life—lack of jobs, lack of money, lack of housing (like this)—and the consciousness associated with those objective conditions—lack of choice and lack of human individuality in being forever perceived as a member of a group rather than as an individual. The perpetrator perspective sees racial discrimination not as conditions, but as actions, or series of actions, inflicted on the victim by the perpetrator. The focus is more on what particular perpetrators have done or are doing to some victims than it is on the overall life situation of the victim class.

The victim, or "condition," conception of racial discrimination suggests that the problem will not be solved until the conditions associated with it have been eliminated. To remedy the condition of

The original version of this chapter appeared in *Minnesota Law Review* 62, 1978. Reprinted by permission of the author and the Minnesota Law Review.

racial discrimination would demand affirmative efforts to change the condition. The remedial dimension of the perpetrator perspective, however, is negative. The task is merely to neutralize the inappropriate conduct of the perpetrator.

In its core concept of the "violation," antidiscrimination law is hopelessly embedded in the perpetrator perspective. Its central tenet, the "antidiscrimination principle," is the prohibition of race-dependent decisions that disadvantage members of minority groups, and its principal task has been to select from the maze of human behaviors those particular practices that violate the principle, outlaw the identified practices, and neutralize their specific effects. Antidiscrimination law has thus been ultimately indifferent to the condition of the victim; its demands are satisfied if it can be said that the "violation" has been remedied.

The perpetrator perspective presupposes a world composed of atomistic individuals whose actions are outside of and apart from the social fabric and without historical continuity. From this perspective, the law views racial discrimination not as a social phenomenon, but merely as the misguided conduct of particular actors. It is a world where, but for the conduct of these misguided ones, the system of equality of opportunity would work to provide a distribution of the good things in life without racial disparities, and where deprivations that did correlate with race would be "deserved" by those deprived on grounds of insufficient "merit." It is a world where such things as "vested rights," "objective selection systems," and "adventitious decisions" (all of which serve to prevent victims from experiencing any change in conditions) are matters of fate, having nothing to do with the problem of racial discrimination.

Central to the perpetrator perspective are the twin notions of "fault" and "causation." Under the fault idea, the task of antidiscrimination law is to separate from the masses of society those blameworthy individuals who are violating the otherwise shared norm. The fault idea is reflected in the assertion that only "intentional" discrimination violates the antidiscrimination principle.

The fault concept gives rise to a complacency about one's own moral status; it creates a class of "innocents," who need not feel any personal responsibility for the conditions associated with discrimination, and who therefore feel great resentment when called upon to bear any burdens in connection with remedying violations.

Operating along with fault, the causation requirement serves to distinguish from the totality of conditions that a victim perceives to be associated with discrimination those that the law will address. These dual requirements place on the victim the nearly impossible burden of isolating the particular conditions of discrimination produced by and mechanically linked to the behavior of an identified blameworthy perpetrator, regardless of whether other conditions of discrimination, caused by other perpetrators, would have to be remedied for the outcome of the case to make any difference at all.

The perpetrator perspective has been and still is the only formal conception of a violation in antidiscrimination law. Strict adherence to that form, however, would have made even illusory progress in the quest for racial justice impossible. The challenge for the law, therefore, was to develop, through the usual legal techniques of verbal manipulation, ways of breaking out of the formal constraints of the perpetrator perspective while maintaining ostensible adherence to the form itself. This was done by separating violation from remedy, and doing through remedy what was inappropriate in cases involving only identification of violations. But since one of the principal tenets of the perpetrator perspective is that remedy and violation must be coextensive, it was necessary to state that tenet and violate it at the same time, no mean task even for masters of verbal gamesmanship. For a while, the remedial doctrines seemingly undermined the hegemony of the perpetrator form, threatening to replace it with a victim perspective. In the end, however, form triumphed, and the perpetrator perspective, always dominant in identifying violations, was firmly reasserted in the context of remedies as well.

II. 1954–1965: THE ERA OF UNCERTAINTY, OR THE JURISPRUDENCE OF VIOLATIONS

A. The Equal Protection Clause

There are at least three different "meanings" that one can ascribe to the equal protection clause, each of which appears to explain a particular kind of controversy under that clause. The first, the "means-oriented" approach, regards the clause as nothing more than a judicial check on legislative mistakes. Under this view, the judicial role is to articulate permissible levels of overinclusion or underinclusion in legislative classifications and send back to the legislature those statutes that have exceeded the allowable tolerances. In this pure form, the principle is perfectly abstract, concerned only with questions of neatness; inasmuch as it serves to check technique rather than goal, it is utterly value-neutral. It is, therefore, a principle suited to the demands of a formalistic, positivist jurisprudence that purports to separate rule application from questions of value.

There is some question, however, whether the principle ever has been, or ever could be, applied in its pure form. On the other hand, the degree of overinclusion or underinclusion that will be tolerated necessarily varies with the subject matter of the legislation. This problem gives rise to the necessity of separating the occasions for "strict" scrutiny from those demanding only "minimal" scrutiny. Since any legislative generalization is likely to fall if subjected to strict scrutiny, the choice between these alternatives takes on a highly substantive content, with the judgment involved in that choice becoming the key decision. Alternatively, the technique of means scrutiny may be employed as a cover for condemnation of an inappropriate purpose or for the creation or extension of a new substantive right.

A second meaning of equal protection, which has on occasion produced affirmative remedies for conditions rather than just negative invalidation of practices, is the "fundamental right" rationale. . . . Given a choice between inventing a new constitutional right explicitly and inventing a new constitutional right by pretending simply to enforce the text of the equal protection clause, the Court has on occasion used the fundamental right doctrine to do the latter. Indeed, in its heyday, the fundamental right doctrine seemed to be the vehicle by which the Court would usher in an era of distributive justice. Now that the smoke has cleared, however, all that happened was the affirmation of some formal, procedural rights. Explicitly rejected as fundamental were those rights having more to do with the substantive conditions of life: education, housing, welfare payments, the right to obtain an abortion (as opposed to the right not to be prevented from going out and paying for one), and even the right to the blessings of federal bankruptcy law.

There is no necessary relation between the fundamental right concept and racial discrimination, since the doctrine is principally concerned with the fundamentality of the abstract right involved—a concern that is ostensibly neutral with respect to the race of the claimants. In fact, however, since racial minorities bear so disproportionately the burdens of economic class in the United States, any claim for substantive distributive justice is in essence a claim on behalf of those minorities. For practical reasons alone, the rejection of those claims forms part of the history of antidiscrimination law.

The third meaning of equal protection is the oldest one, and the one that speaks directly to discrimination against black people in the setting of American history. . . . I prefer to call it "substantive equal protection" to emphasize both its centrality in relation to the other versions of equal protection and its clear focus on ends and purposes, and not just means or legislative rationality. Of the three versions of equal protection, this is the only one that, in employing phrases like "oppressions," "implying inferiority," or "condition of a subject race," speaks to the concrete historical situation of black people in the United States.

B. *BROWN* v. *BOARD OF EDUCATION*[69]

1. COLOR-BLIND CONSTITUTION

To explain *Brown* by invoking the slogan that the "Constitution is color-blind" reflects the means-oriented view of the equal protection clause. On this view, what was wrong with school segregation was that government was employing an irrational classification—race. This approach, however, does not explain why it was irrational to classify people by race if the purpose was to prevent blacks and whites from going to school together. How else could one rationally achieve segregation by race in public schools? One answer is that the purpose itself is illegitimate, that it is no business of government to seek to segregate by race in public schools. If that is the answer, however, the color-blind constitution theory is not a means-oriented approach at all, but rather one that collapses into substantive equal protection. If that is the case, however, one must consider not legislative rationality, but particular relationships between blacks and whites in the context of American history.

A ploy that avoids the quick collapse into substantive equal protection is to bootstrap the means-oriented principle into its own substantive principle. This is done by starting with the means-oriented assumption that racial classifications are almost unrelated to any valid governmental purpose (purpose here being the wholly abstract world of possible purposes). Since such classifications are likely to be irrational, they should be treated as "suspect" and subjected to "strict scrutiny," which they will survive only if found to satisfy a "compelling governmental interest." If the degree of scrutiny is so strict and the possibility of a sufficiently compelling governmental interest so remote that the rule operates as a virtual per se rule, we then seem to have a means-oriented principle that explains the *Brown* case.

The problem with this second formulation of the color-blind theory is that it still contains a substantive assumption: racial classifications are almost always unrelated to any valid governmental purpose. As an abstract matter, this is hardly intuitively obvious. One could easily envision a society where racial or other ethnic classifications are unrelated to any pattern of oppression or domination of one group by another and, in fact, promote feelings of group identity. Thus, the initial assumption cannot be made except in the context of a particular historical situation, and the source of the assumption that underlies the color-blind theory must originate in a notion of substantive equal protection.

Despite this fact, the color-blind theory has tended to become a reified abstraction, to gain a life of its own, and finally to turn back on its origins. Thus, a pure form of the color-blind theory would outlaw any use of racial classifications, no matter what the context, thereby providing easy answers to questions like whether a black community can refuse to participate in an integration plan or whether black students at a public university can establish their own housing units from which whites are excluded. The answers remain easy only as long as the theory remains divorced from its origins in the actuality of black-white relations. By abstracting racial discrimination into a myth-world where all problems of race or ethnicity are fungible, the color-blind theory turns around and denies concrete demands of blacks with the argument that to yield to such demands would be impossible since every other ethnic group would be entitled to make the same demand. . . .

2. EQUALITY OF EDUCATIONAL OPPORTUNITY

Brown can also be viewed as a case concerned with equality of educational opportunity. This approach corresponds with the fundamental right concept of equal protection. Under this view, *Brown* did not merely outlaw segregation in public schools; it also guaranteed that black children would have an affirmative right to a quality of education comparable to that received by white children.

By way of hindsight, the case stood for both more and less than a guarantee of equal educational quality. It came to stand for more insofar as its holding was quickly extended to other forms of state-imposed segregation. But it stood for a great deal less insofar as black children today have neither an affirmative right to receive an integrated education nor a right to equality of resources for their schools, which, ironically, was a litigable claim under the regime of de jure segregation.

For the Court to have recognized affirmative claims to resources or integrated classrooms would have been to adopt explicitly a victim perspective on racial discrimination. Essential to this perspective is the conferral upon the members of the formerly oppressed group a choice that is real and not merely theoretical with respect to conditions over which they have no control under the regime of oppression. Instead, under the perpetrator perspective, the Court recognizes only the right of the black children to attend schools that are not intentionally segregated by the jurisdiction that runs them. This right, it is argued, is all the *Brown* stands for anyway, since all the case did was outlaw de jure segregation. . . .

3. WHITE OPPRESSION OF BLACKS

On this view, the *Brown* case was a straightforward declaration that segregation was unlawful because it was an instance of majoritarian oppression of black people, a mechanism for maintaining blacks as a perpetual underclass. This approach begins and ends with historical fact instead of trying to find a neutral abstraction from which one can deduce the invalidity of segregation. . . .

As a method, the white oppression of blacks approach would ask in each case whether the particular conditions complained of, viewed in their social and historical context, are a manifestation of racial oppression. Such an approach would reflect adoption of the victim perspective. It is not an approach congenial to a system of law that wishes to rationalize continued discrimination just as much as it wants to outlaw it. That goal, if it is to be accomplished through a practice that can be convincingly described as "law," requires a gap between social reality and legal intervention, with that gap mediated by an abstract, objective principle against which particular instances of discrimination can be tested and upheld or struck down, depending on the results. . . .

4. FREEDOM OF ASSOCIATION

The "freedom of association" view sees *Brown* not as an equal protection case at all, but as a case dealing with the due process right of people to associate with one another free of state interference. . . . The freedom of association theory is as much a statement about the right to discriminate as it is about the right not to be discriminated against. All it outlaws is state action. The autonomous individual remains free to discriminate, or not, according to personal preference. Racial discrimination is thus wrenched from its social fabric and becomes a mere question of private, individual taste. Because of the constraints of the state-action principle, there was nothing illegal, as a matter of *national* law, about blatant and explicit discrimination in employment, housing, or public accommodations, as long as such practices were "private." The freedom of association theory legitimizes that tolerance of racial discrimination by transforming it into a freedom to discriminate. . . .

On its own terms, the theory became moot with the subsequent demise of the state-action doctrine through legislation and constitutional decisions expanding the list of responsible perpetrators. . . . Where it does apply, the freedom of association theory implies a notion of racial equivalence similar to the color-blind theory's idea that blacks and whites have equal grounds for complaint about instances of racial discrimination. In this sense, the two theories share a world view—the abstract utopia where racial discrimination has never existed and where, ironically, both theories would probably be irrelevant. The only way that discriminations by whites against blacks can become ethically equivalent to discriminations by blacks against whites is to presuppose that there is no actual problem of racial discrimination. It is just like saying today that the principles of freedom of association and color-blindness govern relationships between long- and short-ear-lobed people.

5. THE INTEGRATED SOCIETY

This view is not so much another way of explaining the *Brown* decision as it is an additional perspective from which to regard all of the other theories and explanations. It begins with the assumption that a decision like *Brown*, which merely outlaws a particular practice, nevertheless implies that the practice is being outlawed to achieve a desired end-state where conditions associated with the outlawed practice will no longer be evident. If particular practices are to be outlawed as deviations from a norm, then the norm must include within it a vision of society where there would not be such deviations. It should then be possible to test current conditions against the desired end-state to decide whether progress is being made. The end-state usually associated with antidiscrimination law is some version of the "integrated society."

Any such vision of the future reflects the achievement of a casteless, if not classless, society in which there is no hierarchy of status that corresponds with racial identification. The essential defect in the color-blind theory of racial discrimination is that it presupposes the attainment of one of these futures. It is a doctrine that at the same time declares racial characteristics irrelevant and prevents any affirmative steps to achieve the condition of racial irrelevance. The freedom of association theory, to the extent it is antidiscrimination at all, also presupposes an already existing future, but it is the tolerance model that it contemplates.

These theories are not alone in presupposing the goal that one is supposedly working toward. Suppose one were to visit the future society of racial irrelevance and discover conditions that in any other society might be regarded as corresponding with a pattern of racial discrimination. Among such conditions might be that one race seems to have a hugely disproportionate share of the worst houses, the most demeaning jobs, and the least control over societal resources. For such conditions to be fair and accepted as legitimate by the disfavored race in future society, they would have to be perceived as produced by accidental, impartial, or neutral phenomena utterly disassociated from any racist practice. Otherwise the future society would fail to meet its claim of racial irrelevance and would not be a future society at all.

Any theory of antidiscrimination law that legitimizes as nondiscriminatory substantial disproportionate burdens borne by one race is effectively claiming that its distributional rules are already the ones that would exist in future society. From the perspective of a victim in present society, where plenty of explicitly racist practices prevail, the predictable and legitimate demand is that those ostensibly neutral rules demonstrate themselves to be the ones that would in fact exist in future society. The legitimacy of the demand is underscored by the fact that those very rules appealed to by the beneficiaries to legitimize the conditions of the victims were created by and are maintained by the dominant race. From the perpetrator perspective, however, those practices not conceded to be racist are held constant; they are presumed consistent with the ethics of future society, and the victims are asked to prove that such is not the case. This is a core difference between the victim and perpetrator perspectives. . . .

C. Post-*Brown* Developments

The remainder of the era of uncertainty offered almost no occasions for resolving any of the ambiguities of *Brown* or exposing the difference between the perpetrator and victim perspectives. Instead, the major task for that era, which put off the question of remedy, was to increase the list of perpetrators against whom antidiscrimination law might be directed. . . .

On one of the few occasions that the Court did have a chance to elaborate on the emerging antidiscrimination principle, it opted for steadfast adherence to the perpetrator perspective. In *Swain* v. *Alabama*,[117] a black man in Talladega County, Alabama, who had been convicted of rape and sentenced to death, brought to the Supreme Court a claim of jury discrimination. He offered three facts in support of this claim: first, that while blacks accounted for 26 percent of the relevant local population, only 10 to 15 percent of the Grand and Petit Jury panels had been black since 1953; second, that in the immediate prosecution, the prosecutor had used his peremptory challenges to exclude all blacks from the jury that tried the defendant; and, third, that no black had ever served on an actual Petit Jury in a civil or criminal case in the county.

The Supreme Court denied the claim, rationalizing all three facts into irrelevance and invoking much of the doctrine associated with the perpetrator perspective. The Court began by acknowledging that purposeful exclusion of blacks from juries had been unconstitutional since *Strauder* v. *West Virginia*[119] had been decided in 1880, but then reminded the defendant that "purposeful discrimination may not be assumed or merely asserted. . . . It must be proven." As for the statistical disparity, the Court concluded: "We cannot say that purposeful discrimination based on race alone is satisfactorily proved by showing that an identifiable group in a community is underrepresented by as much as 10 percent." Why not? Was it a matter of mere accident or random factors? Perhaps that would be the case in the future color-blind society, but this was Alabama in the 1950s and 1960s.

With respect to the peremptory challenges, the Court found merit in Alabama's contention that the practice "affords a suitable and necessary method of securing juries which in fact and in the opinion of the parties are fair and impartial." Again adopting the perspective of future society, the Court justified the actual results of the peremptory challenges in the case before it by deeming those results the product of a fair, neutral, and impartial system of selection. And in typical fashion the Court dragged out the color-blind theory to support this conclusion, approving Alabama's position that "This system, it is said, in and of itself, provides justification for striking any group of otherwise qualified jurors in any given case, whether they be Negroes, Catholics, accountants or those with blue eyes."

On the final claim that no black had ever served on a Petit Jury in the county, the Court invoked the principle of causation, reasoning that while such proof might support a prima facie case that "the peremptory system is being used to deny the Negro the same right and opportunity to participate in the administration of justice enjoyed by the white population," in this case the mere fact that no blacks had served on juries was not a prima facie case of anything since there was no showing that the result was directly attributable to the peremptory system.

Thus an affirmative claim for representation directed against a *system* that was obviously denying that representation was neatly transformed into a burdensome and elusive hunt for the particular villains within that system who were "causing" the result. Necessarily, the Court ignored the results of the system and presumed, despite the obvious fact that blacks were not represented, that the system was operating impartially. To answer what was the core of the defendant's claim—that regardless of causes, it was the results that were the problem—the Court again appealed to the color-blind theory:

> But a defendant in a criminal case is not constitutionally entitled to demand a proportionate number of his race on the jury which tries him nor on the venire of jury roll from which petit jurors are drawn. . . . "Obviously the number of races and nationalities appearing in the ancestry of our citizens would make it impossible to meet a requirement of proportional representation."

Swain points up a deep contradiction in antidiscrimination law that sees no absurdity in legitimizing the precise result that would occur under the regime of de jure exclusion struck down in *Strauder*. Strict adherence to the perpetrator form makes results irrelevant; a concern with results violates the form, while pretending not to, to produce some results. In the third and present era, the Court returns to strict adherence, pretending never to have deviated from it, while pretending to have produced some results in the interim.

III. 1965–1974: THE ERA OF CONTRADICTION, OR THE JURISPRUDENCE OF REMEDY

A. An Overview

A growing tension between the concepts of violation and remedy characterized the second era of modern antidiscrimination law. While the form of the law, with one possible exception, remained squarely within the perpetrator perspective, its content began to create expectations associated with the victim perspective. The perpetrator perspective remained the basic model for a violation, without which there could be no occasion for remedy. Given that finding, however, remedial doctrine took over and, in so doing, subtly changed the concept of violation by addressing itself to substantive conditions beyond the scope of the original violation. . . .

D. Employment: The *Griggs* Case

Griggs v. Duke Power Co.,[183] the Court's first substantive decision under Title VII of the Civil Rights Act of 1964, is as close as the Court has ever come to formally adopting the victim perspective; it is the centerpiece of the era of contradiction. . . . While the actual decision in *Griggs* may be explained in at least two ways that are consistent with the perpetrator principle, the case seems to go beyond that perspective to the extent that it requires neutral practices to justify themselves, radically alters the concept of "intention" in antidiscrimination cases, and implies a demand for results through affirmative action. The Court posed the issue in *Griggs* as:

> whether an employer is prohibited by the Civil Rights Act of 1964, Title VII, from requiring a high school education or passing of a standardized general intelligence test as a condition of employment in or transfer to jobs when (a) neither standard is shown to be significantly related to successful job performance, (b) both requirements operate to disqualify Negroes at a substantially higher rate than white applicants, and (c) the jobs in question formerly had been filled only by white employees as part of a longstanding practice of giving preference to whites.

A unanimous Court, speaking through Chief Justice Burger, answered that question in the affirmative.

That the case was rooted firmly in the perpetrator perspective may be inferred from the behavior of the employer in the case. Prior to July 1965, the employer had blatantly discriminated against black workers, permitting them to work in only one of its five departments, where the highest-paying job paid less than the lowest-paying job in any of the other four departments. In 1965, the employer abandoned its policy of explicit discrimination. In the same year, however, the employer added a high school diploma requirement for transfer out of the previously "black" department and a requirement that a person had to "register satisfactory scores on two professionally developed aptitude tests, as well as . . . have a high school education" for placement in any department except the previously "black" one. These newly imposed requirements operated to limit severely the opportunities available to black employees and applicants. Thus, the case posed the problem of the "ostensibly neutral practice" introduced as a substitute for blatant racial discrimination and achieving substantially the same results.

By making its rationale dependent on the prior explicit discrimination the Court could have stayed within the perpetrator perspective.

But this would have been somewhat disingenuous. For one thing, the prior discriminatory conduct in *Griggs* was legal when it occurred and could not by itself have given rise to a violation. Moreover, to have made the illegality of the test and diploma requirements dependent upon the prior discrimination would have meant that absent such a history the very same practices would be valid however disproportionate their impact. In any event, the Court chose to sever its rationale from any dependence on the prior discrimination, and in so doing left the perpetrator perspective as explaining, at most, why, but not how, the Court intervened in *Griggs*.

Alternatively, the Court in *Griggs* might have remained closer to, but not clearly within, the perpetrator perspective by straying no further than it had in *Gaston County*. On this view, the tests and diploma requirements were not violations in and of themselves, but only to the extent that they penalized blacks for the inferior educations they had received in segregated schools. Some language in *Griggs* even supports this view: "Basic intelligence must have the means of articulation to manifest itself fairly in a testing process. Because they are Negroes, petitioners have long received inferior education in segregated schools and this Court expressly recognized these differences in *Gaston County* v. *United States*." Had this rationale emerged as the dominant one in *Griggs,* the case would have been just another school desegregation case, with the formal violation not the employee selection procedures invalidated but the preexisting system of de jure segregated schools. The *Gaston County* rationale, however, while supportive of the result in *Griggs,* could not be easily transferred to the *Griggs* circumstances.

A straightforward application of *Gaston County* to *Griggs* would have invalidated all test and diploma requirements until the day when black applicants no longer suffered the residual impacts of inferior education. But while the Court was willing to say that all citizens could vote regardless of literacy, they were not equally willing to say that all applicants should be hired, regardless of qualifications. The Court clearly needed a rationale that would describe the instances where tests or other job qualifications could be validly applied even as against black applicants who had suffered inferior educations. To develop such standards, the Court had to take a look at the tests on their merits. Almost inadvertently, then, the opinion switched from blaming the victim to scrutinizing the neutral practices themselves with respect to their claims of rationality. . . .

Thus, the central rationale of *Griggs* is that selection procedures, even ostensibly neutral ones, that disadvantage minority applicants are not valid unless they can demonstrate themselves to be rational: "The Act proscribes not only overt discrimination but also practices that are fair in form, but discriminatory in operation. The touchstone is business necessity. If an employment practice which operates to exclude negroes cannot be shown to be related to job performance, the practice is prohibited." The standard of rationality set by the Court seemed to be a tough one, demanding a showing of job relatedness, the removal of "artificial, arbitrary, and unnecessary barriers," and standards that "measure the person for the job and not the person in the abstract." In short, the opinion amounts to a demand that the myth of a meritocratic scheme of equality of opportunity be transformed into a reality.

Thus for the first time the Court held that a neutral practice, not purposefully discriminatory, that nevertheless failed to admit blacks to jobs had to justify itself or else be declared invalid. Although the opinion was decided under Title VII, its logic did not seem easily confined. The Court even took one general swipe at the workings of meritocracy:

> The facts of this case demonstrate the inadequacy of broad and general testing devices as well as the infirmity of using diplomas or degrees as fixed measures of capability. History is filled with examples of men and women who rendered highly effective performance without the conventional badges of accomplishment in terms of certificates, diplomas, or degrees.

Since the case was concerned not with remedy but with the meaning of "violation" under Title VII, it seemed reasonable to conclude that a discriminatory practice under Title VII would also be a discriminatory practice under the Fourteenth Amendment in areas not subject to Title VII. Read this way, the case becomes a generalized demand that all objective selection procedures under the coverage of some antidiscrimination law be required to justify themselves as consistent with the notion of equality of opportunity. *Griggs* in no way contradicts the meritocratic model, but assumes that it can be made to work, that those who are deserving can be objectively separated from those who are not.

In addition to legitimizing the assertion of an affirmative claim directed at a systemic practice, *Griggs* changed the notion of "intentional" in antidiscrimination law. This aspect of the opinion derives from the Court's severance of its rationale from the prior discriminatory practices of the defendant employer. The opinion makes it clear that "good intent or absence of discriminatory intent does not redeem employment procedures or testing mechanisms that operate as 'build-in headwinds' for minority groups" and that "Congress directed the thrust of the Act to the *consequences* of employment practices, not simply the motivation." Under the notion of "intention" that emerges from the opinion, then, one is intentionally discriminating if one continues to use a practice or maintain a condition that disadvantages a minority group without being able to justify the rationality of the practice or condition. This idea, too, did not seem easily confined within the employment area to tests alone, nor easily within the employment area at all.

When applied to ostensibly rational practices, the *Griggs* notion of intention merely demands a showing of rationality. When applied to nonrational practices, such as school or voter districting, jurisdictional boundaries, or zoning decisions, all of which are inherently arbitrary, the *Griggs* notion becomes a demand for results and, therefore, an adoption of the victim perspective. If, for example, there are a number of ways to divide a community into districts for school assignment purposes, and the one currently employed produces a great deal of racial concentration in schools, to perpetuate the existing scheme with the knowledge of the racial concentration produced becomes intentional discrimination—unless there is a sufficiently good reason for having chosen that scheme. To follow out the analogy to *Griggs,* such a reason would have to be one that tells the black children, who are confined to schools segregated in fact, why it is *legitimate* that they be so confined. Absent such a reason, the children would have the right to a redistricting that did not produce racial concentration.

The third outstanding feature of *Griggs* is that it virtually coerces employers (and others affected by its rationale) into adoption of affirmative action programs. The *Griggs* rationale, with its attendant demand for justification, is not even triggered unless the practice complained of produces a disproportionate impact on a minority group. A potential defendant who wishes to avoid litigation, or who wishes to avoid the adoption of different or more cumbersome selection procedures, need only negate the disproportionate impact by adopting different procedures from the minority groups disproportionately excluded. While such an approach in no way legitimizes the original procedure under the rationale of *Griggs,* it does at least neutralize its illegitimacy by offering an alternative. Thus *Griggs* implicitly offers a choice: either make the meritocracy work on its own terms or make up for its flaws through affirmative efforts.

IV. 1974–?: THE ERA OF RATIONALIZATION, OR THE JURISPRUDENCE OF CURE

A. An Overview

The typical approach of the era of rationalization is to "declare that the war is over," to make the problem of racial discrimination go away by announcing that it has been solved. This approach takes many forms. Its simplest and most direct version is the declaration that, despite the discriminatory appearance of current conditions, the actual violation has already been cured, or is being remedied, regardless of whether the remedy prescribed can be expected to alleviate the condition. A more sophisticated approach is to declare that what looks like a violation, based on expectations derived from the era of contradiction, is not a violation at all. This has been accomplished by isolating statutory discrimination from constitutional discrimination to prevent the former from infiltrating the latter[218] and by weakening the previously created statutory standards under the guise of statutory interpretation.[219] The same results have been achieved by renewing insistence on the always manipulative requirement of causation,[220] by emphasizing the form rather than the results of earlier cases,[221] by invoking the purpose-motive distinction to insulate neutral nonrational decisions,[222] or by presuming the rationality of neutral decisions instead of demanding their justification.[223]

Central to the era of rationalization is the pretense—associated with the color-blind theory of racial discrimination—that but for an occasional aberrational practice, future society is already here and functioning. The contradictions implicit in the earlier cases are thus resolved largely by pretending they were never there. This resolution has in turn facilitated a quick and easy return to the comfortable and neat world of the perpetrator perspective. As a result, the actual conditions of racial powerlessness, poverty, and unemployment can be regarded as no more than conditions—not as racial discrimination. Those conditions can then be rationalized by treating them as historical accidents or products of a malevolent fate, or, even worse, by blaming the victims as inadequate to function in the good society. . . .

D. Employment

If *Griggs* was the most important case of the era of contradiction, the only one offering a genuine threat to the hegemony of the perpetrator perspective, then the major task of the era of rationalization must be the obliteration of *Griggs*. And so it is in the area of employment that one finds the case that will likely become the centerpiece of the era of rationalization: *Washington* v. *Davis*. While not quite obliterating *Griggs*, the Court has so undermined it that it has ceased to be a credible threat. This overall result has been achieved in three discrete steps: *Grigg's* apparent implications for all of antidiscrimination law have been squelched by limiting its doctrine to Title VII; its forceful assault on the system of equality of opportunity from within the structure of Title VII has been blunted by softening the scrutiny required; and its apparent application to analogous Title VII problems has been denied by refusing to extend it to the other major substantive area where it had been applied by the lower courts for some time—seniority. . . .

Washington v. *Davis* involved a test that purported to measure verbal ability, vocabulary, reading, and comprehension. The test was challenged in its role as a criterion for admission to the training program for District of Columbia police officers. Given a failure rate that was four times as high for blacks as for whites, the plaintiffs asserted, in an action commenced before Title VII became applicable to governmental employment, that the test was prima facie unconstitutional. The Court held that absent direct or inferential proof that the test was employed with a design to produce racially disproportionate results, the disproportionate failure rate was not itself significant enough to create a prima facie case and that there was no requirement that the test demonstrate any rationality at all. Using an intriguing kind of inside-out reasoning, the Court quickly rebutted the commonsense notion that racial discrimination under the Fifth or Fourteenth Amendment meant the same thing as racial discrimination under Title VII. Mr. Justice White's terse offering was that "We have never held that the constitutional standard for adjudicating claims of invidious racial discrimination is identical to the standards applicable under Title VII, and we decline to do so today."

To support its position, the Court offered a "parade of horribles" argument that would be embarrassing in a first-year law class: "A [contrary] rule . . . would raise serious questions about, and perhaps invalidate, a whole range of tax, welfare, public service, regulatory, and licensing statutes that may be more burdensome to the poor and to the average black than to the more affluent white." For precedent, the Court turned to cases like *Wright* v. *Rockefeller*, which involved electoral districting, but failed to explain why a conclusion that an inherently nonrational decision like districting need not be justified in rational terms compels the conclusion that an ostensibly rational practice like testing is equally secure from scrutiny.

Thus with quiet efficiency the Court eliminated all extra-Title VII implications of *Griggs*. The alternative holding of *Washington* v. *Davis* went a step further, softening the severe scrutiny thought to be required by *Griggs* to the point where *Griggs* is no longer much of threat even in Title VII cases. . . .

In three respects, the Court in *Washington* v. *Davis* dropped any pretense of strictness with respect to job-relatedness and simultaneously abandoned its posture of deference to the EEOC: the test was ultimately validated by nothing more than intuitive generalization. There may have been evidence that the challenged test correlated with some degree of significance with another test given to trainees at the end of the training program, but there was no evidence that either the entrance test or the final test in any way related to qualities or abilities relevant to being a police officer. In fact, there was no proof that the test given at the end of the training program measured anything taught in that program, even assuming that the program was related to future performance as a police officer. The most that was established was that the test correlated with another test, which in itself is hardly surprising. But that other test may or may not have anything to do with the job for which the training program is supposed to prepare those who pass the initial test. In this context, the Court's conclusion, shared with the district court, that "some minimum verbal and communicative skill would be very useful, if not essential, to satisfactory progress in the training regimen" seems little more than an assumption of the desired conclusion.

Thus, while *Griggs* remains good law with respect to Title VII cases involving tests and other objective hiring criteria, it has lost a good deal of its force even in those areas. And last term the Court rejected the unanimous views of eight courts of appeals by refusing to apply the *Griggs* approach to its other major area of application—seniority. In *International Brotherhood of Teamsters* v. *United States,* the Court conceded that the *Griggs* approach to neutral practices under Title VII would serve to invalidate seniority systems that perpetuated the effects of prior racial discrimination even where such discrimination was not proved or provable as a separate violation of the Act.

NOTES

69. 347 U.S. 483 (1954).
117. 380 U.S. 202 (1965).
119. 100 U.S. 303 (1880).
183. 401 U.S. 424 (1971).
218. See *Washington* v. *Davis,* 426 U.S. 229, 238–39 (1976).
219. See *Dothard* v. *Rawlinson,* 433 U.S. 321, 334–35 (1977); *International Bhd. of Teamsters* v. *United States,* 431 U.S. 324, 348–55 (1977); *General Elec. Co.* v. *Gilbert,* 429 U.S. 125, 133–36 (1976); *Washington* v. *Davis,* 426 U.S. 229, 238–39, 248–52 (1976); *Beer* v. *United States,* 425, U.S. 130, 138–42 (1976).
220. See *Rizzo* v. *Goode,* 423 U.S. 362, 376–77 (1976); *Warth* v. *Seldin,* 422 U.S. 490, 502–7 (1975).
221. Compare *Pasadena City Bd. of Educ.* v. *Spangler,* 427 U.S. 424 (1976), and *Milliken* v. *Bradley,* 418 U.S. 717 (1974), with *Keyes* v. *School Dist. No. 1,* 413 U.S. 189 (1973), and *Swann* v. *Charlotte-Mecklenburg Bd. of Educ.,* 402 U.S. 1 (1971).
222. See *Village of Arlington Heights* v. *Metropoïitan Hous. Dev. Corp.,* 429 U.S. 717, 744–47, 747 n.22 (1974).

PART III

Confronting Contradiction

As the earlier work of Kennedy and Unger suggested (see Part 1), social relations and individual consciousness in modern society are riven with contradictory feelings and practices. By postulating a resolvable solution to this self-generated conflict, liberal theory has lent an appearance of smooth rationality to legal doctrine and has managed to paper over the cracks in social life. A major device for subduing and mediating the tension between the contradictory demands of order and freedom has been rights analysis. Yet despite its superficial appeal and longevity, it cannot stand up to the strain placed upon it: right talk is indeterminate. As competing claims can be effectively framed in the language of rights, each side can invoke the power of the state in its cause. As liberalism does not and cannot possess a metatheory to bring this conflict to a determinate conclusion, rights talk is thoroughly incoherent and inconsistent. Behind the fragile facade of rights talk is the crude ideological struggle for power; sectarian interests are converted into universal insights and provisional arrangements are made to appear natural and inevitable. Duncan Kennedy lays out the basic dynamics and structures of this contradiction. He identifies it as both the problem and the pivot of liberal thinking and practice. The two other pieces offer a more situated demonstration of the vain attempts by traditional lawyers to overcome this problem.

Using Patrick Atiyah's tome on *The Rise and Fall of Freedom of Contract* as a peg, Elizabeth Mensch hangs a detailed critique of free contracts mythology. As a sophisticated exponent of liberal theorizing, Atiyah manages to exhibit and underline its shortcomings as he seeks to disguise and overcome them. Mensch shows that the princi-

137

ple of free contract is inherently incoherent and that the principle's relation to emerging socio-economic conditions was ambiguous and distinctly noninstrumental. Taking a slightly different tack, Mark Tushnet delves into the rituals of constitutional doctrine and draws out the contradictions that comprise and inhibit the dominant theories of constitutional interpretation. Although ostensibly premised on an individualistic theory of political society and its perfectable realization, constitutional judgments and scholarship cannot achieve coherence without relying on the very communitarian assumptions that liberal theory claims to deny.

8

The Structure of Blackstone's Commentaries

Duncan Kennedy

Everything that I will have to say flows from (but is in no sense logically entailed by) a premise about legal thinking. This premise is that the activity of categorizing, analyzing, and explaining legal rules has a double motive. On the one hand, it is an effort to discover the conditions of social justice. On the other, it is an attempt to deny the truth of our painfully contradictory feelings about the actual state of relations between persons in our social world. In its first aspect, it is a utopian enterprise constituting, in E. P. Thompson's phrase, a "cultural achievement of universal significance."[6] In its second aspect, it has been (as a matter of historical fact rather than of logical necessity) an instrument of apology—an attempt to mystify both dominators and dominated by convincing them of the "naturalness," the "freedom," and the "rationality" of a condition of bondage. . . .

METHODOLOGICAL PRELIMINARIES

The Fundamental Contradiction

Here is an initial statement of the fundamental contradiction: most participants in American legal culture believe that the goal of individual freedom is at the same time dependent on and incompatible with the communal coercive action that is necessary to achieve it. Others (family, friends, bureaucrats, cultural figures, the state) are necessary if we are to become persons at all—they provide us with the stuff of our selves and protect us in crucial ways against destruction. Even

---

Excerpted from its original publication in *Buffalo Law Review* 28, 1979, by permission of the author and the Buffalo Law Review.

when we seem to ourselves to be most alone, others are with us, incorporated in us through processes of language, cognition, and feeling that are, simply as a matter of biology, collective aspects of our individuality. Moreover, we are not always alone. We sometimes experience fusion with others, in groups of two or even two million, and it is a good rather than a bad experience.

But at the same time that it forms and protects us, the universe of others (family, friendship, bureaucracy, culture, the state) threatens us with annihilation and urges upon us forms of fusion that are quite plainly bad rather than good. A friend can reduce me to misery with a single look. Numberless conformities, large and small abandonments of self to others, are the price of what freedom we experience in society. And the price is a high one. Through our existence as members of collectives, we impose on others and have imposed on us hierarchical structures of power, welfare, and access to enlightenment that are illegitimate, whether based on birth into a particular social class or on the accident of genetic endowment.

The kicker is that the abolition of these illegitimate structures, the fashioning of an unalienated collective existence, appears to imply such a massive increase of collective control over our lives that it would defeat its purpose. Only collective force seems capable of destroying the attitudes and institutions that collective force has itself imposed. Coercion of the individual by the group appears to be inextricably bound up with the liberation of that same individual. If one accepts that collective norms weigh so heavily in favor of the status quo that purely "voluntary" movement is inconceivable, then the only alternative is the assumption of responsibility for the totalitarian domination of other peoples' minds—for "forcing them to be free."

Even this understates the difficulty. It is not just that the world of others is intractable. The very structures against which we rebel are necessarily within us as well as outside of us. We are implicated in what we would transform, and it in us. This critical insight is not compatible with that sense of the purity of one's intention which seems often to have animated the enterprise of remaking the social world. None of this renders political practice impossible, or even problematic: we can identify oppression without having overcome the fundamental contradiction, and do something against it. But it does mean proceeding on the basis of faith and hope in humanity, without the assurances of reason.

The fundamental contradiction—that relations with others are both necessary to and incompatible with our freedom—is not only intense, it is also pervasive. First, it is an aspect of our experience of every form of social life. It arises in the relations of lovers, spouses, parents and children, neighbors, employers and employees, trading partners, colleagues, and so forth. Second, within law, as law is commonly defined, it is not only an aspect, but the very *essence* of every problem. There simply are no legal issues that do not involve directly the problem of the legitimate content of collective coercion, since there is by definition no legal problem until someone has at least imagined that he might invoke the force of the state. And it is not just a matter of definition. The more sophisticated a person's legal thinking, regardless of her political stance, the more likely she is to believe that all issues within a doctrinal field reduce to a single dilemma of the degree of collective as opposed to individual self-determination that is appropriate. And analyses of particular fields tend themselves to collapse into a single analysis as soon as the thinker attempts to understand together, say, free speech and economic due process, or contracts and torts.

The History of the Contradiction (a)

The all-pervasiveness of the sense of contradiction is the endpoint (by which I do not at all mean the "goal") of a long process of historical change. It is very difficult to conceptualize that history. I propose to begin with a shockingly crude model, and see where it will lead. Suppose that the fundamental contradiction has "always" existed, in its present degree of intensity and pervasiveness. We then need to account for the obvious fact that it has either not been experienced at all, or not acknowledged, by *any* of the succeeding generations of Western legal thinkers between the time of the sophists and the very recent past. Let us suppose that the reason for this has been that during that whole period there have existed processes of mediation, or denial, that have functioned to hide or disguise it from those engaged in the enterprise of legal thought.

Mechanisms of Denial: (a) Types of Legal Thinking

Here is a preliminary statement of how legal thinking can be a mechanism for denying contradictions. Imagine a description that portrays the making of decisions in our situation of contradictory feelings as involving a tension between conflicting values that we must balance rationally. Such a description is untrue to our experience. Indeed, a person who so described the experience might well appear to be hiding from its reality. The bland rhetoric of tension and balance is so clearly false that we suspect a person who employs it of wanting to minimize or conceal the elements of paradox, stalemate, and desperation we experience when we try to decide what kind of collective coercion is legitimate and what illegitimate.

There are at least two other modes for describing the situation that are even more patently untrue than balancing. The first of these is functionalism. In the functionalist mode, we decide which forms of collective action are legitimate by identifying tasks that supposedly must be performed in any social organization. We can then explain, and either justify or criticize, the types of collective action that usually occur by asking how well they fit into the idealized scheme of functions thus identified.

A second mode is sometimes called formalism, by which is meant a system of thought that identifies some forms of collective intervention, such as the defense of private property and the enforcement of contracts, with the protection of individual freedom. This identification serves to legitimate some legal rules while delegitimating others (for example, minimum wage legislation "violates freedom of contract"). That is, formalism resembles balancing and functionalism in that it allows us to deny the contradictory state of our feelings by asserting that there is a proper place for collectivism, and that that place can be determined by the rational analysis of the content of legal rules.

Mechanisms of Denial: (b) Categorical Schemes

While modes of legal reasoning are an important aspect of legal thinking, they are no more and perhaps less important than the structure of categories available at any given moment for classifying different incidents of collective coercion. It is impossible to think about the legal system without some categorical scheme. We simply cannot grasp the infinite multiplicity of particular instances without abstractions. Further, the edifice of categories is a social construction, carried on over centuries, which makes it possible to know much more than we could know if we had to reinvent our own abstractions in each generation. It is therefore a priceless acquisition. On the other hand, all such schemes are lies. They cabin and distort our immediate experience, and they do so systematically rather than randomly.

The very existence of historically legitimated doctrinal categories gives the law student, the teacher, and the practitioner a false sense of the orderliness of legal thought, of our practices, and of our reasons for those practices. But the particular schemes adopted convey more particular falsehoods. The dichotomy of contract and tort, for example, has for generations conveyed the message that in the private sector, individuals freely structure their relationships as long as they obey a set of ground rules that are enforced by the state but prescribed by elementary moral principles. The segregation of real property law from the rest of contract and tort law tells us that both limitations on contractual freedom and instances of strict liability with respect to land are a historical anomaly. The distinction between public and private law replicates the hidden message of tort versus contract: that the state stands outside civil society and is not implicated in the hierarchical outcomes of private interaction.

The notion of "a mode of legal reasoning" and the notion of "a categorical scheme" are not altogether distinct. Categorical schemes are products of the activity of legal thinkers. When thinkers are creating them, they employ modes of reasoning. Thus a thinker may find it necessary to justify the maintenance of a distinction between public and private law, and a particular choice about where to place, say, administrative regulation. She will appeal to the "nature" of things, or to the "functions" of the categories, or to a "balancing test," depending on the mode of reasoning then in use. If lawyers consciously made and remade the categories to fit their purposes, there wouldn't be much point in analyzing them apart from the reasoning process itself.

But even when we profess an extreme nominalism of this kind, we cannot maintain it in practice. Categorical schemes have a life of their own. Most legal thinkers in any given period take both the existing structure and myriad particular categorizations for granted. They deploy their efforts at reasoning new situations into the category that will lead to the outcome they desire. The motives that underlie the structure as a whole are therefore likely to be buried deep, if not altogether inaccessible. In periods when there is little self-consciousness about the artificial character of *all* categories, even a legal thinker who knows she is engaged in a major effort to redefine the structure may have no idea how much choice is implicit in her activity. For these reasons, the study of categorical schemes is particularly fertile ground for the method of interpretation I am proposing.

The History of the Contradiction (b)

Now let us return to our hypothesis about the history of legal thought as the history of the fundamental contradiction. We left off with the notion that previous generations did not experience or did not acknowledge the contradiction because the forms of mediation hid it from them, or allowed them to deny it. We can conceptualize the process that led us to the present impasse as follows.

There have always been many different legal modes of mediation, many forms of legal reasoning, many categorical schemes. Many modes coexist in a given period; different modes dominate from period to period. The single constant has been the gradual accretion of *criticisms* of each of the modes of mediation. The process of criticism has had two simultaneous tendencies: to reduce the multiplicity of modes to a smaller and smaller number, and to undermine the efficacy of the survivors in the very process of demonstrating their generality.

The participants did not *experience* this process as one of descent into contradiction. Indeed, they experienced the activity of discrediting most modes of mediation while developing the survivors into more and more powerful, general, and pervasive mechanisms for ordering the legal universe as enormously fulfilling. It was unimaginable to them that the very process of abstraction that made generalization possible would lead *us* ultimately to lose the ability to deny the contradiction.

I will use the term "liberalism" to describe the mode of mediation or denial that gradually killed off its rivals, before it finally succumbed to the problems it was designed to solve. Liberalism was initially a revolutionary mode not of *legal* thought, but of thinking about politics. It became, through works like Blackstone's *Commentaries,* a mode of legal thought as well. The history of legal thought in our culture is the history of the emergence of this legal version of the liberal mode, its progressive abstraction and generalization through the nineteenth century until it structured all legal problems, and its final disintegration in the early twentieth century.

For the moment, I hope it is enough to define liberalism very roughly in terms of a splitting of the universe of others into two radically opposed imaginary entities. One of these is "civil society," a realm of free interaction between private individuals who are un-threatening to one another because the other entity, "the state," forces them to respect one another's rights. In civil society, others are available for good fusion as private individual respecters of rights; through the state, they are available for good fusion as participants in the collective experience of enforcing rights. A person who lives the liberal mode can effectively deny the fundamental contradiction.

The Apologetic Aspect of Legal Thought

Such a hypothesis about the history of the fundamental contradiction can provide us with a framework for the investigation of a particular work, such as Blackstone's *Commentaries.* For there is more to the enterprise of interpreting legal thought than the history of mechanisms of denial or mediation. Denial or mediation is not necessarily *apologetic.* The element of apology comes in because legal thought denies or mediates with a bias toward the existing social and economic order. It asserts that we have overcome the fundamental contradiction through our existing practices. Or that we can achieve that blissful state through minor adjustments of a legal regime that is basically sound, and needs only a little tinkering to make it perfect. Or that there are many and serious flaws in the existing order that we can remedy by bringing our tawdry practice into line at last with our noble (noncontradictory) ideals.

It is important to keep clearly in mind the lack of necessary connection between the task of mediation and the apologetic enter-prise. For example, a lot of revolutionary Marxist theory consists of the dogmatic denial of our contradictory feelings combined with violent denunciation of the status quo. Seventeenth-century English liberal political theory (Locke, Harrington, the Levelers) was a mode of mediation or denial, but it was also revolutionary. It is simply wrong to insist that because these bodies of thought are or once were radical rather than apologetic, they must necessarily avoid the pitfalls of denial. By contrast, the "tragic view of life" espoused by the leading critics of modernist culture claims to *accept* contradiction. It is nonetheless apologetic for all of that.

The Connection Between Mediation and Apology

A complete account of legal thought would *explain* the contingent but historically determinate association between liberal legalism as denial and liberal legalism as apology. It would get at the merger of the two intentions in the experience of legal thought itself. I would like to do this, but it does not seem possible to me, at least for the moment. For the moment, I am content with some rather vague slogans. The people doing legal thought have always been members of a ruling class. Implicit loyalty oaths have always been a condition of admission to the inner circles of legality. The enterprise of merely understanding the legal order is not one likely to be taken up by a person radically opposed to the status quo. Opposition to the status quo does not easily survive the kind of identification with the legal system that seems to be a psychological precondition for really understanding it. . . .

Contrast with Other Methodologies

It may be helpful in understanding my method if I try to draw a sharp contrast between it and the two alternatives that dominate contemporary legal historiography. The first alternative is the natural law approach practiced in most law school classrooms. It consists of analyzing the rationale of a decision to see if it "makes sense." If it does, we move on to the next. If it does not, we attempt to formulate an alternative rationale that satisfies us of the rationality and justice of the outcome. If we can construct no such rationale, we conclude that the decision was wrong, propose a different outcome, and explain why it would be better. This method attempts to use the analysis of past cases to advance the enterprise of discovering the requirements of justice in particular social circumstances.

My method is like the natural law method in that it requires the analysis of the coherence of judicial explanations of outcomes. It uses exactly the same critical techniques as the natural lawyers. But the goal is neither an alternative rationale nor a criticism of the outcome. It is to discover not what should have been done, but, first, the apologetic motive that the formal rationale was designed to disguise and, second, the contribution of the reasoning process to the creation and maintenance of the liberal mode of mediation. Since the apologetic motive is one the judges could not admit and still retain their legitimacy, the analysis makes no direct contribution to the discovery and elaboration of principles of justice. The most it can do is put us on guard against implications of the rationalizing process that would otherwise have remained unconscious.

The second alternative method is that of instrumental or interest analysis, and it is common to most academic Marxist and liberal historians. The goal of instrumental analysis is to show that the conscious or unconscious motive of the judge was to further some particular interests, either of the judge himself or of a group with whom he identified. The point about interests is that they are selfish, and that they need no further explanation. For example, once it is clear that the purpose of the nineteenth-century rule of caveat emptor was to favor the merchant/capitalist class against the masses of agriculturalists and consumers, the instrumentalist rests his case. The most conclusive evidence of motive, in his view, consists of effects of decisions on the interests of social groups, with the character of the interests affected treated as largely self-evident to a person with a cynical view of human nature. The instrumentalist treats formal rationales of decisions as largely obfuscatory, except when they inadvertently or naively refer to selfish aims.

My method resembles instrumentalism in that it is concerned with hidden motives that the judges themselves would treat as illegitimate if forced to confront them. But the motives that interest me are those that lie behind the forms of legal reasoning and categorization, rather than those that animate the choice between plaintiffs and defendants acting as stand-ins for social classes. This is not to say that the latter kind of motives do not exist—it is their very obviousness that distracts us from the deeper patterns I want to elucidate. What I am after is the logic of obfuscation, rather than the struggle of conflicting interests that gives it energy.

The motives that guide choices among patterns of rationalization are both less conscious and less particular than those on which the instrumentalists focus. They have to do with maintaining and legitimating the general (but biased) ground rules of class struggle rather than with the outcomes day to day or even decade to decade. By looking closely at them, I hope to overcome what seems to me a crippling instrumentalist error: that of attributing so much importance to particular outcomes within the framework that the framework itself becomes invisible. The blanking out of the framework turns instrumental critical thought itself into a form of apology, because it denies the *current reality* in our own thinking of the contradictions it is happy to recognize in particular past decisions.

Some Disclaimers

My focus on interpreting the larger framework as simultaneous mediation and legitimation means that what I have to say is descriptive, and descriptive only of thought. It means ignoring the question of what brings a legal consciousness into being, what causes it to change, and what effect it has on the actions of those who live it. My only justification for these omissions is that we need to understand far more than we now do about the content and the internal structure of legal thought before we can hope to link it in any convincing way to other aspects of social, political, or economic life. There are dangers to deferring the task, but I think them well worth risking.

Given this limitation of focus, it would be a delusion to think that the study of the history and prehistory of our contradictory feelings can resolve the contradiction, provide a basis for political action, or even help us in the task of formulating and reformulating our goal. Even if we *could* resolve the contradiction at the level of theory, we would still be subject to its influence in practice. The examples of Stalinism and fascism have a force on its behalf greater than that of any body of abstract speculatons. The same is true of the commonplace that existing bureaucracies, ostensibly under popular control, develop and pursue interests incompatible with their public purposes. And it is important to remember that, even on the level of thought, legal ideology is only a small, though not insignificant, part of the total complex of ideas that seem to render egalitarian socialism a utopia.

The enterprise thus appears twice defeated before it is begun: we cannot resolve the contradiction within legal theory, and even if we could, the accomplishment would be of limited practical importance. Yet it may nonetheless be worth undertaking. It is true that the categories of individual and collective, and freedom and power, represent an insuperable contradiction within our experience. But it is also true that we embrace, generalize, and intensify the contradiction by accepting it uncritically as part of the nature of things. To *some* extent, we are the victims of our own reification rather than our historical circumstances. To this extent, thinking makes it so. The task of criticism is to demystify our thinking by confronting us with the fact that the contradiction is an historical artifact. It is no more immortal than is the society that created and sustains it. Understanding this is not salvation, but it is a help.

NOTES

6. E. P. Thompson, *Whigs and Hunters: The Origin of the Black Act* (London: Allen Lane, 1975), p. 265.

9

Contract as Ideology

Elizabeth Mensch

Despite our current mode of legal sophistication ("we are all realists now"), American readers should be enlightened by Atiyah's detailed examination of free contract mythology in England. After all, until recently that same mythology dominated American legal thought: upon its coherence hinged the claim that a formal system of rights could intelligibly define a boundary separating each individual's private sphere of legally protected autonomy from arbitrary public or oppressive private power. The legal protection of that boundary was once held out as the best and only definition of freedom we could hope to achieve.

Of course, as classical contract doctrine collapsed, so too did the pretense that the boundary was real. Yet the effort to erect a new contract doctrine on the ruins of the old, like the effort, more generally, to reclaim for liberal legalism its lost coherence, has not transcended the forms and vocabulary of older orthodoxy. Freedom of contract has been conclusively labeled a naive myth, but the forms of that mythology still bind. Atiyah's book, *The Rise and Fall of Freedom of Contract,* is a striking illustration of that fact.

Atiyah explicitly sets out to describe the relation between modern legal thought and recent intellectual and economic developments. The exact nature of those relationships has always eluded precise definition. Perhaps wisely, given the complexity of the theoretical debate on the subject, Atiyah avoids aligning himself with any particular school of thought: his goal is description, not explanation. As a result, his model of the relationship between law and social life is peculiarly amorphous. He blends an instrumental, active model (law as promoting or facilitating the needs and values of a changing society) with a reflective, passive one (law as depicting through its

Excerpted from its original publication in *Stanford Law Review* 33, 1981, by permission of the author and the Stanford Law Review.

forms an otherwise intact social reality). This vague model has the virtue of absorbing Atiyah's many eclectic observations; it also allows him to maintain a balanced, liberal viewpoint throughout the book. Atiyah's model of relationships breaks down, however, with respect to two problems: contradiction and discontinuity. Contradiction means that the principle of free contract is incoherent *on its own terms.* This is different from saying that free contract's historical and intellectual strengths and weaknesses can be balanced. Discontinuity means that comparing the classical model of free contract to the social and economic reality of nineteenth-century England reveals opposition and denial, not mere reflection. . . .

CONTRADICTION IN CONTRACT DOCTRINE

The integrity of classical formalism depended upon the coherence of three highly abstracted categories: freedom of contract, property and, more generally, liberty. These three categories were capable, however, of generating obviously contradictory arguments about specific issues. One of the most painful symptoms of the disintegration of formalism was the recognition of this contradiction. Even a judge determined to decide a case according to free contract principles (or for that matter, to decide a case according to the market principles) could find himself pulled in two quite opposite directions.

The covenants in restraint of trade issue is a clear example of this contradiction. As Atiyah points out, judges soon realized that the process of free contracting could destroy itself through agreements eliminating the threat of competition, and therefore eliminating all pretense of free exchange on an open market. Reluctant to adopt the suspiciously paradoxical view that the law should interfere with freedom of contract in order to save it, English courts enforced obviously anticompetitive agreements.

During the same period, Americans enacted the Sherman Act—which prohibited all contracts in restraint of trade—to preserve the model of free competition. Yet, as Justice White noted in *Standard Oil Co.* v. *United States,*[13] if taken literally, the Act's language would destroy contract law: *all* contracts are in restraint of trade. This is true because enforcing secured risk allocation and protecting reasonable expectations necessarily conflict with market freedom and unregulated value-enhancing exchanges—the arguments upon which the legitimacy of free contract rests. Thus, the restraint of trade issue is not simply an outside, limiting case, different in kind from the inner core of contract law. *In every case,* a contract that is no longer value-enhancing to one party can be impeached by the claim that free traders would no longer agree to the exchange: only *competing* principles of security can justify enforcement.

Every doctrinal dispute within the classical model is reducible to conflicting claims of security and freedom. Each such conflict might be perceived as a problem of messiness, caused by the common denominator of time. If formation and performance are not simultaneous, the world will have changed by the time performance comes due. Freedom logic requires a new formation process whenever performance is no longer in accord with the will of the parties. Only security logic can step in to demand enforcement. Ostensibly undertaken in the name of a barely remembered exercise of freedom, enforcement is inevitably coercion—freedom has become unfreedom. The relation between coercion and freedom ultimately destroys the core of classical contract assumptions.

The doctrinal intractability of the problem is evident. Expanding doctrines of mistake and commercial impracticability, plus problems of modification, underscore the dilemma. Typically, one party seeks to escape a hard bargain by demanding discharge or modification. Notably, the arguments usually advanced in favor of free bargain and value-enhancing exchange are equally favorable to discharge or modification. Discharge and modification pose no threat to free value-enhancing exchange, which would be promoted; only the other party's security is threatened. Current doctrine resolves the conflict by asking whether the excuse advanced for modification or discharge is within the scope of actually or reasonably foreseen risk.[14] That resolution, however, seems simply another vocabulary for choosing between security and market freedom: the complaining party is either free to renegotiate or unfreely bound by the prior bargain. The point here is that free contract logic offers no solution.

Of course, the formal contract model hid this internal contradiction by positing a magic moment of formation, when individual wills created a right whose enforcement was necessary for the protection of free will itself: state coercion dissolved when viewed as merely protecting individual rights. This is why Fuller and Perdue devastated the formal model by showing that enforcing the expectation right is no more than a series of economic policy choices by the state.[15] Moreover, those policy choices are inevitably choices between *conflicting* rights: enforcement is always drawn somewhere between the absolute protection of security and the total market freedom allowed by complete immunity.

Gilmore pointed out that when some unanticipated loss occurs (often the case when legal authority is invoked, since parties generally expect things to work well), the supposed "expectation" of buyer and seller are at odds.[16] If a seller breaches, courts have to choose between the buyer's right to complete security and the seller's expectation of a more limited liability.[17] For example, *Hadley* v. *Baxendale*[18] used the device of foreseeability to mediate the complete security demanded by Hadley, and Baxendale's "right" to assume he had undertaken a less extensive risk. In each choice, for all the good arguments of the

Hadleys of the world—about protecting the full security of transactions, and imposing the burden of loss upon the breaching party—there is a counterargument from the Baxendales about the stifling effects of such liability upon vigorous commercial activity. Those arguments can be reproduced at every level of choice;[19] in the process, the reified right of classical doctrine disappears.

The policy of enforcing the expectancy right involves choices not significantly different from basic formation decisions. Despite the mystical moment of formation posited by the classical model, when the offeror's and the acceptor's free wills meet in full accord, those decisions are not decisions *about* freedom, but *between* the claim for freedom and the need for security. To say the offeror's offer is irrevocable because of the promisee's acceptance is merely to say that the promisee's security is favored over the offeror's freedom to make a better deal elsewhere (or to withdraw from an exchange that is no longer value-enhancing). Modern formation doctrine, which favors "reasonable expectation" over formalistic claims of indefiniteness and lack of mirror-image acceptance, would be viewed by a classical theorist as curtailing the offeror's complete control over the offer, and thereby arbitrarily invading his or her legally protected sphere of private autonomy. Yet formalist recognition of a binding contract at the moment of formation was also a choice between contradictory alternatives. The fixed, formal line drawn between contract and no contract obscured that choice; but as the boundary becomes mushy, the choice becomes more apparent.

Notably, early liberal theorists like Adam Smith and David Hume recognized the internal contradiction which now expresses itself in doctrinal form, although they also sought to conceal it. Exchange, they claimed, was based on natural impulse and (subjective) desire. Like eating, drinking, and sex, it takes place without state or moral compulsion: it requires only release, not enforcement, for it provides a direct and "immediate" utility for the parties. Promise keeping, they thought, does not rest on the same foundation of desire. Instead, it requires the reasoned and objective justification of "ultimate" (rather than "immediate") utility, and its performance depends upon both moral discipline and state enforcement. Unlike the natural impulse to barter and to trade, promise keeping, like property, is part of the "artificial" virtue of justice.

This mix allowed market theorists to argue for subjectivity and freedom as against overt state regulation in the name of an objective moral standard of fairness, yet still to argue for reasoned justice and objectivity as against the self-interested desire to break promises and (perhaps more important) seize the property of others. The result was a structure of thought which presupposed a world of voluntarism, subjective choice, and freely willed mutuality while *also* presupposing a world of objective external control, secured expectation, and a freedom constrained by the inequality of legally protected, accumulated advantage. The allusion to property is more than a metaphor, for in securing promises contract logic begets property logic, which defeats the premises of freedom thought to underlie contract logic. To recognize expectancy rights ostensibly generated by willing parties and to enforce them even against the will of one of those parties amounts to a generation of property rights over time. Their protection invokes the rhetoric of property doctrine—primarily through the language of secured expectation. The result is objectively protected advantage, with its inherent tendency toward accumulation and hierarchy. Every exercise of will, so essential to the freedom of contract model, must take place under the constraints of both property and expectancy rights generated by the same system.

The problem of will reveals the ultimate contradiction of the model. At one level, there is simply the problem of ascertaining states of mind. To protect the subjective by insisting on the objective seems inconsistent. Yet, classical contract doctrine sought to protect autonomy by a system of formal, predictable rules, which excluded extensive inquiry into the particulars of concrete circumstance, especially a moralistic inquiry into actual states of mind. Thus there was a quick classical shift from a factual determination (by juries) of actual subjective intent to a legal determination of intent as formally expressed and reasonably interpreted. When the two differed (an area impossible to define with any precision), liability for breach of contract was, strictly speaking, liability for the tort-like negligent use of language. This meant protection for the security of those who relied on formal written contract terms, and seemed, by its formal predictability, to be protecting rights, and therefore free will itself. Yet that formal protection was necessarily delivered at the expense of any claim that might be made in the name of its *actual* protection. The current parol evidence rule debate indicates that the subjective and objective dilemma remains unresolved.

But the free will contradiction goes deeper than the problem of formal rules; ultimately, it impeaches the coherence of the free value-enhancing exchange mechanism. In theory, exchanges are a function of autonomous will, not legal force: while state control is required to secure *future* performance, a present exchange of goods or promises is a pure expression of voluntarism. In turn, this expression of voluntarism required intelligible legal rules to separate free bargains from those formed under fraud, duress, or undue influence.[28] Dawson's brilliant essay convincingly demonstrated, however, that a natural separation simply does not exist. Instead, the legal boundary identifying freedom is a function of legal decisionmaking, and has varied over the course of history.[29]

In particular, it has arbitrarily excluded economic pressure from the legal definition of duress. That exclusion concealed the fact that coercion, including legal coercion, lies at the heart of *every* bargain. Coercion is inherent in each party's legally protected threat to withhold what is owned. The right to withhold creates the right to force submission to one's own terms. Since ownership is a function of legal entitlement, every bargain (and, taken collectively, the "natural" market price) is a function of the legal order—including legal decisions about whether and to what extent bargained-for advantages should be protected as rights. It is therefore wrong to dissociate private bargaining from legal decisionmaking: the results of the former are a function of the latter. This conclusion dissolves the theoretical distinctions between public and private spheres, and between free and regulated markets. Since the inner sphere of free bargaining and the outer framework of fixed rules collapse into each other, the problem of state coercion in the ideal of free contract is not simply a messy inconvenience caused by temporal change; it is a problem deep in the core of the ideology itself. The assumption that the state was not implicated in the outcomes of free market bargaining was *never* true—a quite different point from saying, as Atiyah does, that it is *no longer* true.

Still, the image of the autonomous bargainer was a powerful one, profoundly believed in by those who added to its credibility by constructing around it the elaborate structure of contract law. There may be reasons in concrete experience that made this particular myth more credible in the early nineteenth century than it is today.[31] Nevertheless, the problem of contradiction undercuts the conclusion that legal doctrine mirrored reality and progressively served its needs. The legal myth was too obviously only an ideological myth. If the free contract ideal seemed to accurately reflect life under capitalism, that is surely in large part attributable to the power of the ideology, rather than to the accuracy of the reflected image.

DISCONTINUITY IN CONTRACT DOCTRINE

The classical model of contract formation could never have matched social and psychological reality. Simply as a matter of language, parties cannot fully communicate with each other; nor can their words completely capture the future. The language they use is as much social as individual, its meaning colored by context and, at the time of enforcement, by judicial hindsight and interpretation. Thus, all contracts are in part implied contracts; all express conditions really constructive covenants. Future exchange based entirely upon individual promise is nonexistent—and always has been.[35] The individual is never wholly autonomous from social life.

Moreover, the picture Atiyah draws of commercial life in nineteenth-century England does not depict the discrete, autonomous units of classical doctrine. Rather, he notes that it was the *interdepen-*

dence of commercial life which prompted the use of executory contracts as a planning device. His description of commercial decision-making as dictated by the momentum of capital investment conveys an almost Marxist image of control, not an image of freedom.[37]

Atiyah points out that early nineteenth-century businesses were either sole proprietorships or partnerships. Individualism ended with the emergence of giant corporations and other hierarchically organized institutions. The observation is useful; but it is also true that these "individuals" were hardly self-reliant units. Instead, their size and instability made their survival utterly dependent on the fluctuating economy.

Within this context of interdependence, Atiyah suggests that actual business practice never fit the model of cutthroat competition. Rather, nineteenth-century practice was more akin to modern commercial behavior than to a model of fixed rights and formality. Indeed, it would be surprising if the need for flexibility and good-faith dealing were new to commercial life.

Atiyah also argues that successful commercial development required the classical model rules. Like contract doctrine itself, however, this instrumental argument raises contradictory arguments about what commercial classes really need. For example, they supposedly want secured expectations for the sake of future planning, but they also require that liability be limited by the *Hadley* rule and by statutory provision for the limited liability of corporations.

Moreover, the actual results of the particular rules associated with commercial class interest are difficult to gauge. Part of the problem lies with the discontinuity, not only between legal doctrine and social practice, but also between treatise law and the law as applied. For example, the rule of *caveat emptor* seemed to favor commercial classes; nevertheless, it was never applied with any rigor in England, and as between merchants, could always be countered by a security-based argument for protecting reasonable expectations of decent quality. At any rate, commercial development did not come grinding to a halt because the judiciary ignored *caveat emptor*.

Atiyah downgrades the substantive inequality of contracts between employers and workers during the nineteenth century, insisting that the real freedom of workers has been underestimated. But even Adam Smith admitted that contracts between owners and workers were far from free. And a striking irony emerges from Atiyah's own description of the process of disciplining the nineteenth-century working class. The virtues of independence and free choice were preached to workers as part of this disciplining process, even while industrial life disrupted their lives and imposed oppressive workplace conditions. Ironically, Atiyah suggests that had workers been *really* free, they would have chosen to retain their pre-industrial patterns of life, not to submit to the brutal coercion of nineteenth-century factory discipline. There is nothing original in observing the irony of coercion imposed in the name of freedom. Atiyah *almost* recognizes that irony, yet he never explores contract law's role in making actual domination appear free, natural, and rational. Atiyah's failure to explore this irony derives from his nostalgia for the myth of past economic freedoms.

NOTES

13. 221 U.S. 1, 63 (1911) (opinion of the Court).

14. See, e.g., RESTATEMENT (FIRST) OF CONTRACTS §§ 454-69 (1932) (unchanged in tentative drafts of the Second Restatement).

15. L. L. Fuller and William R. Perdue, "The Reliance Interest in Contract Damages: 1," *Yale Law Journal* 46 (1936): 52.

16. F. Kessler and G. Gilmore, *Contracts: Cases and Materials*, 2d ed. (Boston: Little, Brown, 1970), pp. 1041–43.

17. Complete security could mean full consequential damages even if they are hopelessly speculative, or full performance even if ridiculously wasteful. Conversely, where the buyer breaches, the court may have to choose between the seller's complete security—a captive buyer at a captive price—and the buyer's reasonable "expectation" that the seller will mitigate in the case of buyer breach.

18. 9 Ex. 341, 156 Eng. Rep. 145 (1854).

19. I.e., no liability versus the standard market price/contract price differential, market price/contract price versus consequential, foreseeable consequential versus full consequential. The market price/contract price differential is generally preferred, but apparently as a convenient and seemingly objective compromise. While it helps to objectify the market price as a substitute for the older fair price, it usually bears little relation to actual loss caused by seller breach, except in the commodities and stock markets.

The arguments over strict versus limited liability for expectation, doctrinally stated in terms like foreseeability, mitigation, and unreasonable waste, seem generally to reproduce the arguments in tort for strict liability versus negligence, contributory negligence versus no contributory negligence, etc.

28. These rules were necessary to maintain that judicially enforced contracts had been freely made. The classical claim was that doctrines like fraud and duress merely identified a pre-existing line between freedom and coercion.

29. John P. Dawson, "Economic Duress—An Essay in Perspective," *Michigan Law Review* 45 (1947): 253.

30. See, e.g., Peter Gabel, "Intention and Structure in Contractual Conditions: Outline of a Method for Critical Legal Theory," *Minnesota Law Review* 61 (1977): 601, 607–14; Morton J. Horwitz, "The Legacy of 1776 in Legal and Economic Thought," *Journal of Law and Economics* 19 (1976): 621, 628–29.

35. I. MacNeil, *The New Social Contract* (New Haven: Yale University Press, 1980), p. 8.

37. Atiyah describes the interdependence of economic entities: "Now in the highly volatile commercial and industrial activity I have described . . . , it does not seem surprising that businessmen came to demand a greater degree of legal protection for careful planning. Vast sums of money depended on the skill with which men could now plan; the mill owner needed to buy his supplies of cotton in advance, so that it would be available in a continuous flow; he needed to be assured of his labor supply in advance

for the same reasons. Or again, the landowner thinking of investing in the mining of coal on his lands, might need the safety of forward contracts relating to the carriage of coal, when it was dug. Merchants exporting and importing the hugely increased flow of commodities had to plan future shipments with some regularity with the aid of the new brokers who were springing up everywhere." (p. 421). Apparently the commercial need for continuous relations rather than just one-shot transactions has not been only a twentieth-century phenomenon. If so, the tendency to exclude the relational element from contract doctrine would not be attributable to reflection of reality, but perhaps to the internal pressure of the ideology itself.

10

Following The Rules Laid Down: A Critique of Interpretivism and Neutral Principles

Mark V. Tushnet

Interpretivism and neutral principles, as the two leading dogmas of modern constitutional theory, are designed to remedy a central problem of liberal theory by constraining the judiciary sufficiently to prevent judicial tyranny. But it turns out that the two theories are plausible only on the basis of assumptions that themselves challenge important aspects of the liberal world view. Interpretivism attempts to implement the rule of law by assuming that the meanings of words and rules are stable over extended periods; neutral principles does the same by assuming that we all know, because we all participate in the same culture, what the words and rules used by judges mean. In this way, interpretivism and neutral principles attempt to complete the world view of liberalism by explaining how individuals may form a society.

I argue below, however, that the only coherent basis for the requisite continuities of history and meaning is found in the communitarian assumptions of conservative social thought—that, in fact, only these communitarian assumptions can provide the foundations upon which both interpretivism and neutral principles ultimately depend. Conservative social thought places society prior to individuals by developing the implications of the idea that we can understand what we think and do only with reference to the social matrix

Excerpted from its original publication in *Harvard Law Review* 96, 1983, by permission of the author and the Harvard Law Review Association.

within which we find ourselves. If I am correct, the liberal account of the social world is inevitably incomplete, for it proves unable to provide a constitutional theory of the sort that it demands without depending on communitarian assumptions that contradict its fundamental individualism. . . .

INTERPRETIVISM AND HISTORICAL KNOWLEDGE

It is commonplace to observe that interpretivism has its roots in *Marbury* v. *Madison*, the Supreme Court's first assertion of the power of judicial review. In that case the Court thought it essential to decide whether a section of the statute organizing the federal court system was consistent with the distribution of judicial authority dictated by the Constitution. Chief Justice Marshall justified the exercise of the power of judicial review by a number of arguments, prominent among which was his appeal to the idea of a written constitution. According to the Chief Justice, the Constitution was law, albeit supreme law, and thus was to be treated just as other legal documents were. Therefore, when the Court was asked to determine the meaning of the Constitution, it was to do what it did when faced with other legal instruments. This enterprise is characteristically "interpretivist": judges must look both to the words of the document and, because such words as "equal protection" and "due process of law" are too opaque, to the intent of those who wrote the document.

Like other theories of constitutional argumentation, interpretivism is subject to both external and internal critiques. The external critique of interpretivism argues that the theory, though it may constrain judges effectively, in fact fails to constrain the legislature (or the executive) in a manner both flexible enough to fit changed circumstances and stringent enough to avoid realistic threats of oppression. The internal critique attempts to determine the maximum coherent content of the theory in order to demonstrate that the story is conceptually incapable of providing the constraints on judicial tyranny that its advocates claim it offers.

The External Critique

For about thirty years, roughly from 1940 to 1970, interpretivism had a bad reputation, largely because, allied as it was to politically conservative positions, it seemed too vulnerable to external critique. That critique is captured by counterposing "the dead hand of the past"—interpretivism—to the need for "a living Constitution." That is, a strict adherence to interpretivism seems to require that we find legislation valid unless it violates values that are both old-fashioned and seriously outmoded. The interpretivist deflects this criticism by invoking the specter of judicial tyranny.[17] Of course, the response goes, interpretivism does mean that we will be subject to the risk that the legislature will develop novel forms of tyranny. Empirically, however, novelty in tyranny is relatively rare, and because the framers of the Constitution were rather smart, they managed to preclude most of the really troublesome forms of tyranny through the Constitution they wrote. Some risk of novel forms of tyranny remains, but that risk is significantly smaller than the risk of judicial tyranny that would arise were we to allow judges to cut free from interpreting the text. In this sense, according to the interpretivist, we are indeed better off being bound by the dead hand of the past than being subjected to the whims of willful judges trying to make the Constitution live.

This response is, I think, fairly powerful. But it rests in part on an empirical claim about novelty, a claim that is open to obvious external attacks. First, the possibilities of innovative legislative tyranny are in fact great because the social and material world in which we live has changed drastically since 1789. The drafters of the Fourth Amendment obviously could not have contemplated wiretapping when they thought about searches.[18] Yet if interpretivism means that we cannot respond to that kind of innovation, it fails to guard against legislative tyranny.

Moreover, if we look to the historical record, we discover that, at least according to the interpretivist account, the framers had a fairly limited conception of legislative tyranny. For example, Leonard Levy, the most careful recent student of the history of the First Amendment, concludes that the framers did not intend it to prohibit sedition laws, that they meant it to prohibit only prior restraints on publication and not subsequent punishment, and that they did not intend the amendment to insulate speech from regulation simply because the speech was political.[20] Similarly, the Bill of Rights provided protection, such as it was, against encroachment only by the national government, not by the states. Because a genuine interpretivism would thus protect only against limited varieties of legislative tyranny, it fails to achieve its objective. When the real risks of legislative tyranny are recognized, they appear more serious than the prospects of judicial tyranny.

Now the external critique begins to bite hard: interpretivism seems to constrain judges only at the cost of leaving legislatures too little constrained. One might expect critics to abandon interpretivism as an inadequate bulwark, but the power of the ideas underlying interpretivism moves them instead to attempt to rescue it with its own tools. Revisionist critics such as Ely and Douglas Laycock accuse interpretivists of being halfhearted in their commitment to their theory. These critics contend that, if we examine the Constitution closely, we will discover clauses concerning which the framers intended the courts to have a free, noninterpretivist hand. Ely relies on the portion of the Fourteenth Amendment that bars the states from making "any law whch shall abridge the privileges or immunities of citizens of the United States."[23] Laycock relies on the Ninth Amendment: "The enumeration in the Constitution, of certain rights, shall not be construed to deny or disparage others retained by the people."[24]

But, on two counts, the interpretivists condemn this proposed route to salvation. First, because the revisionists are trying to play the game of theory on the interpretivists' terms, they are vulnerable to attack on historical grounds. When the revisionists invoke the privileges and immunities clause or the Ninth Amendment, they are met by a barrage of evidence from interpretivists that these supposedly broad clauses actually had narrow and well-defined meanings. The Ninth Amendment, for example, is said to mean merely that the Constitution itself does not authorize judicial denial of other rights and to have no implications for legislative authority to deny those rights.

The second response is more interesting. The interpretivist concedes the possibility that some provisions of the Constitution license noninterpretivist theories. But, he contends, we can at least rule out some results under those theories on interpretivist grounds. Suppose that the framers, while they were drafting one of the noninterpretivist provisions, were aware of a specific practice. Suppose further that, as far as the record shows, they agreed overwhelmingly that the provision would not make the practice unconstitutional. Surely, the interpretivist claims, given these assumptions we could not rely on the noninterpretivist provision to invalidate the practice even if the provision might otherwise authorize invalidation. This claim seems hard to dispute. Unhappily for the revisionist, though, this second interpretivist response states in general terms the relevant history of the Fourteenth Amendment with respect to school segregation. As Michael Perry puts it, "segregated public schooling was present to the minds of the Framers; they did not intend that the [equal protection] clause prohibit it; and no historical evidence suggests that they meant to leave open the question whether the clause should be deemed to prohibit the practice."[27] If noninterpretivist constitutional interpretation must rest on an interpretive warrant, then *Brown* v. *Board of Education* seems unjustifiable.

Interpretivism is alluring enough that, even at this point, revisionists need not throw up their hands, and they usually do not. Instead they can try to rely on Ronald Dworkin's distinction between generic "concepts," such as equality, and specific "conceptions," such as ideas of what equality meant in particular circumstances.[28] Dworkin argues that the Fourteenth Amendment enacts the concept of equality, not specific conceptions. The framers had a conception of equality that regarded segregated schools to be equal, but they enacted something more general, something that they knew would develop in ways they knew not. Constitutional provisions that embody concepts rather than conceptions license (and demand) noninterpretivist approaches.

Here again the interpretivist has two reasons not to embrace the revisionists' position. First, like Ely and Laycock, Dworkin can be called upon to live up to the interpretivists' historiographic standards if he wants to play their game. He therefore can be required to produce evidence of an interpretivist sort that the framers knew that they were enacting provisions that embodied a moral content richer than their own moral conceptions. And, simply put, there is no evidence at all that they did. The distinction relies on modern theories of law that, I am certain, were quite foreign, indeed probably incomprehensible, to the framers of the Bill of Rights and the Fourteenth Amendment. Their theories of law were at the same time both more positivistic and more allied to theological versions of natural law theories than is the secularized vision of moral philosophy from which Dworkin draws his distinction.

The second objection rests on a frontal attack on the proposed distinction between concepts and conceptions, a distinction that reflects a general problem in constitutional theory. Frequently an analysis turns completely on the level of generality at which some feature of the issue under analysis is described. But the choice of that level must be made on some basis external to the analysis. For example, why describe the concept of equality on a level of generality so high that it obliterates the specific intention to permit segregation? After all, the concept is—at least in part—built up from particular experiences of what is seen as equal treatment; it is to that extent derived from conceptions of equality. . . .

The external critiques developed thus far do not demolish interpretivism. But the responses to those critiques have the effect of weakening the theory seriously. The most coherent version of interpretivism protects against only the few specific forms of legislative tyranny that the framers had in mind. Interpretivism might have been quite protective had the framers been more visionary. But that is not how things were. Still, interpretivists can argue with some force that interpretivism is better than the alternatives. Interpretivism gives us a Constitution with many opportunities for legislative tyranny, some, though few, limits on legislatures, stringent limits on judges, and few opportunities for judicial tyranny. The alternatives provide many opportunities for judicial tyranny, few limits on judges, and an unknown mixture of opportunities for and limits on legislative tyranny. As is true of all external critiques, those of interpretivism do not themselves make it impossible to defend the theory; everything depends on the balance we think appropriate.

The Internal Critique

The internal critique cuts deeper; it undermines in several steps the plausibility of interpretivism as a constitutional theory. The first step is an argument that interpretivism must rest on an account of historical knowledge more subtle than the naive presumption that past attitudes and intentions are directly accessible to present understanding. The second step identifies the most plausible such account, the view—sometimes called hermeneutics—that historical understanding requires an imaginative transposition of former world views into the categories of our own. The third step is an argument that such an imaginative transposition implies an ambiguity that is inconsistent with the project of liberal constitutional theory (and interpretivism). The project of imaginative transposition can be carried through in a number of different ways, with a number of different results, none of which is more correct than the others. The existence of such an indeterminacy means that interpretivism, unless it falls back on nonliberal assumptions, cannot constrain judges sufficiently to carry out the liberal project of avoiding judicial tyranny.

1. *Interpretivist History*—We can approach the problems of historical knowledge by noting the standard criticism of "law office" history. Interpretivism calls for an historical inquiry into the intent of the framers. That inquiry is conducted by lawyers imbued with the adversary ethic. The standard criticism is that lawyers are bad historians because they overemphasize fragmentary evidence and minimize significant bodies of conflicting evidence in the service of their partisan goals.

Though some lawyers surely deploy the kind of history thus criticized, interpretivism need not rest on that sort of bad history. But the difficulty goes deeper. Interpretivist history requires both definite answers (because it is part of a legal system in which judgment is awarded to one side or the other) and clear answers (because it seeks to constrain judges and thereby to avoid judicial tyranny). The universal experience of historians, however, belies the interpretivists' expectations. Where the interpretivist seeks clarity and definiteness, the historian finds ambiguity. I have already mentioned the interpretivist view of the history of the First Amendment. But if we were able to sit down for a talk with Thomas Jefferson about civil liberties, a good historian will tell us, we would hear an apparently confused blend of assertions: libertarian theory, opposition to the enactment of sedition laws, the use of sedition laws once in office, and so on. Jefferson's "intent" on the issue of free speech is nothing more than this complex set of responses.

Because evidentiary materials are frequently incomplete and fail to yield answers of sufficient clarity, interpretivists must rely on supplementary evidentiary rules. Raoul Berger, for example, proposes a burden of proof: one who claims that the framers of the Fourteenth Amendment intended to alter substantially the relations that existed in 1871 between state and national government must provide more persuasive evidence than must one who claims that the amendment's framers did not intend such alterations. Similarly, Berger invokes lawyers' rules about legislative debate: statements made on the floor of the Senate, for instance, are to be given more weight than statements made in private letters.

These supplementary evidentiary rules are simultaneously helpful and misleading. The rules may have two functions. First, they may be crystallized expressions of what more detailed inquiries have shown usually to have been true. Berger's federalism burden-of-proof rule, for example, is partly justified by the fact that, upon examining the range of uncontroversial situations in which national-state relations were altered, we discover much more evidence about the relevant intent in the situations in which those relations were altered substantially than in the situations in which they were altered less substantially. In fact, the federalism rule may turn out to be merely an instance of the generally useful historiographic principle that it is reasonable to require more evidence to show a radical discontinuity than to show a steady continuity in history.

Second, the rules may embody policy judgments that are independent of the rules' role in promoting accurate reconstructions of the past. The intent rule, for instance, may be justified on the ground that the interpretivist should look for a "special" kind of intent—the kind exhibited on relatively formal occasions and expressed in relatively formal terms, rather than the "private intent" of letters and the like. To restrict the focus of the inquiry to such a "special" kind of intent is to make a policy judgment that expressions of opinion on relatively formal occasions ought to be given special weight. The federalism rule can also serve as an example: it is partly justified by a policy preference for maintaining the distribution of authority between state and nation.

These justifications for supplementary rules, however, in the end distort the interpretivist inquiry. An historian interested in the history of the Fourteenth Amendment might conclude that, on balance and taking into account the supplementary rules to the extent that they are based on a concern for accuracy, Senator X's private letters provide a better guide to his intentions and to those of his colleagues than do his statements on the floor of the Senate. The historian might conclude that, all things considered, a stray expression about federalism really does reveal what the framers intended. And to the extent that the supplementary rules are based on policy grounds, the liberal project itself is defeated; justifying the rules on policy grounds directly confronts liberalism with the anomaly of relying on a particular political or social vision to support interpretation.

2. *Intentions and Liberal Thought*—The interpretivist project requires the discovery and use of unambiguous historical facts; the only
way that interpretivists can find such facts is to embrace what are
fundamentally flawed historiographic methods. Underlying the interpretivists' reliance on these methods is the view that individuals are
the primary units of human experience and history and that larger
social wholes are best understood as aggregates of such individuals.
From this view, it follows that an individual's beliefs, intentions, and
desires have their character independent of, or prior to, the larger
social and conceptual context in which they occur, a context that the
liberal vision sees as a product of all antecedent individual perspectives. The project of the liberal historian thus is to study the historical
record for evidence of what the intentions and beliefs of historical
actors actually were.

On this account, intentions must be real, determinate entities; the
interpretivist must be able to identify and understand specific intentions of the framers with respect to one part of the Constitution or
another.

In fact, the richest kinds of historical understanding do not rest on
the isolation of discrete and determinate beliefs or intentions of
historical actors. Here I can use as an example Leon Litwack's *Been in
the Storm So Long*,[44] one of the great works of American history.
Litwack examines emancipated slaves' response to freedom in the
immediate aftermath of the Civil War. He presents incredibly rich
detail, drawn from letters by former slaves, Federal Writers' Project
interviews with over two thousand ex-slaves, newspaper interviews,
and government records. We are forced to conclude that the response
to freedom was extremely complex. The ambiguity and contradiction
that Litwack discloses in individual responses to emancipation demonstrate the impossibility of singling out specific past intentions or
beliefs without denying the shifting, complex circumstances that led
each person to develop such ambiguous and contradictory understandings of his or her world. One cannot finish Litwack's book
without gaining some historical understanding. Yet that understanding is not gained because Litwack has somehow captured the thoughts
or feelings of particular former slaves. Rather, he has provided us
with a wealth of materials from which we can piece together a tenuous
and readily displaced sense of the slaves' perspectives and predica-
ments.

3. *The Hermeneutic Alternative*—These examples raise doubts about
easy acceptance of an interpretivism whose theory of historical knowledge presumes that past beliefs and intentions are determinate and
identifiable. Those doubts can be deepened by comparing this theory
of history to its main rival, the hermeneutic tradition. In that tradition, historical knowledge is seen as "the interpretive understanding
of [the] meaning" that actors give their actions.[47] The historian must

enter the minds of his or her subjects, see the world as they saw it, and understand it in their own terms. For my purposes, Litwack's book is a paradigmatic hermeneutic history. Justice Brandeis's eloquent opinion in *Whitney* v. *California*,[49] which recreates one version of the world view of the framers, is the best example in the case law of a hermeneutic effort to understand the past. Brandeis's reconstruction, though partial and largely unsupported by specific references to what any framer actually said, does in the end bring us into the framers' world:

> Those who won our independence believed that the final end of the State was to make men free to develop their faculties; and that in its government the deliberative forces should prevail over the arbitrary. They valued liberty both as an end and as a means. They believed liberty to be the secret of happiness and courage to be the secret of liberty. They believed that freedom to think as you will and to speak as you think are means indispensable to the discovery and spread of political truth; that without free speech and assembly discussion would be futile; that with them, discussion affords ordinarily adequate protection against the dissemination of noxious doctrine; that the greatest menace to freedom is an inert people; that public discussion is a political duty; and that this should be a fundamental principle of the American government. They recognized the risks to which all human institutions are subject. But they knew that order cannot be secured merely through fear of punishment for its infraction; that it is hazardous to discourage thought, hope, and imagination; that fear breeds repression; that repression breeds hate; that hate menaces stable government; that the path of safety lies in the opportunity to discuss freely supposed grievances and proposed remedies; and that the fitting remedy for evil counsels is good ones. Believing in the power of reason as applied through public discussion, they eschewed silence coerced by law—the argument of force in its worst form. Recognizing the occasional tyrannies of governing majorities, they amended the Constitution so that free speech and assembly should be guaranteed.

Here Brandeis recalls to us the framers' belief in a republic dominated by civic virtue. It matters not very much that their views on specific aspects of governmental design may have differed in detail from Brandeis's reconstruction; what matters is that the framers designed a government that comported with their sense of a world in which civic virtue reigned. The significance and the ramifications of this sense are what Brandeis strove to capture, and they are what interpretivism, too, must recognize to be central. The ways in which people understand the world give meaning to the words that they use, and only by recreating such global understandings can we interpret the document the framers wrote.

The dilemma of interpretivism is that, if is to rely on a real grasp of the framers' intentions—and only this premise gives interpretivism its intuitive appeal—its method must be hermeneutic, but if it adopts an hermeneutic approach, it is foreclosed from achieving the determinacy about the framers' meanings necessary to serve its underlying goals. The interpretivists' premise of determinate intentions is essential to their project of developing constraints on judges. But the hermeneutic approach to historical understanding requires that we abandon this premise. In imaginatively entering the world of the past, we not only reconstruct it, but—more important for present purposes—we also creatively construct it. For such creativity is the only way to bridge the gaps between that world and ours. The past, particularly the aspects that the interpretivists care about, is in its essence indeterminate; the interpretivist project cannot be carried to its conclusion. . . .

The hermeneutic tradition tells us that we cannot understand the acts of those in the past without entering into their mental world. Because we live in our own world, the only way to begin the hermeneutic enterprise is by thinking about what in our world initially seems like what people in the past talked and thought about. Usually we begin with a few areas in which we and they use the same rather abstract words to talk about apparently similar things. Thus, we and the framers share a concern for democracy, human rights, and limited government. But as we read what the framers said about democracy and limited government, we notice discontinuities: they described their polity as a democratic one, for example, when we would think it obviously nondemocratic. As we examine this evidence, we adjust our understanding and attempt to take account of the "peculiarities." With a great deal of imaginative effort, we can indeed at the end of the process understand their world, because we have become immersed in it. But the understanding we achieve is not the unique, correct image of the framers' world. On the contrary, our imaginative immersion is only one of a great many possible reconstructions of that segment of the past, a reconstruction shaped not only by the character of the past, but also by our own interests, concerns, and preconceptions. The imagination that we have used to adjust and readjust our understandings makes it impossible to claim that any one reconstruction is uniquely correct. The past shapes the materials on which we use our imaginations; our interests, concerns, and preconceptions shape our imaginations themselves. . . .

Nonetheless, the hermeneutic tradition does identify something that constitutional theory should take seriously. The point is not, as some fanatic adherents of hermeneutic method might have it, that, because the world of the past is not the world in which we have developed our ways of understanding how others act, we can never understand that past world. That view would go too far. We can gain an interpretive understanding of the past by working from commonalities in the use of large abstractions to reach the unfamiliar particulars of what those abstractions really meant in the past. The commonalities are what make the past *our* past; they are the links between two segments of a single community that extends over time. The commonalities are both immanent in our history and constructed by us as we reflect on what our history is. Interpretivism goes wrong in thinking that the commonalities are greater than they really are, but we would go equally wrong if we denied that they exist. The task is to think through the implications of our continued dedication to the large abstractions when the particulars of the world have changed so drastically. That project will lead us to face questions about the kind of community we have and want.

NEUTRAL PRINCIPLES AND THE RECOGNITION OF RULES

The hermeneutic tradition suggests that historical discontinuities are so substantial that interpretivism must make incoherent claims because it can achieve the necessary determinacy of past intentions only at the cost of an implausible claim about consistency of meaning across time. The theory of neutral principles fails for similar reasons. It requires that we develop an account of consistency of meaning—particularly of the meaning of rules or principles—within liberal society. Yet the atomistic premises of liberalism treat each of us as autonomous individuals whose choices and values are independent of those made and held by others. These premises make it exceedingly difficult to develop such an account of consistent meaning. The autonomous producer of choice and value is also an autonomous producer of meaning.

The rule of law, according to the liberal conception, is meant to protect us against the exercise of arbitrary power. The theory of neutral principles asserts that a requirement of consistency, the core of the ideal of the rule of law, places sufficient bounds on judges to reduce the risk of arbitrariness to an acceptable level. The question is whether the concepts of neutrality and consistency can be developed in ways that are adequate for the task.

Neutral Content

Robert Bork's version of neutral principles theory would require that decisions rest on principles that are neutral in content and in application.[65] Bork's formulation may be an attempt to generalize Wechsler's definition, which characterizes neutrality as judicial indifference to who the winner is. For Wechsler, such indifference was a matter of judicial willingness to apply the present case's rule in the next case as well, regardless of whether the beneficiary in the later case was less attractive than the earlier winner in ways not made relevant by the rule itself.[66] Neutral content for Bork might mean a similar indifference, but not within the case: the principle governing the case should be developed in a form that employs only general terms and that avoids any express preference for any named groups. This outcome, however, is impossible. We might coherently require that rules not use proper names, but there is no principled way to distinguish between the general terms that in effect pick out specific groups or individuals and those that are "truly" general. Any general term serves to identify some specific group; hence if the notion of content neutrality is to make any sense, it must depend on a prior understanding of which kinds of distinctions are legitimately "neutral" and which are not. The demand for neutrality in content thus cannot provide an independent criterion for acceptable decisions.

Standing alone, the theory that principles must be neutral in content cannot constrain judicial discretion. But it could be coupled with some other theory—such as interpretivism, Ely's reinforcement of representation, or a moral philosophy. When coordinated with some such substantive theory, the demand for neutral principles stipulates that a decision is justified only if the principles derived from the other theory are neutrally applied. Yet to require neutral application of the principles of the other theory is merely to apply those principles in given cases; the requirement of content neutrality adds nothing.

Neutral Method

If neutrality is to serve as a meaningful guide, it must be understood not as a standard for the content of principles, but rather as a constraint on the process by which principles are selected, justified, and applied. Thus, the remaining candidate explications of neutrality all focus on the judicial process and the need for "neutral *application*." This focus transfers our attention from the principles themselves to the judges who purport to use them.

One preliminary difficulty should be noted. All versions of the demand for neutral application of principles ultimately rest on the claim that, without neutrality, a decision "wholly lack[s] legitimacy." Legitimacy, though, has at least two possible meanings. One is common in the sociological literature on government. Legitimate actions are those that are accepted by the relevant public. Decisions that lack legitimacy in this empirical sense are undesirable, because a court's critical resource in effectuating its decisions is public acceptance and illegitimate decisions deplete the court's limited capital. It is implausible, however, that the neutral application of principles is an important source of public acceptance of judicial decisions. The general public is, I suspect, unlikely to care very much about a court's reasoning process, which is the focus of the neutral principles theory; the public concern is with results. . . .

The second meaning of legitimacy is more normative and conceptual. Wechsler claimed that neutral principles are an essential component of the practice of judging in our society. To the extent that it is not a mere throwback to the sociological concept of legitimacy, such an appeal to the essence of a social practice draws a vision of how ideal courts act, a vision stimulated by reflection on the proper place of the courts in our social fabric. In this second sense, legitimacy is a matter of concordance with the demands of this ideal. In the ensuing inquiry, it is this second sense of legitimacy that is of interest: the claim that neutrality is a prerequisite for legitimacy means that, in our society, institutions must use neutral principles if we are to regard them as courts. This demand, however, ultimately proves empty, for rather than constrain the proper role of courts, the concept of neutrality instead presupposes a shared understanding and acceptance of any constraints.

1. *Prospective Application*—What then are methodologically neutral principles? To Wechsler, such principles are identified primarily by a forward-looking aspect: a judge who invokes a principle in a specific instance commits himself or herself to invoking it in future cases that are relevantly identical.

There are two levels of problems with the idea that commitment to prospective neutral application constrains judicial choices. First, there are two features of our judicial institutions that dissipate any constraining force that the demand for prospective neutrality may impose. Second, there is a conceptual problem that robs the very idea of prospective neutrality of any normative force.

(a) *Institutional Problems*—The first institutional problem is that Supreme Court decisions are made by a collective body, which is constrained by a norm of compromise and cooperation. Suppose that in case 1 Justices M, N, and O have taken neutral principles theory to heart and believe that the correct result is justified by principle A. Justices P, Q, R, and S have done likewise but believe that the same result is justified by principle B. Justices T and V, who also accept principle A but believe it inapplicable to case 1, dissent. The four-person group gains control of the writing of the opinion, and the three others who agree with the result accede to the institutional pressure for majority decisions and join an opinion that invokes principle B. Now case 2 arises. Justices T and V are convinced that, because case 2 is relevantly different from case 1, principle A should be used. They join with Justices M, N, and O and produce a majority opinion invoking principle A. If principle B were used, the result would be different; thus, there are four dissenters.

A second institutional problem is that prospective neutrality involves unreasonable expectations concerning the capacities of judges. Every present case is connected to every conceivable future case, in the sense that a skilled lawyer can demonstrate how the earlier case's principles ought to affect (although perhaps not determine) the outcome in any later case. In these circumstances, neutral application means that each decision constrains a judge in every future decision;

the import of the prospective approach is that, the first time a judge decides a case, he or she is to some extent committed to particular decisions for the rest of his or her career.

There are two difficulties here. First, even if we confine our attention to cases in the same general area as the present one, this formulation of the neutrality requirement is obviously too stringent. We cannot and should not expect judges to have fully elaborated theories of race discrimination in their first cases, much less theories of gender, illegitimacy, and other modes of discrimination as well. Second, to the extent that perceptions of connections vary with skill, the theory has the curious effect of constraining only the better judges. The less-skilled judge will not think to test a principle developed in a race-discrimination case against gender-discrimination or abortion cases; a more-skilled judge will.

(b) *Conceptual Difficulty*—The third, largely conceptual difficulty with the theory of neutral principles was foreshadowed, by the example of a case whose result could be justified by either of two principles. Neutral application requires that we be able to identify *the* principle that justified the result in case 1 in order to be sure that it is neutrally applied in case 2. This requirement, however, cannot be fulfilled, because there are always a number of justificatory principles available to make sense of case 1 and a number of techniques to select the "true" basis of case 1. Of course, the opinion in case 1 will articulate a principle that purports to support the result. But the thrust of introductory law courses is to show that the principles offered in opinions are never good enough. And this indefiniteness bedevils—and liberates—not only the commentators and the lawyers and judges subsequently dealing with the decision; it equally affects the author of the opinion. . . .

2. *Retrospective Application*—Although Wechsler framed the neutral principle theory in prospective terms, it might be saved by recasting it in retrospective terms. The theory would then impose as a necessary condition for justification the requirement that a decision be consistent with the relevant precedents. This tack links the theory to general approaches to precedent-based judicial decisionmaking in nonconstitutional areas. It also captures the natural way in which we raise questions about neutrality. The prospective theory requires that we pose hypothetical future cases, apply the principle, and ask whether the judges really meant to resolve the hypothetical cases as the principle seems to require. Because the hypothetical cases have not arisen, we cannot know the answer; we can do little more than raise our eyebrows, as Wechsler surely did, and emphasize the "really" as we ask the question in a skeptical tone.

In contrast, the retrospective theory encourages concrete criticism. We need only compare Case 2, which is now decided, with case 1 to see if a principle from case 1 has been neutrally applied in case 2. But if the retrospective demand is merely that the opinion in case 2 deploy some reading of the earlier case from which the holding in case 2 follows, the openness of the precedents means that the demand can always be satisfied. And if the demand is rather that the holding be derived from the principles actually articulated in the relevant precedents, differences between case 2 and the precedents will inevitably demand a degree of reinterpretation of the old principles. New cases always present issues different from those settled by prior cases. Thus, to decide a new case, a judge must take some liberties with the old principles, if they are to be applied at all. There is, however, no principled way to determine how many liberties can be taken; hence this second reading of the retrospective approach likewise provides no meaningful constraints.

The central problem here is that, given the difficulty of isolating a single principle for which a given precedent stands, we lack any criteria for distinguishing between cases that depart from and those that conform to the principles of their precedents. In fact, any case can compellingly be placed in either category. Although such a universal claim cannot be validated by example, examples can at least make the claim plausible. Therefore, the following paragraphs present several instances of cases that simultaneously depart from and conform to their precedents.

The first is *Griswold* v. *Connecticut,* in which the Supreme Court held that a state could not constitutionally prohibit the dissemination of contraceptive information or devices to married people.[100] *Griswold* relied in part on *Pierce* v. *Society of Sisters,*[101] which held unconstitutional a requirement that children attend public rather than private schools, and *Meyer* v. *Nebraska,*[102] which held that a state could not prohibit the teaching of foreign languages to young children. In *Griswold,* the Court said that these cases relied on a constitutionally protected interest, conveniently labeled "privacy," that was identical to the interest implicated in the contraceptive case.

On one view, *Griswold* tortures these precedents. Both were old-fashioned due process cases, which emphasized interference "with the calling of modern language teachers . . . and with the power of parents to control the education of their own." On this view, the most one can fairly find in *Meyer* and *Pierce* is a principle about freedom of inquiry that is rather narrower than a principle of privacy. Yet of course one can say with equal force that *Griswold* identifies for us the true privacy principle of *Meyer* and *Pierce,* in the same way that the abortion funding cases identify the true principle of *Roe* v. *Wade.* Just as hermeneutic interpretivism emphasizes the creativity that is involved when judges impute to the framers a set of intentions, so the retrospective approach to neutral principles must recognize the extensive creativity exercised by a judge when he or she imputes to a precedent "the" principle that justifies both the precedent and the judge's present holding.

A second example is *Brandenburg v. Ohio*.[104] The state of Ohio had prosecuted a leader of the Ku Klux Klan for violating its criminal syndicalism statute, which prohibited advocating the propriety of violence as a means of political reform. The Court held that the conviction violated the First Amendment which, according to the decision, permits punishment of advocacy of illegal conduct only when "such advocacy is directed to inciting or producing imminent lawless action and is likely to incite or produce such action." Remarkably, the Court derived this test from *Dennis v. United States,* in which the Court had upheld convictions of leaders of the Communist Party for violating a federal sedition law.[10] This reading was, to say the least, an innovative interpretation of *Dennis,* which explicitly stated a different test—"the gravity of the 'evil', discounted by its improbability"— that left the decision largely to the jury. Putting aside the obvious effects of cold war hysteria on the 1951 decision in *Dennis,* a dispassionate observer would find it hard to reconcile the results in *Dennis* and *Brandenburg.* But again the requirement of retrospective neutrality may be satisfied if we interpret *Brandenburg's* use of *Dennis* as the creative reworking of precedents within fair bounds. . . .

Once again the examples illustrate a general point. In a legal system with a relatively extensive body of precedent and with well-developed techniques of legal reasoning, it will always be possible to show how today's decision is consistent with the relevant past decisions. Conversely, however, it will also always be possible to show how today's decision is inconsistent with the precedents. This symmetry, of course, drains "consistency" of any normative content. Just as we were forced to abandon content neutrality and prospective neutrality of application, we are now also forced to abandon retrospective neutrality of application as a source of meaningful constraints in a mature legal system like ours.

The difficulties with this variety of neutral principles theory are on a par with the problems in understanding interpretivism that were noted earlier. Understanding the intentions of the framers required a special kind of creative recreation of the past; the creativity involved in such a re-creation dashed any hopes that interpretivism could effectively constrain judicial decisions, because many alternative re-creations of the framers' intentions on any given issue are always possible. In the same way, the result of the inquiry into retrospective neutral principles theory indicates that, though it is possible to discuss a given decision's consistency with previous precedents, requiring consistency of this kind similarly fails to constrain judges sufficiently and thereby fails to advance the underlying liberal project.

3. *The Craft Interpretation*—This critique of the retrospective-appli-

cation interpretation points the way to a more refined version—what I will term the craft interpretation—of the calls of the neutral principles theorists for retrospective consistency. The failings of this final alternative bring out the underlying reasons that the demand for consistency cannot do the job expected of it.

The preceding discussion has reminded us that each decision reworks its precedents. A decision picks up some threads that received little emphasis before, and places great stress on them. It deprecates what seemed important before by emphasizing the factual setting of the precedents. The techniques are well known; indeed, learning them is at the core of a good legal education. But they are techniques. This recognition suggests that we attempt to define consistency as a matter of craft. When push comes to shove, in fact, adherents of neutral principles simply offer us lyrical descriptions of the sense of professionalism in lieu of sharper characterizations of the constraints on judges. . . .

If the craft interpretation cannot specify limits to craftiness, another alternative is to identify some decisions that are within and some that are outside the limits in order to provide the basis for an inductive and intuitive generalization. As the following discussion indicates, however, it turns out that the limits of craft are so broad that in any interesting case any reasonably skilled lawyer can reach whatever result he or she wants. The craft interpretation thus fails to constrain the results that a reasonably skilled judge can reach, and leaves the judge free to enforce his or her personal values, as long as the opinions enforcing those values are well written. Such an outcome is inconsistent with the requirements of liberalism in that, once again, the demand for neutral principles fails in any appreciable way to limit the possibility of judicial tyranny.

The debate over the propriety of the result in *Roe* v. *Wade*[120] illustrates this problem. It seems to be generally agreed that, as a matter of simple craft, Justice Blackmun's opinion for the Court was dreadful. The central issue before the Court was whether a pregnant woman had a constitutionally protected interest in terminating her pregnancy. When his opinion reached that issue, Justice Blackmun simply listed a number of cases in which "a right of personal privacy, or a guarantee of certain areas or zones of privacy," had been recognized. Then he said, "This right of privacy, whether it be founded in the Fourteenth Amendment's concept of personal liberty . . . or . . . in the Ninth Amendment's reservation of rights to the people, is broad enough to encompass a woman's decision whether or not to terminate her pregnancy." And that was it. I will provisionally concede that this "argument" does not satisfy the requirements of the craft.

But the conclusion that we are to draw faces two challenges: it is either uninteresting or irrelevant to constitutional theory. Insofar as

Roe gives us evidence, we can conclude that Justice Blackmun is a terrible judge. The point of constitutional theory, though, would seem to be to keep judges in line. If the result in *Roe* can be defended by judges more skilled than Justice Blackmun, the requirements of the craft would mean only that good judges can do things that bad judges cannot without subjecting themselves to professional criticism. . . .

There is in fact a cottage industry of constitutional law scholars who concoct revised opinions for controversial decisions. Thus, the craft interpretation of neutrality in application is ultimately uninteresting for reasons that we have already seen. At most it provides a standard to measure the competence of judges, a standard that by itself is insufficient to constrain adequately the risk of tyranny.

The other difficulty with the craft interpretation runs deeper. Craft limitations make sense only if we can agree what the craft is. But consider the craft of "writing novels." Its practice includes Trollope writing *The Eustace Diamonds,* Joyce writing *Finnegan's Wake,* and Mailer writing *The Executioner's Song.* We might think of Justice Blackmun's opinion in *Roe* as an innovation akin to Joyce's or Mailer's. It is the totally unreasoned judicial opinion. To say that it does not look like Justice Powell's decision in some other case is like saying that a Cubist "portrait" does not look like its subject as a member of the Academy would paint it. The observation is true, but irrelevant both to the enterprise in which the artist or judge was engaged and to our ultimate assessment of his product.

Rules and Institutions

We can now survey our progress in the attempt to define "neutral principles." Each proposed definition left us with judges who could enforce their personal values unconstrained by the suggested version of the neutrality requirement. Some of the more sophisticated candidates, such as the craft interpretation, seemed plausible because they appealed to an intuitive sense that the institution of judging involves people who are guided by and committed to general rules applied consistently. But the very notions of generality and consistency can be specified only by reference to an established institutional setting. We can know what we mean by "acting consistently" only if we understand the institution of judging in our society. Thus, neutral principles theory proves unable to satisfy its demand for rule-guided judicial decisionmaking in a way that can constrain or define the judicial institution; in the final analysis, it is the institution—or our conception of it—that constrains the concept of rule-guidedness.

Consider the following multiple choice question: Which pair of numbers comes next in the series 1, 3, 5, 7? (a) 9, 11; (b) 11, 13; (c) 25, 18. It is easy to show that any of the answers is correct. The first is correct if the rule generating the series is "list the odd numbers"; the second is correct if the rule is "list the odd prime numbers"; and the third is correct if a more complex rule generates the series.[131] Thus, if asked to follow the underlying rule—the "principle" of the series—we can justify a tremendous range of divergent answers by constructing the rule so that it generates the answer that we want. As the legal realists showed, this result obtains for legal as well as mathematical rules. The situation in law might be thought to differ, because judges try to articulate the rules they use. But even when an earlier case identifies the rule that it invokes, only a vision of the contours of the judicial role constrains judges' understanding of what counts as applying the rule. Without such a vision, there will always be a diversity of subsequent uses of the rule that could fairly be called consistent applications of it.

There is, however, something askew in this anarchic conclusion. After all, we know that no test maker would accept (c) as an answer to the mathematical problem; and indeed we can be fairly confident that test makers would not include both (a) and (b) as possible answers, because the underlying rules that generate them are so obvious that they make the question fatally ambiguous. Another example may sharpen the point. The examination for those seeking driver's licenses in the District of Columbia includes this question: What is responsible for most automobile accidents, (a) the car; (b) the driver; or (c) road conditions? Anyone who does not know immediately that the answer is (b) does not understand what the testing enterprise is all about.

In these examples, we know something about the rule to follow only because we are familiar with the social practices of intelligence testing and drivers' education. That is, the answer does not follow from a rule that can be uniquely identified without specifying something about the substantive practices. Similarly, although we can, as I have argued elsewhere, use standard techniques of legal argument to draw from the decided cases the conclusion that the Constitution requires socialism,[134] we know that no judge will in the near future draw that conclusion. But the failure to reach that result is not ensured because the practice of "following rules" or neutral application of the principles inherent in the decided cases precludes a judge from doing so. Rather, it is ensured because judges in contemporary America are selected in a way that keeps them from thinking that such arguments make sense. This branch of the argument thus makes a sociological point about neutral principles. Neither the principles nor any reconstructed version of a theory that takes following rules as its focus can be neutral in the sense that liberalism requires, because taken by itself, an injunction to follow the rules tells us nothing of substance. If such a theory constrains judges, it does so only because judges, before they turn to the task of finding neutral principles for the case at hand, have implicitly accepted some image of what their role in shaping and applying rules in controverted cases ought to be.

There is something both odd and important here. The theory of neutral principles is initially attractive because it affirms the openness of the courts to all reasonable arguments drawn from decided cases. But if the courts are indeed open to such arguments, the theory allows judges to do whatever they want. If it is only in consequence of the pressures exerted by a highly developed, deeply entrenched, homeostatic social structure that judges seem to eschew conclusions grossly at odds with the values of liberal capitalism, sociological analysis ought to destroy the attraction of neutral principles theory. Principles are "neutral" only in the sense that they are, as a matter of contingent fact, unchallenged, and the contingencies have obvious historical limits.

CONCLUSION

The critiques of interpretivism and neutral principles have each led to the same point. To be coherent, each theory requires that our understandings of social institutions be stable. Interpretivism requires that judges today be able to trace historical continuities between the institutions the framers knew and those that contemporary judges know. The theory of neutral principles requires that judges be able to rely on a shared conception of the proper role of judicial reasoning. The critiques have established that there are no determinate continuities derivable from history or legal principle. Rather, judges must choose which conceptions to rely on. Their choice is constrained, but explaining the constraints demands a sociological explanation of the ways in which the system within which they operate is deeply entrenched and resistant to change. If this sociological explanation is to have not merely descriptive validity, but normative force as well, we find ourselves drawn into the domain of conservative social theory, in which variable individual conceptions are seen to be derivative from—and subsidiary to—an underlying societal perspective.

The problem faced by both judge and constitutional theorist is how to find or construct the requisite shared conceptions. This problem is analogous to the interpretive difficulties that confront us in many aspects of our social experience. Consider an ordinary conversation between two people. Alice hears Arthur use the word "arbogast." She thinks she knows what he means, but as the conversation continues Alice realizes that Arthur is using the word in a way that comes to seem a little strange. She interrupts, so that Arthur can explain what he means. But things get worse. His explanation shows that his entire vocabulary rests on the way that he has lived until that moment. Because Arthur's life is by definition different from Alice's, Alice finds herself left with only an illusory understanding of what Arthur says. Her task is then to identify the point at which she can, so to speak, think her way into Arthur's life, so that she can understand what he means through understanding how he has developed. In this story, "understanding what Arthur means when he says 'arbogast' " plays the role of "following the rule in *Roe* v. *Wade*" or "remaining faithful to the framers' meaning of "due process.' "

The question in each case is how to overcome the gaps that reflection has revealed. Of course, we go along each day with some taken-for-granted understandings of the world. But anyone can disrupt what is taken for granted simply by placing it in question. Courts are institutions in which challenges to the taken-for-granted may be made as a matter of course, and the individualist premises of the liberal vision both make such challenges inevitable and demand that they be heard. But if society is to be stable, those challenges must be rebuffed in ways that preserve the shared societal understandings.

Here the parable of the conversation is central. As experience has taught us, Alice and Arthur need not give up in despair; if they keep talking, they can build bridges between their two idiosyncratic dialects. Just as the historian can understand the past through hermeneutic efforts, so can we understand each other by creating a community of understanding. But the parable also reminds us that we cannot assume that people who talk to each other are part of such a community merely because they seem to be speaking the same language. Similarly, communities of understanding are not defined by geographical boundaries or by allegiance to a single constitution. They are painstakingly created by people who enter into certain kinds of relations and share certain kinds of experiences.

Some have argued that such relations demand complete equality of power and of access to material resources; others identify the requisite experiences as confrontations with scarcity or similar natural kinds of human experience. For my purposes, I need not identify exactly what the prerequisites for a community of understanding are. It is enough simply to recognize that we must develop a shared system of meanings to make either interpretivism or neutral principles coherent. But in developing such a system, we will destroy the need for constitutional theory, predicated as that need is on liberal individualism; the problem identified by Hobbes, Locke, and liberal thought in general disappears in a society in which such a shared understanding exists. In the end we may decide to retrieve individualism in order to reaffirm its insistence on the otherness of other people, but we can do so only after we have thought through the implications of our dependence on each other.

NOTES

17. See, e.g., R. Berger, *Government by Judiciary* (Cambridge, Mass.: Harvard U. Press, 1977).

18. See, e.g., Michael J. Perry, "Interpretivism, Freedom of Expression, and Equal Protection," *Ohio State Law Journal* 42 (1981): 261, 281.

20. L. Levy, *Freedom of Speech and Press in Early American History: Legacy of Suppression* (Cambridge: Belknap Press of Harvard U. Press, Torchbook ed., 1963.

23. J. Ely, *Democracy and Distrust* (Cambridge, Mass.: Harvard U. Press, 1980) (quoting U.S. Constitution, Fourteenth Amendment, § 1), pp. 22–30.

24. Douglas Laycock, Book Review, *Texas Law Review* 53 (1975): 343.

27. Perry, "Interpretivism," p. 300 (footnote omitted).

28. R. Dworkin, *Taking Rights Seriously* (Cambridge: Harvard U. Press, 1977), pp. 134–36.

44. L. Litwack, *Been in the Storm So Long: The Aftermath of Slavery* (New York: Vintage Books, 1979).

47. R. Keat, *The Politics of Social Theory* (Oxford: Basil Blackwell, 1981), p. 3.

49. 274 U.S. 357, 372 (1927) (Brandeis, J., concurring).

65. Robert H. Bork, "Neutral Principles and Some First Amendment Problems," *Indiana Law Journal* 47 (1971): 1, 6–7.

66. Herbert Wechsler, "Toward Neutral Principles of Constitutional Law," *Harvard Law Review* 73 (1959): 1, 11–12, 15.

100. 381 U.S. 479 (1865).

101. 268 U.S. 510 (1925).

102. 262 U.S. 390 (1923).

104. 395 U.S. 444 (1969).

106. 341 U.S. 494 (1951).

120. 410 U.S. 113 (1973).

131. One possible rule is the following: $f(1) = 1$; for n greater than 1, if n is divisible by 5, $f(n) = n^2$; if $(n - 1)$ is divisible by 5, $f(n) = f(n - 1) - f(n - 2)$; if neither n nor $(n - 1)$ is divisible by 5, $f(n) = 2n - 1$.

134. Mark V. Tushnet, Book Review, *Michigan Law Review* 78 (1980): 694, 696–98.

PART IV

Beyond Rationality

The Rationalist tradition dominates legal and political thought, and most thinking about that thinking. The virtues of reason as the universal solvent for social conflict and moral disharmony are embodied in the Rule of Law. Aping the vaunted rigor of the natural sciences, the central premise is that, in order to command any moral authority or intellectual allegiance, there must be a solid epistemological foundation on which to build moral theory if people are to be expected to live and be bound by its ethical maxims. Without an objective ahistorical grounding, knowledge and truth would allegedly become prey to radical skepticism, behind which lurks the specter of social chaos and tyranny. As part of a broader intellectual attack on Western metaphysics, CLS reasserts the inescapable connection between philosophy and history by showing that there is no privileged ground for philosophers to stand or build on. In the constructed world of social action, there is no position of theoretical innocence or political neutrality. Criticism is intended to deconstruct the constructs of philosophy so as to better reveal their constructedness and potential for reconstruction.

In his piece, Gerald Frug introduces the deconstructive technique by explaining how it takes constructs seriously and works to collapse them from within. As a focus for his argument, he looks to the historical attempts to justify the efficacy and appropriateness of controls over private and public bureaucracy. In different ways, each model attempts to define, distinguish, and render mutually compatible the subjective and objective aspects of life. Using a Derridean style of deconstruction, Frug brings to light the failure of this futile ambition. After outlining the basic force and operation of this critical technique, he suggests the transformative potential that this revelation of the constructedness of legal categories and social life can have. As part of a larger analysis of contract doctrine, Clare Dalton applies

179

a similar deconstructive critique to the judicial treatment of nonmarital agreements by cohabitants. She shows how doctrinal stories simplify and render abstract the lived complexity of human relationships and disguise the indirect attempts to resolve the central problems of power in intimate relations. In understanding doctrine as an impoverished effort at world-making, she indicates how this might enable us to see in what way existing stories empower some at the expense of others and how they could be retold to empower more in different ways.

Finally, Mark Kelman makes a general defense of a particular version of this critique—what he calls "trashing"—against its critics. He emphasizes CLS's focus on ambiguity and its refusal to seek total syntheses. Moreover, he sees in the work of traditional scholars the very utopianism and vagueness that they are so quick to condemn within CLS work. Pushing these concerns and commitments in an uncompromising manner, he surveys critically the scope of CLS work. By way of conclusion, he encourages a localized critique of micropractices throughout the legal establishment and society and reminds CLS of the seductive, but dangerous, allure of utopian speculation.

11

The Ideology of Bureaucracy in American Law

Gerald E. Frug

I. THE ARGUMENT

A. The Stories That Justify Bureaucracy

From the time of their introduction into American life, large-scale business corporations and the administrative state that regulated them have raised profound questions about the kind of nation we are creating and the kind of people we are becoming. One way to understand the nature of these questions is to examine the ways dissident political movements have contested the foundation, growth, and predominance of bureaucratic entities. From the republicans of the revolutionary period through the Jacksonians, populists, and labor organizers of the nineteenth century, to modern writers on economic and political democracy, dissidents have charged that public and private power has become vested in the hands of the few. This concentration of power, they have argued, threatens fundamental ideals of liberty and equality, whether these ideals are understood in terms of an economy founded on widespread individual entrepreneurship, a polity based on democratically controlled decisionmaking, or a theory of the self that emphasizes the ability of individuals to control the nature of their work and their essential life choices. . . .

Dissidents have also charged that the emergence of large-scale bureaucratic enterprise has transformed day-to-day-life experience. Sometimes this criticism refers to the alienation that has invaded ordinary human activity: the lack of fulfillment people derive from their work, the sense of dealing with organizations seemingly beyond

---

Excerpted from its original publication in *Harvard Law Review* 97, 1984, by permission of the author and the Harvard Law Review Association.

their own, even anyone's, control. At other times, this criticism is directed at the increasing sameness and conformity within everyday life. People act by reference to their roles in life, and these roles are reproduced endlessly: McDonald's, McDonald's everywhere. Whether they emphasize the problems of human estrangement or those of conformity, critics charge that the bureaucratization of life has diminished the possibility of an authentic experience of the self.

Dissidents' complaints about the growth of large-scale public and private enterprise, however, have been simply a subtheme in American political discourse, one that has been overwhelmed by the growth of these enterprises and the voices of their defenders. The defenders of bureaucracy have allied its emergence with the idea of progress, the advances of the technological age, and the realities of a modern, complex society. Bureaucracy, we are told, is a necessary, inevitable feature of modern life. Only a foolish romantic—a reactionary who idealizes a past that never really existed and could not conceivably exist—could hope to dismantle or radically to alter current public or private bureaucratic organizations. Once they establish this argument of necessity, defenders of bureaucracy then typically demonstrate why these organizations constitute desirable forms of human association. Here, more than in mass meetings or even in the family, personal domination is subject to checks and balances. Moreover, far from creating a diminished sense of self, modern large-scale organizations have made possible an unparalleled expansion of people's opportunity to choose their own lifestyle. Never have people had more options in life or more time to pursue them. Indeed, the modern workplace has been portrayed as the place where classical republican ideals can actually be put into practice.

The history of the conflict over bureaucratic organization in America is important because it affects our current stance toward these institutions. Subordinate dissident concerns about the exercise of managerial power and about the dangers of bureaucracy to personal freedom have influenced both the growth and the defense of large-scale organizations. Indeed, one can understand the changing forms of justification offered for bureaucratic organization in terms of an historical progression fueled by a dialectic of critique and response. But one can also view our relationship to the historical controversy over bureaucracy in less causal terms. From this perspective, the historical debate simply replicates our own ambivalent feelings about the desirability and the danger of bureaucratic institutions: the debate between bureaucracy's defenders and dissidents is one we still carry on—within ourselves.

Like the historical defenders of bureaucratic organizations, we have adopted only a limited number of ways to reassure ourselves about these institutions. These limited attempts to justify bureaucracy, I claim, are the basis on which corporate and administrative law are built. I identify four different attempts to understand and defend corporations and administrative agencies. These four approaches represent responses to the critique of both managerial domination and the erosion of the space for personal self-expression. . . .

The first of these [bureaucratic] models, which I call the formalist model, can be associated with the work of late nineteenth and early twentieth-century bureaucratic theorists such as Max Weber, Frederick Taylor, and Ernst Freund. These theorists portrayed bureaucracy as a rationalized, disciplined mechanism for implementing the wishes of its creators, whether stockholders or legislators. They saw bureaucratic power as unthreatening because they understood bureaucratic organizations to be objective instruments under the control of those who delegated power to them. Indeed, constituent control not only prevented abuse of managerial power but also preserved a sphere for the full expression of subjective experience in the activity of those outside the bureaucracy whose wishes the bureaucracy carried out.

The second form of bureaucratic legitimation, which I call the expertise model, developed in response to the critique of the formalist model. Progressives and certain New Dealers—including organization theorists like Philip Selznick, corporate managerialists like Chester Barnard, Elton Mayo, Peter Drucker, and Douglas McGregor, and administrative law scholars like Woodrow Wilson and James Landis—agreed with the charge that bureaucracies were not in fact controlled by commands issued from outside. They recognized the enormous range of discretion exercised by bureaucratic managers; indeed, they argued that this discretion was not only an unavoidable ingredient of bureaucratic life but also its very raison d'être. Instead of fearing bureaucratic discretion, these thinkers welcomed it because they perceived the managers and employees who exercised it to be "experts" whose professionalism simultaneously limited the scope of their power, prevented personal domination, and made possible the creativity and flexibility necessary to the effectiveness of the bureaucratic form.

The third theory of bureaucratic legitimacy, which I call the judicial review model, was a reaction against the "excesses" of the expertise model. Those who articulated this point of view, including such legal scholars as Felix Frankfurter, Lon Fuller, Louis Jaffe, and Kenneth Culp Davis, expressed doubts that either constituent control or managerial expertise could limit the exercise of bureaucratic power. That limit had to be located instead in the ability of the courts to review and, when necessary, to overturn the actions of bureaucratic organizations. Bureaucracy could be rendered nonthreatening, in their view, only if adequately subject to the rule of law. Because the intrusion of the courts would be limited, however, managers and constituents would retain primary control over bureaucratic activities.

Finally, in the 1960s and 1970s, liberal democrats and conservative representatives of the "Chicago School" criticized the effectiveness and credibility of the judicial review model. These theorists, who espouse what I call the market/pluralist model, ground the legitimacy of administrative and corporate structures on the operation of either political or market mechanisms within bureaucratic structures. As they see it, either interest-group politics or market forces intervene to discipline bureaucratic management; in addition, these mechanisms allow people to express themselves about how bureaucratic organizations should operate. . . .

Each model of bureaucratic legitimacy is a story designed to tell its listeners: "Don't worry, bureaucratic organizations are under control." All of administrative and corporate law can, in my view, be understood as an expression of one of these stories or of a combination of them. These bodies of law comprise, in other words, a series of assurances that the legal system can overcome the perennial concerns about bureaucratic organizations. The most prominent concern that these areas of legal doctrine address is the fear that bureaucratic managers—whether public or private—can control bureaucratic power in a manner adverse to the interests of the shareholders or citizens whom they purport to serve. . . . These bodies of law also seek to assure us that bureaucratic organization allows ample room for self-determination and self-development. This aspect of legal doctrine, although often less apparent than the focus on managerial power, is no less important.

Many readers may find it odd to talk of corporate and administrative law as a series of stories that assure us about the acceptability of bureaucratic organizations. They may think that the decision to create these organizations takes place outside the legal system—that bureaucracy is the product of political choice or of market forces. The law, under this view, merely reflects social life; it functions only to correct the problems that bureaucratic organizations generate. Other readers, however, may recognize the claim that the legal system itself shapes the development of bureaucratic organization through the "legitimating function" of law, to use Alexander Bickel's well-known phrase.[30] According to one definition, "Legitimacy means that there are good arguments for a political order's claim to be recognized as right and just. . . . *Legitimacy means a political order's worthiness to be recognized.*"[31] For these readers, the process of distinguishing legal from illegal activity in corporate and administrative law has been a source of bureaucratic power in American society. . . .

B. The Subjective/Objective Dichotomy

In my view, all of the stories that seek to explain and defend bureaucratic organization have undertaken two tasks. First, they have sought to respond to the fear of managerial control by demonstrating that bureaucratic power is constrained by some kind of objectivity. Objectivity is thought to protect people within the bureaucracy from domination and to ensure that the interests of constituents are not threatened by the consolidated power exercised by the bureaucracy itself. The definitions of objectivity adopted in these stories have varied widely—"neutrality" and "pursuit of a common purpose" are examples—but all of them have emphasized values of organizational life that everyone is considered to hold in common. It is the fact that these values are shared that makes them "objective." Accordingly, any intrusion of subjective, personal values into this objectivity has been treated as inconsistent with it. . . .

Second, each of the stories has tried to show that bureaucratic organization does not limit the opportunity for personal self-expression. They have responded to the concerns about personal freedom by illustrating how bureaucracy can provide us with an improved ability to control our own lives in our own way. This side of the agenda, then, attempts to make bureaucracy consistent with subjectivity—with the values of individuality associated with the unique desires that distinguish each person from others in the world. Like the pursuit of objectivity, the search for subjectivity has taken many forms. Some stories, for example, emphasize constituents' ability to ensure that the bureaucracy does what they want it to do, and others emphasize the freedom of bureaucratic officials to apply their own expertise and training in their work. To be persuasive, however, this appeal to subjectivity must provide some assurance that individuals can escape from the enforced commonness of objectivity and be themselves. Above all else, then, the presence of subjectivity in organizational life must be protected from the demands of objectivity.

All the stories of bureaucratic legitimation, in short, share a common structure: they attempt to define, distinguish, and render mutually compatible the subjective and objective aspects of life. All the defenses of bureaucracy have sought to avoid merging objectivity and subjectivity—uniting the demands of commonness and community with those of individuality and personal separateness—because to do so would be self-contradictory. Moreover, it has never been enough just to separate subjectivity and objectivity; each must also be guaranteed a place within the bureaucratic structure. As a result, the "line" between the two realms has become the critical focus of all efforts to legitimate bureaucracy. It is this line that allows bureaucratic theorists simultaneously to separate and combine the values of subjectivity and objectivity—to present bureaucracy as both an enhancement and a protection of liberty—and that therefore permits them to present bureaucracy as legitimate.

I argue that this project of bureaucratic legitimation is a failure. Theorists have not been able to distinguish and render compatible the subjective and objective aspects of organizational life because no line between subjectivity and objectivity can ever be drawn. Instead, as each model of bureaucratic legitimation has developed, it has included subjectivity on the objective side of the boundary and objectivity on the subjective side. The facets of organizational life that need to be subjective have become so constrained by objectivity that they cannot convincingly represent the expression of human individuality. Similarly, the facets that need to be objective have become so riddled with subjectivity as to undermine their claim to represent common interests. Indeed, opponents of each individual story of bureaucratic legitimation have usually lodged precisely this form of criticism against it. Yet these critics themselves have generally sought only to legitimate bureaucracy more convincingly by substituting their own combination of objectivity and subjectivity; later, the same critique has been lodged against them. . . .

At this point it may seem difficult to understand why bureaucratic theorists have never been able to find a way to ensure that the bureaucratic organization can combine-yet-separate the realms of objectivity and subjectivity. The explanation that I shall offer relies on the term "a dangerous supplement" found in the work of Jacques Derrida.[37] In each of the four stories of bureaucratic legitimation analyzed, the relationship between subjectivity and objectivity can best be understood by conceiving each of them as the "dangerous supplement" of the other.

What, then, is "a dangerous supplement"? The idea can most easily be grasped through an example, and my example shall be the relationship of law to society. It is not uncommon to think of the law as a supplement to the normal operation of social life. A supplement, the dictionary tells us, is "something added, especially to make up for a lack or deficiency." Law seems to be something added to society; one often hears of social life existing before there was a legal system. The addition of law, far from being optional, seems necessary to cure defects in the social order. Without law, society cannot operate properly; without it, according to one account, there would be a war of each against all. Yet law is also a threatening supplement; it gives certain individuals—the lawgivers—the ability to impose on society a new form of oppression. It is, then, a dangerous supplement. And, paradoxically, the only apparent way to curb this new danger is through the law itself: the threat posed by the law has to be restrained by law. "A terrifying menace, the supplement [here, the law] is also the first and surest protection against that very menace."[41]

This familiar way of understanding the relationship of law and society presents a picture of a supplement that is simultaneously necessary to the preservation of society and threatening to its survival. The dangerous supplement is avidly sought because it seems the only way to make society what it ought to be. The very idea of society without law is permanently "deferred," to use Derrida's term: we can attain society-without-law—if we can attain it at all—only by establishing society-under-law. Law and society become inextricably interlinked; law, dangerous yet unavoidable, becomes part of what we mean by society.

This story of the supplemental relationship between law and society needs now to be retold so that society becomes the dangerous supplement of law. After all, one can establish law only through the actions of society, yet society—the activity of human beings—poses a threat to the ideal of legality. This process of seeing both society and law as dangerous supplements of each other strips the concepts of "law" and "society" of their apparently separate identities. Neither society-without-law nor law-outside-of-society seems a meaningful possibility in the world; the use of one of these terms always seems to imply the existence of the other. Moreover, the notion that either law or society existed in history without the other becomes subject to a similar process of doubt; it seems that this relationship between law and society has "always already" existed.[42] If so, one can see why the task of "drawing a line" between law and society becomes an incoherent, meaningless task. Society is constituted, in part, by law, and law is constituted, in part, by society.

Every attempt to separate objectivity and subjectivity in bureaucratic thought has instead resulted in a relentless intermixing of them. This intermixing—this insertion of subjectivity and objectivity into their antithesis as dangerous supplements—has actually been brought about by the very people who sought to prevent it. This supplemental structure has been as necessary and unavoidable—and as threatening—as the interweaving of law and society. In an attempt to overcome the combination of subjectivity and objectivity, legal theorists have sought new lines between subjectivity and objectivity *within* both the objective and the subjective realms of bureaucratic form. But this line-drawing enterprise has reproduced the same relentless intermixture of subjectivity and objectivity, each becoming the dangerous supplement of the other. Rather than drawing a line between subjectivity and objectivity, bureaucratic theorists have concealed their failure to overcome the conflict between subjectivity and objectivity through an endless series of unsuccessful attempts to combine-yet-separate the two spheres of life.

This inability of bureaucratic theorists to draw a subjective/objective boundary can readily be understood in terms of the dangerous supplement. After all, the idea of subjectivity usually refers to the sphere of the self, but we can define ourselves only through relationships with the world in which we live. To find ourselves, we seek ideas through the commonly created world of language, knowledge through interaction with others, and an affective life through loving and being loved by those close to us. . . . But these others also threaten to eliminate our separate sense of identity. The influence of others can be so powerful that our identity becomes a product not of what *we* want to be but of what others have made us. Indeed, there is no way to escape from the world in order to distinguish what "we" want from what "they" want. The world we share in common—the objective world—is both necessary to and incompatible with our subjective identity.

The same story can be told by starting with the notion of objectivity. Objectivity is usually associated with the ideas of impersonality or commonality rather than with those of the self—with the perspective of universality rather than that of particularity. But any reference to what we share collectively must take into account each of the individual components that make up the collectivity. There can no more be universal, collective, or shared goals separate from the particular goals advanced by specific people, than there can be an objective world of nature separate from the individual features of the world sought to be described. Yet separateness and individuality threaten to break apart the notion of objectivity. The individual aspects that are sought to be combined can be understood not only in terms of what they have in common but also in terms of how they differ from each other. For example, you and I share much in common—we are human, we can read English, even the kind of English printed in the *Harvard Law Review*—but our differences rather than our similarities can always be emphasized. If they are, the notion that we together create a world of objectivity can be destroyed simply by emphasizing the differences embodied in our particularity. The world of individual subjectivity is a necessary part of the objective world but one that is dangerous to any sense that "objectivity" is possible.

Once the reader grasps the inability to separate subjectivity and objectivity, the reason I do not elaborately define these terms should become clear. What defines our particularized selves—our subjectivity—and what defines the outside world of objective truth is problematic: who we are is up for grabs. Indeed, bureaucratic theorists have taken a vast array of features of life and described them as elements of either "subjectivity" or "objectivity." Yet these features could just as easily have been described in the opposite terms because the categories themselves lack specific content. Moreover, once one understands the relationship between subjectivity and objectivity, it should also be clear that we can never draw a line between them. Therefore, my critique of bureaucratic theorists' reliance on the subjective/objective dichotomy is not designed to propose a better way of combining subjectivity and objectivity or even to suggest that we substitute a recognition that everything is subjective for the theorists' relentless search for objectivity. Instead, I suggest that we should abandon the attempt to understand the world in terms of the subjective-objective dichotomy; we should deal with the problems of human association in other ways. It is important to realize that we need not understand the world in terms of subjectivity and objectivity—that this dichotomy, like so many other categories through which we experience the world, is a human creation and not a reflection of what the world "is really like.". . .

C. The Nature of Legal Argument

It may still be unclear why the inability of bureaucratic theorists to combine-yet-separate subjectivity and objectivity is so destructive to legal argument about bureaucracy. The reason, briefly stated, is that this relentless attempt to divide and redivide subjectivity and objectivity has produced a form of legal doctrine that restates the very problems of bureaucratic domination and personal self-expression that it was created to solve. Instead of providing a way to decide whether a concrete bureaucratic activity should be approved or condemned, legal doctrine simply presents a structure that lawyers can use to formulate arguments for and against the activity under review. Because every aspect of bureaucratic life that must be objective also must be subjective, lawyers can argue endlessly over which of these conflicting yet essential ingredients should be focused on. The law either oscillates between seeing the subjective or the objective side as the more important or offers alternative, but inconsistent, schemes for combining-yet-separating both sides. Legal doctrine thus provides a justification for both a particular course of action and its opposite. Moreover, any attempt to determine the result of appealing to the "facts of the case" provides no escape from this problem. The interpretation of the facts suffers from the same intermixture of subjectivity and objectivity that plagues bureaucratic theory. The facts, too, can be construed either to justify or to condemn any bureaucratic activity.

Results produced by this kind of legal argument can be convincing only if they present an artificially partial view of the world as if it were complete. If the entire structure of argument were apparent, we could see that the imagined resolution of a legal problem is made possible only by concealing the elements of subjectivity and objectivity that would produce the opposite result. More important, a system that can be used to legitimate so much can hardly be convincing in its effort to legitimate anything. If one can deduce from a doctrine or induce from a "fact situation" contradictory conclusions, the results of legal discourse lose their power to persuade. The arguments that generate these results are revealed to be a stylized form of rhetoric, one that can be invoked to approve or disapprove any action taken by the bureaucracy. This rhetoric can assure its advocates and their audience of the legitimacy of bureaucratic power only as long as its manipulability is concealed. . . .

D. The Phenomena of Abstraction and Reification

If the creation of an effective subjective/objective dichotomy is both the basis of bureaucratic legitimation and a failure, how has legal argument concerning bureaucracy been able to convince anyone? The answer, I suggest, is that bureaucratic theorists have relied on a peculiarly deceptive kind of rhetoric in their attempts to combine-yet-separate subjectivity and objectivity.

This kind of rhetoric has two components. Sometimes it involves appeals to abstractions and suggests that one can deduce from an abstraction a specific form of bureaucratic organization. For example, the concept of "expertise" could be invoked to suggest the possibility of an organization that constrains the exercise of subjective discretion within the bounds of professional objectivity. This kind of reasoning, associated particularly with legal formalism, is the most familiar and widely criticized of the two forms of rhetoric, and I shall not subject it to a general discussion here. Suffice it to say that one of the triumphs of legal realism was to demonstrate that there is no method to deduce from an abstraction ("expertise") any particular form of social life. Instead, contradictory forms of life can be consistent with the same abstract goal. . . .

It is the other component of legal rhetoric that I want to introduce at this point. This component treats abstractions such as "subjectivity" and "objectivity" as if they themselves were something concrete and specific—like some *thing*, concrete and specific. For example, bureaucratic theorists discuss subjectivity in terms of people's "incentives," "interests," or "values" as if these words referred to actual things that could have determinate content; similarly, they describe objectivity in terms of the "needs" or "goals" of an organization, or speak of what "society requires," as if these too were actual things to be scrutinized. Once this vocabulary is adopted, a theorist might then show how people's "incentives," the organization's "goals," and society's "needs" can all be mutually consistent. S/he might say, for example, that both people's incentives and the organization's goals are motivated by a search for profit, and that this kind of profit seeking meets one of society's important needs.

This way of talking has two characteristics. First, by reducing abstractions to a more concrete form, it helps make them more understandable. The concrete terms acquire the power—as does a metaphor ("The growth of a large business is merely a survival of the fittest")—to capture the imagination so completely that they seem to become the abstraction itself. This gives the rhetoric its power to persuade. Second, because the concrete terms can never capture all aspects of the abstraction, they remain vague and manipulable ("What do you mean by survival? Fittest?"). This manipulability allows them to be shaped in a wide variety of ways to make bureaucratic organization appear natural and necessary. As long as the manipulation is not too obvious, this characteristic helps rather than hinders the rhetoric's ability to persuade.

This form of rhetoric, however, is always deceptive. The reduction of human ideals to the status of things and the consequent mistaken treatment of the things as if they were the ideals themselves—a process often called reification—falsify human experience by leading people to think that a form of life they are leading is the equivalent of life itself. People think of themselves as "employees" and act according to their conception of what an employee is (for example, someone loyal to the organization's goals), thereby adapting themselves to forms of experience instead of recognizing that they can create for themselves what these forms should be. But without the trick of reification, bureaucratic theorists would never be able to "add together" different "facets" of life to devise a "structure" that "satisfies" the "subjective desires" and "objective needs" of the individual. Nor could they find "needs of society" that "demand" certain forms of organization to "satisfy" them. Life would retain its complex character: all aspects of life would simultaneously contain possibilities for change and frustrations that impede those possibilities. Human relationships within the bureaucracy would both threaten to dominate the individual and give her/him fulfillment—both restrain and enhance her/his sense of freedom. If the contradictory nature of these relationships were fully recognized, people would treat all bureaucratic structures as permitting and needing revision. Moreover, the object of this transformation would not be merely to find the right structure or to replace one structure with another but permanently to alter the relation of structure and freedom. Only by continually overcoming the structures that falsify her/his human potential could the individual engage in the self-transforming, self-creating process of freedom. Thus, the very project of bureaucratic theorists—to find a structure that is necessary to promote and defend human freedom and to rely on the device of reification to make such a structure intelligible—is itself an impediment to human liberation. By constraining the possibilities of life within false forms, all such structures deny individuals the ability to create and re-create their own form of life. . . .

E. The Choice Between Bureaucracy and Democracy

These assertions about legal argumentation apply to much more than bureaucratic legitimation. . . . Bureaucracy is the primary form of organized power in America today, and it is therefore a primary target for those who seek liberation from modern forms of human domination. The ideology that reassures us that bureaucracy is legitimate is demobilizing because it conceals the need to reorder American society to bring to life better versions of the ideal of human freedom. Critical theory seeks to undermine this ideology by exposing the false consciousness through which people understand the world. Such an exposure is itself an act of liberation.

Of course, this sort of liberation cannot alone ensure human freedom. New forms of human association designed to take the place of bureaucracy must themselves be subject to the same critique. But this critique has its limits—there is a stopping place. This would be reached when people abandoned abstract arguments that seek to defend some form of life as a structure that can protect human individuality—when people jointly recognize that no structure can protect us from each other given the variable, intersubjective, interdependent nature of human relationships. The forms of organization that would then be created would not be understood as an answer to the human predicament. They would be transparently open to transformation (no form of organization is necessary) and always in need of transformation (all forms of organization create forms of domination that need to be combated).

I use the ideal of participatory democracy to represent this different kind of social organization. Of course, some proponents of participatory democracy reduce it to a concrete structure that "solves" the problems of social life.[53] These proponents should be subjected to the same critique that I lodge here against the proponents of bureaucracy. But other advocates of reinvigorating the notion of democracy are not vulnerable to the critique advanced here.[54] They understand the term "democracy" to refer to the process by which people create for themselves the form of organized existence within which they live. Only by creating these forms together can people confront the intersubjective nature of social life. Moreover, unless people do so *themselves,* the artificial structures through which they operate will threaten to function beyond their control. In this view, the term "participatory democracy" does not describe a fixed series of limited possibilities of human organization but the ideal under which the possibilities of joint transformation of social life are collected.

III. SOME CONCLUDING THOUGHTS

What does this article suggest that bureaucratic theorists *do,* given the impossibility of drawing a line between subjectivity and objectivity? What alternative is there to seeking, the best one can, a basis for building some objective limits on power and for allowing needed subjective discretion? My answer to this line of questioning must start with isolating the fundamental project undertaken by bureaucratic theorists. Their effort can be characterized as an attempt to defend a controversial feature of social life—bureaucracy—by tying it to a more basic aspect of social life that is itself noncontroversial. Such an effort to ground social institutions on some unchallengeable foundation is not new; one need only think of the attempts to derive the appropriate organization of society from the will of God. Moreover, it is not surprising that the bureaucratic theorists' foundation embraces some notion of objectivity: how can people trust these concentrations of power unless they can be shown to be objective in some way? Nor is it surprising that the foundation must include subjectivity as well: why should anyone want bureaucracies unless they are responsive in some way to individual desires? Thus, bureaucratic theorists base their models of bureaucracy on aspects of social life that seem to promise an appropriate mix of objectivity and subjectivity. . . .

This article suggests that such a search for a foundation for social life is a futile and empty project. If subjectivity can be understood only as the dangerous supplement of objectivity and objectivity only as the dangerous supplement of subjectivity, each of these concepts is based on the other. If so, neither concept can possibly be the "foundation" of the other. No foundation can support an item it rests on. And if law and society relate to each other as dangerous supplements, neither of them can provide a stable basis on which to construct the other. . . .

There is nothing particularly novel about this critique of the search for a foundation for social life. . . . But it is not a form of social theory likely to be tolerable to the theorists of bureaucracy. Their efforts have concentrated on finding a basis on which bureaucracy can be justified. Without a foundation, they cannot claim that bureaucratic organizations provide the objectivity needed to protect us from bureaucratic power; they cannot assure us of room within the bureaucracy to be free of its restraints. Without a foundation, they cannot persuade us to accept bureaucratic organizations by tying them to any less controversial feature of social life. Yet if my critique is convincing, bureaucratic theorists must abandon their relentless search for a foundation on which to construct a viable defense of bureaucracy. . . .

It may be hard for readers to think it worthwhile to give up the search for a foundation that would render human relationships unthreatening. They may, for example, believe that we risk tyranny without such a foundation. It is certainly true that, without foundations, there is no guarantee against tyranny; its likelihood will depend on what people do. But foundations have never protected us against tyranny either; there are no such things. Even the fabrication of foundations hasn't helped; we have never been able to "deduce" from some ultimate foundation the things that are worth fighting for and worth fighting against. Without a (mythical) foundation for our views, we admittedly are (still) unable to say what our choices are based on. But social choices are certainly not arbitrary: choices about how to live and what kind of world to create are neither "objective" nor "subjective," neither certain nor meaningless. They cannot be characterized either way once we recognize how crucially the nature of human relationships and institutions affect who we are. The alternative to

194

"foundations" is not "chaos" but the joint reconstruction of social life, the quest of participatory democracy. Acting together, we could begin to dismantle the structure of bureaucratic organizations—not all at once, but piece by piece. In their place we could substitute forms of human relationship that better reflect our aspirations for human development and equality. . . .

NOTES

30. See A. Bickel, *The Least Dangerous Branch* (Indianapolis: Bobbs Merrill, 1962), pp. 29–33.
31. J. Habermas, *Communication and the Evolution of Society*, trans. T. McCarthy (Boston: Beacon Press, 1979), p. 178.
37. See J. Derrida, *Of Grammatology* (Baltimore: Johns Hopkins Univ. Press, 1976), pp. 141–64.
41. Ibid., p. 154.
42. Ibid., pp. 157–64.
53. See, e.g., J. Cohen and J. Rogers, *On Democracy: Towards A Transformation of American Society* (New York: Penguin Books, 1983), pp. 146–83; I. Markovic, "New Forms of Democracy in Socialism," *Praxis International* 1 (1981): 23.
54. See, e.g., H. Pitkin and S. Shumer, "On Participation," *Democracy* 2 (1982): 43; see generally, B. Barber, *Strong Democracy: Participatory Politics for the New Age* (Berkeley: Univ. of California Press, 1984).

12

An Essay in the Deconstruction of Contract Doctrine

Clare Dalton

IV. CONCLUSION: DOCTRINE, THE COHABITATION CONTRACT, AND BEYOND

Doctrinal arguments cast in terms of public and private, manifestation and intent, and form and substance continue to exert a stranglehold on our thinking about concrete contractual issues. By ordering the ways in which we perceive disputes, these arguments blind us to some aspects of what the disputes are actually about. By helping us categorize, they encourage us to simplify in a way that denies the complexity, and ambiguity, of human relationships. By offering us the false hope of definitive resolution, they allow us to escape the pain, and promise, of continual reassessment and accommodation.

I will illustrate the poverty of traditional doctrinal arguments by examining the use of contract doctrine in recent cases involving the agreements of nonmarital cohabitants. Distinctions between private and public realms, between contracts implied-in-fact and contracts implied-in-law, play an important part in the decisions. Interpretive questions and questions about the basis for enforcement—about consideration—also loom large, reiterating the concern with private and public, but couching that concern in the competing terms of subjective and objective, form and substance.

Significantly, the opinions largely ignore the aspect of the public-

Excerpted from its original publication in *Yale Law Journal* 94, 1985, by permission of the author and the Yale Law Journal.

private debate that appears in contract doctrine as the set of rules governing duress and unconscionability. The concerns of those doctrines—preventing oppression of each party by the other, while preventing oppression of both by the state—are nonetheless highly relevant. For at the heart of these cases lies the problem of power. It is only because the exercise of power in this context is not seen as fitting the traditional rubrics of duress and unconscionability that courts are able to ignore and avoid it.

Once the convoluted play of doctrine in this area has been exposed, we can see that traditional doctrinal formulations are not the only means for understanding how and why decisionmakers reach their decisions. At this point, other inquiries become both possible and legitimate. In suggesting what some of those other inquiries might be, my conclusion points toward possible ways of expanding our thinking about the issues of contract law.

A. The Cases

State courts have increasingly confronted cases involving various aspects of the cohabitation relationship, and their decisions have attracted a fair amount of scholarly attention. I focus on two such decisions: that of the California Supreme Court in *Marvin v. Marvin*,[432] and that of the Illinois Supreme Court in *Hewitt v. Hewitt*.[433]

In *Marvin*, Justice Tobriner addressed the question of whether plaintiff Michelle Triola, who had lived with the defendant, Lee Marvin, for seven years, could recover support payments and half the property acquired in Lee Marvin's name over the course of the relationship. The court found that the plaintiff, in alleging an oral contract, had stated a cause of action in express contract, and further found that additional equitable theories of recovery might be applicable. On remand, the trial court found that there existed neither an express contract nor unjust enrichment, but awarded the plaintiff equitable relief in the nature of rehabilitative alimony. The court of appeals then struck this award on the theory that relief could be granted only on the basis of express contract or quasi-contract.

The alleged oral agreement provided that plaintiff and defendant would, while they lived together, combine their efforts and earnings and share equally any property accumulated. They agreed to present themselves publicly as husband and wife. Triola also undertook to serve as the defendant's companion, homemaker, housekeeper, and cook. A later alleged modification to the contract provided that Triola would give up her own career in order to provide these services; in return, Marvin promised to support Triola for the rest of her life. The relationship ended when Marvin threw Triola out.

The plaintiff in *Hewitt* was in many respects a more sympathetic figure than Michele Triola. When she and Mr. Hewitt were both college students, she became pregnant. He then proposed that they live together as man and wife, presenting themselves as such to their families and friends, and that he thereafter share his life, future earnings, and property with her. She borrowed money from her family to put him through professional school, worked with him to establish his practice, bore him three children and raised them, and otherwise fulfilled the role of a traditional wife. After more than fifteen years he left her. She sought an equal division of property acquired during the relationship and held either in joint tenancy or in the defendant's name.

The appeals court ruled that she could have an equitable share of the property if she were able to prove her allegation of an express oral contract, although it did not preclude the possibility of alternative equitable theories of recovery in appropriate circumstances. The Supreme Court of Illinois reversed, basing its decision principally on considerations of public policy.

B. Express and Implied Agreement

The opinions in the cohabitation cases indicate that the distinction between the intention-based express contract and the public institution of quasi-contract may be central to the question of whether to grant relief. Techniques for interpreting the express contract are indistinguishable from techniques used to determine the presence of a quasi-contractual relationship. If the interpretive techniques employed highlight factors external to the parties and their actual intentions, even express contracts seem very public. If, in contrast, the techniques used have as their stated goal the determination of the parties' intentions, then quasi-contracts appear no less private or consensual than express contracts. The cohabitation opinions employ both public-sounding and private-sounding arguments to reach a variety of conclusions. In some cases courts determine that the parties are bound by *both* real and quasi-contractual obligations, in others that they are bound by neither, in yet others that they are bound by one but not the other. The arguments do not determine these outcomes— they only legitimate them.

In these cases, as in *Hertzog*, there is a common presumption that agreements between intimates are not contractual.[442] While this model of association was developed in husband-wife and parent-child cases, nonmarital cohabitants are assumed, for these purposes, to have the same kind of relationship.[443] As in *Hertzog*, express words are taken to be words of commitment but not of contract; conduct that in other circumstances would give rise to an implied-in-fact contract is instead attributed to the relationship. These cases also reach a conclusion only intimated in *Hertzog*: they find no unjust enrichment where one party benefits the other.

One possible explanation for this presumption against finding contracts is that it accords with the parties' intentions. It can be argued that cohabitants generally neither want their agreements to have legal consequences nor desire to be obligated to one another when they have stopped cohabiting. It can further be presented as a matter of fact that their services are freely given and taken within the context of an intimate relationship. If this is so, then a subsequent claim of unjust enrichment is simply unfounded.

This intention-based explanation, however, coexists in the opinions—indeed sometimes coexists within a single opinion—with two other, more overtly public explanations that rest on diametrically opposed public policies. The first suggests that the arena of intimate relationships is too private for court intervention, through contract enforcement, to be appropriate. In *Hewitt*, for example, the Illinois Supreme Court suggests that "the situation alleged here was not the kind of arm's length bargain envisioned by traditional contract principles, but an intimate arrangement of a fundamentally different kind."[448]

While it has some intuitive appeal, the argument that intimate relationships are too private for court enforcement is at odds with the more general argument that all contractual relationships are private and that contract enforcement merely facilitates the private relationships described by contract. To overcome this apparent inconsistency, we must imagine a scale of privateness on which business arrangements, while mostly private, are still not as private as intimate arrangements. But then the rescue attempt runs headlong into the other prevailing policy argument, which separates out intimate arrangements because of their peculiarly public and regulated status. Under this view, it is the business relationship that by and large remains more quintessentially private.

According to this second argument, the area of nonmarital agreements is too public for judicial intervention. The legislature is the appropriate body to regulate such arrangements; courts may not help create private alternatives to the public scheme. In *Hewitt*, the supreme court directly follows its appeal to the intimate nature of the relationship with an acknowledgment of the regulated, and hence public, character of marriage-like relations. With respect to intimate relations conceived as public, the judiciary can then present itself as either passive or active. The argument for passivity is that judges should "stay out" of an arena already covered by public law. The argument for activity is that judges should reinforce public policy by deterring the formation of deviant relationships, either because they fall outside the legislative schemes organizing familial entitlement and property distribution or because they offend public morality.

Neither the private nor the public arguments for the absence of contract in this setting are conclusive. Both private and public counterarguments are readily available. If the absence of contract is presented as flowing from party intention, competing interpretations of intention can be used to argue the presence of contract. If, within a more public framework, the court categorizes the concerns implicated by the relationship as private, then an argument can be made that within the boundaries expressly established by legislation, the parties should be free to vary the terms of their relationship without interference by the state. If the focus is the place of cohabitation agreements within the publicly regulated sphere of intimate relationships, then an argument can be made that certain kinds of enforcement in fact extend and implement public policy rather than derogate from it.[455]

The availability of this range of intention-based and policy-based arguments makes possible virtually any decision. A court can find or not find a "real" contract. It can decide that enforcement of a real contract is or is not appropriate. It can decide that while real contracts should be enforced, there is no basis for awarding quasi-contractual relief in the absence of an expressed intention to be bound. It can decide that even in the absence of real contract, the restitutionary claim of the plaintiff represents a compelling basis for quasi-contractual relief. Further, the competing public and private strands of argument—each of which connects to both enforceability and non-enforceability arguments—can be used within the same opinion or other legal text, without the inconsistencies being so apparent as to undermine the credibility of the final result.

C. Manifestation and Intent

Some identifiable, particular patterns do emerge from this overall confusion of public and private arguments. As with all agreements, for example, every aspect of a cohabitation agreement raises interpretive questions that will drive a court to search for the elusive correspondence between subjective intent and manifested form. Even this most private exercise of contractual interpretation thereby opens the doors to the imposition of public values, norms, and understandings. Two interpretive issues in particular recur in the cases. The courts repeatedly consider how to evaluate the relationships out of which the agreements arise. They also repeatedly consider how to evaluate the role of sex in those relationships and in these agreements.

Courts frequently invoke the context of cohabitation relationships to avoid enforcing agreements arising out of them. The argument here is essentially that even if such agreements use language of promise, or commitment, or reciprocal obligation, that language must be understood, *in the intimate context in which it is employed,* as not involving any understanding that one party might use a court to enforce a duty forsaken, or a promise broken.

In theory, if the parties make perfectly clear their intention to be legally bound by their agreement, then their intention governs. But this leaves open the question of when a court will find objective manifestations of such an intention to be bound. Will a written agreement be more susceptible to legal enforcement than an oral one? Will an agreement in which the reciprocal obligations relate to a particular piece of property or to a transaction that can be separated out, however artificially, from the affective context of the relationship convince a court that it has crossed the boundary between intimate unenforceability and business-like enforceability? These approaches all find some support in the cases, although their manipulability and their imperfect correspondence to questions of motivation and intention are obvious.

A second common theme employing notions of manifestation and intent is the specific role of sex in the parties' arrangement. The boundaries of this debate are set both by the tradition that precludes enforcement of prostitution contracts for reasons of public policy, and by the acknowledgment that even cohabiting parties may form valid contracts about independent matters. In the case of cohabitation agreements, the question therefore becomes whether the sex contemplated by the parties contaminates the entire agreement to the point where it is seen to fall within the model of the prostitution contract, or whether other features of the agreement can be seen as independent and enforceable.

Judges' differing interpretations of virtually identical agreements seem to depend quite openly on either their views of what policy should prevail or their own moral sense. Rarely does a judge even appear to make a thorough attempt to understand and enforce what the parties had in mind. For Justice Underwood in *Hewitt*, for example, nothing but "naiveté" could explain the assertion that "there are involved in these relationships contracts separate and independent from the sexual activity, and the assumption that those contracts would have been entered into or would continue without that activity."

Justice Tobriner in *Marvin*, on the other hand, rejects the idea that the sexual relationship between parties to a cohabitation contract renders the contract as a whole invalid. He explicitly uses the divide between objective and subjective, form and substance, to carve out a much larger space for enforceable agreements than that envisaged by Underwood. Tobriner's test has two components: contracts between nonmarital partners are enforceable unless they *explicitly* rest "upon the immoral and illicit consideration of meretricious sexual services"; furthermore, such contracts are unenforceable only "*to the extent*" that they rest on this meretricious consideration.

Tobriner is not so naive as to suppose that the Triola-Marvin agreement did not contemplate a sexual relationship. But he feels that the "subjective contemplation of the parties" is too "uncertain and unworkable" a standard. He relies instead on formal criteria of intent—on the manifestations of agreement alleged by Triola—to determine if his two-part test of enforceability has been met. For the purposes of this analysis Tobriner describes the agreement as follows: "the parties agreed to pool their earnings, . . . they contracted to share equally in all property acquired, and . . . defendant agreed to support plaintiff." None of this strikes Tobriner as necessitating a conclusion that sex invalidates the agreement.

Of course the formal criteria are themselves empty of significance until given meaning by judicial analysis. The very same language construed by Tobriner had been given very different effect in an earlier decision. In *Updeck v. Samuel*, a California District Court of Appeal considered the statement that the woman would make a permanent home for the man and be his companion as indicating precisely the sexual character of the relationship.[469] Unwilling or unable to disapprove *Updeck*, Tobriner is forced to distinguish this case in a fashion that directly undercuts the legitimacy of his stated reliance on form or manifestation. He argues that the *Updeck* agreement was found invalid because the Court "[v]iew[ed] the contract as calling for adultery." But the very act of "viewing" the contract, or interpreting its terms, involves an explanation of substance. The court in *Updeck* supplied sexual substance, while Tobriner supplies economic substance. *Jones v. Daly*,[472] a case subsequent to *Marvin*, provides another striking illustration of the manipulability of form. In *Jones*, which involved a homosexual partnership, a California Court of Appeal denied relief on the ground that an agreement, in other respects almost identical to the *Marvin* agreement, contained the word "lover."

As the courts wrestle with these interpretive questions, we see them apparently infusing a public element, external to the parties' own view of their situation, into their assessment of cohabitation agreements. We also can see how this is a necessary result of the tension between manifestation and intent, of the way in which intent requires embodiment in manifested forms, even while the forms require an infusion of substance before they can yield meaning. Indeed, to accuse judges of moving from the private to the public sphere is only to accuse them of the inevitable. If there is force behind the accusation, it is not *that* they have made the transition from private to public, but that they have made the transition *unselfconsciously*, and that the particular values, norms, and understandings they incorporate are different from the ones we would have favored, or different from the ones we think would correspond with those of one or both of the parties to the agreement.

D. Consideration: Its Substance

Consideration doctrine offers yet other opportunities for the conflation of public and private, and the introduction of competing

values, norms, and understandings into the resolution of these cohabitation cases. Just as in the area of interpretation, the crucial additions
are judicial conceptions of sexuality, and of woman's role in her
relationship with man. Two aspects of consideration doctrine recur in
the cases. Each illustrates the proposition that formal consideration
doctrine cannot be implemented without recourse to substance. Substance, here as elsewhere, can be provided by assessments of objective
value or by investigations into subjective intent. It is with respect to
these substantive inquiries that ideas about sexuality and relationship
come to play so potentially important a part.

The first use of consideration doctrine in this context shows up in
the disinclination of courts to enforce contracts based on "meretricious" consideration.[474] Courts frequently search beyond the express
language of the agreement in order to "find" that sex is at the heart of
the deal—specifically that the woman is providing sexual services in
return for the economic security promised by the man. Insofar as this
investigation depends on divining what the parties had in mind,
consideration turns on subjective intent. For these purposes, it matters not at all that "intent" has been derived from the judge's own
feelings about such relationships, even when the express language of
the parties would appear to point in an opposite direction.

The treatment of meretricious consideration also illustrates how
consideration may depend on a finding of objective value. When
courts refuse to enforce contracts based on the exchange of sexual
services for money, they are, for long-standing policy reasons, declining to recognize sexual services as having the *kind* of value that they
will honor. This decision, based on an objective measure of value, is
no different from the decision that "nominal" consideration will not
support a contract. There, too, courts disregard intention in the name
of a policy that depends upon societal recognition of certain sorts of
values and delegitimation of others.

The second aspect of consideration doctrine of interest in this
context is the traditional conclusion that the woman's domestic service
cannot provide consideration for the promises made to her by the
man. This is usually linked to the idea that the relationship itself is not
one the parties see as having a legal aspect. The standard explanation
is that the woman did not act in expectation of gain, but rather out of
affection, or that she intended her action as a gift.

Tobriner in the *Marvin* decision rejects this conclusion by recasting
the issue as one properly belonging in the selfish world of business.
Unless homemaking services are considered lawful and adequate
consideration for a promise to pay wages, the entire domestic service
industry will founder. Just as plainly, such services can provide the
consideration for an agreement concerning property distribution.
Tobriner thus appeals to the substance of objective value: there is a
market in which domestic services receive a price; when intimates

arrange that one will deliver those same services to the other, that promise is therefore capable of supporting a return promise.

Even as Tobriner uses ideas of objective value, however, his reasoning reveals that the ultimate rationale for this aspect of consideration doctrine depends upon arguments of subjective intent. Like the promise in the *Michigan* case,[481] the services could constitute consideration if they were offered with the intention of bargain or exchange. It is only the altruistic context, revealing the beneficent intention, that invalidates them.

Thus, while one route of access into this issue threatens to expose the public determination of what values the law will and will not recognize, that route is apparently closed off by the reminder that it is private intention, not public power, that assigns value. But then the very public role abjured in the context of objective value is played out instead through the "finding" of intent according to criteria that are essentially and inevitably public rather than private.

E. The Question of Power

Under duress and unconscionability doctrines, policing the "fair" exchange is tied irretrievably to asking whether each party entered into the contract freely, whether each was able to bargain in equally unconstrained ways, and whether the deal was a fair one. I suppose that any of us would find these questions even harder to answer in the context of intimate relationships than in other contexts—harder in that we would require a much more detailed account of the particulars before we could hazard an opinion, and harder in that even this wealth of detail would be likely to yield contradictory interpretations. Yet we acknowledge the importance of these questions in the area of intimate relations; we do not imagine either that most couples wind up with a fair exchange, or that most couples have equal bargaining power vis-à-vis one another.

The doctrinal treatment of cohabitation agreements, however, like the treatment of contracts in general, usually pays little attention to questions of power and fairness. Duress and unconscionability are the exceptions that prove the rule. These doctrines identify the only recognized deviations from the supposedly standard case of equal contracting partners. Intimate partners are conceived of as fitting the standard model. One consequence of this conception is that courts can justify the failure to enforce cohabitation arrangements as mere nonintervention, overlooking the fact that the superior position in which nonaction tends to leave the male partner is at least in part a product of the legal system. Another is that courts can idealize the private world in which their "nonintervention" leaves the parties, disregarding the ways in which the world is characterized by inequality and the exercise of private power. Yet another is that courts can talk blithely about the intentions of "the parties" in a fashion that ignores the possibility that one party's intentions are being respected at the expense of the other's.

Not all of the cohabitation contract opinions ignore the issues of fairness and power. They are more likely to receive explicit attention when a judge frankly invokes "public policy" instead of relying exclusively on contract doctrine. They appear, for example, when the Illinois appeals court in *Hewitt* explains why enforcement of such agreements promotes rather than undermines the institution of marriage. When a judge casts his opinion in traditional doctrinal terms, using intention, for example, or consideration, then any sensitivity he has to questions of power and fairness must be translated—translated, for example, into a willingness to assume that the parties did intend to enter a relationship of reciprocal obligation or that the woman has provided services that require compensation. Frequently this involves construing the male partner's intentions *as if* he were the concerned and equal partner the law assumes him to be. Again, these devices parallel those used by courts across the range of contract decisions. But only when judges move outside the framework of traditional contract doctrine will they be in a position to grapple with the full range of problems posed by these disputes.

* * *

There are several ways to begin a richer examination of the cohabitation cases. First, we can learn from the truths underlying contract doctrine while rejecting the idea that that doctrine alone can lead us to correct answers. The dichotomies of public and private, manifestation and intent, form and substance, do touch on troubling questions that are central to our understanding of intimate relationships and the role of the state in undermining or supporting them. The problem with doctrinal rhetoric is twofold. First, it recasts our concerns in a way that distances us from our lived experience of them. Second, the resolution of the cases that the application of doctrine purports to secure offers us a false assurance that our concerns can be met—that public can be reconciled with private, manifestation with intent, form with substance.

Once we realize that doctrinal "resolutions" are achieved only by sleight of hand, consideration of the identified dichotomies helps us to explore more fully the cohabitation agreement. What is the nature of this relationship, or what range of cohabitation arrangements precludes us from making general statements about the nature of the relationship? To what extent do these relationships need protection from authority, and to what extent do they require nurturing by authority? To what extent do they reflect the shared expectations of their participants, and to what extent the imposition of terms by one party on another? How can we harbor intimacy within institutions that offer the flexibility to accommodate individual need, while at the same time providing a measure of predictability and stability? What stake does the society have in limiting the forms of association it will recognize? Given our dependence on our social and cultural context, what freedom does any of us have to reimagine the terms of human association?

Study of the play between public and private, objective and subjective, shows us that these same dichotomies organize not only the strictly doctrinal territory of contract interpretation or consideration, but also the broader "policy" issues that are folded into the cases. Questions of judicial competence, for example, turn out to involve precisely the question of whether a private sphere can be marked off from the public sphere. Similarly, whether enforcement of cohabitation agreements is a pro-marriage or an anti-marriage position turns out to depend on questions of intention and power. Even as this analysis illuminates the policy dimension of the cases, it refutes the claim that the addition of policy considerations can cure doctrinal indeterminacy.

If neither doctrine nor the addition of policy can determine how decisionmakers choose outcomes in particular cases, the next question is whether the opinions contain other material that illuminates the decision-making process. The dimension of these cohabitation cases that cries out for investigation is the images they contain of women, and of relationship . . .

I am not claiming that judges decide cohabitation cases on the basis of deeply held notions about women and relationship in the sense that these notions provide a determinate basis for decision. For this to be true, attitudes toward women and relationship would have to be free from contradiction in a way that doctrine and policy are not. I believe instead that these notions involve the same perceived divide between self and other that characterizes doctrine, and are as internally contradictory as any doctrine. My claim, therefore, is only that notions of women and relationship are another dimension of the opinions. These notions influence how judges frame rule-talk and policy-talk; in a world of indeterminacy they provide one more set of variables that may persuade a judge to decide a case one way or another, albeit in ways we cannot predict with any certainty. . . .

One powerful pair of contradictory images of woman paints the female cohabitant as either an angel or a whore. As angel, she ministers to her male partner out of noble emotions of love and self-sacrifice, with no thought of personal gain. It would demean both her services and the spirit in which they were offered to imagine that she expected a return—it would make her a servant. As whore, she lures the man into extravagant promises with the bait of her sexuality—and is appropriately punished for *her* immorality when the court declines to hold her partner to his agreement.

Although the image of the whore is of a woman who at one level is seeking to satiate her own lust, sex—in these cases—is traditionally presented as something women give to men. This is consistent both with the view of woman as angel and with the different image of the whore as someone who trades sex for money. In either event, woman is a provider, not a partner in enjoyment. When a judge invokes this image, he supports the view that sex contaminates the entire agreement, and that the desire for sex is the only reason for the male partner's promises of economic support. If sex were viewed as a mutually satisfying element of the arrangement, it could be readily separated out from the rest of the agreement. In most cases, the woman's career sacrifices and childrearing and homemaking responsibilities would then provide the consideration for the economic support proffered by the man.

Marriage is often presented in the cases as the only way in which men and women can express a continuing commitment to one another. This suggests that when men do not marry women, they intend to avoid all responsibility for them. Women therefore bear the burden of protecting themselves by declining the irregular relationship. At the same time, the institution of marriage as an expression of caring is portrayed as so fragile that only the most unwavering support by the state will guarantee its survival. This could mean that other expressions of caring would entirely supplant marriage without vigilant enforcement of the socially endorsed forms of relationship, although that would be inconsistent with the portrayal of marriage as the only expression of commitment. Alternatively, it could mean that men and women would not choose to enter relationships of caring without pressure from the state.

These nightmarish images have much in common with what other disciplines tell us men think about women and relationship. The conception of women as either angels or whores is identified by Freud,[502] and supported by feminist accounts.[503] The evil power of female sexuality is a recurrent subject of myth and history.[504] The contrast of men who fear relationship as entrapping and women who fear isolation is the subject of Carol Gilligan's work in the psychology of moral development;[505] others have explored the origins of that difference in the context of psychoanalytic theory.[506] Raising these images to the level of consciousness and inquiry therefore seems to me an important aspect of understanding this particular set of cases. It is also a way of stepping beyond the confines of current doctrine and beginning to think about other ways of handling the reciprocal claims cohabitants may make of one another.

EPILOGUE

The stories told by contract doctrine are human stories of power and knowledge. The telling of those stories—like the telling of any story—is, in one sense, an impoverishing exercise: the infinitely rich potential that we call reality is stripped of detail, of all but a few of its aspects. But it is only through this restriction of content that any story has a meaning. In uncovering the way doctrine orders, and thereby creates, represents, and misrepresents reality, I have suggested and criticized the particular meaning created by doctrinal stories, the particular limitations entailed in the telling of those stories.

My critique is in turn a story, which itself creates order and meaning. My story, too, is subject to the charge that it has reduced the richness of contract law and the multiplicity of its concerns to a few basic elements, that it misrepresents as much as it reveals. And, in fact, I do not believe that my story is the only one that can be told about contract doctrine. I insist only that it is *an* important story to tell.

My story reveals the world of contract doctrine to be one in which a comparatively few mediating devices are constantly deployed to displace and defer the otherwise inevitable revelation that public cannot be separated from private, or form from substance, or objective manifestation from subjective intent. The pain of that revelation, and its value, lies in its message that we can neither know nor control the boundary between self and other. Thus, although my story has reduced contract law to these few basic elements, they are elements that merit close scrutiny: they represent our most fundamental concerns. And the type of analysis I suggest can help us to understand and address those concerns.

By telling my story, I also hope to open the way for other stories— new accounts of how the problems of power and knowledge concretely hamper our ability to live with one another in society. My story both asks why those problems are not currently addressed by doctrine and traditional doctrinal analysis, and suggests how they might be. By presenting doctrine as a human effort at world-making, my story focuses fresh attention on those to whom we give the power to shape our world. My story requires that we develop new understandings of our world-makers as we create them, and are in turn created by them. This kind of inquiry, exemplified for me by feminist theory, can help us see that the world portrayed by traditional doctrinal analysis is already not the world we live in, and is certainly not the only possible world for us to live in. And in coming to that realization, we increase our chances of building our world anew.

NOTES

432. 18 Cal. 3d 660, 557 P.2d 106, 134 Cal. Rptr. 815 (1976).

433. 77 Ill. 2d 49, 394 N.E.2d 1204 (1979). The lower appeals court opinion in *Hewitt,* 62 Ill. App. 3d 861, 380 N.E.2d 454 (1978) (reversing dismissal on ground that public policy did not disfavor grant of mutually enforceable property rights to

knowingly unmarried cohabitants in nonmeretricious relationship), provides a perfect counterpoint to its supreme court successor.

442. *Hertzog* v. *Hertzog,* 29 Pa. 465 (1857); see also *Balfour* v. *Balfour,* [1919] 2 K.B. 571.

443. See *Keene* v. *Keene,* 57 Cal. 2d 657, 668, 371 P.2d 329, 336, 21 Cal. Rptr. 593, 600 (1962).

448. *Hewitt,* 77 Ill. 2d at 61, 394 N.E.2d at 1209.

455. See, e.g., *In re Marriage of Cary,* 34 Cal. App. 3d 345, 353, 109 Cal. Rptr. 862, 866 (1973) (court's holding that property should be divided between unmarried couple would not necessarily discourage marriages).

469. *Updeck* v. *Samuel,* 123 Cal. App. 2d 264, 267, 266 P.2d 822, 824 (Dist. Ct. App. 1954) (ending oral contract based on immoral consideration where both parties legally married to other spouses).

472. 122 Cal. App. 3d 500, 176 Cal. Rptr. 130 (Ct. App. 1981).

474. See, e.g., *Hill* v. *Estate of Westbrook,* 95 Cal. App. 2d 599, 603, 213 P.2d 727, 730 (Dist. Ct. App. 1950).

481. *Wisconsin & Mich. Ry. Co.* v. *Powers,* 191 U.S. 379 (1903).

502. S. Freud, "A Special Type of Choice of Object Made by Men," in *The Standard Edition of the Complete Psychological Works of Sigmund Freud,* vol. 7, trans. and ed. J. Strachey (1957); ibid., "On the Universal Tendency to Debasement in the Sphere of Love," p. 179.

503. See, e.g., A. Dworkin, *Woman Hating* (New York: Dutton, 1974).

504. Ibid., especially pp. 31–46, 118–50.

505. C. Gilligan, *In a Different Voice* (Cambridge: Harvard Univ. Press, 1982), pp. 24–63.

506. N. Chodorow, *The Reproduction of Mothering* (Berkeley: Univ. of California Press, 1978).

13

Trashing

Mark Kelman

Here's one account of the technique that we in Critical Legal Studies often use in analyzing legal texts, a technique I call "Trashing": take specific arguments very *seriously* in their own terms; discover they are actually *foolish* ([tragi]-*comic*); and then look for some (external observer's) *order* (*not* the germ of truth) in the internally contradictory, incoherent chaos we've exposed. . . .

Today's "law and economics" sorts have applied cost-benefit analysis to entitlements, purportedly creating a coherent general picture of an apolitical legal method. But, in reality, the analysis is utterly indeterminate: although the analysis purports to establish a rights framework *ex nihilo*, it in fact requires a preexisting rights framework in order to generate concrete results. Further, the analysis is unselfconsciously limited, blinded by a pompous scientism. Here too, however, there is external order: cost-benefit analysis does hold at bay problems about the separation of law and politics and of courts and legislatures that have nagged for centuries. The technique also has enabled reformist liberals to turn the tables on the antiinterventionist right. While the Coase Theorem seems to be intended partly as a plea for a noninterventionist state (because it identifies at least an unreal condition in which state action may have no significant effects), recognizing high transaction costs in manifesting moralisms enabled liberal interventionists to justify pretty much any result they desired.

And here is one account of the most frequently recurring theme in the attacks on our own technique, the more-or-less hysterical counterrevolution against Trashing. We take arguments too seriously; the arguments really aren't so bad after all; there is a germ of truth, a

Excerpted from its original publication in *Stanford Law Review* 36, 1984, by permission of the author and the Stanford Law Review.

kernel of genuine wisdom, embedded in each of them, even if they are, as are all human products, imperfect and therefore subject to smart-alecky mockery. Moreover, it is pointless or irresponsible or infuriating to trash if the ultimate task is political reconstruction; only by comparing Our State (our dad? our team?) with Their State can we (legitimately? as a purely tactical matter?) hope to prod people to a new political commitment. The attack on CLS trashing has a secondary aspect. When we're not "merely" trashing, we switch to uselessly general utopian theorizing. That is, when we are both positive and constructive, we're so vague that it is impossible for anyone to know what concrete steps would satisfy our demands. Thus, we never fit into the "acceptable" category of being both constructive and concrete at the same time.

I'd like first to look reasonably closely at this attack—to treat the typical argument that we are either destructive or vague as yet another text to be trashed. But I have a strong antitrashing streak myself that I have never wanted or tried to hide. What strikes me as most distinctive about Critical Legal Studies, especially in comparison with left academic movements of the past, is its focus on ambiguity, its resolute refusal to see a synthesis in every set of contradictions. We may well feel, at once, a need for agitated utopian hope and more peaceful resignation to an inevitably tragic world; we may simultaneously seek solace in rational expertise/control and a mystical faith that is divorced from a need for exacting answers. Thus, no program satisfies all of our hopes for our work. The next section, is an internal account of the debates on trashing within CLS; while I will, once more, basically align myself with the trashers among us, I do so with more than a modicum of regret that trashing is, above all, simply the best *available* academic posture.

TRASHING ANTITRASHING

Our answer to the accusation that we're some combination of worthless wreckers and hopelessly vague visionaries is hard to pin down, purposefully slithery and evasive (the lure of the guerrilla *image*, updated for those made too pessimistic by the Vietnamese, Cambodians, and Iranians to trust too many actual guerrillas), but it goes something like this First, we don't do what you say we do or at least we don't do it all the time (we are often quite constructive and concrete); second, to the extent that we suffer from the problems you ascribe to us, you do too (although you don't trash arguments, you are generally quite vague and utopian); and third, even if we do something you don't, it's a good thing that we do, for reasons you don't even begin to consider (trashing is good).

CLS Work Is by No Means as Invariably Destructive or Vague and Utopian as Its Critics Seem to Believe

It seems to me important to note what should be an obvious point: the academics and practitioners in CLS are role-restricted actors. Role restriction should certainly be a familiar concept. . . .

Just as the [left] lawyer may frequently act in a role that makes it hard to distinguish his or her work from that of a practitioner with very different political beliefs, so there will be times when a CLS scholar's work is fundamentally indistinguishable from that of colleagues with very different agendas. This confusion is most likely when the CLS academic addresses the "live" policy issues of the day. Of course, we can also adopt roles in which our work looks more "different," but this work is no less *constructive* or *concrete*. At times, for instance, we will, in a more radical mode, advocate particular legal reforms, hoping both to better the short-term position of the reform's beneficiaries *and* to expose the limits of legal reform. This second aim, political education, is perfectly concrete and constructive, even though it is far less relevant to those interested only in whether the reform ought to be enacted to help the beneficiaries. At other times, in our role as purely descriptive academics, hoping to *explain* the legal culture we all live in, we may simply deconstruct arguments in a way that is of no obvious immediate help whatsoever to those trying to pick and choose particular institutions they might find most desirable, except insofar as they are freed to evaluate their choices differently when their current cultural blinders are labeled, exposed, and, perhaps as a result, partly lifted.

With the preliminary points about role restriction in mind, let's take a quick survey of CLS work done in various roles. CLS academics often address the typical legal-political controversies between liberals and conservatives, usually, though not always, tending to argue for relatively traditional liberal positions, usually in reasonably traditional ways. For instance, academics who have associated themselves with CLS have used traditional neoclassical economic analysis to question the *a priori* conservative assumption that housing code enforcement or compulsory (nonwaivable) warranties will either be of no moment to or detrimental to their purported beneficiaries,[14] offered arguments against replacing the income tax with an almost inevitably less redistributive consumption tax,[15] been wary of efforts to truncate the income tax base in ways that would contravene progressivity;[16] defended affirmative action programs;[17] . . . and pressed for state reforms of work rules and childcare programs that would better permit working mothers to maintain their careers.[20]

As "policy analysts" with a concern for redefining the proper scope of "live" legal and political issues, CLS people have been able to connect inevitably partial legal reform efforts with more radical consciousness-raising pro' ims. Thus, some of our proposals have both met short-term meliorist goals *and* expanded our understanding that the meliorist programs are limited—that there are problems that the legal remedies will not address. Perhaps most notable among these efforts has been the work of feminist lawyers/academics in developing legal theories of sexual harassment,[22] which were designed not only to reform practice so as to enable women to use state power to squelch one of the most extreme forms of exploitation (quid pro quo sex-for-advancement) and also to trigger collective exploration into the more general issue of sexual objectification as the form of the expropriation of female sexuality. . . .

CLS academics have proposed a number of other concrete reform packages that would serve both to bolster partially the positions of particular unnecessarily injured parties and to help focus attention on the structural deficiencies of legal/social relations as currently constituted. For instance, CLS writers have produced proposals . . . to expand the rights of workers to strike over mid-term grievances, instead of relying on union stewardship of collective bargaining;[27] to expand municipal powers so as to enable publicly established productive institutions to flourish;[28] and to reformulate our ideas about the meaning of informed consent in the medical area.[29]

At other times, though, we abandon *legal, state-focused* reform without abandoning what we think of as politics. In this role, we naturally have little advice to give judges or legislators or administrators regarding the policy questions that might conceivably confront them. . . .

Finally, since many CLS people are academics, it is appropriate to recall that they are often engaged *as* academics in the perfectly concrete and constructive enterprise of trying to understand human behavior, whether or not that understanding will directly help us reformulate legal practice. . . .

Mainstream Legal Thought Is Vague and Utopian, Not Concrete

To listen to the critics of CLS, one might forget oneself for a moment and imagine that the typical mainstream legal arguments to which we are routinely exposed are concrete, detailed, empirically grounded justifications for the social/legal system around us or for the particular alteration of a particular rule that the author is urging. How droll.

Let me divide the claims of mainstreamers into two sorts: micro claims—arguments for particular institutional forms or rules (e.g., for or against enforcing liquidated damage clauses, for or against allowing criminal procedure rules to be applied prospectively, for or against respecting the state sovereign's right to exemption from

federal wage or retirement rule regulations) and macro claims—
arguments for some grand cent⁓ꞏ   ꝛr conservative world view (generally a variant of the notion that because people are a self-interested lot
with widely varying productive capabilities, all attempts to make the
world a radically better place will fail dismally). I would argue that the
micro claims are inevitably grounded in the emptiest generalities
imaginable, except arguably when they are grounded in economic
theory. But in that case they are grounded in what should be recognized as openly unempirical utopian speculation about the nature of
self-interest and the harmonizing effects of efficient backdrop entitlement rules and markets. Claims of the macro sort could be grounded
in one of two sorts of conservative functionalism—sociobiology or
microeconomics—or in detailed historical study. Because I cannot
imagine that any reasonably self-critical mainstreamer would argue
that there have been any trenchant uses of sociobiology, microeco-
nomics-as-social-theory, or historical studies of failed reform or revolutionary efforts by legal scholars that would justify the assertion that
the prevailing mainstream anti-Utopianism is any more or less an
article of faith or assertion than the left Utopianism of the CLS, I will
focus on the micro claims.

LAW AND ECONOMICS AS UTOPIAN THOUGHT

At its core, economics gives us only a *vision* of human fulfillment,
not a "scientific" or richly textured descriptive account of actual
fulfillment. Economists simply *assume* that observed behavior in fact
maximizes self-interest. They do not explain in any serious way why
we should believe that to be the case, especially in light of the fact that
one can observe common behavior that one might well describe as
unfulfilling. But I want to ignore the core for now. For even if we
believed with Posner that the goal of the law was to maximize wealth
(and could understand what he might mean by such a blatantly empty
concept), the fact remains that the typical analysis of the relationship
between particular rules and wealth-maximizing ends has been almost entirely devoid of real world references. Law-and-economics
studies of private law rules have not actually analyzed the concrete
implications of rule choices on particular occasions, pretensions of
policy relevance to the contrary. Instead, they have again and again
simply derived apologies for existing arrangements from a highly
general and theoretical economic vision. . . .

STRANGE INTERLUDE: FORMALISM, LEGAL PROCESS, AND HUNCHES

I could, of course, discuss seriously the other noneconomic garden
variety of legal academic "policy analysis": the residual formalism in
nominally post-Realist legal thought. Or I could try, in a perfectly
somber fashion, to find some argument worth destroying in the
standard public law side of the Legal Process school, which posits

(quite unfathomably) a strong relationship between certain more-or-less accidental and/or trivial American institutional developments (e.g., federalism, "balance of powers" between the branches of government, a relatively aggressive court with the power to squelch legislative and executive actions) and more general liberal ideals of personal autonomy and the Rule of Law (political openness and experimentation coupled with stability and competent administration). The protection of certain significant processes is supposed to have some content or bite in preserving cultural virtues; attempts to trample over these processes lead to some variant or other of unpleasantness or social chaos. I could even attempt to catalogue the out-of-thin-air empirical assertions routinely made by conventional law teachers in "justifying" some existing rule or institution or pet legal reform proposal. For example, I might subdivide these "empirical" hunches into (a) those that are arguably falsifiable, assuming that we can still imagine running some elaborate tests and experiments that we know perfectly well can never actually be run (e.g., hunches about the purported inability of jurors to properly weigh the probative value of hearsay evidence); and (b) those that, while *sounding* descriptive or empirical, refer fairly openly to concepts with no discernible external reference whatsoever (e.g., a contract may not be "mutually beneficial" to the contracting parties when there is "unequal bargaining power").

I *could* take all this seriously (Tricky Dick, you were so right), but it would be wrong, that's for sure. Arguing that standard legal argument is vague, nonempirical, windbag rhetoric is just not worth it. . . .

Trashing Is Good

There are any number of reasons why CLS people might be right to debunk ordinary legal argument, even if they offered no well-grounded proposals for institutional change (as is not the case) while others routinely made detailed, concrete arguments for particular institutions (as is not the case).[68] I want to focus, though, on only two.

TRASHING AS AN ANTI-HIERARCHICAL STRATEGY
WITHIN THE LAW SCHOOLS

Many of us have been interested in understanding power in its most local manifestations ("micropractices"); for me, trashing is above all a technique of seeing (and undermining) illegitimate power in the most comprehensible and immediate institutions I see—the law schools where I've studied and worked.

Let me try to get at this point by starting with a list of typical left/idealist CLS-style propositions about the instrumental significance of coherent doctrine. The first proposition is the most localized, the second is more global, and the third is more global still.

1. The first argument is that the elegance and coherence of legal

argument is an issue primarily to its full-time producers—legal academics—and that attempts to discredit or trash these arguments are predominantly a threat to the producers' prestige. Most of the arguments that law professors make are not only nonsensical according to some obscure and unreachable criteria of Universal Validity, but they are also patently unstable babble. The shakiness of the argumentative structure is, quite remarkably, readily elucidated. All the fundamental, rhetorically necessary distinctions collapse at a feather's touch—distinctions between substance and process, voluntary and involuntary action, public and private, legislative and adjudicative. Those who routinely use these distinctions "know" of their vulnerability, at least in the limited sense of being able to recognize it without being forced to look at the world in radically different ways. Law professors are, in fact, a kiss away from panic at every serious, self-conscious moment in which they don't have a bunch of overawed students to kick around.

At the same time, the prestige of law professors—for instance, their ability to inspire generally self-assured senior partners at ritzy law firms to tell remarkably heartfelt, awestruck rite-of-passage stories when these partners gather for reunions thirty years after the first shock—is intimately connected to their (purported) capacity to make arguments (both legal and social/political) that seem not only better than nonsensical but seem even downright wise.

This prestige, however, may be based on an illusory hierarchical legitimacy. The stability of hierarchical divisions—the social acceptance of inequality—is generally premised on purported distinctions in capacity to produce. Our well-honed ability to distinguish easily and objectively between two people in different status slots (teacher vs. student, elite professor vs. nonelite professor, lawyer vs. layman) will make hierarchies appear legitimate or inevitable, even when we are (or could be made to be) at least dimly aware that the distinctions, though clearly *discernible*, are *irrelevant*. (A "great" law professor may discuss affirmative action with an obvious elegance that most laymen clearly lack. But whether he has more insight into the substantive issues at stake or privileged access to the "right" answers is quite another question.)

2. While the greatest desire of the producers of "good rhetoric" may be that people think their rhetoric good so that such producers can stay atop some pyramid, producers of apology also have a reasonably, perhaps unusually, strong belief that *general* status differentials are justified at a general level, and that legal arguments are, in essence, about desert, that is, whether benefits are merited or punishments deserved. Thus, the acceptability of "good arguments" is significant to the professional producers of apology in justifying significant social institutions. Criminal law professors, for instance, typically believe it is important that those we label criminals are "blameworthy"

and believe that they have "proven" this in a fairly elaborate and technical way. Other professional functionaries who hold positions in which they purvey civic myth—judges, teachers, editorial writers, clergymen—also find it reasonably important to believe that the legal system is well-grounded, that the particular legally based disabilities and privileges they dimly perceive to frame one's social position are distributed according to an orderly scheme that has been honed in some high-quality debate.

3. Finally, relatively well-off citizens generally are more prone to be self-righteous and immune from crises of conscience because they sense that people are generally treated fairly—that, for both better or worse, people in this country pretty much get what they deserve. To a discernible degree, the idea that legal rules of the most general form are defensible and are being defended (somewhere) by experts bolsters this belief. . . . Even citizens who are badly off are a bit more prone to accept rather passively their bad lot as reasonable if it seems to flow from a legal system that is not obviously personally focused on abusive, since they've just gotten—for better and worse—what they were "entitled to" according to legitimate rules.

We in CLS are prone to defend our focus on debunking rhetoric against both mainstream "policy analysts" and traditional marxists who believe in the vital significance of the material base (and the corresponding triviality of cultural artifacts like legal argument, if not bottom-line case results) by referring to the more global of these propositions. But my point here is that I am most willing to defend debunking at the local level, in part because I am decreasingly certain of each proposition as one goes down the list (from local to global): In fact, by the time one reaches the third proposition, I am currently agnostic as to the truth of the assertion and even as to how one could hope ever to have much of an opinion about its truth, although I feel certain it would be an important proposition if it were indeed valid. From my vantage point, which is the vantage of "micropractices," the primary thrust of the CLS enterprise at an academic level should be to explore, in a very concrete, particular setting, the vital general point that status hierarchies are founded, at least in significant part, on sham distinctions.

We are not just trying to "prove" an abstract or academic point about the phoniness of hierarchy. (Nor do we really believe that the debunking of technical rhetoric can fully and adequately demonstrate the contingent, potentially unstable position of rhetoric's producers and guardians.) . . . We are also engaged in an *active*, transformative anarcho-syndicalist political project, and it is only the project's success that serves as real proof of egalitarian possibilities. At the *workplace* level, debunking is one part of an explicit effort to level, to reintegrate the communities we live in along explicitly egalitarian lines rather than along the rationalized hierarchical lines that currently integrate them. We are saying: Here's what your teacher did (at you, to you) in contracts or torts. Here's what it was really about. Stripped of the mumbo-jumbo, here's a set of problems we *all* face, as equals in dealing with work, with politics, and with the world.

If there is a problem with this project, it is that the techniques of mystification have become so complex that we demystifiers may often end up sounding at least as highfalutin', technical, and ritzy as the people we critique. The fear is that there is a less-than-voluntary CLS elitism, parasitic on the dominant legal culture's elitism: those who can deconstruct the most elaborate of the traditional arguments, those who resimplify and politicize the most obscurred disputes, are lionized precisely like the original obscurantists. The problem is within as well as outside us; too few are immune to the charms of status and prestige.

Trashing May Destabilize Pervasive Complacency-inducing Rationalizations

One goal, if not an inevitable effect, of trashing is to destabilize a variety of theoretical world views (and thus, one would hope, related commonsense world views) that imply the beneficence or inexorability of social life as we see it. Of course, asserting that there must be a *causal* connection between the high-level apologetics of the intelligentsia and the everyday mediating "political" ideals that help us organize and make sense of daily interactions would be patently ridiculous. But one can discern, without straining credulity, at least a close family resemblance between elaborate, mandarin apologetics and the more ordinary, complacency-inducing, "commonsensical" bits of wisdom.

Events cannot be perceived without the mediation of theory. As an abstract, bookish, epistemological proposition, this observation is routine, unbelievably boring, and so acceptable as to be meaningless. Here's the punch, though—the sort of thing we think we really *mean* when we gush on about paradigms or theory-impregnated observations or antipositivist hermeneutic views of knowledge: There's a male boss and a female secretary, and he makes sexual remarks and touches her a lot; she voices some (slightly guilty, nervous) complaints to a bunch of the other women workers (or just her best friends), and maybe she said "Thank you" after her new hairdo was complimented, and it sounded like she was really touched that such changes were noticed, etc., etc., etc. Whether all this adds up to something like sexual harassment—more concretely, whether it adds up to something one would bother to notice, talk about, organize about, or sue about—depends in some significant degree on whether the woman's failure to leave the office means the workplace is okay. Now this idea—that "it must not bother her that much or why does she take it?"—is just an everyday, commonsense filtering mechanism, but there are corresponding, far more complex versions of much the same idea in mandarin thought. The academic theory may, in the overtly right-wing law and economics camp, be a theory of labor market perfection (so that, at a minimum, workers are harassed only to the extent they are compensated for it). Or the academic theory may draw on traditional notions of implied consent to all conditions imposed in the private sphere, notions which reached their zenith in the expansive doctrine of assumption of risk.

Because the causal link between theory and commonsense is, at best, obscure, one can hardly know for sure whether even the most successful assault on high theory will ever disturb those who organize the world around the usual homilies; criticizing the assumptions behind the more *elaborate* justifications for the status quo is not obviously fruitful. The belief that "it must not bother her so much or why does she take it?" may not truly depend on the stability of the more complex models that assert much the same thing. Complacency may survive because it is desired in itself, just as hierarchy may not depend on any of its particular justifications. Discovering that a routine sense of complacency, when fully articulated, rests on inde-fensible premises may not ultimately free us from that complacency. But it surely is *not* the case that the full articulations of complacency are *removed* from daily life; they are not *totally* isolated and irrelevant. Thus, we argue in law reviews that one has to draw an indefensibly bright line between public and private life to justify the notion that only "state" institutions can exercise true coercive powers. We argue that the labor market equilibrium depends upon the permissibility of harassment and cannot be ascertained without regard to the underly-ing structure of legal rights; we also note, in response to more typical law and economics sorts, that the level of what arguably constitutes harassment will depend upon whether women initially are entitled to be free from unwanted sexual attention; and we note that the ques-tion of whether the sexual attention is desired is not a straightforward question, given the complexity of desire. But what we are really saying, in these particular contexts, is don't be too quick to accept that all pain is chosen.

Thus, much of the "trashing" work within CLS is designed to counter beliefs (which appear quite clearly in daily life) that the world is running smoothly: for example, that we have intellectually stable practices of blaming wrongdoers, or can rely on adherence to rule-like legality to govern social interaction. The impetus for collective transformation is in part the *perception* that the world is excessively imperfect; high-level liberal ideology corresponds to, even if it may not cause, "commonsense" organizations of the perceptions of daily life that block the recognition of imperfection.

ANTITRASHING WITHIN CLS

The Matrix: A Typology of Prototypical Academic CLS Stances

	Utopian/Forward-Looking	Descriptive/Analytical/Backward-Regarding
Intellectual	1. Empirical studies of progressive communities or experiments 2. Grand philosophical or social/theoretical: specification of the content of the better state.	3. Formal empirical work; law & society studies of "law in action." 4. Social/theoretical accounts of broad social practices (e.g., rule of law; informalism and monopoly capitalism). 5. *Micropractice-oriented highly theoretical analyses of the self-deceiving, mystifying practices of particular actors, assumed to be important enough to study though by no means asserted to be representative of a place, time, or class.*
Non- or Anti-Intellectual	7. *Jokes, costumes, snippets.*	6. *Thick description, exemplary anecdotes, casual empiricism.*

Note: Those academic postures that are listed in italics are those I associate with what the Critical Legal Studies movement labels internally as "trashing"; I see these postures as most likely to succeed at this time.

Commentary: A Trasher's Reluctant Critique of the Alternatives

Within CLS, we self-proclaimed trashers are condemned, on what might be best characterized as aesthetic grounds, as an antiintellectual cultural affront or, more politically/instrumentally, as wasting our residual unbanished intellectual gifts on the useless and compulsive ordering of a triviality—the justificatory practices of a bunch of uninteresting, politically peripheral, windbag rhetoricians. It is also true that our utopian "work" has been strictly anti- or nonintellectual. And it is true that our descriptive work has partaken neither of formal, quantitative empirical accounts of the "law in action" (exhaustive descriptions of the nitty-gritty of daily social life) nor of grand social theoretical accounts of megatrends (Legality, Formality, or the Welfare State). Rather, our work tends either to consist of wholly impressionistic, nonacademic descriptions of what we consider revealing snippets of everyday interactions (an empiricism, of sorts, but one too casual to satisfy self-identified Empiricists) or, when we are most obviously orderly and intellectual, to deal with legal rules or doctrines that are very limited in scope. Surely the objects of our studies of justificatory micropractices are not *utterly* random, but we make little *systematic* attempt to locate precisely our objects of study, whether as opinion leaders who affect others, fair representatives of a (powerful or not) class, or spokespeople for an epoch. . . .

Empirical Work (with a particular focus on utopian empiricism)

I would literally *love* to be able to do empirical utopian work, and I am reasonably sure that *none* of us trashers has fully abandoned the following positivist/adolescent academic fantasy. Trekking about, toting lab coat, clipboard, and stopwatch, we discover an isolated community, culturally enough like our own for our findings not to be dismissed as more curious than relevant. In this community, work is organized nonhierarchically, rough equality of material reward prevails, there are few discernible race or gender distinctions in the assignment of those tasks that remain differentiated, etc., etc., etc. The community is clearly materially prosperous, its citizens all bouncy and cheerful, and the regime generally stable. Further, there are no brainwashers or hypnotic drug peddlers about that would make us wary of *Brave New World*-style, high-tech anti-Utopias. Nearby, we find two communities that once functioned just like our recently discovered little gem but that somehow got swallowed up in either a corporate capitalist or state socialist expansionist push. In the "Americanized" community, we see dire poverty among a violent, barely socialized subproletariat, rampant drug and alcohol abuse, constant low-level, intrafamily violence among the alienated proletarian workforce, and a self-defeating materialism among those deemed most successful. In the "Soviet" community, we see a visible collapse of production, cynically fake public-spirited rhetoric coupled with staggeringly corrupt self-serving practice, and near-total repression of cultural diversity.

We have, of course, no such beacons to study nor paradises to dissect. (Perhaps that fact *proves* that life on this earth is inevitably miserable. Consequently, we should not be disappointed with our pitiful capacity to study but should instead renounce the romantic delusion of ever finding anything particularly good to study. But I don't think there's any intellectually compelling reason to jump to that conclusion: only [bad socio]biology is destiny.) And once one tries to study the more imperfect, actual communities we see, one realizes that the task can never be done in such a way as to truly satisfy a full-blown vision of the keys to human fulfillment. The technical problems are just too great.

The problem of weighting social welfare functions alone—disregarding the deep normative conflicts, the difficulty of labeling even any single life as well-lived—would be insuperable. The United States, for instance, is hardly one political community.

Even the much less ambitious attempt to understand the effects of some isolated institutional shift is, I fear, further beyond our technical skills than we like to believe. Although I am highly sympathetic to the *aims* of the "Law and Society" people, I can't honestly say I've ever read anything in the Law and Society literature that persuaded me beyond something far less demanding than a reasonable doubt that they really knew what went on out there. I can't give a detailed critique of the dozens of articles in, say, the *Law and Society Review*, but I should give a few *typical* reactions to some of the focused, *descriptive* formal empirical pieces.

I think no one would accuse me of attacking an inferior product if I quibble with Whitford and Grau's generally superior study of self-help repossession in Wisconsin. The fact is, though, that the authors can't even begin to tell us whether interest rates rose as a result of the judicialization of repossession.[106] Nor can we tell whether more wholly informal resolutions (work-outs) of customer disputes with lenders occurred after the legislation so that self-help repossession was not as fully supplanted by formal adjudication as the legislation's advocates might have intended. To the extent that the data are convincing, they seem to show a trend toward work-outs in the first year after the legislation that promptly disappeared in the second year. . . .

The most important problem in realizing my own yearning for good utopian empiricism, though, may well be theoretical rather than practical. I'm just not convinced it really leads anywhere if one is trying to think about the radical transformation of daily social life. The standard vision of empirical utopian work is not just a vision of *academic procedure*, a vision of what one ought to write about if one is to be "useful" to those with political ideals, but a particular substantive path to Utopia. . . .

Nor does a descriptive empiricism combined with utopianism seem more promising than the vision of generalizing from little empirical studies. Traditional marxists implicitly sought to find a quasi-utopian logic immanent in a careful empirical *description* of current conditions and "laws of historical motion." While they always condemned the full specification of communist society as a nonscientific, bourgeois, sentimentalist venture (in part on the "scientific" supposition that communist society was posthistorical, that is, beyond the domain of determinism), one could, in fact, suspect a good deal about the nature of such a society simply by extending the analysis of capitalism's breakdown. (Certain forms of exploitation and business cycle crises, for instance, would disappear.) But Marx's "laws" of motion all seem to me either undeniably wrong (falling profit rate, the decline of the petit bourgeoisie) and/or too vaguely specified to make sense of. I see too little reason to believe either that history *has* a significantly predetermined teleological path, particularly a progressively bettering one, or that we could discern such a path if it did exist, to believe that the precise nature of our better tomorrows can be understood by looking more carefully at the hands we've already been dealt.

Philosophical/Social Theoretical Utopian Work

The critique that we trashers do too little empirical utopian work seems to be fundamentally an engineer's complaint. Big deal, so everybody wants unalienated, joyful, cute-as-a-button lives; the *real* question is, can you get us from here to there without going over the actual retail price? The philosopher/social theorist's complaint, on the other hand, is that we ought to specify far better what it is that everybody supposedly wants, in case being cute as a button is not everyone's idea of a good time.

Within CLS, there are certainly anti-trashers who have engaged in the enterprise of utopian specification, an enterprise that is both solemn in tone and well rooted in high culture. Though I will take examples from two particular people for argumentative convenience, every single one of us has made moves exactly like those I am attributing to Gabel and Unger.

The content of Peter Gabel's ideal is so elusive as to be nondiscernible. He says things like "The project is to realize the unalienated relatedness that is immanent within our alienated situation."[116] But I see too few concrete references to lived experience in this "specification" to know if he is actually describing a blissful state-of-mind or a small household appliance. To the extent that one can discern content, the perils of tautology loom: If what we seek is simply "human fulfillment," the group can quickly adjourn, both unanimous and groggy. Furthermore, Peter's technique seems almost cruelly ironic, given that his primary critique of "mainstream" judicial thought is that it lacks concreteness—that by conceiving of the parties to a dispute as idealized role-players in a "fact situation" (for instance, "buyers" and "sellers" in a breach of contract suit assumed to be acting in accord with idealized, social expectations of such actors), it elevates their abstract characteristics. But Peter's "real" characters, lurking behind the juridical abstractions, feel at least as abstract and lifeless to me. My mind goes utterly blank when I try to picture Peter's characters glimpsing liberation by way of unalienated relatedness.

Roberto Unger's early utopian speculations strike me as more concrete, but they seem affirmatively misleading. I read the latter part of *Knowledge and Politics* as posing the problem of discerning moral truth (separate either from believing in false Platonic objectivism or ungrounded subjective preference assertion) as *the* fundamental human problem and correlatively as picturing Utopia as the neighborhood in which we could discern moral truth through some combination of nondominative discourse with our fellow citizens and sensitivity to divine revelation. But why did I ever believe that *a*, let alone *the,* fundamental feature of Utopia was its moral lucidity? Once again, I suspect that much of the plausibility of the utopian account is its pedigree: because Unger was talking about the sorts of issues one always talks about when "doing social theory," it is extremely hard to force oneself to focus on the more relevant issue of whether or not Unger is talking about anything one discerns as "society."

As I see it, then, theoretical utopian writing is either empty or puzzling. But I think that every trasher within CLS has at least *tried* utopian specification. I strongly suspect that we would all be far less capable of maintaining our political commitments if we hadn't. But that puts me, a more-or-less trasher, skeptical of grand theory, in a paradoxical position. Is philosophy, like mumps, an affliction which it is perversely good to get early on but bad to get once one has grown up?

There are surely times in our lives and stages in political movements when it is essential to learn what Marx thought would become of the division of labor. Similarly, if I had not studied all the formal arguments about equality and argued with interest and ferocity about when it was permissible or impermissible to tolerate distinctions in material rewards, I doubt I would *perceive* hierarchical relationships, like those between teachers and students, as I do today. The trasher's counterclaim is simply that there are also times when it is imperative to stop incessantly *repeating.* To continue *now* to try to specify what a "reasonable commitment to equality" does and does not entail would ensnare me in a numbing recitation of internally referential rhetorical ploys, eternally responding to good old argument *X* with good old argument *Y*.

Constructing careful lists of one's enemies' rhetorical strategies calls on all one's part learning of theory. Without Weber and Freud and Marx, for example, surely no one I know would ever have thought of Apology. So, too, does the most impressive and influential work of trashing, the first part of Unger's *Knowledge and Politics,* result from a careful rethinking and reintegration of past social/theoretical efforts. Because subsequent deconstructive works within CLS are incredibly indebted to Unger both for his particular substantive insights into liberal theory and his method of "total criticism," the world *we* see has been greatly clarified by the systematic social theorists from whom we now partly distance ourselves. But the actual detailed content of our deconstructive agenda, our lists of others' ploys, is not as immediately accessible, not just another rehash of a familiar framework. It requires far more liberatory, creative energy than one more recitation of the social theory that may well have actually created it.

The problem with rejecting Peter's empty slogans or Roberto's puzzling ones, even if it "feels" more creative and liberating to break away from a world of slogan and counterslogan, is that we may readily become passive unless we try (pretend?) to specify goals. It is passivating enough to recognize that one flunks the strongest engineer's test, that one can't draw a road map to our destination; but if we can't even talk coherently about what our destination looks like . . . The danger may be inertia and/or complacency. Trashers presumably assume that the status quo is dominantly stabilized by *rationalization*. Take the ground out and we're all in some sort of potentially transformative free float. But the status quo could just as well be stabilized by *resignation*. If that's the case, the more ground that's undercut, the less reason there is to be anything but cynical and resigned.

I have two very tentative and, in my mind, obviously inadequate responses to this criticism: (a) I never really claimed to be a good organizer anyway; in fact, I suspect that I'm a lousy one. I actually believe that the crudest Marxist sociology can adequately account for that: I am an isolated bourgeois academic, removed from daily struggles, etc., etc. (b) If it really is true that political action falters unless it is more-or-less obviously grounded in grandiose (and false)' First Theorems, then I'm not at all sure I really want to be political. It may be that you do painful but morally exalted dirty work with more than ordinary fervor if you have big beliefs that purport to tell you both what's going on and what you ought to do. But this sort of deceptive belief seems to me so hard to sustain that radicals who ostensibly believe it will say it out loud only in safe groups of other believers, and even then, I suspect, each individual secretly thinks he or she is talking mumbo-jumbo. I suppose I sense that when we claim to be squarely in favor of "unalienated relatedness" or against the opposition of reason and desire, we hope only our friends are listening, and they not too closely. Still, it seems true that people have been far more willing to die (and kill) for Nation, against Infidels, against Westernization, etc., etc., than for Critical Theory. To quote innumerable law professors, though, "Which way does that cut?"

NOTES

14. See Duncan Kennedy, "Distributive and Paternalist Motives in Contract and Tort Law, with Special Reference to Compulsory Terms and Unequal Bargaining Power," *Maryland Law Review* 41 (1982): 563, 599–602, 604–14, 655–58.

15. See Mark Kelman, "Time Preference and Tax Equity," *Stanford Law Review* 35 (1983): 649.

16. See Thomas L. Heller, "The Importance of Normative Decisionmaking: The Limitations of Legal Economics as a Basis for Liberal Jurisprudence—as Illustrated by the Regulation of Vacation Home Development," *Wisconsin Law Review* (1976): 385, 421–38 (urging the abolition of the mortgage interest deduction for second homes); Mark Kelman, "Personal Deductions Revisited: Why They Fit Poorly in an 'Ideal' Income Tax and Why They Fit Worse in a Far from Ideal World," *Stanford Law Review* 31 (1979): 831 (arguing against the medical and charitable contributions deduction).

17. See, e.g., Derrick A. Bell, "In Defense of Minority Admissions Programs: A Response to Professor Graglia," *Univ. of Pennsylvania Law Review* 119 (1970): 364.

20. See Mary J. Frug, "Securing Job Equality for Women: Labor Market Hostility to Working Mothers," *Boston Univ. Law Review* 59 (1979): 55, 94–103.

22. See C. MacKinnon, *Sexual Harassment of Working Women: A Case Study of Sex Discrimination* (New Haven: Yale Univ. Press, 1979); idem, Book Review, *Stanford Law Review* 34 (1982): 703, 705.

27. See, e.g., Karl Klare, "Critical Theory and Labor Relations Law," in *The Politics of Law: A Progressive Critique*, ed. D. Kairys (New York: Pantheon Press, 1982) pp. 65, 78–80.

28. See Gerald E. Frug, "The City as a Legal Concept," *Harvard Law Review* 93 (1980): 1057, 1127–28, 1150.

29. See Rand E. Rosenblatt, "Health Care, Markets and Democratic Values," *Vanderbilt Law Review* 34 (1981): 1067, 1094–1100.

68. For a fuller exposition of certain defenses of "trashing," see Alan D. Freeman, "Truth and Mystification in Legal Scholarship," *Yale Law Journal* 90 (1981): 1229. Freeman's defenses of trashing include the following: It is "fun"; we gain the greatest amount of insight into our values not by expounding on them but by stepping back from them (which we do in trying to undermine them); and we cannot engage in utopian speculation until we stop referring all of our practices to the justifications to which we've become overly accustomed. My decision to defend trashing affirmatively on the particular grounds that I do in the text is based in significant part on the fact that I have little to add to what Freeman says about the issues he addresses.

106. William C. Whitford and Harold Laufer, "The Impact of Denying Self-help Repossession of Automobiles: A Case Study of the Wisconsin Consumer Act," *Wisconsin Law Review* (1975): 607, at 635: "it seems reasonable to suppose that rates on indirect loans have increased more dramatically for these borrowers than for others. We emphasize, however, that we have no direct evidence of the latter phenomenon."

116. Peter Gabel and Duncan Kennedy, "Roll Over Beethoven," *Stanford Law Review* 36 (1981): 1.

PART V

On Ideology

A crucial plank in the Critical platform is the need to appreciate the operation of law as ideology or as a particular mode of consciousness. CLS writers go beyond the marxist notion of ideology as "false consciousness"—that an intellectual veil that presently covers social life must be stripped away so as to permit people to comprehend the true and enslaving nature of social reality. Instead, CLS insists that ideology is as much a lived relation in the world as a detached filter for viewing that world; law does not so much falsely describe the world, as inscribes it with its own image. Law and legal consciousness are constitutive features of social life and change. The challenge is to reveal the interests that are identified with universal claims, to uncover the processes by which contradictions are denied and the status quo presented as a natural, rather than contingent, state of affairs, and to explore other ways of thinking about and acting in the world as a prelude to changing it.

Focusing on the judicial treatment of the epochal Wagner Act, Karl Klare investigates the complex relation between the industrial crucible of competing social forces and the judicial forum of legal interpretation. He relates a sorry tale of lost judicial opportunity. In its efforts to give political substance to the statutory scheme, the judiciary established a powerful mode of legal consciousness and reinforced the contradictory relations of modern industrial society. Frances Olsen explores the ways in which the opposed institutions of market and family with their intrinsic values have pervaded our attempts to come to terms with and change our personal and social existence. Because they have failed to recognize fully the central nature of this dichotomy, reform methods to improve women's lives have been trapped within a limiting set of alternatives and have produced mixed results. After documenting these traditional strategies for change, she outlines a different way of thinking about the problem and develops a

227

vision of human relations that transcends the constraints of traditional consciousness. In his essay, Richard Abel pursues the manifold and complex relations between the industrial economy and the compensation of accident victims. Strongly influenced by neo-marxist theory, he reveals how people are treated as another commodified variable in the production-consumption equation. In place of the dehumanizing effects of existing law, Abel suggests a socialist approach that offers a more integrated and person-centered response to risk and misfortune.

14

Judicial Deradicalization of the Wagner Act and the Origins of Modern Legal Consciousness, 1937–1941

Karl E. Klare

. . . .

The Wagner Act and the rise of organized labor unquestionably effected profound changes in the American political economy. Collective bargaining became fairly widespread, unions attained a significant role in the partisan political system, the labor market was rationalized in certain important ways, many people improved their standard of living and job security, and millions of workers experienced a new sense of participation and dignity.

Nevertheless, at the beginning of labor's New Deal, many employers feared that the Act would lead to state control of business and compulsory arbitration of the terms and conditions of employment, if not a usurpation of the prerogatives of private property ownership itself. These fears proved to be exaggerated, however, for whatever its achievements, the Act did not produce a fundamental transformation of the premises and institutions of capitalist society. True, private ownership was burdened by state regulation that allowed most workers the right to organize and bargain collectively. But state regulation is characteristic of advanced capitalism; rather than radically revising property relations or the social distribution of power, it protects them. Likewise, although workers in unionized industries generally enjoy a higher standard of living and more security now than did most workers a generation ago, the Act did little to enhance their decision-making role regarding the use of society's means of production, the

Excerpted from its original publication in *Minnesota Law Review* 62, 1978, by permission of the author and the Minnesota Law Review. © 1978 by Karl E. Klare.

organization of the work-process, and other decisions that affect their industrial lives. Moreover, New Deal reform appears to have fostered the co-optation of the workers' movement and, with the exception of certain periods such as the post-World War II strike wave, a diminution of labor's combativeness. Indeed, it has been argued that collective bargaining has become an institutional structure not for expressing workers' needs and aspirations but for controlling and disciplining the labor force and rationalizing the labor market. One need not accept these claims fully to recognize that, since World War II, organized labor has become more integrated into the economic system of advanced capitalism, progressively more dependent on its erstwhile corporate adversaries, and largely conventional in the political arena.

How this transformation of the labor movement took place is the broad underlying question motivating this essay. Obviously many processes were at work—political, social, economic, and cultural. I will make no attempt to canvass them here. I will focus only on what was contributed to the deradicalization and incorporation of the working class by developments within the relatively autonomous dimension of legal consciousness, legal institutions, and legal practice, as revealed in the Supreme Court's early Wagner Act decisions.[11] I do not argue that there is a direct causal relationship between the Supreme Court's decisions and the integration of the working class into the postwar social order. But those decisions did have two more indirect consequences worth noting. First, they provided the beginnings of the conceptual integration of the working class by laying the intellectual groundwork upon which were later erected the prevailing political theories of the postwar period, which in turn have in significant measure been internalized by and become the self-conception of the leadership of the labor movement.[12] Second, in the process of adopting some and foreclosing other paths of doctrinal development under the relatively general terms of the Act, the Court began to elaborate the boundaries of "legitimate" labor activity. This process not only had some immediate political consequences in the 1930s but its ultimate, more enduring, significance was the creation of the rudiments of what later became an increasingly formalized and regulated institutional structure for the state administration of the class struggle.

It is not suggested that the Supreme Court engaged in a plot or conspiracy to defeat or co-opt the labor movement, nor do I think that the Court can adequately be understood as an instrument of particular economic interests.[13] I emphatically reject any such reductionism or determinism. That the Court did so much to guide the long-run development of the labor movement into domesticated channels and, indeed, to impede workers' interests is, in fact, ironic precisely because it was so often attacked by contemporaries as overly friendly to labor. Many decisions of the prewar period were intended to be, and were then understood as, tremendous victories for organized labor. But these prolabor victories contained the seeds of long-term defeats, because through them the Court, including its most liberal members, set in motion a distinctive style of legal analysis characteristic of modern American legal consciousness that came to stand, whatever the intentions of its authors, as an ineluctable barrier to worker self-activity.

II. THE SETTING

. . . .

C. The Wagner Act: Goals and Perceptions

It is not easy to discern and articulate the goals of the NLRA.[16] The legislative history is often vague and inconclusive, and on many issues that were subsequently the subject of burning debate, Congress simply expressed no legislative intent. Nonetheless, from the "Findings and Policy" incorporated in section 1 of the Act and from the labor law cases and literature, it is possible to identify at least six statutory goals:

1. *Industrial Peace:* By encouraging collective bargaining, the Act aimed to subdue "strikes and other forms of industrial strife or unrest," because industrial warfare interfered with interstate commerce; that is, it was unhealthy in a business economy.[53] Moreover, although this thought was not embodied in the text, industrial warfare clearly promoted other undesirable conditions, such as political turmoil, violence, and general uncertainty.

2. *Collective Bargaining:* The Act sought to enhance collective bargaining for its own sake because of its presumed "mediating" or "therapeutic" impact on industrial conflict.

3. *Bargaining Power:* The Act aimed to promote "actual liberty of contract" by redressing the unequal balance of bargaining power between employers and employees.

4. *Free Choice:* The Act was intended to protect the free choice of workers to associate among themselves and to select representatives of their own choosing for collective bargaining.

5. *Underconsumption:* The Act was designed to promote economic recovery and to prevent future depressions by increasing the earnings and purchasing power of workers.

6. *Industrial Democracy:* This is the most elusive aspect of the legislative purpose, although most commentators indicate that a concept of industrial democracy is embedded in the statutory scheme, or at the least was one of the articulated goals of the sponsors of the Act. Senator Wagner frequently sounded the industrial democracy theme in ringing notes, and scholars have subsequently seen in collective

bargaining "the means of establishing industrial democracy. . . . the means of providing for the workers' lives in industry the sense of worth, of freedom, and of participation that democratic government promises them as citizens."[60] Indeed, one carefully argued study has gone so far as to conclude that

> Congress viewed the objective of the Act as establishing throughout the country as the normal relationship between employer and employees, a system whereby employees would participate through their representatives in governing all matters affecting their conditions of work. . . . When judges and the public become more familiar with the principles of industrial democracy it is to be expected that any autocratic conduct by an employer will come to be viewed as a serious breach of the employees' rights to self-organization and collective bargaining.[61]

Enumerating the statutory premises in this manner makes apparent why the Wagner Act was, at first, perceived by employers as such a radical threat. Although it demands an effort of historical imagination sufficient to penetrate the narcotic haze of hindsight to understand this perception, the Act by its terms apparently accorded a governmental blessing to powerful workers' organizations that were to acquire equal bargaining power with corporations, accomplish a redistribution of income, and subject the workplace to a regime of participatory democracy. The Act's plain language was susceptible to an overtly anticapitalist interpretation.[62]

To corporate management, the Act was unquestionably the most unpopular piece of New Deal legislation affecting industry. The bill was denounced in vivid terms by representatives of a wide spectrum of business interests, and most employers, large and small, opposed its passage. The *Commercial and Financial Chronicle* had called Senator Wagner's predecessor bill "one of the most objectionable, as well as one of the most revolutionary, pieces of legislation ever presented to Congress," while the Associated Industries of Oklahoma thought the new bill would "out-SOVIET the Russian Soviets." Nor was opposition to the Act limited to verbal assaults. The business community embarked upon a path of deliberate and concerted disobedience to the Act between 1935 and 1937, a response marked by determination and often by violence. Large and respected corporate employers engaged vast resources in systematic and typically unlawful antiunion campaigns involving such tactics as company unionism, propaganda, espionage, surveillance, weapons stockpiling, lockouts, pooling agreements for the supply of strikebreakers, and terrorism.

What provoked this extraordinary campaign of lawlessness and opposition to the statute? It is difficult to say with certainty whether the dominant motive was simply opposition to the Act's promotion of unionism and redistribution of bargaining power or a more fundamental fear that the Act was a prelude to state regulation of the substantive terms of the wage-bargain and the loss of management's exclusive right to direct the production process. From the available evidence, however, it is at least possible to conclude that, in addition to the purely economic costs of collective bargaining, business opposition to the Act was in significant measure prompted by two fundamental considerations. First, the Act's radical potential justifiably produced a fear that collective bargaining meant the loss of control over the production process, the fatal subversion of the hallowed right of managerial freedom to run the enterprise. In short, business took the Act's rhetoric of industrial democracy seriously. This common denominator of fear of loss of managerial control runs through much of business' perceptions of the Act. Business was particularly outraged because the statute went beyond merely legalizing union activity and providing for representation elections, but in addition created an affirmative *duty* on the part of employers to bargain with the employees' exclusive representative over terms and conditions of employment. This requirement raised the spectre that section 8(5) could lead to administrative scrutiny of the substantive terms of employment contracts, indeed, to compulsory arbitration of the terms of employment, and was viewed as a dramatic departure from the concept of managerial control.

The other motif prominent in expressions of business opposition to the Act was the fear that the Act would encourage and promote labor radicalism and class conflict as a necessary consequence of promoting any kind of unionism. A Cleveland Chamber of Commerce resolution of the era, for example, expressed concern about "professional labor agitators whose primary objective is to foment antagonism, with a view to an organized power, socially, politically and economically dangerous to the American Commonwealth." In fact, business had good reason to fear that the Act would lead, at least in the short run, to labor conflict and, therefore, in the context of the times, to the possibility of increased working-class militancy and political radicalism. As the sponsors of the Act themselves must have foreseen, their rhetoric of industrial peace notwithstanding, the inevitable short-run impact of the Act would be a substantial increase in strikes.

It is even more difficult accurately to specify working people's perceptions of, and attitudes toward, the Wagner Act. Conventional labor historiography has tended to equate the aspirations and goals of working people with those of the leadership of organized labor and, apart from the well-known rivalry between the AFL and the CIO over the craft versus industrial models of unionization, has assumed widespread consensus among working people as to what was desired: legal protection of the right to organize; equalization of bargaining power by—and to the extent of—promoting unions as units of countervailing economic power; use of this power to achieve higher standards of living through wage-bargaining; and an industrial democracy limited to the notion that the bargaining unit is a political constituency to which should be extended the traditional democratic right to vote for or against representation, but that democratic participation is largely exhausted by that choice. From this perspective, it follows that the Wagner Act embodied the highest aspirations of labor and that its passage and success not only marked the irreversible emergence of labor as a political force in American life, but was triumphant testimony to the possibilities of democratic reform within the framework of capitalism.

Recent reexaminations of the American labor history of the 1930s suggest, however, that, whereas the foregoing goals may have reflected the attitudes of union leadership, a vastly more complicated and variegated situation is revealed beneath the plane of articulate historical actors at the level of ordinary, historically anonymous, working people. The conventional view exaggerates the unitary character of what labor sought generally in the 1930s and particularly from the collective bargaining law. It appears that the leadership of labor was in many respects quite distant from the rank and file and often acted at cross-purposes to its desires. There is evidence to support the claim that the collective bargaining model that eventually prevailed in the United States may not accurately reflect the aspirations of at least a significant number of those who were footsoldiers in the industrial battles of the New Deal era. Rather, these working people may have contemplated a far more radical restructuring of relationships within the workplace in which industrial democracy, as an ongoing, participatory process both in the factory and the union, was at least as important as improved living standards. From this perspective, working people fought with determination to make the Act a reality—many giving their lives—because it imported more to them than the right to engage in endless economic combat for whatever benefits could be wrung from their corporate adversaries; it meant a commitment of government assistance toward the achievement of an objectively decent living standard and some control over the industrial decisions that affected their lives. At the very least, it can be asserted that the Act meant many different things to different people and groups on the labor side and that, for a substantial number, although they may have had only a vague idea of what the statute actually said, it nevertheless symbolized a significant opening in the direction of radical change.[79]

An important conclusion emerges from the foregoing discussion: the indeterminacy of the text and legislative history of the Act, the political circumstances surrounding its passage, the complexity and fluidity of working-class attitudes toward collective bargaining and labor law reform during the period, and the hostility and disobedience of the business community make it clear that there was no coherent or agreed-upon fund of ideas or principles available as a conclusive guide in interpreting the Act. The statute was a texture of openness and divergency, not a crystallization of consensus or a signpost indicating a solitary direction for future development. This situation presented first the Labor Relation's Board and the lower courts, but ultimately the United States Supreme Court, with the task of plotting the contours of the nation's new labor law. In doing so, the Court had to select one set of principles from among the Wagner Act's possible meanings and give to it the imprimatur of law. This task was unavoidably a *political* enterprise that thrust the Court into a central role in shaping the ideological and institutional architecture of the modern capitalist workplace.

Of course, the Court was not presented with treatises on political philosophy or industrial sociology in the argument of cases, nor was it asked to write such treatises in its decisions. The Court decided issues of law in particular cases. Yet in many cases, the Court easily could have reached one or more alternative results, while employing accepted, competent, and traditional modes of judicial analysis and remaining well within the boundaries of the legislative history of the Act. In a number of cases, the Court overruled decisions of the Board that were fully "responsible" in any traditional sense of appropriate legal discourse and thereby pushed the law in a markedly different political direction. To justify not one result but the entire set of results, the Court was obliged to articulate a new legal consciousness respecting labor matters, a new intellectual outlook on the nature of the wage-bargain. As this world view matured, it began to set boundaries on the type of questions the Court would ask and the possible scope of results it could reach in the labor field; that is, future decisions were mediated through, and in part determined by, the new legal consciousness. At a certain point, this mediation of legal consciousness may explain particular results in particular cases, where the mere logic of precedent or legislative history, on the one hand, or political result-orientation, on the other, are unable to do so. Though it changed and adapted throughout the postwar period, the outlines of the Court's modern outlook on labor issues were established in the crucible of the late 1930s. To the extent that the vision of the law is a form of legitimating ideology supportive and protective of the institutional structure of the workplace, this vision itself serves as a form of political domination.

The remainder of this essay will attempt to demonstrate that, in shaping the nation's labor law, the Court embraced those aims of the Act most consistent with the assumptions of liberal capitalism and foreclosed those potential paths of development most threatening to the established order. Thus, the Wagner Act's goals of industrial peace, collective bargaining as therapy, a safely cabined worker free choice, and some rearrangement of relative bargaining power survived judicial construction of the Act, whereas the goals of redistribution, equality of bargaining power, and industrial democracy—although abiding in rhetoric—were jettisoned as serious components of national labor policy. This process will be discussed in terms of three central aspects of the Court's deradicalization of the Wagner Act and articulation of a more modern legal consciousness: its emphasis on contractualism; its development of the "public right" doctrine; and its promulgation of certain limitations on the legal protection of employee concerted activity.

III. JUDICIAL TREATMENT OF THE WAGNER ACT: FROM THE SIT-DOWNS TO PEARL HARBOR

A. The Contractualist Phoenix: The Labor Law Revolution as the Revival of Lochner v. New York

In 1931, Walton Hamilton argued that the days of "freedom of contract" were numbered. When the Wagner Act was passed, commentators and courts saw in it the fulfillment of this prophecy with respect to labor contracts. Indeed, it is widely believed today that the Wagner Act effected a detachment of labor relations from the law of contracts that had previously governed it. This notion is seriously misleading. Contract is alive and well in the law of labor relations. To be sure, the collective bargaining agreement is a special kind of contract, with peculiar legal incidents, but despite the strongly anti-contractualist overtones of the Act, the Supreme Court ensured from the start that contractualism would be the jurisprudential framework of the law of labor relations. . . .

The central moral ideal of contractualism was and is that justice consists in enforcing the agreement of the parties so long as they have capacity and have had a proper opportunity to bargain for terms satisfactory to each. Contractual justice is, therefore, formal and abstract: within the broad scope of legal bargains it is disinterested in the substantive content of the parties' arrangements. . . .

The foremost task of the Supreme Court, in the wake of the Wagner Act, was to resolve whether the wage-bargain would remain fundamentally within the contractualist, private ordering framework. This task was accomplished in the very first cases decided under the Act. *NLRB v. Jones & Laughlin Steel Corp.*[103] and its companion cases[104] are chiefly remembered for their far-reaching innovations in the areas of federalism, the commerce power, and the scope of judicial review, but this fact must not obscure their crucial historical role in updating and preserving the freedom of contract ideal.

Jones & Laughlin began by establishing that employees would be allowed to pool their bargaining power to offset the superior economic position of the employer and that the employer would not be permitted to interfere with its employees' decision whether to adopt a collective posture for wage-bargaining or their choice of a representative for that purpose. Chief Justice Hughes's conception appeared to be that employees had a privilege to create a quasi-fiduciary or protected economic relationship between each of them individually and the others by constituting a collective bargaining unit and designating an "agent" or "agency" (a word commonly used to refer to unions in the early opinions) to represent them. The designation of the bargaining agency constituted the creation of the "protected" relationship, and the unfair labor practices proscribed in section 8 were conceived essentially as torts of injurious interference with the privileged relationship. That is, employer interference with employee choice of a bargaining representative was treated conceptually as similar to employee interference with the employer's protected relationship with its representative, such as would occur, for example, if an employee intercepted the employer's communications with counsel:

> [Legitimate] collective action would be a mockery if representation were made futile by interference with freedom of choice. Hence the prohibition by Congress of interference with the selection of representatives for the purpose of negotiation and conference between employers and employees, "instead of being an invasion of the constitutional right of either, was based on the recognition of the rights of both."

But the Court emphatically rejected any suggestion that the Act abolished private-ordering as the framework of relationships in the workplace:

> The Act does not compel agreements between employers and employees. It does not compel any agreement whatever. It does not prevent the employer "from refusing to make a collective contract and hiring individuals on whatever terms" the employer "may by unilateral action determine." . . . The Act does not interfere with the normal exercise of the right of the employer to select its employees or to discharge them. The employer may not, under cover of that right, intimidate or coerce its employees with respect to their self-organization and representation, and, on the other hand, the Board is not entitled to make its authority a pretext for interference with the right of discharge when that right is exercised for other reasons than such intimidation and coercion.

In the Court's view, the Act did not infringe on normal managerial prerogatives except insofar as the employer was prohibited from invading the employees' privilege to pool their bargaining power and to choose and act through a bargaining agent. The Act was no warrant for a regime of governmental supervision of normal managerial decisions. The Court rejected any inference that the law would inquire into the substantive justice of labor-management relations or the fairness of the wage-bargain. In short, the opinion of Chief Justice Hughes really went no further than the dissenting opinions in the classical freedom of contract cases of *Adair v. United States*[113] and

Coppage v. Kansas;[114] his conceptual universe was akin to that which inspired those opinions.

Subsequent cases of the period preserved this framework, with a bloc composed of Chief Justice Hughes and Justices Roberts and Stone continuing to adhere to contractualism and a conceptualist style of analysis. In *NLRB v. Mackay Radio & Telegraph Co.,*[116] for example, the Court established the crucial strategic right of struck employers to offer permanent positions to workers hired to replace strikers (so long as the strike was not provoked or prolonged by unfair labor practices). The manner in which the Court reached its conclusion is instructive. The issue before the Court was whether, as a matter of labor policy, the employer should have the weapon of permanent replacement at its disposal. The Court, however, never candidly addressed this question, saying only that it did not follow from section 13 "that an employer, guilty of no act denounced by the statute, [had] lost the right to protect and continue his business by supplying places left vacant by strikers." This statement is a paradigmatic representation of the vices of conceptualist legal reasoning because the question whether the employer was "guilty of [an] act denounced by the statute" was precisely the matter to be decided, and the question whether the employer had a right to protect his business, if to do so would invade the right of his employees to engage in concerted activity, likewise required explicit analysis from the standpoint of the society's labor policy. In each case, the Court merely assumed its conclusion, presenting as compelled by the words of the Act, or by Reason, or simply as a priori true, judgments involving debatable choices from among competing economic and political values. Thus, the conceptualist tradition was upheld and continued as the Court masked the unavoidably ideological content of judicial action.[120]

The *Mackay* rule remains the prevailing law. It is historically important because it was one of the earliest manifestations of the developing premise that once an employer lawfully bargains to impasse, it is free unilaterally to impose terms and conditions of employment, if it has the economic staying power to defeat a strike. Thus, the decision furthered the principle that the Act is disinterested in the substantive justice of the labor contract, since it taught that not only would the wage-bargain not ordinarily be subject to substantive scrutiny, but also that the economic combat of the parties had replaced a "meeting of the minds" as the moral basis of labor contractualism.

NLRB v. Sands Manufacturing Co.[123] was another example of this trend. In *Sands,* a dispute arose between the union and the employer during the term of a collective bargaining agreement. The Court held that the statutory duty to bargain attached in such situations. The dispute in question remained unresolved after discussion, however, and a work-stoppage was threatened. The company thereupon discharged the entire workforce and reopened the plant with a wholly new complement of employees. It was contested whether the initial dispute went to a question of contract application or to a proposed modification; in any event, the union refused to compromise its position. Interpreting the contract *sua sponte*, the Court announced that its terms favored the employer's version and that, therefore, the union was unilaterally insisting upon a mid-term modification. The Court held that employees may not use economic power to impose their demands in such a situation, despite the fact that the contract did not contain a "no-strike" clause and, in fact, reserved full liberty of action to the employees in case of impasse in attempts to resolve "misunderstandings" between the company and the workforce.[127] The employees' insistence that they would not work except under their interpretation of the contract was held to be a "breach" or "repudiation" of an implied contractual obligation, sufficient to divest the workers of their statutory right to engage in concerted activity. The Court stated,

> The Act does not prohibit an effective discharge for repudiation by the employee of his agreement. . . .
>
> . . . .
>
> . . . If, as we have held, the respondent was confronted with a concerted refusal on the part of [the union] to permit its members to perform their contract there was nothing unlawful in the company's attempting to procure others to fill their places.

The Court's opinion in *Sands* relied on a highly formalistic and contractualist reading of the statute to legitimize the inequalities of bargaining power arising from the unequal social distribution of property ownership. The ban on the use of economic power by the union was, given the record presented, presumably meant to apply equally to attempts to impose a union interpretation of an agreement as well as to achieve a mid-term modification of the agreement. That is, if an impasse is reached, the employer could use its economic power, namely its ownership and control of the business, to get its way, but the workers could not use their primary economic weapon, the work-stoppage.

The Court's initial period of contractualist formalism under the Wagner Act was followed by a series of realist victories, written chiefly by Justices Black and Douglas. One series of these cases concerned the definition of "free choice," an essential ingredient of traditional contract doctrine, in the context of alleged employer domination of labor organizations.

The old-fashioned company union was one of the preeminent weapons employers used to defeat the labor movement. Therefore, section 8(2) of the Act was a crucial battleground in the 1930s. If the Act were to fulfill its functions, the company union had to be eliminated. To this end, the Board and the courts developed the remedy of "disestablishing" organizations found to be employer-dominated. The realists pushed this remedy to its limits. In *NLRB v. Falk Corp.*,[133] for example, one issue was whether the remedy of "disestablishment" meant that the company union was to be denied a place on the ballot in an election to choose a new bargaining representative. Justice Black, writing for the Court, upheld the Board's conclusion that the "company-created union could not emancipate itself from habitual subservience to its creator, and that in order to insure employees that complete freedom of choice guaranteed by § 7, [the dominated union] must be . . . kept off the ballot." In other words, if the workers voted for the company union in a fair election, that would not be "free choice." This free choice had a *substantive* content, determined by the history of the workplace, not merely a formal content determined by the mechanics of secret balloting.

The realist tide swept away other formalistic doctrines. In *NLRB v. Waterman Steamship Co.*,[136] Justice Black held that the formalities of the typical seaman's contract, under which each voyage constitutes a separate and distinct contractual relationship, were not controlling under the Act. . . . The Court held that, although the employer had a clear contractual right to discharge his employees after a voyage for any reason whatsoever or no reason at all, it could not exercise that right in such a way as to chill union activity.

Similarly, in *International Association of Machinists v. NLRB*,[140] the Court developed a broad doctrine of "imputed liability" in order to safeguard worker free choice. The Court stated that the technicalities of *respondeat superior* were not applicable to proceedings under the Act. . . .

Undoubtedly, the free choice decisions overrode certain traditional doctrines governing the employment contract, but they did not attack contractualism as such. They sought to achieve what the Court saw as the preconditions of "true" or "actual" private-ordering; they were designed to make contractualism work, not to abolish it. There is no intimation in these decisions that, once the preconditions of "actual liberty of contract" were realized, the law would inquire into the substantive results of bargaining. Thus, the new realism preserved the formal and abstentionist posture of traditional contract doctrine, and the political function of labor contractualism—the creation of an institutional framework in which social relations of domination appear in the guise of free exchange—was reaffirmed.

Only the uncertain shadow of the section 8(5) duty to bargain clouded this contractualist horizon. The legislative history of section 8(5) contains repeated indications that the Act was not intended to require the parties to agree to anything, but just to meet and bargain. Nevertheless, it was clear from the pre-NLRA experience of the National Labor Board and the "old" National Labor Relations Board under section 7(a) of the National Industrial Recovery Act, that the duty to bargain would have to mean more, if it were to mean anything, than just a minimal duty physically to meet with employee representatives. The Board and the courts, however, largely avoided setting the parameters of the duty during the period under discussion, because the primary battleground of the 1930s was the field of union organization and recognition, not collective bargaining as such. . . .[151]

The rudimentary foundations of a new jurisprudential synthesis, "social conceptualism," began to appear on two levels in the process of development of the new labor contractualism. On a substantive level, the Court recognized that state regulation of the wage-bargain could coexist with private-ordering. This outlook at once affirmed two seemingly contradictory social values: that it is appropriate and just for the state to rearrange the relative bargaining strengths of capital and labor because the pre-existing disparity of power produced substantively unacceptable results, and that the state ought not to intervene in private wage-bargaining to encourage or assure any particular substantive outcome. In logic, these competing social values may be mutually exclusive, but not so in the new judicial consciousness, which accommodated both regulation and private-ordering by refusing to push either principle to its limits.

On a second, methodological level, the emerging legal consciousness became sensitized to the social and political ramifications of legal rules and decisions, but the Supreme Court was not prepared simply to assimilate legal reasoning to social policy analysis. The political realism that indicated the necessity of state intervention in labor bargaining did not inexorably lead to legal realism as an adjudicatory method. On the contrary, the process at work was the reification of ad hoc social policies into "values" or "first principles" that were then conceived to provide determinate—and therefore legitimate—solutions to legal problems, as, for example, with Justice Roberts's concept of the employer's right to protect the business and Justices Douglas's and Black's notion of free choice.

B. The Public Right Doctrine: New Deal Administrative Law as a Contribution to Pluralist Political Theory

A classical problem of liberal political theory has been to preserve the neutrality of the state in a world understood to be dominated and motivated by the conflict of private interests. Liberal political theory has always conceived of the state as being radically divorced from, or rising above, civil society, the realm of private and group interest. During the early years of the Great Depression, however, the purported neutrality of the state, particularly the federal judiciary, was, as had happened before, called into widespread doubt. The New Dealers eventually appointed to the Court confronted a massive crisis of legitimacy. Their difficult task, therefore, was to make the law more responsive to pressing social priorities and the constituencies that the reform programs of the New Deal were designed to aid, while restoring the purported neutrality of the state. That is, although the law was to be mobilized to carry out new regulatory and welfare functions representing the triumph of a particular political coalition, the rhetoric of liberal legalism had to be repaired and enhanced, proving that Americans did, indeed, live under the rule of law, not men.

The articulation of a comprehensive modern administrative law was one of the New Deal jurists' most creative responses to this dilemma. In this jurisprudence, the actions of administrative agencies and tribunals were considered subject to the rule of law and not mere reflections of the shifting interests of partisan power, yet administrative bodies were also conceived to be relatively emancipated from rule-formalism insofar as their responsiveness to changing crystallizations of public interest and policy was deemed legitimate. This uneasy merger of formalism and result-orientation required careful and articulate justification. New doctrinal formulas were needed to enable progressive courts to brush aside some of the finer concerns and details of traditional private adjudication in reviewing the work of the agencies, while at the same time avoiding any appearance of capitulation to partisan interest.

A second challenging aspect of rehabilitating the state's image as neutral arbiter above group conflict was to provide a theoretical justification for the delegation of the lawmaking function (i.e., the setting of enforceable standards of conduct) to socially significant groups. If the Wagner Act and the other New Deal reform measures were to succeed, the law had to allow for some notion of legitimate private lawmaking. The radical disjunction between public and private that characterized classical liberal political theory was no longer tenable in the late capitalistic welfare state in which the government systematically and pervasively intervened in the private sector and, conversely, in which institutions, such as corporations and unions, hitherto deemed to be purely private in nature, increasingly assumed the functions, attributes, or powers of quasi-governmental agencies. On the other hand, the public/private distinction could not be abandoned altogether without subverting the basic philosophical premises of the liberal democratic state. The preservation of the public/private distinction in a world in which it was becoming increasingly incoherent, at least in the classical liberal formulation, became one of the central projects of the new jurisprudence of social conceptualism. One minor but significant early episode in the process was the strategy developed in the NLRA cases of maintaining the forms of private conflict-resolution in the administrative and legal process while superimposing on them a new version of higher law through the public right doctrine.

In *Jones & Laughlin,* Chief Justice Hughes made a remarkable claim:

> Thus, in its present application, the statute goes no further than to safeguard the right of employees to self-organization and to select representatives of their own choosing for collective bargaining or other mutual protection without restraint or coercion by their employer.
> *That is a fundamental right.* Employees have as clear a right to organize and select their representatives for lawful purposes as the [company] has to organize its business and select its own officers and agents. Discrimination and coercion to prevent the free exercise of the right of employees to self-organization and representation is a proper subject for condemnation by competent legislative authority.

Hughes's choice of language implied that the rights guaranteed by the Act were not created by it. Rather, they were basic or inherent rights deriving from a source of law much more fundamental than mere statute. Hughes conceived of the Act as providing for the protection, as a matter of public policy, of a *right inhering in private law* and as striking a general balance between the respective private rights of adverse parties, with the Board assigned the detailed task of weighing and resolving clashes of *private* interests in particular factual settings.

Of course, the historical record flatly contradicted the view that the right to organize was recognized by law prior to 1935 as a fundamental, extrastatutory right, or, indeed, as a right at all. Perhaps Chief Justice Hughes was motivated to use this schema by a desire to depreciate the momentousness of what the Court was actually doing in *Jones & Laughlin.* In any case, the opinion reflects the inertia of legal concepts, the difficulty of conceptualizing radical change even at the moment it is experienced or brought about. Though everyone knew the Act was a marked political departure, the radical innovations it implied in legal theory were at first only dimly understood. The idea of a right had theretofore been associated with a private law conception of adjudication, and it is no surprise, therefore, that Hughes interpreted the Act within this conceptual framework. Moreover, his account of the Act had, in retrospect, a great virtue: it focused attention on the raw fact of class (group) conflict, rather than on the nebulous, and ideological, conception of a public interest rising above such conflict.

The Hughes formulation, however, was short-lived. The outline of an alternative scheme first appeared, implicitly, in *American Federation of Labor v. NLRB.*[160] The case was a political bombshell, because the Court, in effect, allowed Harry Bridges's International Longshoremen's & Warehousemen's Union (CIO) to have a Pacific Coast-wide bargaining unit over the outraged opposition of the rival International Longshoremen's Association (AFL), which stood to lose its small base on the Pacific Coast. The Court's holding was that judicial review of Board decisions in representation proceedings was not available unless and until the employer was charged with an unfair labor practice and raised a section 9 issue as a defense. This decision implicitly rested on the idea that the statutory scheme does not protect private entitlements but protects certain public interests. A private litigant was entitled to the orderly completion of the Board's processes, but it had no individual right, entitlement, or claim to the section 9 unit determination preferred by it. Thus, no deprivation of any right was involved in forbidding the courts to hear the claims of aggrieved private parties except under the circumstances provided by the statutory scheme. Under other circumstances, there was literally no claim to be heard.

The case was widely viewed as a prolabor victory, notwithstanding the wrath of the AFL, because the ruling put an end to one of the employers' favorite antiunion delaying tactics. But it had an unfortunate consequence, which CIO as well as AFL leaders were quick to see. If the party aggrieved in the section 9 proceeding was the union, for example, a union that later lost an election because of an improper definition of the bargaining unit, it would have *no* remedy under the Act because it would never be in a position to defend a refusal-to-bargain charge.

The new public right schema was explicitly articulated less than two months later in *Amalgamated Utility Workers v. Consolidated Edison Co.*[164] Alleged employer disobedience to a Court of Appeals enforcement order prompted the union to move that the employer be cited for contempt. Although the Board had standing to make such a motion, it had declined to do so. The issue, therefore, was whether a *private party* could vindicate its rights under the Act by this means. A unanimous Supreme Court said no. Chief Justice Hughes wrote,

> The Board as a public agency acting in the public interest, not any private person or group, not any employee or group of employees, is chosen as the instrument to assure protection from the described unfair conduct in order to remove obstructions to interstate commerce.
> When the Board has made its order, the Board alone is authorized to take proceedings to enforce it.
> . . . .
> It is the Board's order on behalf of the public that the court enforces. It is the Board's right to make that order that the court sustains. The Board seeks enforcement as a public agent, not to give effect to a "private administrative remedy."

As a result, if a successful charging party was aggrieved but the Board refused fully to enforce its order through contempt proceedings, that party was without remedy to protect its rights or even to obtain a hearing. The fundamental rights spoken of in *Jones & Laughlin* were transmuted in the space of three years into privileges created by the statute and therefore measured by the Board's discretion and largesse in administering the statutory scheme. The rights of employees were now conceived to be held and defined at the pleasure of an agency of the federal government.

Once launched, the public right doctrine exhibited a potent power to override private interests. The Court allowed the Board to adjudicate certain contract rights without requiring the Board to join or afford a hearing to one of the contractual parties, employed the public right doctrine to justify its previously mentioned rulings that the technicalities of *respondeat superior* do not apply to section 8 proceedings, and invoked the doctrine to justify the breakdown of traditional concepts of remedies.

The culmination of the public right conception occurred in *Pittsburgh Plate Glass Co. v. NLRB*.[173] In that case, a CIO affiliate had an overall majority and a majority in each of five of PPG's six flat glass plants. An independent union, with a history of employer domination, claimed a majority in the sixth plant. The Board found appropriate a single bargaining unit encompassing all six plants, thus writing off the independent union for practical purposes. The Court affirmed the Board's action, relying in part on the view that it was permissible for the Board to consider in deciding the case that, if the sixth plant were placed in a separate bargaining unit, the employer could use it to maintain operations in the event of a strike in the larger unit and thereby tip the balance of economic power in its favor.

The Court's holding itself was of modest significance, especially since the Board had receded from its policy of certifying such massive units prior to the *Plate Glass* decision. But the Court's conception of the Board's role under the Act was of preeminent importance. Read broadly, *Plate Glass* implied that determinations as to the appropriateness of bargaining units were strictly reserved to the Board's discretion and that in making such determinations, the Board was authorized to include in its calculations a balancing of the relative economic power of the opposed class forces. Presumably, the balancing of relative economic forces was deemed a matter of neutral, expert judgment, although the Court never explained how one might define or identify a public interest in one or another balance of power between capital and labor. In practice, *Plate Glass* placed enormous political power in the hands of the Board to delimit the contours of legitimate class struggle. Not only was the Board granted wide discretion in enforcing the Act, but it also had the power to define the balance of opposing economic forces on which the substantive outcome of collective bargaining depends.

Of course, it is not suggested that the Court granted the Board carte blanche to restructure American class relations; the historical impact of the case should not be exaggerated. Rather the effort here is to recover the Court's conceptualization of the statutory scheme, in which the Court recognized that as a practical matter the Board had the power dramatically to shape the terrain on which private-ordering will take place and thereby crucially to influence its outcome. In *Plate Glass* the Court endowed this de facto power with the imprimatur of law. Although institutional and political considerations have led the Board generally to utilize this power discreetly over the years, in the context of the late 1930s, *Plate Glass* brought to fruition an intellectual movement to conceptualize employees' rights as public rights, measured by the discretion of the Board. Unavoidably, the decision in *Plate Glass* created an intellectual justification for the dependency of labor on the state, thereby reinforcing the cultural hegemony of liberal political theory. This dependence hindered labor from conceiving of itself, or acting, as an autonomous movement capable of fundamentally transforming the established social relations of production. The public right doctrine created a justification in political theory for labor's dependence on government, thereby tending to transform a contingent historical relationship into a moral destiny.[184]

C. The Inhibition of Worker Self-Activity

Labor was the beneficiary of an exciting series of legal victories in the early years of Wagner Act interpretation. In procedural matters, the scope of judicial review of Board findings under section 10 was narrowly confined, and the courts were forbidden to review or interdict Board proceedings until they had run their proper course. Thus, the Court made clear that it would protect the Board's processes from judicial invasion and employer stalling tactics. In substantive matters, the Court liberalized the law of picketing and endowed ordinary union activities with immunity under the antitrust laws. The latter action brought an end to what for generations had been one of the primary legal weapons used by employers against the labor movement.

Intermixed with these cases, however, were several decisions narrowing and limiting legally protected union activity and hampering the effective enforcement of the Act. Chief among these decisions were *NLRB v. Fansteel Metallurgical Corp.*, condemning the sitdown strike; *NLRB v. Mackay Radio & Telegraph Co.*, allowing permanent replacement of economic strikers; *NLRB v. Sands Manufacturing Co.*, withdrawing section 7 protection from certain strike activity in the context of an existing collective bargaining relationship; and *Phelps Dodge Corp. v. NLRB*, establishing the mitigation rule.

The early Wagner Act cases had a much more momentous consequence than can be captured in this simple tally of labor's immediate gains and losses. The unprecedented privileges granted to labor created discord in conventional legal thought. In generating doctrines to justify this new legal status, the Court was called upon to develop a conception of the proper role of unions in the reformed social order.

Two motifs are paramount in the Court's portrait of "legitimate" union activity. First was the fiduciary theme, the Court's view that unions have an institutional role setting them apart from their members. Initially this idea was but a conceptual corollary of the "quasi-tort" schema Hughes articulated in *Jones & Laughlin,* namely, the view that the union was something separate and apart from the employees and the purpose of the Act was to prevent unwarranted employer invasion of the privileged relationship between the employees and their "agent." But the theme soon developed a life of its own. The delineation of legitimate forms of concerted activity contained the unstated proviso that unions wishing the protection of the Board had to keep their members in line. *Sands Manufacturing* and *Fansteel* were abrupt warnings that what, from a management perspective, were the more spontaneous or undisciplined forms of concerted activity, the mid-term strike and the sit-down strike, would not be protected by the Act. The public right doctrine implied that union conduct would not be judged solely against the backdrop of competing employer and employee interests, but against the public interest in industrial peace as well. The ideological premise that there is such a general societal interest in the smooth operation of the industrial system was always taken for granted. The union was seen not just as a private fiduciary vis-à-vis the membership of the bargaining unit, but also as a "trustee" of this public interest, and "responsible behavior" by unions became a quid pro quo for the legal privileges extended by the Act.

Second, the Court's wage-bargain theme represented, as the term implies, a conception that the function of a union was to make a wage-bargain: that is, its role was limited to the sphere of exchange. The very power that unions had in arranging the sale of labor power signaled their inevitable participation in reproducing the alienation that characterized the work-process itself and negated the alternative historical and moral claims they might have advanced with respect to the sphere of production.

The negative implications of these two themes provided the underpinnings of a narrow conception of the social relations of the workplace in three fundamental and interrelated ways. First, the treatment of workers as sellers of labor power and as consumers of commodities, but not as producers, hindered them from achieving an alternative perspective in which worker self-activity, the process by which workers produce value by embodying their labor power in things, services, and relationships, would be recognized as the basis of all production in, and reproduction of, society. The Court's vision countered the corollary of this alternative premise, that workers' organizations ought to affirm and advance the proposition that those whose collective efforts make social production possible should have a decisive say in the decisions that affect the process, that they pose themselves morally and institutionally as the authors of their own destinies in the workplace.

Second, since it was imagined that there was an overall societal interest in maintaining the prevailing industrial system, the Court's fiduciary theme encouraged responsible unions to accept the social order as given and to seek to defend and better the lot of their members only within its ground rules. Here again, the fact that the social fabric is itself produced and reproduced through the activity of society's members was obscured and denied.

Finally, since union activity was denominated as something separate from members' self-activity in the workplace, unions could not function as participatory institutions in which workers continuously articulated and redefined their aspirations for the governance and transformation of the work-process. The union was not expected to foreshadow the organizational form of a democratic workplace, nor to provide the workers with an "experiment . . . in self-organization, in initiative and collective decision-making, in short, an experiment in the possibility of their own emancipation."[199] In sum, the Court's narrowly restricted vision of legitimate union activity stood in every sense as a barrier to the possibility that labor would participate in bringing about fundamental social change.

These themes are vividly illustrated by the extraordinary case of *NLRB v. Fansteel Metallurgical Corp.*,[201] which condemned the sit-down strike. In *Fansteel,* massive and undisputed employer unfair labor practices designed to defeat unionization of the plant provoked the employees to stage a sit-down strike in their factory. They were evicted by the police, and many strikers were fined or jailed under state law. The employer then encouraged the formation of a company union, continuing its course of illegal conduct. The Board attempted to undo the effects of the employer illegality by ordering the company to bargain on request with the bona fide union and to reinstate the strikers. The Court agreed that the employer had committed unfair labor practices, but overruled the reinstatement of the sit-down strikers, holding that under the Act the company could legally discharge the strikers for occupying the plant and that the Board lacked authority under section 10(c) to order reinstatement. . . .

The extreme formalism underlying the *Fansteel* opinion is evident in Hughes's focus on the legal aspects of the discharge, rather than on the scope of the Board's remedial powers. Hughes reasoned that the strikers' tortious conduct was independent from the employer's unfair labor practices and an adequate basis for divesting them of their status as employees, notwithstanding the language of section 2(3), which provides for the continuation of employee status in contemplation of law notwithstanding its cessation in fact in connection with current labor disputes or unfair labor practices. Accordingly, it followed that the strikers could not avail themselves of the protection and remedies of the statute. Hughes, however, belatedly recognized that the remedial powers of the Board were not limited to the assistance of employees; the ultimate test under section 10(c) was whether reinstatement would serve, under the circumstances, to effectuate the policies of the Act. Responding briskly in the negative, Hughes argued that reinstatement would only give license to tortfeasors and discourage the peaceful settlement of industrial disputes. Concluding this formalist tour de force, Hughes castigated the workers for their sit-down tactic. . . .

The realists bitterly counterattacked, contending that the real question was the Board's expert assessment, arguably proper under section 10(c), that the purposes of the Act would best be served by reinstating the strikers. Since any unlawful acts committed by the strikers had already been punished quite severely under state law, to impose the futher penalty of allowing the company permanently to sever the employment relationship would permit employers to subvert the Act by provoking sit-down strikes or other tortious conduct and then reaping the benefits of their unfair labor practices by immunizing themselves from the Board's remedial powers. This, at any rate, was the Board's considered judgment. The real issue of the case, brusquely avoided by the Court, was the soundness and legitimacy of this judgment of social policy.

The best that can be said for Hughes's view is that it blatantly ignored historical and social reality. The Court ignored the fact that the sit-down strikes were essentially a reaction to the widespread and often violent refusal by employers to obey the law between 1935 and 1940. The historical record is clear that the sit-down strikes were an indispensable weapon with which workers stemmed the tide of employer resistance to unions and to the law; inferentially, they thereby helped create the political conditions for the Court's leftward shift in *West Coast Hotel Co. v. Parrish* and *NLRB v. Jones & Laughlin Steel Corp.* That is, the sit-down strikes contributed to, rather than detracted from, whatever law and order existed in industrial life in 1939 when Hughes delivered *Fansteel*. Moreover, in sharp contrast to contemporary but traditionally conducted strikes, the sit-downs in 1936–1938 caused no deaths and little property damage.

The sit-down strike was important not only because it was so effective tactically, but also because it minimized the risks of picketline violence. The traditional strike separates the employees from the workplace and from each other. Typically, striking workers come together only serially, on the picket line. In the sit-down, however, workers posed themselves as collectively capable of organizing the workplace. The logistics of the sit-down required the constant participation of all in decisionmaking and fostered a spirit of community, cooperation, and initiative. The sit-downs nurtured a new psychological and emotional experience: " 'The fact that the sit-down gives the worker in mass-production industries a vital sense of importance cannot be overemphasized.' "[222] The sit-downs were a utopian breach in the endless regularity and pessimism of everyday life, a "dereifying" explosion of repressed human spirit.

By ignoring these social realities and condemning the sit-down strike, the Court interpreted the Act as standing against the possibility of emancipatory workplace experiments. *Fansteel* condemned a tactic designed to transcend the disjunction between the union and its members; it bolstered the forces of union bureaucracy in their efforts to quell the spontaneity of the rank and file. As such, it marked the end of the radical potential of the 1930s by demarcating the outer limits of disruption of the established industrial order that the law would tolerate. The utopian aspirations for a radical restructuring of the workplace, engendered by enactment of the Wagner Act and the intoxicating experience of the rise of the CIO, were symbolically thwarted by *Fansteel*, which erected labor law reform as a roadblock in their path.

D. The Roots of Modern Legal Consciousness

The contours of a more modern legal consciousness, hinted at in the earliest Wagner Act cases, were clearly visible by the beginning of the 1940s as the legal crisis of the previous decade drew to a close. The Court could be divided, somewhat schematically, into three groups. Chief Justice Hughes and Justices Stone and Roberts continued the conceptualist tradition. They were reluctant to abide by the Board's expert judgment and fearful, to some extent, of the new power of labor. Justices Black, Douglas, and Murphy, sometimes joined by Reed, formed the realist contingent. Their opinions evinced a purposive style of legal analysis and a willingness to defer to the discretion of the Board. There is a curious correlation between legal styles and these Justices' understanding of the fundamental purposes of the Act. The conceptualist group persistently emphasized what is probably the most instrumental goal of the Act, industrial peace, whereas the realists stressed the more ethereal goal of employee free choice. Since bringing social policy explicitly into legal analysis was already disturbing to the more traditional judicial mind, the conceptualists probably felt most comfortable coming to grips with urgent and undiscriminating priorities rather than trying to elaborate on more philosophical themes requiring a more thorough-going transformation of their personal assumptions. On the other hand, in Douglas's and Black's emphasis on free choice, an abstract, highly conceptual term, can be seen an intimation of future movement away from their early realism. In the postwar period Black's labor opinions evinced a rigid contractualist formalism, whereas Douglas's disillusionment with Big Labor led him to adopt a stance of tenacious individualism or "anti-institutionalism."

It is appropriate to put Justice Frankfurter in a separate category. Though his opinions sounded the themes of legal realism, he was a legalist through and through, and the roots of his later attempt to mediate between realism and conceptualism were already apparent. Much sooner than Blacks's or Douglas's, Frankfurter's work showed glimpses of the emerging "social conceptualism." . . .

A microcosm of modern legal consciousness, [the Court's labor opinions just prior to Pearl Harbor] contained a chaotic amalgam of conceptualism and realism, ruleboundedness and ad hoc balancing, deference to nonjudicial sources of law and unhesitating faith in the superiority of the judicial mind. This jurisprudential mélange transcended political lines and attitudes as to whether the proper judicial role is one of activism or restraint. I believe that all of modern legal consciousness partakes of this hodge-podge character. It is a consciousness in which contrasting styles of legal reasoning are simultaneously and unreflectively employed by the same court or even the same judge; in which the public/private distinction is invoked as the basis of judicial decisions, as though it were a concept of scientific precision and with no apparent recognition that the distinction has assumed formidable ideological and mystificatory functions in the welfare state; in which state regulation of private economic activity is assumed to be a legitimate and even compelling mode of achieving progressive reform, while the ideal of the free market is simultaneously upheld as the proper basis of social organization; and in which the antinomy of reason and fiat is understood to pervade the legal process, while at the same time it appears to be a veritable public responsibility of the judge to obscure or veil this fact. The formalist and realist traditions are continued *sub silentio* in judicial decisions, but in a manner consistent with neither legal vision. The rule of law is preserved, though in an updated, more socially responsive form.

The full rehabilitation of legalism awaited the relative social stability of the Cold War era, when it again became possible to attempt a totalizing jurisprudence, a merger of realism and the social policies it imported into the law with the traditions of formalist jurisprudence.[276] No doubt such attempts to revitalize legalism have dominated postwar American legal thought, to some extent quelling the residual disquiet left over from the legal crisis of the 1930s. For this reason, it is appropriate to conceive of modern legal consciousness as a relatively unified whole, although this is a unity that consists chiefly in a willingness to merge approaches and methods that, if pushed only slightly, appear to be antagonistic. The preeminent characteristic of modern legal consciousness, transcending all political battlelines, is its unreflective and uncritical quality, its attempt to accommodate yet obscure the contradictions of legal thought, which reflect the contradictions of social life in late capitalist society. . . .

NOTES

11. By focusing on the Supreme Court, I do not mean to imply that other legal institutions, notably the National Labor Relations Board, did not also contribute to the integrative process here described. I have emphasized the Court because some of the most significant issues in this process are highlighted by the Court's several attempts to define its relationship to the Board and to other courts.

12. The argument relies on the theory of hegemony articulated in the work of the Italian Marxist philosopher Antonio Gramsci. See A. Gramsci, *Selections From the Prison Notebooks*, ed. and trans. Q. Hoare and G. Nowell Smith (London: Lawrence & Wishart, 1971). See generally C. Boggs, *Gramsci's Marxism* (London: Pluto Press, 1967); Perry Anderson, "The Antinomies of Antonio Gramsci," *New Left Review* (November 1976– January 1977), at 5; Gwyn A. Williams, "The Concept of 'Egemonia' in the Thought of Antonio Gramsci: Some Notes on Interpretation," *Journal of the History of Ideas* 21(1960): 58. By "hegemony" Gramsci meant "the permeation throughout civil society . . . of an entire system of values, attitudes, beliefs, morality, etc., that is in one way or another supportive of the established order and the class interests that dominate it."

13. I adopt the concept of the "relative autonomy" of legal consciousness, institutions, and practice notwithstanding my obvious commitment to the view that the legal process is deeply imbedded in the political process and not only reflects the political and class structure of American capitalism but serves to maintain and reproduce it. The view that law reflects the political and class structure does not require or imply the reductionist argument that the legal process is directly responsive to the needs and preferences of dominant social and political actors. See Isaac D. Balbus, "Commodity Form and Legal Form: An Essay on the 'Relative Autonomy' of the Law," *Law and Society Review* 11 (1977): 571, 572–73. Indeed, though determinism regrettably remains the popular conception of Marxist method, the most creative work on law within the Marxist tradition begins with the rejection of economic determinism as an explanatory mode. This intellectual tradition has sought to develop a theory adequate to explain the way in which law ultimately reflects and sustains the social order, yet has its own internal logic and unique modes of discourse and institutional patterns that are to some extent independent of the will of powerful, nonlegal, social and political actors and that represent an important constitutive element of the social totality in their own right.

16. This article will consider the work of the Court from the 1937 decision upholding the Act, NLRB v. Jones & Laughlin Steel Corp., 301 U.S. 1 (1937), to Pearl Harbor. After Pearl Harbor, the creation of the National War Labor Board on January 12, 1942, see Exec. Order No. 9017, 3 C.F.R. 1075 (1938–1943 compilation), reprinted in 9 L.R.R.M. 945 (1943), and such other wartime enactments as the War Labor Disputes Act, ch. 144, 57 Stat. 163 (1943), so radically altered the legal status of labor that the conceptual scheme of the NLRA was temporarily abandoned. . . .

53. Ironically, section 13 of the Act emphatically affirms the right to strike, and its sponsors must have known that in the short run the Act would encourage workers to exercise this right on a massive scale, which is exactly what happened. Thus, the industrial peace rationale only makes sense on the assumption that employers would eventually come to their senses and accept collective bargaining as more productive from the long-run standpoint of the business system than intransigent efforts to hold back the clock. In other words, the Act gave workers a powerful weapon in industrial warfare so that industrial warfare would, in the long run, be dissipated. . . .

Not surprisingly, once section 13 served its purpose, the Court and Congress began to impose elaborate restrictions on the right to strike and other potentially disruptive activity. See, for example, Hudgens v. NLRB, 424 U.S. 507 (1976) (picketing rights subordinated to property rights); Emporium Capwell Co. v. Western Addition Community Organization, 420 U.S. 50 (1975) (minority concerted activity unprotected); Linden Lumber Div. v. NLRB 419 U.S. 301 (1974) (restriction of the recognitional strike); Gateway Coal Co. v. UMW, 414 U.S. 368 (1974) (restrictions on safety strikes); Boys Mkts., Inc. v. Retail Clerks Union Local 770, 398 U.S. 235 (1970) (revival of the labor injunction); Local 174, Teamsters v. Lucas Flour Co., 369 U.S. 95 (1962) (implication of no-strike clause); NLRB v. Wooster Div. of Borg-Warner Corp., 356

U.S. 342 (1958) (barring strike to win demand on "permissive subject"); Labor Management Relations (Taft-Hartley) Act ss. 8(b) (4), 303, 29 U.S.C. ss. 158(b) (4), 187 (1970) (prohibiting secondary activity); idem ss. 206–210, 29 U.S.C. ss. 176–180 (restrictions on strikes imperiling national health or safety).

60. Harry Shulman, "Reason, Contract, and Law in Labor Relations," *Harvard Law Review* 68 (1955): 99, 1002.

61. Ruth Weyand, "Majority Rule in Collective Bargaining," *Columbia Law Review* 45 (1945): 566, 599.

62. Obviously such a radical reading of the Act is not compelled by the legislative history. It does, however, find substantial support in that history and in the text of the Act, . . . and moderate and conventional interpretations of the Act, however more plausible they may seem now, cannot conclusively be said to be *commanded* by the legislative history either.

79. The evidence on which these claims typically are based comes in part from oral histories given by participants in the events of the 1930s and in part from a fresh review of the record of working-class action. . . . Key points often made in support of the new viewpoint are that (1) the sit-down strikes—particularly in rubber and auto—resulted from spontaneous militancy on the part of the rank and file, who often acted against union advice and received only reluctant and belated support from the leadership of the CIO; (2) many crucial strikes were precipitated by issues concerning control of the work-process (e.g., the speed of the assembly line; work discipline) rather than wage issues; (3) militant rank-and-file groups often expressed disillusionment during the period with both the CIO leadership and the government, and they expressed a perspective of reliance on their own concerted activity as the primary resource for achieving reform; (4) the positive and often leading role played by left-wing activists (Communists, Trotskyists, and others) has been distorted and underplayed in conventional historiography; and, the most problematical claim, (5) the conduct of workers during the sit-downs—particularly their efforts to create collective forms of social life during the building occupations—intimates a yearning for, and the possibility of, a democratic reorganization of the workplace on the basis of a workers' control model. By contrast, it is argued, CIO leaders moved swiftly after union recognition to suppress the more spontaneous and participatory expressions of working-class militancy so as to be able to present themselves to management as competent guarantors of labor discipline.

Although this new labor history adds an important dimension to our understanding of the era, as with corporate liberalism theory, it is important to maintain a critical distance. Even accepting the claims of the new histories, it remains to be explained why collective bargaining was almost universally and uncritically viewed by working-class activists, both within and outside of the organized left-wing groups, as the cornerstone of all programs for social justice and why, in contrast, the concept of workers' control as such, and workers' councils, public ownership, state planning or decentralized planning, and direct state regulation of the terms and conditions of employment never became dominant rallying cries. . . . The argument of this Article is that the law itself, as a legitimating ideology and a system of institutions, played a role in the deradicalizing process.

Regardless of the strength of [the explanations discussed], however, the new labor history provides convincing support for the proposition that the possibilities of, and support for, working-class radicalism going beyond the quest for reforms within the boundaries of capitalism existed during the 1930s to a far greater degree than is customarily supposed.

103. 301 U.S. 1 (1937).

104. NLRB v. Fruehauf Trailer Co., 301 U.S. 49 (1937); NLRB v. Friedman-Harry Marks Clothing Co., 301 U.S. 58 (1937); Associated Press v. NLRB, 301 U.S. 103 (1937); Washington, Va. & Md. Coach Co. v. NLRB, 301 U.S. 142 (1937).

113. 208 U.S. 161 (1908).

114. 236 U.S. 1 (1915). . . .

116. 304 U.S. 333 (1938) (Roberts, J.).

120. The point is not that a realist analysis would have guaranteed a different or

better result in *Mackay*. An explicit sociopolitical analysis might have more candidly addressed the real issues involved, but ultimately a realist balancing of competing interests in light of Congress' labor policy might have led to the same result. Neither conceptualism nor realism succeeds in immunizing adjudication from politics, nor is either a method that provides a determinate answer to every legal problem. The effort here is simply to delineate the texture and vision of the legal consciousness developing in the cases under discussion.

123. 306 U.S. 332 (1939) (Roberts, J.).

127. Ibid., 343. It is curious that *Sands* is no longer remembered in terms of its actual facts, but rather is commonly assumed to reflect the case in which the union *has* agreed to a no-strike clause. For example, one prominent casebook cites *Sands* for the proposition that "although a strike during the term of a labor contract, in violation of a no-strike clause, is not prohibited by the Labor Act, it is unprotected." A. Cox, D. Bok, & R. Gorman, *Labor Law*, 935–36 (8th ed. 1977).

In 1947 Congress provided statutory guidelines relating to the midterm modification problem with the addition of section 8(d) (1)-(4), 29 U.S.C. s. 158(d) (1)-(4) (1970).

133. 308 U.S. 435 (1940).

136. 309 U.S. 206 (1940).

140. 311 U.S. 72 (1940) (Douglas, J.).

151. The foregoing discussion is not a legal argument that the Board should have been granted the power of substantive scrutiny over wage-bargaining. Nor is it contended that substantive review of the wage-bargain would have been the answer to labor's problems or a guarantee of justice for the American worker. From a theoretical standpoint, the idea of a democratic process establishing what the community regards as fair and just terms of employment is attractive compared to leaving such decisions to the outcome of the raw conflict of class power. I do not share the premise of liberal political theory that there is an inherent contradiction between community intervention and individual or group self-actualization and freedom. Nevertheless, in society as presently constituted, there is no reason to assume that a grant of substantive review powers to an administrative agency would, with any likelihood, result in a democratic process or just terms of employment. The Board is a priori no more likely to serve the needs of employees (or employers) than the courts or the private collective bargaining process.

My political claim, therefore, does not rest on a preference for the assumption by the Board of substantive review powers. Rather my claim is that, had the Court permitted and encouraged the Board to assume such powers, a potentially radicalizing force would have been introduced into the law by the making of a *public political issue* of the substantive terms of the wage-bargain. Public discussion and criticism of Board decisions respecting the fairness of terms of employment would have had a politicizing and destabilizing impact on the labor movement by creating greater public understanding of the contingent nature of social relationships and the way in which the purportedly neutral decisions of government reflect the preponderant influence of class power on the state. In this sense, the Court's preference for a formal, proceduralist model represented a deradicalization of the potential of the Wagner Act.

160. 308 U.S. 401 (1940) (Stone, J.).

164. 309 U.S. 261 (1940) (Hughes, C.J.). . . .

173. 313 U.S. 146 (1941) (Reed, J.).

184. As a postscript to this discussion and a prelude to the next section, it should be noted that the public right doctrine was applied selectively. That is, when the Court disapproved of the Board's action in a particular case, it suddenly reverted to the more exacting standards of traditional private adjudication. Most often, this latter approach was used to defend the property rights of employers from encroachment by the public rights supposedly protected under the Act. The result was severe limitations on the protection of employee concerted activity. See, e.g., Phelps Dodge Corp. v. NLRB, 313 U.S. 177 (1941), . . . NLRB v. Fansteel Metallurgical Corp., 306 U.S. 240 (1939). . . .

199. André Gorz, "Reform and Revolution," in *The Socialist Register* 125 (1968).

201. 306 U.S. 240 (1939) (Hughes, C.J.). . . .

276. Central to the process of the mutual assimilation is the inevitable tendency of

realism to evolve into a species of formalism. This tendency arises for several reasons. First, because liberal political theory and social science are unable candidly to confront the reality of class power and class domination in capitalist society, they necessarily serve an ideological and mystificatory role; in particular, the tendency of liberal social thought (which is harnessed by, but ultimately contributes to the transformation of, legal realism) is to present, as scientifically necessary, answers to questions involving choices between competing political values and interests. Second, and more generally, all legal decisions are necessarily made within a context of assumptions (i.e., a "concept-less" jurisprudence is an epistemological impossibility), and the historical tendency is for these underlying assumptions periodically to become reified. Finally, the aforementioned tendencies are exacerbated by the formal character of law itself in the liberal tradition, that is, its requirement that the grounds of decision in particular cases be capable of presentation in a general, suprahistorical rule-form. . . .

15

The Family and the Market: A Study of Ideology and Legal Reform

Frances E. Olsen

I. THE IDEOLOGY OF THE FAMILY AND THE MARKET

. . .

E. Summary

With the decline of feudalism there arose the dichotomies between the state and civil society and between the market and the family. The free market combined an egalitarian ideology with an individualistic ethic. The private family combined a hierarchical ideology with an altruistic ethic. In both the market and the family, state activity has tended to moderate these characteristics. Welfare state reforms in the market have reduced individualism while promoting a new kind of hierarchy. Regulation of the family has undermined the hierarchical ideology and at the same time promoted individualism.

The market and the family reflect a parallel development with respect to the dichotomy between state and civil society. The ideologies of both the free market and the family tried to legitimate actual inequality by emphasizing the equality of all with respect to the state. Inequality was said to result from the private relations among people and was thus a natural attribute of civil society rather than the responsibility of the state. It is currently asserted that the state is promoting as much equality as it reasonably can in both the family

---

Excerpted from its original publication in *Harvard Law Review* 96, 1983, by permission of the author and the Harvard Law Review Association.

and the marketplace and that any remaining inequality is a private or particularized matter.

The market and the family also relate to each other inversely. While the values of the market provide the basis for a critique of the family, the values of the family provide the basis for a critique of the market. The state intervenes in the market to make it more like the family, and in the family to make it more like the market.

Viewed from a perspective that favors democratic, intersubjective relations, these state interventions have two distinct effects. Intervention in the market is desirable insofar as it promotes altruism, but is undesirable insofar as it takes the form of the family hierarchy and legitimates and particularizes inequality instead of eliminating it. The state steps in to protect workers; the workers do not assert their own control through local organization and consolidation of power. Similarly, intervention in the family is desirable insofar as it promotes women's claims for greater power and tends to undermine formal family hierarchy; it is undesirable insofar as it promotes individualism and particularizes and legitimates hierarchy rather than eliminates it. Intervention exposes family members to market exploitation. Further, it entails the state's stepping in to equalize the results of family interaction; it does not democratize the family.

II. IDEOLOGY AND LEGAL REFORM

The dichotomization of market and family pervades our thinking, our language, and our culture. It limits and impoverishes the ways we experience our affective and productive lives, the possibilities we can imagine for restructuring our shared existence, and the manner in which we attempt change.

A wide variety of reforms aimed at improving the lives of women have been undertaken in the last two centuries. The reform efforts discussed are familiar, as are their successes and failures. Less familiar are the reasons the reforms have not been more successful—the reasons they have damaged as well as improved women's lives. By approaching this issue from the perspective of the dichotomization of market and family, I hope to cast new light on the attempts at reform and their mixed results. . . .

A. Strategies for Improving the Status of Women by Reforming the Family

Family reforms aimed at improving women's status tend either to encourage the family to emulate the egalitarianism of the market, or to protect the family from the selfish, individualistic tendencies of the market and to encourage husbands to treat wives better.

I. Greater Equality via the Market Critique.—(a) *Independence and Equality.*—Blackstone's well-known aphorism about the suspension of the wife's legal existence during marriage found support in early common law provisions that appeared to merge the wife's legal personality into the husband's. . . .

Reformers condemned these provisions for being feudal and oppressive, and worked to develop for the married woman a legal personality and existence separate from her husband's. . . .

Reformers establishing the wife's independent and equal existence have continued to the present day and have benefited women in a number of ways. They have promoted equality for women in marriages by undermining the legitimacy of family hierarchy and the oppressive prerogatives claimed by husbands. At the same time, however, the results of such reforms have often proved detrimental to women. Although the reforms promote equality, they also undermine the altruistic bases of the family and thus leave women open to the kind of individualized, particularized domination characteristic of market relations. The reforms have tended to give women equal rights, but they have not democratized the family.

For example, the married women's property acts did not force the husband to share his power over the family's wealth, but instead provided that each spouse owned his or her separate property. Given that women performed vast amounts of unpaid labor while men owned most of the propery and earned most of the money, the acts had little effect on the lives of most women. Similarly, when the law declared wives to be equal guardians of their children, this pronouncement did not by itself prevent the husband from making every important decision about the children. The basis for the father's authority changed from juridical superiority to other forms of power, such as financial control and physical force, but the authority nonetheless continued. The mother might no longer be powerless simply because she was a wife, but she might well remain powerless for reasons that would seem more particular to her situation. . . .

While reformers were trying to establish a separate and equal legal status for married women, they were also struggling to enable women to leave unsatisfactory marriages. After liberalizing the grounds for separation, reformers began working on the grounds for divorce. Legislative reform increased the grounds upon which divorce could be granted, and the new statutes sometimes included vague "catch-all" grounds like "incompatibility" or "cruelty." The reforms also tended to make divorce law more gender-neutral. Reformers persuaded trial courts to grant uncontested divorces on increasingly scanty evidence, and encouraged a liberal policy for recognizing out-of-state divorces granted in jurisdictions with less stringent laws. These reforms have enhanced the ability of women to obtain a divorce and have reduced the need for perjury or forum shopping. . . .

Although these reforms enable women to leave unsatisfactory marriages, they fail to address the economic, social, and emotional impact that divorce has on women. Moreover, the reforms do little to help women prevent their marriages from becoming unsatisfactory in the first place. In fact, the reforms may adversely affect women by increasing the ease with which *men* can get out of marriages and by undermining the power some wives once had when a husband needed his wife's consent and cooperation to obtain a divorce. A man's earning power typically increases during the course of his marriage, while a woman's often remains constant or even decreases. If a couple divorces after twenty years of marriage, the wife is likely to experience a sharp drop in her living standard, despite provisions for alimony, while the husband's living standard often rises. Marital instability may also have a more pronounced social and emotional impact on women than on men: a divorced forty-year-old man occupies a decidedly different position in society from that of a divorced forty-year-old woman.

(b) *Legalization.*—Reforms tending to establish the husband and wife as juridical equals also tend to "legalize" the relationship—that is, to allow rights to be enforced between husband and wife just as rights are enforced between people in the marketplace. Legalization requires that any deviation from the treatment of husband and wife as strangers be based on their voluntary agreement, not on any state-imposed definition of marriage.

In marriage as in the market, the will of the contracting parties is increasingly considered to be the appropriate basis for their relationship. Contracts between husband and wife are no longer treated as illegitimate efforts to alter terms and conditions of marriage that are properly imposed by the state. . . . Even if many courts will not enforce a marital contract during marriage, they will usually give some effect to the agreement upon the death of one of the parties or the dissolution of the relationship.

At the same time that contracts between husband and wife have become enforceable, torts and crimes perpetrated by one spouse against the other have become actionable. Reformers have steadily eroded doctrines of intrafamily immunity and what used to be considered the husband's right of "correction" is now recognized as assault and battery. . . . Even if few husbands or wives sue their spouses and interspousal crimes are rarely prosecuted, the removal of the immunities barring such actions represents an important legalization of the husband-wife relationship. In both criminal law and tort law, the state is undertaking to enforce the basic rights of individual women, even against their own husbands.

These reforms are beneficial in two ways. First, legalization serves generally to improve the wife's status and to protect individual women. Wife beating and marital rape, for example, lose some of their social approval and probably take place less often. Second, the reforms that legalize the husband-wife relationship do enable some individuals to negotiate better marriage terms than those provided by the state. People have more options available to them, and they are freer to experiment with new forms of family relationships.

The reforms, however, do not go far enough. The state will enforce individual rights of women, but the position of women in society may make these rights meaningless. For example, a battered wife may be legally entitled to send her husband to jail, but her economic incentive not to do so may be overwhelming. Although the reforms end certain specific kinds of domination, they legitimate others. A wife who does not press criminal assault charges against a battering husband, for example, may be blamed for allowing herself to be a victim. . . . The husband and wife are treated as if they were equal bargaining partners, even though women are in fact systematically subordinated to men.

Further, although these reforms promote legal equality and individual freedom, they may discourage altruistic behavior. When a relationship is legalized, parties are left to look out for themselves, and unless the contract provides otherwise, the sharing behavior of one party may not be reciprocated by the other. If a marriage may easily be dissolved, whoever sacrifices for the sake of the marriage is taking a greater risk than she or he would be taking for a permanent relationship.

Finally, in the same way that contracts in the marketplace may formalize domination as much as they express the will of the parties, contracts among lovers and friends may reflect and perpetuate the inequalities in their relationships. Similar legal treatment of situations involving married couples and those involving strangers may not promote equality or independence for women. Just as advocates of the welfare state argued that special legislation was necessary to protect the rights of workers and create real equality, so advocates of the regulated family have argued that special provisions are necessary to create real equality in families and to protect the individual rights of family members.

(c) Regulation.—Designed to create "real equality" within the family, a number of reforms replace rules of formal juridical equality between husband and wife with regulations that treat relations between married couples differently from relations between strangers; these regulations tend to make the family more like the welfare state market. One of the earliest forms of such regulation was aimed at ensuring that marital contracts expressed the "true will" of the parties. Courts recognizing and enforcing contracts that altered the financial consequences of marriage frequently devised special rules regarding undue influence. Some courts have based their special treatment of marital contracts on openly paternalistic appeals and stereotyped images of conniving men and unworldly women,[156]

whereas other courts have held that the marriage relationship imposes certain fiduciary obligations on both spouses.[157] . . .

2. *Increased Altruism and Solidarity Through State Regulation.*—An alternative strategy seeks to reform the family not by making it more like the market, but rather by making the family more like the ideal image of the family and enforcing an altruistic ethic. Generally, these reforms tend to widen the separation between the market and the family, and they frequently increase sexual hierarchy. Some of the reforms create financial interdependence within the family; others substitute for a regime of individual rights of family members a strategy of detailed regulation of family behavior on a case-by-case basis.

(a) *Financial Dependence.*—Community property laws, enacted in eight states, have established community ownership both of property gained by the spouses' joint efforts and of wages earned by the husband or wife during the marriage. These laws provide for shared ownership of property by the husband and wife. Whereas the married women's property acts were individualistic, community property laws are altruistic. The shortcomings of community property laws stem from their tendency to undermine equality and promote hierarchy. As originally enacted, most of these laws provided that the husband would manage the property owned by the marital community. A married woman's wages would thus become community property subject to the control of her husband.

. . .

(b) *"Deformalization."*—The clearest example of "deformalization" as a reform strategy is the family court movement that began at the turn of the century. Family courts were established to deal in an informal and sensitive manner with problems that arise in a family. Frequently, social workers and other "helping" professionals who emphasize adjustment and reconciliation serve on the staffs of family courts. Disputes are to be approached on a case-by-case basis, with resolutions carefully tailored to the particular family. The point is not to protect the individual rights of each spouse against infringement by the other, but to use the state apparatus to promote family solidarity.

Deformalization should be recognized as an alternative strategy, different from both delegalization and legalization. The delegalized private family instituted a limited "state of nature" in which the husband, if he was stronger or more powerful, could dominate his wife. Legalization of the family establishes the husband and wife as individuals with rights against each other and places the enforcement mechanisms of the state at their disposal. In both of these strategies, the state avoids making ad hoc adjustments in the outcomes of family relations.

Delegalization threatens individual rights by refusing to enforce them, and legalization threatens family solidarity by enforcing individual rights against the family. Deformalization tries to protect family solidarity without destroying individual rights. The anarchy of delegalization is avoided: the state does undertake to protect one spouse from the other. Moreover, because the state does not blindly and impersonally protect abstract rights, the protection is supposed to be less subversive of family solidarity. Rather than require the state to remain formally neutral, deformalization allows the state to make ad hoc readjustments in the outcomes of family relations. Thus, deformalization may avoid both the brute-force domination possible in the delegalized private family and the free market domination possible in the modern legalized family.

At the same time, though, the deformalization reform strategy may have adverse effects on women. First, it fails to provide full protection for individual family members because, in encouraging agreement between the parties, it may force the weaker party to accept a resolution that gives her far less than she would be entitled to in a formal adjudication. Women who try to deal with battering husbands through the family court system may well find themselves the victims of continued battering. Thus, although the aim of deformalization is altruism and family solidarity, the actual result is too often the perpetuation of hierarchy and domination. Second, deformalization violates notions of the rule of law and may result in ad hoc readjustments that are themselves oppressive. The welfare of family members may come to depend upon the uncontrolled discretion of state agencies, with the result that the state may directly dominate family life. . . .

B. Strategies for Improving the Status of Women by Reforming the Market

* * *

1. Eliminating Discrimination Against Women: Making the Market Less like the Family.—Reformers generally conceive of antidiscrimination law as a strategy to enable women to participate in the market as freely and effectively as men do. For women to participate in the market at all, it was necessary first to change the state laws that made women objects in the market or mere agents of their husbands or that barred them from the market. The futher project of making women equal participants in the market is the subject of continuing political and legal battles. The market, despite its egalitarian theoretical premises, reproduces the inequality of the family. This reproduction takes place for a number of reasons and through a number of mechanisms. Efforts to combat it are thus also varied in their intentions and their effects.

One reason women are disadvantaged in the market is that some market actors intentionally discriminate against them. Before such discrimination was outlawed, there were frequent efforts to justify it. The justifications ranged from protecting the family and women from the corruption of the market, to protecting men and the market itself from the ill effects said to result from women's participation in the market. These concerns are generally no longer considered adequate justifications for state policies excluding women from working in the market, but they continue to appear in various forms and in some cases operate to rationalize differential treatment of men and women.

Even when these concerns are rejected as justifications for differential treatment, they are often accepted as explanations for the patterns of pervasive inequality and sexual segregation that continue in the market. Thus, it may be admitted that the market reproduces the inequality of the family but denied that this inequality is caused by intentional discrimination against women. Rather, unequal results in the market are explained as the effect that growing up and living in families has upon the behavior of men and women in the market. These inequalities may be referred to as "sex-blind" discrimination.

There are two general mechanisms by which sex-blind discrimination operates. First, differing family obligations and expectations about men and women prejudice women. Second, the particular upbringings girls receive in families and the roles women have played in the past do in fact leave women ill prepared to succeed in the market, as it is now organized.

An important aspect of both mechanisms is that the market was constructed primarily by men, and the roles available in the market as well as the rewards associated with those roles were created in a sexist and discriminatory environment.

(a) Reforms Designed to Integrate Women into the Free Market.—. . . Laws forbidding conscious sex discrimination in employment, education, credit, and housing, as well as laws and regulations prescribing hiring procedures that employers must follow to protect women from such discrimination, can also be viewed as efforts to make the market more like the free market ideal. Three of the four classic reasons for intentional discrimination against women—protecting women from the corruption of the market, insulating the family from market pressures, and protecting men's position in the marketplace—are factors that ideal free market actors would not take into account in purely profit-motivated activity. Only the fourth concern—that women are in general less valuable or less productive in the market— provides a market justification for intentional discrimination. Even that argument, however, is weak support for discriminating against all women. Thus, requiring market actors to abandon their irrational

biases against women or their misplaced, altruistic inclinations to protect women, family life, or men can be seen as a way of forcing these actors to behave as rational profit maximizers.

Even affirmative action for women can be justified on free market grounds as a measure to eliminate irrational discrimination against women. First, a target or quota may be set to approximate the number of women who would be hired or promoted in the absence of irrational discrimination; such a quota serves as a proxy for gender-neutral decisions, especially in areas, like academic hiring, that are difficult to police. Furthermore, even when affirmative action is intended to compensate individual women for prior discrimination or to create a sexually integrated marketplace by rewarding women beyond what they individually merit, it is conceived of as a temporary, stopgap measure. It may be seen as a brief departure from the free market system, a departure designed to correct a malfunction caused by irrational, intentional discrimination and to restore free-market, profit-maximizing rationality.

Finally, reforms eliminating facially neutral policies that serve to handicap women are sometimes supported as efforts to purify the free market. For example, under the principles established in *Griggs v. Duke Power Co.*,[203] courts have invalidated minimum height, weight, and strength requirements that have a disproportionate impact on women and that cannot be demonstrated to be job-related. The very fact that the requirements are not job related suggests that from a free market perspective they are irrational. . . .

The major benefit of reforms that attempt to integrate women into the free market is their tendency to promote freedom and equality for women. Such reforms help to free women from economic dependency on men, expand the career options available to women, and increase the salaries and advancement possibilities of certain groups of women workers. Further, laws requiring equal treatment tend to undermine demeaning and debilitating stereotypes of women and their roles. Finally, antidiscrimination law legitimates women's complaints of unfair treatment and provides women with a vehicle for fighting back against institutions that oppress them.

The reforms, however, do not go far enough toward real equality or empowerment of women. Moreover, they encourage market individualism. Antidiscrimination law does not end the actual subordination of women in the market but instead mainly benefits a small percentage of women who adopt "male" roles. Meanwhile, it legitimates the continued oppression of most women: the reforms maintain the status quo by particularizing and privatizing inequality and encouraging women to blame themselves for their failures in the market.

Antidiscrimination law promotes market individualism and promises each individual woman that she can win success in the market if only she chooses to apply herself. It obscures for women the actual causes of their oppression and treats discrimination against women as an irrational and capricious departure from the normal objective operation of the market, instead of recognizing such discrimination as a pervasive aspect of our dichotomized system. The reforms reinforce free market ideology and encourage women to seek individualistic, inward-looking solutions to social problems.

(b) Welfare State Reforms Designed to Help Women.—A second common understanding of antidiscrimination law is that it moderates the effects of the free market in order to promote women's equality. If intentional discrimination is considered rational but socially irresponsible, laws against such discrimination can be seen as an effort to counteract the individualistic ethic of the market and to force market actors to behave more responsibly. Similarly, affirmative action can be considered more than just an effort to eradicate irrational discrimination: it can be viewed as a method of combating sex-blind discrimination or even as an attempt to restructure the workplace.

Another category of welfare state reforms designed to counteract sex-blind discrimination seeks to reduce the discriminatory impact that the unequal division of family responsibilities has on women in the market. Probably the most important reform in this category has been the amendment of Title VII to include as sex discrimination most forms of pregnancy discrimination. . . .

These reforms share the advantages of the welfare state. Like other welfare state provisions, antidiscrimination law can promote more than mere formal equality. By recognizing women's subordination, the law can account for and counteract sex-blind discrimination. Because affirmative action acknowledges the common themes in the oppression that each woman suffers, it encourages women to recognize their shared interests and can serve to empower women as a group. The reforms compensate women for their unequal family roles, improve women's market opportunities, and spread to employers and to the government some of the costs of bearing and raising children, costs that would otherwise fall disproportionately on women. Finally, by acknowledging the unfair treatment accorded women, antidiscrimination law can counteract the tendency of both men and women to lay the blame for a woman's failure in the marketplace on the woman herself rather than on a systemic bias against women.

The disadvantages of these reforms are related to the limitations of the welfare state. Although the state claims to promote greater equality, its efforts to do so have been inadequate. Antidiscrimination law helps only a small group of successful women but fails to change the basic pattern of sexually segregated employment and thus ensures that most women will remain in dead-end jobs. Yet the success of a few is used to justify a system that continues to oppress most women. Although the doctrine of affirmative action presupposes prior discrimination against women, affirmative action policies pretend to have ended such discrimination. Affirmative action thus creates another reason for women to blame themselves when they fail in the marketplace. Moreover, although affirmative action may expand women's social roles, it also tends to reinforce the ideology of inequality and to reintroduce problems of paternalism.

2. *Forcing the Market to Respond to Human Needs: Making the Market More Like the Family.*—Reforms that seek to improve the status of women by moderating the individualism of the market often improve conditions for women, but they also reinforce sexual stereotypes, augment hierarchy, and therefore undermine the quality of women's lives. Labor legislation that protects women illustrates well the advantages and drawbacks of this reform strategy. Such legislation, enacted around the turn of the century, often singled out women for special treatment, especially after *Muller v. Oregon*[228] established the validity of laws that would have been unconstitutional under the freedom-to-contract principles of *Lochner v. New York*[229] had they applied to men as well as to women.

Changed social conditions have made it easy in recent years simply to condemn *Muller* for its blatant sexism and offensive stereotyping, but at the time the case was decided, it was recognized that the case itself and the gender-based labor legislation it authorized had more complex and ambiguous implications. On one hand, *Muller* was part of the attack upon the laissez-faire policies associated with *Lochner* and upon the *Lochner* case itself. *Muller* admitted what *Lochner* had tried to deny—that protective labor legislation can benefit workers and society. . . .

On the other hand, *Muller* undermined the struggles of women for equality and, paradoxically, even offered support for the *Lochner* free market principle by carving out a limited exception to it based on a view of women's frail physique and unique role in the family. One effect of this exception was to relieve pressure for broader reforms by making laissez-faire more acceptable. Indeed, associating the need for protective labor legislation with the frailty of women offered ideological support for the claim that legislative protection was unmanly. Moreover, protective labor legislation is effective only when its beneficiaries have no choice but to receive the protection; if individual workers or a whole group can waive the benefits, they can compete more effectively in the market, and the protective legislation loses much of its value. As long as employers can hire workers who waive protection, the employers will have insufficient incentive to improve working conditions. Thus, by restricting the protective legislation to women, *Muller* placed women at a competitive disadvantage and achieved the same effect that might have been expected had the states passed gender-neutral labor legislation but allowed men to waive the protection. Protective labor legislation fell victim to the vicious circle characteristic of much reform: if a reform is too limited in its application, it is unlikely to be very effective; because it appears ineffective, its application is less likely to be extended.

. . .

The same basic pattern of possibility and risk illustrated by *Muller* is repeated in other reforms that try to make the market less individualistic. Paid maternity leave requirements, for example, provide an immediate benefit to many women workers because they force employers to moderate profitmaking to accommodate family needs. Yet they create only a minor exception to the normal operation of the market and relieve the pressure for broader reforms that would allow workers to take leaves whenever it might be socially desirable for them to do so. Focusing on maternity leave implies that having babies is the only legitimate reason for temporarily withdrawing from the marketplace. Finally, both blatant and subtle forms of prejudice continue to operate against women who take maternity leave. Maternity leave provisions tend to encourage stereotyping and hierarchy, and thus operate as *Muller* did, though far less offensively. . . .

III. TOWARD A NEW VISION

Up to this point I have described a particular structure of consciousness—the market/family dichotomy—and have explored the destructive effects it has on various reform strategies intended to improve the lives of women. As long as our discourse and our thinking remain constrained within this dominant conceptual scheme, we are faced with a kind of stalemate. Like the characters in the story from the first-grade reader, we are trying to build two different playhouses out of the same set of bricks; each effort to improve one aspect of our lives inflicts loss upon some other aspect.

I now examine the possibility of breaking out of this stalemate and speculate upon alternative ways of conceiving and experiencing our affective and productive lives. My aim is simply to begin a conversation about such alternatives.[241]

. . .

C. Transcending the Dichotomies

. . . .

Criticisms of the family are often misinterpreted as attacks upon humanization, connectedness, and parenthood, just as criticisms of the market may be misunderstood to be attacks upon efficient production of goods and services. Yet the production of goods and services is a worthwhile goal, just as it is worthwhile to express personality and to satisfy human desires to relate with others. At present, production is carried out primarily by the market, and the opportunity for expressing personality occurs mostly in the family. My argument is that this separation and polarization of functions reinforces the status quo and limits the possibilities of human association.

People who support the market/family dichotomy argue that life will be impoverished if all of it "falls under a single set of terms."[257] The problem, however, is that life all too often is circumscribed by a double set of terms. The market and the family are seen as correlatives, each opposing yet reinforcing the other. But it is my contention that we do not need inhuman environments in order to enjoy human ones, nor do we need unproductive or impractical associations in order to enjoy productive or practical ones. Polarizing the family and the market does not increase the possibilities available to individuals and to the human personality. Instead it reifies the abstractions of "the market" and "the family" and renders us powerless.

. . .

I do not advocate replacing the present dichotomies with an all-powerful state and an all-embracing market any more than I would advocate making women just like men. The state as it now exists must be ended at the same time that civil society as it now exists is ended; and when we transform the contemporary family, we must simultaneously transform the market.

I favor neither a romantic return to a simpler form of life nor a regression to an earlier, undifferentiated world. It would not be a solution to reestablish cottage industries, to have both parents at home working and caring for the children. I am not envisioning an escape from the complications of existing in the world as conscious free-willed beings, nor do I advocate an evasion of the conflict that may be painful but is inherent in human growth. Rather, I have in mind a situation in which conflict can take place more effectively. The dichotomies stunt human growth by avoiding and displacing conflict—conflict within the individual psyche and among people. The problem of externalizing conflict through compartmentalization, and the advantages to be gained by transcending the dichotomies, can be illustrated by an examination of the male/female dichotomy.

The differences between men and women are as natural as starvation, religion, and brutality. Inequality between men and women has existed throughout recorded history and has persisted across widely divergent cultures. So too have starvation, religion, and brutality. That each of these phenomena has been long lived does not mean that any of them is immutable. . . .

(a) *Problems of Love.*—Feminists have long argued that our present gender system, with its inequality and domination, makes true love between the sexes difficult, perhaps impossible.[276] What currently passes for love has been described as "a one-sided pathological dependency of women on men."[277] Men are seen to be strong and powerful, women to be weak and dependent.

In addition, in our present society women are economically and socially dependent upon men. The chief determinants of a woman's status are her acceptance by and associations with men. Under these circumstances, romantic love plays an apologetic role; it mystifies women about their dependency on men and reinforces male hegemony. . . .

Drawing on Rousseau, [Elizabeth Rapaport] suggests that achieving equality of power and influence between men and women would not by itself solve the problems of love. Love begins with a healthy attraction, a recognition of like sensibilities. But lovers then focus on differences, she argues, because they are seeking to find in their partners the qualities they fear they lack in themselves, and are thus in some sense seeking to gain possession of those qualities. They do not choose the partner with whom they have most to share, but rather seek the "pre-eminent" member of the opposite sex. Each person hoping to be loved must strive to appear to be that preeminent person. Consequently, even if there were equality between men and women, a relationship of dependency might lead to a false presentation of the self as well as to a fear of exposing the real, flawed self. The lover thus loses his or her identity and autonomy. . . .

Thus, the real issue is not dependency, but rather one's attitude toward oneself. It is important that one be self-sufficient, but not that one be independent. The choice is not between being a complete, independent individual and being dependent and incomplete.

Rapaport contends that healthy love is impossible not only because of the inequality between men and women, but also because of the individualist assumptions of liberalism and the actual competitive and hierarchical conditions of capitalist society. Thus, she argues, socialism and women's equality hold the promise of healthy love. Rapaport is correct to reject dependency and autonomy as polar choices. An adult can and should be "autonomous" in the sense of being a full and complete human being. Yet social life is richer than isolation; sharing and intimacy enable a person to enjoy life more fully. To the extent that our social interactions enrich the quality of our lives, we can be said to be "dependent" upon others for this enhanced existence. To have to depend on another to fulfill immediate emotional needs can be a bad thing; to be able to depend on another to enrich one's life is a good thing. To be autonomous means not to need another in order to feel complete; it does not mean that one is incapable of enriching one's life through social interaction.

Socialism and sexual equality together, however, are not enough to rehabilitate love. We must also counter the selfalienation inherent in our present gender system. When we project human traits separately upon men and women, we ensure that we remain incomplete beings. Our attraction for the opposite sex has a quality of urgency because a relationship with a member of that sex is necessary for our own completion. Our present gender system tends to foster relationships based on need rather than desire. To need another to complete oneself is ultimately unsatisfactory; it interferes with the intimate sharing that is possible between human beings, a sharing that leads us to want contact with others.

(b) *Problems of Domination.*—The domination of women by men is self-perpetuating. Women's unfamiliarity with aspects of the world to which they have been denied access has justified their continued exclusion. Menstruation, pregnancy, and childbirth have been made to operate as disadvantages to women and have allowed women to be dominated by men and to need their protection. The degradation of women in the real world was matched by their exaltation in a fantasy world. Women were seen as wonderful and terrible.

The world came more generally to be viewed as a series of complex dualisms—reason/passion, rational/irrational, culture/nature, power/sensitivity, thought/feeling, soul/body, objective/subjective. Men, who have created our dominant consciousness, have organized these dualisms into a system in which each dualism has a strong or positive side and a weak or negative side. Men associate themselves with the strong sides of the dualisms and project the weak sides upon women. In the same way that men simultaneously exalt and degrade women and the family, they simultaneously exalt and degrade the concepts on the weak sides of the dualisms. Nature, for example, is glorified as something awesome, a worthy subject of conquest by male heroes, while it is simultaneously degraded as inert matter to be exploited and shaped to men's purposes. Irrational subjectivity and sensitivity are similarly treasured and denigrated at the same time.

Another important aspect of the way these dualisms are viewed in dominant culture is that the inferior half of any dualism is often seen to pose a constant danger to the stronger half. Man is warned to do battle with the flesh, with nature, even with women. Irrationalism is regarded as something that must be conquered, like nature. The weak sides of the dualisms are simultaneously indispensable and threatening to men.

The limited choices that seem available to women may be described in terms of women's relationship to those dualisms. One feminist strategy accepts the identification of women with their traditional side of the dualisms but tries to deny the hierarchy men have established between the two sides. Another strategy struggles to identify women with the stronger side of the dualisms instead of challenging the devaluation of the side traditionally associated with women. . . . Although neither of these two feminist strategies is necessarily inconsistent with a rejection of the dualisms themselves, such a rejection has not in practice been emphasized.

The traditional identification of women with the weak side of the dualisms—with nature, subjectivity, nurturance—has been a legacy of oppression. Accepting this identification may be tantamount to embracing women's subordinate position. Yet the identification is also a potential source of power and insight. To reject the weak side of the dualisms is to neglect the qualities that women have been allowed to cultivate. Both approaches may be considered to accept, perhaps even to reinforce, the dualisms.

The answer that I endorse is not to reject identification with the strengths and values of women, but to recognize the incompleteness of the traditional roles of women and of women's identification with one side of the dualisms. Thus, I would not repudiate the traditional values and roles of women, but would refuse to give those values and roles a privileged place. It is the acceptance and the sexualization of the dualisms that is the chief problem. When one side of a dualism is forced upon us, it is not enough to insist upon the right to choose the opposite side. Nor, of course, is it helpful to grab the weak side of the dualism voluntarily before it is forced upon us. We cannot choose between the two sides of the dualism, because we need both. Similarly, we cannot choose between men's roles and women's roles, because both are essential to us. We can never win if we fight for the bigger portion or even an equal portion of a body torn in two; we must prevent the initial destruction.

3. Criticisms and Conclusions.—As early as the nineteenth century, feminists became aware of the idea of abolishing sex roles. The rebirth of the women's movement has again brought this idea into popular discourse, and critics have leveled a variety of attacks against what has been loosely labeled "androgyny." In order to clarify my position, I shall briefly set forth two of these attacks and my response to them.

First, opponents of androgyny warn that the elimination of the present gender system will diminish the possibilities for passion and variety in human association by making everyone boringly the same. It is true that as long as we sexualize dichotomies and constitute ourselves as incomplete beings, we must depend on finding other, correlatively incomplete beings in order to reclaim wholeness. As incomplete beings, we find it threatening to consider the sudden loss of other incomplete beings who are our inverse. . . . With respect to the division between male and female, whole people do not need correlatives and will find their social wants more readily satisfied by other complete beings. We can recognize that we would not increase diversity by chopping off the right arms of all women and the left arms of all men; yet what some opponents of androgyny argue is no more sensible. Sex roles limit human potential far more than they expand it.

A second objection to androgyny suggests that the union or transcendence of the male/female dichotomy may be undesirable because it would require that women accept what men have been as a part of the wholeness women seek. Instead, this argument runs, women should reject what men have been and find strength in women's culture and the values of our foremothers. My response to this is that most of what is wrong with what men have been is what they have not been. The point is not that the passions are superior to reason, subjectivity to objectivity, nature to culture, and so forth. To reverse the dualisms may secure for women a fairer portion of the divided psyche, but to reject the polarization of the dualistic pairs is to create the possibility of wholeness. Although I share the rejection of much of what men have been (or rather what they have *not* been), I feel that I must also reject much of what women have not been (and thus, in the same sense, what we have been).

When I speak of transcending the male/female dichotomy, I have in mind creating a new referential system for relating men and women to the world, a systemic departure from the ordinary image of male and female as correlatives. This does not mean making women more like men, or men more like women. Rather, it means radically increasing the options available to each individual, and more important, allowing the human personality to break out of the present dichotomized system. We have all experienced occasional glimpses of what this might mean—moments of power, sensitivity, and connectedness. We should recognize these fleeting experiences as a source of hope, a foreshadow of the human beings we can become. In some ways women will be *less* like present men, and men will be *less* like present women. Rather than shades of grey as an alternative to all black and all white, I envision reds and greens and blues.

NOTES

156. See Kosik, 253 Or. at 15, 452 P.2d at 560.
157. See In re Estate of Hillegass, 431 Pa. 144, 244 A.2d 672 (1968).
203. 401 U.S. 424 (1971).
228. 208 U.S. 412 (1908).
229. 198 U.S. 45 (1905).
241. None of what I say here is in any sense intended to be a resolution of the dilemmas I have sketched out, nor is it an effort to construct a new system that could become as rigid and oppressive as the market/familly dichotomy. Rather, it is meant to be an example of the kind of speculative thinking that we can and should undertake as a first step in a better direction.
257. J. Elshtain, *Public Man, Private Woman* (Oxford, Martin Robertson, 1981), p. 335.
276. For an excellent summary and evaluation of some of these views, see *Women and Philosophy,* Rapaport, Elizabeth, "On the Future of Love: Rousseau and the Radical Feminists," eds. C. Gould and M. Wartotsky (New York: Putnam, 1980), p. 185.
277. Ibid.

16

A Critique of American Tort Law

Richard Abel

TORT LAW AND CAPITALISM

Tort law is intimately related to the rise of capitalism as both cause and effect. Because capitalism separates those who produce from those who own the means of production, workers lose control over their own safety. Because capitalists have to maximize profit in a competitive market, they must sacrifice the health and safety of others—workers, consumers, those affected by environmental danger. Tort law has reflected this compulsion in many ways: the choice of negligence over strict liability, the fellow servant rule and assumption of risk, exculpatory clauses, the lower standard of care for landowners and professionals. Capitalism fosters injury for another reason: it must constantly expand its markets and increase consumption. Torts contribute to this end, just like planned obsolescence and warfare.

Capitalism is accompanied by industrialization, which confers on capitalists (and only much later on individuals, e.g., car drivers) the power to do extraordinary damage, first through dominion over unprecedented amounts of physical force (factories, railroads), and more recently through the proliferation of toxic chemicals. Concentration of capital and mass production increases the number of workers, consumers, and others who may be harmed by capitalist indifference or miscalculation. Capitalism and technology also distance from their victims those who make the "decision for accidents," so that tortious acts increasingly resemble modern warfare.

Excerpted from its original publication in *British Journal of Law and Society* 8, 1981, by permission of the author and the British Journal of Law and Society.

Capitalism transforms the social structure. Industrialization requires urbanization, which enormously increases the frequency of
interaction among strangers. This is significant because strangers,
unlike acquaintances or intimates, have less incentive to exercise care
not to injure one another inadvertently, and also because strangers
find it more difficult to resolve the differences that arise when such
injury occurs. Both problems are aggravated by the class and racial
differences within the modern capitalist city. At the same time,
interaction among friends and relatives shrinks, ultimately, to the
nuclear family. This is significant because it is intimates who commit
intentional torts: "each man kills the thing he loves." Indeed, inadvertent injuries that cannot be forgiven are often interpreted as intentional, whether in terms of witchcraft in tribal societies or theories of
unconscious ambivalence since Freud. Yet intentional torts within the
nuclear family are rarely resolved by the legal system, both because
the process frequently would destroy the relationship and because
those who commit the torts—men against women, parents against
children—are powerful enough to obstruct legal redress. A separate
but related development alters the legal response to intentional tort:
the growth of the state apparatus as an essential condition of capitalism. The state (in the form of police, criminal courts, and the penal
system) expropriates interindividual conflict and invites, indeed requires, passivity and dependence (consider the invisibility of the
victim in most criminal prosecutions). Crime virtually supplants intentional tort; civil remedies are largely limited to unintentional
behavior.

Capitalism also shapes the experience of injury. First (and this
enumeration is not chronological) capitalism creates a proletariat that
must sell its labor for wages in order to live. It simultaneously destroys
the obligations of mutual support outside the nuclear family and pays
those within it who are gainfully employed a level of wages too low to
support nonproductive members. Because inability to work thus
becomes tantamount to destitution or dependence upon charity, the
core of damages is compensation for loss of earning capacity.[16]
Second, capitalists, petty bourgeois, and more recently unionized
workers are able to accumulate consumer goods which require protection against inadvertent destruction (just as there is greater power
to destroy, so there is more to be destroyed).[17] The capitalist process
of commodification and the industrial process of mass production
make one chattel as good as another (indeed, the newer the better)
and money the equivalent of all; hence money damages come to be
seen as adequate compensation. Third, the family (now shrunk to a
nucleus) is no longer able to care for illness or injury, partly because
its members must seek employment outside the home and partly
because care itself has been commodified and monopolized by the
emergent medical profession. Since this monopoly allows profession-

als to command high fees, injuries come to "cost" a great deal more.[18] Finally, the logic of the commodity form is progressively extended to nonproductive experience (damages for pain and suffering, emotional distress) and intimate relationships (damages for wrongful death, loss of consortium). Thus tort law under capitalism equates labor, possessions, care, emotional and physical integrity, and ultimately love with money.

Capitalist tort law exploits and alienates tort victims in ways that parallel the exploitation and alienation of labor by the capitalist mode of production. In pre-capitalist society injury, like work, creates use value: it elicits care from intimates who are motivated by concern, and it stimulates a demand for an apology backed by a threat of retribution by those who belong to the same community as the victim and are therefore also injured. The capitalist state, which obstructs this latter response by its monopoly of force, simultaneously creates a market for injuries in the form of tort law and the legal system (just as it constitutes the market for the sale of labor, capital, land and commodities). Where capitalism separates the worker from the means of production, the legal profession separates tort victims from the means of redressing their wrongs and the medical profession disables victims and intimates from caring for illness and injury. In each instance a fraction of the dominant class mobilizes the power of the state in its own interests—to protect the property of the capitalist and the monopoly of expertise of the lawyer and physician. The lawyer then combines his expertise with the victim's injury (as the capitalist combines his capital with the worker's labor) to create a tort (a commodity) that has exchange value both in the state-created market (the court) and in the dependent markets it spawns (negotiated settlements). The lawyer (like the capitalist) exercises total control over this process; the victim (like the worker) has virtually no say over which torts are produced or how they are produced. When the transaction is complete, the victim receives the bare minimum necessary for survival (or less)[25] and the lawyer takes the rest as a fee (the capitalist expropriation of surplus value), some of which is shared with physicians.

CRITIQUE OF CAPITALIST TORT LAW

Discriminating Against Class, Race, and Gender

Liberal legalism, the dominant political philosophy under capitalism, decries explicit de jure discrimination. Therefore tort law gradually eliminates distinctions between patients who are injured in charitable and in profit-making hospitals, fee-paying automobile passengers and gratuitous guests, business and social guests injured by landowner negligence, those injured by medical malpractice and other tort victims. But insistence on superficial equality hides the persistence of numerous invisible inequalities. First (and foremost) there is inequality in the incidence of injury and illness: capitalists, professionals, white-, pink-, and blue-collar workers are exposed to vastly different hazards in the workplace;[32] consumers (of household goods, foods, automobiles, medical care, etc.) suffer different risks of injury, depending on the quality of the products and services they buy (necessarily a reflection of class); residential segregation by class determines the level of environmental pollution that members of a household will endure.[34] For the same reasons, ethnic differences in employment, consumption, and residence will produce racial inequalities in incidence. Women are exposed to more dangers in the home than are men but conversely may be "protected" from hazards at work by being excluded from dangerous jobs with higher pay and status.

Second, class, race, and gender will affect the extent to which and the way in which the experience of injury is transformed into a claim for legal redress: the sense of entitlement to physical, mental, and emotional well-being (women only recently began to resist abuse by their husbands; textile workers are just now coming to view chronic shortness of breath as unnatural); the feeling of competence to assert a claim and to withstand retaliation; the capacity to mobilize the legal process, which includes choosing and controlling a lawyer and preparing evidence; and financial and emotional resources, which will affect the quality of legal representation obtained and the ability of the claimant to overcome opposition and delay in order to pursue negotiation or litigation to a satisfactory conclusion.

Third, the law discriminates in the availability and generosity of the remedies it offers. The greatest difference is between tort damages and other compensation systems. An injured blue-collar worker is far more likely than someone from another occupational category to be relegated to workers' compensation, which pays only a fraction of tort damages and rejects some tortious injuries altogether.[45] But other oppressed categories—the poor, the elderly, women, children, and ethnic minorities—are also excluded from tort recovery.[46] Thus the victims of violent crimes, whose assailants are unidentifiable or judgment-proof, are relegated to state compensation schemes that reach very few victims and pay even them inadequate amounts. Women and children who are injured by intimates are left without any remedy. The poor and minorities, who either cannot evade the draft or enlist in the military as an alternative to structural unemployment, are dependent on niggardly veterans' benefits when injured in war. And when they are victims of governmental misconduct—police violence, abuse in prisons, schools, and mental institutions—they may be completely remediless, either because of sovereign immunity or because officials possess substantial tactical advantages in defending against such claims.

Another form of remedial discrimination is internal to the tort system; the quantum of damages preserves, and indeed amplifies, the present unequal distribution of wealth and income. Imagine a car crash between A, who is unemployed and drives a worthless jalopy, and B, who owns a Rolls-Royce and earns a high income. If A is negligent and B non-negligent, A will have to pay for the damage to the Rolls and to B's earning capacity. But if B is negligent and A non-negligent, B will have to pay virtually nothing. This inequality is exaggerated by the fact that damages for pain and suffering are often expressed as a multiple of the pecuniary damages (usually two-to-one). If we make the hypothetical more realistic by giving both parties liability insurance the inequality remains: A's insurance premium will have to reflect the possibility of injury to B and be higher than would be necessary to protect A and others like him, whereas B's premium will reflect the possibility of an injury to A and be lower than would be necessary to protect a world of Bs. A thus pays part of the cost of protecting the privileges of B.

Producing Illness and Injury

Capitalist tort law systematically encourages unsafety. The dynamic of capitalism—competitive pursuit of profit—impels the enterprise to endanger the workers it employs,[52] the consumers of its products and services, and those who inhabit the environment it pollutes. The cost of safety almost always diminishes profits. The capitalist, therefore, must be as unsafe as he can get away with being. Tort law purports to curb these destructive consequences of capitalism. The legal-economic rationale that presently dominates and shapes tort principles is market deterrence, which argues that the most efficient means to promote an optimum level of safety is to internalize accident costs by making those who negligently cause accidents legally liable for their consequences. But there are fundamental theoretical and empirical reasons why market deterrence does not and cannot work. First, the very name is deceptive: there can be no market deterrence because there is no market for injury and illness. The determination of what an accident costs can be decided only collectively, whether by a judge, a jury, or a legislature. Furthermore, the decision necessarily introduces a large margin of error, since it must not only value intangibles but also make predictions about an individual future: lost earnings, inflation, career prospects, change in number of dependents, what would be spent on dependents, change in tax structure, life expectancy, prognosis for recovery, possible medical discoveries, etc. Second, a court is required to decide whether a *particular* injury was negligently inflicted, but the economic conceptualization of negligence as suboptimal safety (epitomized in Learned Hand's formula weighing the cost of accident avoidance against the cost of injury discounted by its probability)[61] can meaningfully be applied only to an ongoing activity. The inevitable errors in determining negligence can lead only to inadequate safety. Third, a court is required to determine whether or not a particular actor *caused* a given injury or illness, a dichotomous decision. But we know that causation is probabilistic and that for any event there are a multiplicitly of contributing causes. The imposition of liability on one party (or even several) necessarily fails to internalize the accident costs in other casual activities.

Fourth, there is an inescapable tension between promoting safety through accident cost internalization and spreading these costs—another goal of tort law.[65] The most important mechanism for spreading costs is liability insurance, which has become so widespread, and which discriminates so crudely among insured in setting premiums, that it alone virtually destroys the capacity of tort liability to optimize safety.

Fifth, in order for liability costs to alter the behavior of entrepreneurs the latter must be unable to pass these costs on to consumers; but this condition will not be satisfied if liability costs are an insignificant percentage of the price of the good or service (as they usually are), if demand is relatively price-inelastic (the good or service is a necessity), or if the market is highly oligopolistic.

Sixth, market deterrence assumes that all actors who "cause" accidents are economic maximizers and consequently argues that victims must be *denied* compensation (in whole or in part) in order to motivate them to protect themselves. This can only diminish the concern of capitalists for the safety of others.

Seventh and the most important, market deterrence assumes that the legal system fully internalizes *all* the costs of negligent accidents. Yet we have just seen in the previous section that capitalist tort law systematically denies compensation for injury and illness and does so in a highly discriminatory manner. Therefore, the theory of market deterrence logically compels the conclusion that capitalist tort law encourages unsafety and subjects the most oppressed sectors of the population to the greatest danger. It motivates the entrepreneur to reduce *liability* costs, not accident costs, to seek to evade the consequences of unsafety, not to enhance safety. Thus we have Ford producing a Pinto with a gasoline tank it knew to be explosive, Johns-Manville continuing to subject its workers to asbestos for decades after it learned they could suffer lung damage and cancer,[75] American Airlines flying the DC-10 that crashed in Chicago when it knew of the faulty pylon and the drug companies selling thalidomide they knew to be dangerous. The capitalist response to the threat of tort liability is to strive to externalize accident costs by concealing information (denying workers access to their medical records), threatening retaliation against those who seek compensation, and using the enormous resources of the enterprise (and of its liability insurer) to coerce victims into accepting inadequate settlements, to overwhelm them in litigation, and to pass legislation that immunizes the enterprise from liability costs (as the nuclear energy industry has done with the Price-Anderson Act). We know from studies of the deterrent effect of criminal sanctions that certainty is more important than severity; because it is so unlikely that damages will ever be paid, tort liability is an empty threat, incapable of promoting safety.

If market deterrence worked the way it claims, state regulation of danger would be wholly unnecessary. The capitalist enterprise would balance the cost of safety against the cost of accidents, and whatever level of danger it chose would, by definition, be optimally efficient. Indeed, the mythical efficiency of the market is often invoked to oppose all regulation, or at least to require agencies to conform to the fictitious criteria of cost-benefit analysis, as in the attacks on OSHA by capitalists, the Supreme Court, and now the Reagan administration. Yet surely the failure of tort as a means of control is visible in the proliferation of regulation in such areas as food and drugs, environmental pollution, toxic wastes, pesticides, air, rail and road transportation, nuclear energy, consumer products, professional services, and the workplace. Virtually everyone concedes the need for rules in at least some of these areas, e.g., traffic laws or the testing of medicines. Indeed, capitalists often welcome regulation as a protection against the competitive market. But we also know that these agencies fail to achieve acceptable levels of safety because, when compared to the capitalist enterprises they seek to regulate, they are inadequately funded, more restrained by legal formalism, denied effective sanctions, and readily captured by the industries they ostensibly control.

The most insidious consequence of dependence upon market deterrence and state regulation has been to undermine collective efforts by those endangered to protect their own safety. Critics have often noted that the regulatory agency can lull citizens into a false sense of security, and hence into passivity, by appearing vigorously to champion public interests. The politics of safety is transformed into the administration of safety, thereby obscuring the political interests the administrative apparatus continues to serve. But if the bankruptcy of government regulation is a familiar tale, the effect of dependence on market deterrence is less widely recognized, and yet such dependence is even more dangerously seductive. Market deterrence, by mandating the payment of money damages to the injured person, subverts collective efforts to exert control over safety. Damages are paid only to individuals (not collectivities) because the injury, like the individual, is viewed as unique; group reparations and class actions are unavailable to those who share the experience of having been injured by the same polluter, manufacturer of a defective product, or employer. Damages are paid only for an injury *caused* by the defendant's act: this means both that unsafe conduct causing no injury is not deterred and that legal attention is focused on the temporally delimited act of an individual rather than on the ongoing activity of a collectivity. Capitalist tort law, like capitalist medicine, is obsessed with individual cure at the expense of collective prevention because (among other reasons) capitalism creates a market only for the former. Money damages undermine the sense of a collective interest in safety both by conveying the (false) impression that they adequately compensate for the injury (so that greater safety is unnecessary) and by arousing jealousy of the victim, thereby dividing those who might be injured in the future from the unfortunate victim who already has suffered.

At the same time that the class of victims (actual and potential) is individualized, those responsible for creating the danger and potentially liable for damages are collectivized—by the corporate form, the doctrine of respondeat superior, an expansive interpretation of proximate cause, and the spread of liability insurance. This aggregation is necessary because tort damages have grown too large to be paid by the individual (again the subversion of control in the name of spreading costs). But the inequality between individual victim and collective tortfeasor is also constructed by the legal system: although the (collective) liability insurer can aggressively badger the victim for a release, the personal injury lawyer cannot solicit the victim for authority to represent him in suing the insurer; group legal service plans, originally formed by automobile owners to provide lawyers for accident victims, were long illegal; corporations often refuse to bargain with unions over safety practices, claiming these as "management prerogatives"; and, of course, most workers, consumers, and citizens are not organized collectively. Thus the legal structure of the struggle over safety pits the individual victim (or potential victim) against a collectivity, whether in the legislature, the regulatory agency, the court, or at the negotiating table.

Reproducing Bourgeois Ideology

It would be a mistake to interpret legal phenomena solely in terms of their instrumental effect upon material conditions. Tort law is also significant in the reproduction of bourgeois ideology. The fault concept upon which that law was built reinforces a central element of bourgeois ideology—individualism. Predicating liability upon the defendant's fault and denying recovery because of the victim's fault perfectly express the bourgeois belief that each person controls his or her own fate. And indeed the bourgeoisie experience this control in their own lives—in their work, their consumption, and their environment—an experience epitomized in the contemporary "sauve qui peut" obsession with *personal* physical, mental, and emotional well-being. But the nineteenth-century concept of fault is too moralistic for today's tastes and too patently inconsistent with the reality that the collective consequences are caused by the confluence of multiple, ongoing, collective activities. As a result of these tensions strict liability has progressively displaced negligence, and the defenses of contributory negligence and assumption of risk have been eroded through doctrinal change and jury nullification. Yet individualism has been saved, if in a modified form. The triumph of economic analysis has redefined fault as the efficient allocation of resources, a concept that appears scientific and apolitical rather than mushy and moralistic. And economic efficiency sees everyone as potentially capable of avoiding accidents, thereby equating the car driver with the automobile manufacturer, the worker with the boss. Fault translated into the language of economics has once again infiltrated strict liability under cover of the requirement of a defect;[104] fault has revived contributory negligence in the guise of doctrines of comparative negligence and unforeseeable use;[105] and it has answered the problem of concurrent causation by comparing the fault of multiple tortfeasors.[106] And individualism also survives in the rejection of affirmative duties, a rejection that asserts that each man is an island, sole unto himself.

Tort law also offers symbolic support for inequality. By compensating owners for property damage it upholds the notion of private property and its concomitant—that a person's worth (as a tort plaintiff) is proportional to the value of the property he owns. By preserving the income streams of those who suffer physical injury (and of their dependents), tort law affirms the legitimacy of the existing income distribution. By excluding certain categories of people from tort recovery, the law suggests that their injuries, and therefore they themselves, are less highly valued. Furthermore, by relegating injured employees to worker's compensation (which is limited to medical expenses and a fraction of lost wages in most jurisdictions), the law treats workers like pure labor value, implicitly denying that they suffer the pain for which we compensate tort victims or enjoy the pleasures whose loss is often a significant element of tort damages. Tort law proclaims the class structure of capitalist society: you are what you own, what you earn, and what you do.

Finally, tort law responds to intangible injury by extending the fundamental concept of capitalism—the commodity form—from the sphere of production to the sphere of reproduction. Damages for pain and suffering extrapolate the Benthamite hedonic calculus to its ultimate extreme, insisting that for every pain suffered there is some equivalent pleasure that will erase it—a pleasure that can be bought with money—and that the jury therefore must simulate a market in sadomasochism by asking themselves what they would charge to undergo the victim's misfortune. Tort thus extracts an involuntary present sacrifice in exchange for future gain (damages), thereby reproducing bourgeois notions of delayed gratification, an instrumental view of the self, characteristics that Weber stressed in his identification of capitalism with the Protestant ethic. They commodify our unique experience by substituting the universal equivalent, money—as when a plaintiff's attorney asks the jury to assign a money value to each *second* of the victim's pain and then aggregate it over a lifetime of suffering.[111] This dehumanization is particularly striking in two extreme (and opposite) situations: when injuries shorten a victim's life expectancy so that money damages are rationalized as enhancing present pleasure in lieu of a future foregone[112]—a secular variation on the Faustian compact; and when the guardian of a child born illegitimate or deformed sues for wrongful life, arguing that money is necessary to compensate the child for the net detriment of a disadvantaged life over never existing.[113] Giving the victim money damages for pain and suffering, especially when the injury is severe and the award proportionately large, has several additional consequences: it salves the guilt the rest of us feel at having been spared such torment (the survivor syndrome); it justifies us in succumbing to the selfish desire to have nothing further to do with the disabled and disfigured; indeed, rather than stimulating compassion for the victim, large awards incite envy for what is seen as a windfall; and they convey the (erroneous) impression that the compensation system is working well—if anything, too well.

If damages for pain and suffering commodify experience, the recent expansion of tort remedies for injuries to relationships commodifies love. Damages are now paid for loss of the society and companionship of a parent in wrongful death actions,[117] for loss of consortium of an injured spouse,[118] lover,[119] parent,[120] or child;[121] for witnessing or learning about an injury to a loved one;[122] for mistreatment of the corpse of a loved one;[123] for negligent misinformation about the death of a loved one;[124] for destruction of community; even for injury to loved objects.[126] Such compensation affirms several symbolic messages. All relationships have a monetary value and hence can be bought and sold. The value of a relationship varies with the extent to which the attributes of the other partner approximate societal ideals of physical beauty, mental acuity, athletic ability, emotional normality, etc. If the other partner is impaired the relationship should be discarded—like any other consumer product in our throwaway society—and a replacement purchased with the money damages received. In effect, all relationships are treated as a form of prostitution—the semblance of love exchanged for money—a generalization of feminist criticism of marriage. Just as society pays pain and suffering damages to the injured victim who is shunned (so he can purchase the commodified care and companionship that will no longer be given out of love and obligation), so it pays damages to those who loved him, compensating them for their lost "investment" in the relationship (so they can invest in other human capital).

A SOCIALIST APPROACH TO INJURY AND ILLNESS

Just as capitalism expropriates from workers, consumers, and citizens the power to control their own health and safety, offering only an inadequate level of compensation in exchange, so the primary concern of socialism must be to ensure that those at risk regain control over the threat of injury and illness; compensation must be subordinated to safety, if it remains important. This reversal of priorities simply reflects our spontaneous response to danger: surely we think first about the safety of those we love and not whether they will be compensated if they are injured. We do not accept—or perversely welcome—injury because it is accompanied by damages. Furthermore, compensating victims by imposing liability on the causal actor *cannot* achieve an acceptable level of safety. Even if we remedied all the defects in the capitalist compensation system, raising damages to adequate levels and increasing rates of recognition, claim, and recovery to 100 percent—and clearly this would require a fundamental social transformation—we would have devised a social democratic rather than a socialist solution to the problem of injuries, one that contains two irremediable and fatal flaws. First we would have spread the *cost* of accidents across society through a social welfare scheme, whereas what we must do is spread the *risk* of accidents more equally. True, accidents would then cost the same, regardless of the victim's identity, and there would be no economic incentive to inflict them on a particular class, race, or gender. But those with greater resources would still be able to buy more immunity from risk and would undoubtedly do so, just as they do now under capitalism. For every social democracy preserves differences of wealth and income that allow the privileged to obtain superior education, health care, cultural and physical amenities—and safety. The social democratic program might better promote the capitalist criterion of allocative efficiency, but it would not realize the distributional goal of equality. Second, the social democratic solution remains paternalistic (like capitalist law, whatever its pretensions to protect individual freedom). The valuation of illness and injury (and the converse, health and safety) is still performed by the state—whether by a legislature, regulatory agency, judge, or jury—and not by the person or group who suffers (or enjoys) it. Respect for personal autonomy demands that the person at risk decide what it is worth to undergo that danger—even bourgeois economics concedes this (which suggests that the bourgeois ideal of optimal efficiency can be realized only under socialism and may not be all that different from the principle "to each according to his needs").

The two requirements of a just approach to illness and injury—equalizing risk and restoring control to those who undergo danger—cannot be satisfied without radical change: in the division of labor (a reduction in specialization and perhaps rotation between hand work and head work, such as occurred during the Chinese cultural revolution and in many intentional communities); and in control over the means of production (which must be transferred from capitalists to workers). The first steps might be forms of cooperative enterprise and worker involvement in improving health and safety in the workplace—*not* nationalization of industry, which simply substitutes the state for capital. Since both reforms would threaten capitalist control, vigorous resistance can be expected and is already visible in the Reagan administration's decision to withdraw funding from the national cooperative bank and in its attacks on OSHA. The strength of capitalist opposition may also explain the timidity of unions. But for precisely these reasons, occupational health and safety is an excellent issue for rank-and-file activists and for organizing unorganized workers. It is harder to see how to equalize exposure to the risks posed by consumer goods and services and by residence (although economic equality and its political and social consequences would advance this goal) and how to empower those exposed to such risks to control their own safety (increased self-reliance may be necessary since consumers are a diffuse category, unlike those who share the same workplace or residential area).

The socialist approach to the problem of safety will still require a reponse to illness and injury, since these will occur even under socialism(!), although their frequency and distribution will be radically altered. Furthermore, because full attainment of the socialist program will have to await the overthrow of capitalism, it is essential to identify other short-run goals that progressives can pursue, as long as there is no reason to believe that these detract from safety or come to be seen as substitutes for prevention. Historically, and perhaps inevitably, there has been a tension between efforts to extend recovery to new victims or new forms of misfortune and efforts to increase the amount of compensation paid to each. Thus both workers' compensation and no-fault insurance for automobile accidents protect more victims but are less generous than tort damages. I believe this is the right choice on grounds of both equity and political tactics. The paramount criterion for a just compensation system should be equality: it should respond to all victims if it responds to any, and the response to each should be equal. The first requirement mandates equality among victims whether or not their misfortunes were caused by fault (their own or that of others), or by human actors at all: those who suffer from tort, unavoidable accident, illness, and congenital disability should be treated alike. After all, that is how we respond to the misfortunes of those we love. The second requirement argues that inequalities of wealth and income should not be reproduced in the level of compensation, for this would maintain those inequalities materially and reaffirm them symbolically. Thus there should be *no* compensation for damage to either property or individual earning power: those who enjoy privileges of wealth or income should pay to protect them against loss. But if the present system of compensating pecuniary loss treats equals unequally (all people are created equal), compensation for intangibles treats unequals equally (human experience is unique). I advocate an end to such compensation, both for this reason and because I believe that damages for intangible injury dehumanize, substituting money for compassion, arousing jealousy rather than expressing sympathy, and contributing to a culture that views experience and love as commodities. We need, instead, to recreate a society that responds to misfortune with personal care rather than relegating the victim to the scrap heap of welfare and custodial institutions: nursing homes, hospitals, "special" schools, and ghettos for the aged and the mentally ill—the sanitized and less visible skid rows of our society.

Implementing these latter recommendations might also enhance our ability to provide a remedy for all—the first (and primary) meaning of equality. By reducing the amount of compensation paid to any one victim (i.e., by excluding property damage, loss of income above some minimum level, and intangible injury)[146] we would free resources that could be distributed to additional victims. Even more important, the extraordinarily high transaction costs of the present system[147] virtually would be eliminated, because there would no longer be any need to adjudicate causation, fault, defenses, or even damages. For the same reason lengthy delays[148] would disappear and victims would no longer be dependent on, or exploited by, lawyers. The politics of injury would be replaced by the administration of care.

To this end I propose that the state provide comprehensive medical care and a guaranteed minimum income. The first would be broadly defined to include all forms of therapy, rehabilitation, physical aids, special education, etc. The second would ensure a minimum standard of living for all members of the society regardless of why their income was otherwise inadequate. Both state responsibilities are mandated by the fundamental requirements of human dignity; they are a response to all forms of misfortune, not just to traumatic injuries. But this proposal, too, will have its opponents who benefit from the status quo: personal injury lawyers (whose greed and hypocrisy have become notorious), the private insurance industry (endowed with enormous assets and substantial political clout), and those who presently enjoy privileges of wealth and income. These are less formidable adversaries than the capitalist class that will resist the reallocation of risk and worker control over safety (indeed, capital might well favor some of these changes); but they are not insignificant enemies, as the dismal history of recent reform efforts shows. It is essential to recognize the limitations of this plan. It would not greatly alter the existing distribution of wealth and income, since the privileged would protect themselves by insuring their property and income expectations. It would not itself encourage greater compassion for the victims of misfortune, although they would less likely become the subjects of misplaced envy. It would not express societal outrage at the victim's wrong, for which purpose a criminal penalty is necessary. And it would do nothing to enhance safety (if there is also little persuasive evidence that externalizing accident costs presently internalized through the tort system would *reduce* safety). Nevertheless, the proposed response to misfortune would be more humane and just and might allow us to concentrate on safety the energies that are presently dissipated in simultaneously pursuing the often inconsistent goals of compensation and the punishment of moral fault.

NOTES

16. Lost earnings constituted about 40 percent of all payments for injury suffered as a result of automobile accidents. A study of almost 2,000 workers' compensation claimants between 1968 and 1971 who had suffered a permanent disability of more than 10 percent found that 36 percent were unemployed five years after the injury. A second study of more than 1,000 claimants whose cases were closed in 1972 and 1973 found that 81 percent of those with permanent and total disability, 46 percent with major permanent partial disability, and 27 percent with minor permanent partial disability were not working two to three years after their claims were settled. Fifty-six percent of the respondents in the second study felt they had experienced job discrimination. Employers avoid hiring injured workers for fear that the pre-existing injury will be aggravated by, or attributed to, present work conditions.

17. The National Safety Council estimated that in 1969 property damage in automobile accidents was $4.3 billion, more than the combined value of wage loss and medical expenses in such accidents.

18. Medical expenses attributable to accidental deaths and injuries in 1969 were estimated at $2.7 billion. Medical benefits represented a third of all workers' compensation payments in 1960, 12 percent of private loss insurance payments, a third of public assistance payments for injury and illness, 30 percent of veteran's benefits, and an overall total of 40 percent of all benefits paid for injury and illness.

25. In the vast majority of claims, the victim's net recovery is less than out-of-pocket expenses. See R.B. Hunting and G.S. Neuwirth, *Who Sues in New York City? A Study of Automobile Accident Claims* (New York: Columbia University Press, 1962).

32. Annual injury rates per 1,000 male employees in British industries in 1972–75 varied from 4 in insurance, banking, finance, and business services, to 198 in mining and quarrying. See *The Report of the Royal Commission on Civil Liability and Compensation for Personal Injury* (1978; Cmnd. 7054) (Pearson Report) Vol. 1, *Report;* Vol. II, *Statistics and Costings;* Vol. III, *Overseas Systems of Compensation.* In particular for annual injury rates, see Vol. II, table 32. Premiums for workers' compensation insurance in California vary from $.125 per $100 payroll for auditing and accounting offices, to $39.70 for wrecking or demolition of structures, D. M. Berman, *Death on the Job* (New York: Monthly Review Press, 1979), 70.

34. For instance, the level of airborne pollutants is between two and ten times as high in poor, working class, and minority sections of Chicago as it is in middle-income, professional/managerial, white sections.

45. Workers' compensation accounted for 5.4 percent of all benefits paid for injury and illness in 1960; tort liability accounted for 7.9 percent. Millions of workers are excluded from coverage under workers' compensation and yet may also lack effective

access to tort remedies. The discriminatory character of workers' compensation is revealed in the hostility with which workers initially greeted it, the success of a few of the better organized groups of workers in retaining their tort remedies or obtaining a compensation system superior to workers' compensation (e.g., railroad workers, sailors, longshoremen, miners), and the strenuous efforts of workers to evade workers' compensation by filing a third-party claim in products liability. There is good reason for these last efforts: in 1974, 1.5 million workers' compensation claims led to payments of $5.5 billion; third-party suits were filed in only 31,500 cases—2 percent—but resulted in tort payments of $1.5 billion—27 percent.

46. In the Oxford compensation survey, although people under 16 and over 65 represented about a third of the sample of accident victims, they constituted only 11 percent of the successful claimants. The low rate of claiming by victims of accidents in the home, who are disproportionately young or elderly, confirms this.

52. It has been estimated that each year there are 390,000 new cases of occupational disease in the United States.

61. *U.S.* v. *Carroll Towing Co.*, 159 F.2d 169 (2d Cir. 1947)

65. To the extent that the costs of injuries are paid by general welfare schemes, internalization is lost. In a study of approximately 2,000 injured workers, almost three-quarters of the non-working male respondents received some welfare benefit payments, and less than one-fifth of those respondents received workers' compensation benefits. Tort and workers' compensation accounted for only 13.3 percent of all benefits paid for illness and injury in 1960; in other words, 86.7 percent of all illness and injury costs not borne by the victim were externalized. In the U.K., only about 40 percent of compensation payments are internalized through tort claims and occupational sick pay and pensions, Pearson Report, *supra* note 32, Vol. I, Table 4.

75. Asbestosis was diagnosed as early as 1906, benzene poisoning in 1909, and the effects of chloroform in 1894.

104. E.g., *Barker* v. *Lull Engineeering Co., Inc.* (1978) 20 Cal. 3d 413,573 P. 2d 443.

105. E.g., *Daly* v. *General Motors Corp.* (1978) 20 Cal. 3d 725, 575 P. 2d 1162.

106. E.g., *Safeway Stores, Inc.* v. *Nest-Kart* (1978) 21 Cal. 3d 322, 579 P. 2d 441.

111. E.g., *Ratner* v. *Arrington*, 111 So. 2d 82 (Fla App. 1959); *Seffert* v. *Los Angeles Transit Lines*, (1961) 56 Cal. 2d 498, 364 P. 2d 337; *Capelouto* v. *Kaiser Foundation Hospitals*, (1972) 7 Cal. 3d 889, 500 P. 2d 880 (damages awarded for pain and suffering experienced by infant during first year of life although infant could not verbalize experience and damages would not be enjoyed until majority).

112. *Downie* v. *United States Lines Co.*, 359 F. 2d 344 (3d Cir. 1966) cert. den. 385 U.S. 897 (1966); John G. Fleming, "The Lost Years: A Problem in Computation and Distribution of Damages," *California Law Review* 50 (1962): 598.

113. *Howard* v. *Lecher* (1977) 42 N.Y. 2d 109, 366 N.E. 2d 64 (parents can recover for medical and funeral expenses of child who died of Tay-Sachs but would have been aborted had they been warned of danger during pregnancy); *Berman* v. *Allan*, 404 A. 2d 8 (N.J. 1978) (parents, but not child, can sue for wrongful life of child born with Down's Syndrome); *Karlsons* v. *Guerinot*, 394 N.Y.S. 2d 933 (App. Div. Fourth Dept. 1977) (same); *Curlender* v. *Bio-Science Laboratories*, 165 Cal. Rptr. 477 (Ct. App. 1980) (wrongful life claim of *child* recognised).

117. E.g., *Zaninovich* v. *American Airlines Inc.* (1966), 26 App. Div. 2d 155, 271 N.Y.S. 2d 866.

118. *Rodriquez* v. *Bethlehem Steel Corp.* (1974) 12 Cal. 3d 382.525 P.2d 699; *Molien* v. *Kaiser Foundation Hospitals*, 167 Cal. Rptr. 831 (Sup. Ct., 1980) (affirming action for negligent infliction of emotional distress and loss of consortium when defendant negligently misdiagnosed plaintiff's wife's condition as syphillis, required her to inform plaintiff of diagnosis, and required plaintiff to submit to blood test).

119. *Bulloch* v. *U.S.*, (U.S. Dis. Ct. N.J., 27 March 1980); but see *Drew* v. *Drake*, 168 Cal. Rptr. 65 (Ct. App. 1980) (rejecting claim because there was no "family relationship" although couple had lived together for three years).

120. *Berger* v. *Weber* (1978) 82 Mich. App. 199, 267 N.W. 2d 124; but see *Borer* v. *American Airlines, Inc.* (1977) 19 Cal. 3d 441, 563 P. 2d 858.

121. *Shockley* v. *Prier*, 225 N.W. 2d 495 (Wis. 1975); but see *Baxter* v. *Superior Court*

(1971) 19 Cal. 3d 461, 563 P. 2d 871; *cf. Gregory P.* v. *Vista Del Mar Child Care Service,* 165 Cal. Rptr. 370 (Ct. App. 1980) (rejecting claim by adoptive parents for damages against adoption agency for failing to disclose emotional problems of adopted child).
    122. *Bliss* v. *Allentown Public Library,* 497 F. Supp. 487 (E. D. Pa. 1980) (recovery allowed where mother heard loud noise and turned to see child on the floor with statue lying across arm); *Dillon* v. *Legg* (1968) 68 Cal. 22d 728.
    123. E.g., *Corrigal* v. *Bail and Dodd Funeral Home, Inc.* (1978) 89 Wash. 2d 959, 577 P. 2d 580; *Allen* v. *Jones,* 163 Cal. Rptr. 445 (Ct. App. 1980) (damages for emotional distress for loss of cremated remains).
    124. E.g., *Johnson* v. *State* (1975) 37 N.Y. 2d 378, 334 N.E. 2d 590.
    126. *Rodriguez* v. *State* (1970) 52 Hawaii 156, 472 P. 2d 509; but see *Van Patten* v. *Buyce* (1971) 37 App. Div. 2d 448, 326 N.Y.S. 2d 197.
    146. It has been estimated that in automobile accident liability payments, 21.5 cents out of every premium dollar are used to pay for intangible losses, and these represent nearly half of the compensation actually received by the victim.
    147. Administrative costs as a percentage of benefits paid for the various compensation systems in 1960 were: tort—49, workers' compensation—30, private loss insurance—18, public welfare programs—5, social insurance—2. In other words, it cost two dollars to pay a tort plaintiff one dollar but only a dollar and two cents to pay the same amount through social insurance.
    In the U.K. it has been estimated that the operating costs of the tort system amount to 85 percent of the benefits paid, i.e., it costs £1.85 to pay a tort plaintiff £1 (see Pearson, *supra* note 32, Vol. I, para 83). The cost of administering the British social security system, by contrast, ranges from 8.5 to 12 percent of the benefits paid (ibid. para 121).
    148. In tort claims in which suit was filed, 96 percent took more than six months to settle, 82 percent took more than a year, and 48 percent took more than three years. In workers' compensation it still takes an average of four months before any payment is made in contested cases and an average of more than one and a half years in contested cases of fatalities. Furthermore, even under this ostensibly no-fault system the insurer contests approximately 8 percent of temporary disability claims, 65 percent of permanent partial disability claims, and 80 percent of permanent total disability claims.

PART VI

Toward a Critical Practice

Critical Legal Studies is not only an intellectual movement, but is also committed to acting as a practical force in radical politics. The Critical oeuvre is replete with critiques of existing arrangements and alternative visions for social life and legal involvement. A necessary complement to these essential theoretical pursuits is the development of a style of legal practice that furthers the Critical project in concrete ways. The challenge is to bridge the gap between the contemporary situation and its future improvement by recommending a vision of practice that can inform and enhance the everyday activities of radical lawyers. The difficulty is to develop a professional modus vivendi that works within the system by allowing the radical to function as a lawyer, but does not become captive to the very system that it strives to overcome.

William Simon draws the general connections between Critical theory and practice. He looks to the different images of practice that are entailed by the larger traditional visions of law and legal theory. In both its liberal and conservative forms, the legal profession is viewed as participating in and responding to a social world that is almost entirely and already made; it depoliticizes lawyers's activities and thereby legitimates their power. In sketching an alternative Critical model, Simon emphasizes the constituent and transformative force of lawyering and its professional implications of personal responsibility and political commitment. Continuing this line in a more concrete way, Peter Gabel and Paul Harris offer particular strategies for integrating radical politics with the day-to-day activities of the lawyer. The ambition of Critical lawyering must be to empower individuals. This means that litigation ought not to concentrate exclu-

289

sively on the expansion and enforcement of legal rights, but should be used principally as an occasion to exploit the potential within law for politicizing conflicts and challenging the structures of social domination that courts and law embody. As part of an overall campaign to change social life, Gabel and Harris recommend a power-oriented rather than a rights-centered approach to law practice.

Finally, in a different and more ambitious vein, Roberto Unger attempts to draw from his critique of formalism and objectivism a proposal for a social program that respects and realizes the Critical insights about the constructed and provisional nature of all social arrangements. Recognizing that existing structures shape ordinary political and economic activity, but are themselves not answerable to any higher logic than their own contingent concerns, he lays out a program of Critical practice that works from within the present context and galvanizes its latent potential for transformative action. His wish is to turn the legal arena into an important venue for the endless debate over the conditions and circumstances of social life. The practice of "enlarged" or "deviationist doctrine" is intended as a vehicle to connect critique to construction, to dismantle the artificial barrier between law and politics, and to work the openings between reform and revolution. In this way, Unger suggests how it might be possible for the engaged revision of the terms of collective existence to become a standard feature of everyday life and for routine legal arguments to be imbued with revolutionary significance.

17

Visions of Practice in Legal Thought

William H. Simon

. . . .

I. REPRESENTATION: THE CONSTRUCTION OF THE CLIENT

In the established professional conception of the lawyer-client relation, the client's identity consists of a bundle of interests. These interests are subjective in the sense that the client is the only legitimate judge of what they are. Most fundamentally, they arise independently of the lawyer-client relation itself. Law practice is instrumental to the advancement of these ends. The lawyer's duty is to manipulate the world outside the attorney-client relation in ways that serve the client's interests. The lawyer violates her duty when she substitutes her own judgment about the client's well-being for the client's judgment (paternalism) or when she takes advantage of the client to further her own interests (exploitation).

Critical legal writing has challenged this conception by suggesting, first, that the client's interests are in fact too indeterminate to play the role assigned to them and, second, that the client's understanding of his interests is affected by the experience of the representation his interests are supposed to determine.

Both problems are reflected in the basic recurring dilemma of professional doctrine on representation. This doctrine proves unable to reconcile or to choose between two competing interpretations of

Excerpted from its original publication in *Stanford Law Review* 36, 1984, by permission of the author and the Stanford Law Review.

the professional notion of the client. One interpretation portrays the client as an actual or potential participant in social relations that represent fulfillment and empowerment. The other portrays the client as an isolated individual for whom social relations represent vulnerability and oppression. These competing interpretations of the client parallel two competing interpretations of the function of legality. One sees legality as a means of dispute resolution and social integration. The other sees legality as a safeguard for the individual against social oppression.

These competing interpretations have produced two distinct versions of the professional understanding of the lawyer-client relation. The first is largely identified with conservatism and has been substantially discredited in elite professional circles, although some of its tenets have resurfaced recently in the politically heterogeneous movement for informal dispute resolution and delegalization. The second, which is generally, though not invariably, associated with liberalism, currently dominates the professional literature. The most intense concern of the conservative approach is that lawyering will undermine intact social relations by fostering alienation and aggressive individualism; the most intense concern of the liberal approach is that lawyering will sacrifice individual interests to collective action. While the anxieties of the conservatives are expressed most clearly in the doctrines of solicitation and maintenance, the anxieties of the liberals are expressed most clearly in the doctrine of conflict of interest.

A. The Conservative View

The conservative view starts from the premise that the bundle-of-interests conception is appropriate only in the distinctive *fallen state* in which people are compelled to seek legal representation. This view sees people as fundamentally cooperative, solidaristic creatures and sees social relations as expressing and fulfilling their basic needs. So long as these relations remain intact, there is little, if any, role for lawyering. Lawyering is associated with litigation and other adversary activity. So viewed, it is not merely useless to intact social relations, but presents a danger to them. . . . By introducing the perspective of egoistic interest calculation and aggressive instrumental strategizing, the lawyer subverts this character and thus threatens the relations. Legality and lawyering can play a productive role only where social relations have broken down. Here egoism and antagonism are already facts of life. In such situations, the legal system, while unlikely to repair the relation, helps the parties work through their hostility and resolves their dispute in a way that contains it and minimizes damage to the social fabric.

The conservative view requires that law practice be confined to the realm of manifest conflict and segregated from the realm of intact social relations. It relies on the rules prohibiting maintenance and solicitation to achieve this segregation. The maintenance prohibition restricts the lawyer's ability to acquire an interest in another's claim and to pursue it for his (the lawyer's) own benefit; the solicitation prohibition restricts the lawyer's ability to propose that he pursue claims for another's benefit. . . . Both prohibitions discourage legal intervention before conventional social relations have broken down; they insure that the client's interest in claim assertion, and in the egoistic, instrumental attitude claim assertion entails, has arisen independently of the lawyer's suggestion.

The most fundamental problems with this view have arisen as it has become acceptable to question that conventional intact social relations are presumptively valuable and that the preeminent purpose of the legal system is dispute resolution. Throughout much of their history, the conservative premises have had to compete with other premises that suggest that some social relations may be oppressive and that it is part of the mission of the legal system to safeguard against such oppression. These contrasting premises are less hospitable to the maintenance and solicitation prohibitions, tolerating them only as a form of consumer protection against the dangers of misinformation and overreaching. With the expansion of explicitly interventionist regulatory and welfare activities during the 1960s and 1970s, the conservative premises came under increasing pressure. And when the Supreme Court struck down the solicitation rules of the *Code of Professional Responsibility* in the late 1970s, it repudiated concerns about generating disputes and suggested that such rules could be justified only to a limited extent and only as a form of consumer protection, not as a safeguard of solidaristic social relations.[5] . . .

One cannot interpret the absence of manifest disputes as presumptive evidence of social health or the provision of dispute-generating legal assistance as mere destructive "intermeddling." People may acquiesce in social relations and fail to seek legal assistance because of ignorance or weakness resulting from the kind of oppression the legal system is supposed to guard against. In failing to confront this basic fact, the conservative response to the problem of reconciling the individual and collective implications of client interest proves unsatisfactory.

B. The Liberal View

The dominant view in professional discourse is not the conservative one, but a liberal one. The liberal view insists that the legal system and lawyering are equally concerned with dispute resolution, with dispute-generating regulatory intervention, and with a third function—facilitation of transactions that are consensual but that would not take place without legal intervention. It insists that the bundle-of-interests notion of the client should not be restricted to the circumstances of a manifest dispute, but it also insists that this notion is compatible with collective and conciliatory, as well as individual and adversarial, practice. It sees cooperative social relations as potentially instrumental to individual interests.

Thus, while the most important challenge for the conservative view is to find a plausible way to distinguish circumstances in which legal intervention is appropriate from those in which it is not, the most important challenge for the liberal view is to derive a way to determine whether a client's interests are best served by relatively individual and adversarial or by relatively collective and conciliatory practice. The conservative view expects the lawyer to take the client as he or she finds him—in the fallen state of alienation and antagonism—and to adopt an individual, adversarial mode of practice. The liberal view aspires to a more flexible approach. It recognizes that at every critical point in the representation, lawyer and client face a range of choices from relatively individual to relatively collective ones. . . .

Lawyer and client will have to make a series of decisions as to whether to go it alone or with others (and if with others, which others) and whether to structure the relation in ways that tend to maximize the client's security at the expense of solidarity and flexibility or in ways that tend to maximize solidarity and flexibility at the expense of security. These choices overlap another series of choices between relatively adversarial and relatively conciliatory ways of dealing with outsiders; lawyer, client, and their allies must decide repeatedly whether to press every immediate advantage regardless of injury to the interests of others or to forgo immediate advantage in the hope of long-term cooperation from, or out of concern for, outsiders. The issue of individual or collective practice and the issue of adversarial or conciliatory practice lead to similar but partially distinct problems. . . .

Because the client is the only authoritative judge of his interests, the best answer the liberal view has to the question of how the lawyer is to find out these interests is to suggest that he ask the client. There are at least two problems with this response.

The first problem is that the process of asking itself tends to narrow the range of practical options. In part, this is simply a matter of material cost. Asking involves explanation and discussion, which take time and effort that cost money. In group litigation, asking can be so expensive as to preclude any sort of action at all. . . . Where the lawyer is dealing with a single individual, the expense may be less, but it is still often a significant factor. Much of the representation available to middle and lower income individuals is economically feasible only through routinized case handling that does not permit elaborate asking. Furthermore, asking alters the range of possibility because it requires the lawyer to disclose all the relevant facts to those he asks. Such disclosure can have strategic consequences. Each member of a group of actual or potential collaborators may have information that, if collaboration does not work out, it would be in his interest to keep from others. Once such information is disclosed in the asking process, the range of alternatives available to the parties has changed. Through the asking process, the lawyer may compromise the client's interests even before she has determined who the client is.

The second problem is that the client's answers are often unreliable. The asking process calls for a decision in which the client relates her own subjective interests to the universe of available courses of action. But the client cannot be presumed to understand the available courses of action, which are defined by the specialized knowledge for which she relies on the lawyer, and the lawyer cannot be presumed to understand the client's interest, which are by definition subjective. Under these circumstances, there is no reason to believe that the lawyer can provide the client with the precise kind and amount of information she needs to decide reliably or that he can avoid shaping the information he gives her in accordance with his own preconceptions of her ends. Thus, the client's encounter with the lawyer may influence her understanding of her ends. . . .

An important body of recent scholarship has emphasized how costly and problematical the asking process is and how much more limited a role it plays in practice than the one assigned to it in the liberal view. This literature has shown that, in addition to asking, lawyers in fact rely on a largely tacit set of presumptions about the interests of people with general characteristics of the client.

Moreover, it is becoming increasingly apparent how dubious some of the presumptions have been. Consider the presumptions that dominated private practice prior to the 1960s. They can be described with only moderate oversimplification as follows: Collective action was presumed to be in the interests of investors, managers, and entrepreneurs pursuing profits and—after 1935 and to a more limited extent—industrial workers pursuing economistic goals; it was presumed not to be in the interest of most other clients. . . .

These presumptions were challenged extensively during the 1960s and 1970s. Professional discourse became more willing to recognize intracorporate conflicts of interest and noncorporate common interests in collective action. Indeed, at their most extreme, these trends occasionally reversed the older presumptions. Activists who found intracorporate conflicts of interest all over the place (because some shareholders were opposed to investing in South Africa, making napalm, or fighting unionization) sometimes spoke in connection with the War on Poverty or the legal services program of the urban low-income "community" in just the way corporate lawyers spoke of the corporation—as if it were a fully constituted entity with determinate, articulated, unitary interests.

The trends of the 1960s and 1970s have slowed and even reversed in the legal literature of the past few years. Reflecting partial disillusionment with the progressive lawyering of those decades, a large conflict of interest literature has emerged criticizing some of this lawyering as too quick to risk client interests in the name of collective action.[23] And while some corporate writing remains more sensitive to intracorporate conflict than the older doctrine, a new literature uses economics to argue that the market neutralizes much intracorporate conflict.[24]

The great virtue of the recent conflicts literature has been to demonstrate how indeterminate the liberal notion of client interests is. But the efforts of this literature to rescue the liberal conception from the problems it has explicated do not seem successful. Two types of solutions have been suggested. The first calls for a more subtle or elaborate asking process. Proponents of psychologically informed interviewing and counseling techniques represent one example of this response; proponents of elaborate notice and intervention procedures in class actions represent another. This response has the disadvantage of encumbering collective action, at best by making it more expensive, at worst by uncovering or engendering conflict among collaborators. Moreover, as its proponents have acknowledged, given the problems of communication, even the most elaborate asking process will not consistently yield reliable answers.

The other solution is to assert that presumptions about interests are inescapable and to embrace them. Presumptions can be redeemed by making them explicit, testing them against knowledge of actual interests, and discarding the ones which correlate poorly with the client characteristics on which they are based. This response so drastically attenuates the principle of the subjectivity of interests that it is doubtful that it can qualify as a revision, rather than a repudiation, of the professional premises. However one characterizes it, the position has evident drawbacks. Most obviously, it requires the sacrifice of atypical clients whose interests do not in fact coincide with the presumptions. In resorting to presumptions, this response dispenses with the most morally appealing feature of the professional doctrine, its aspiration to respect the client as a concrete individual. . . .

Most important, while the presumption approach does not necessarily entail the traditional bias of the liberal view against collective practice, it is in fact linked to that bias in current professional discourse. Despite the insights of the last two decades, the fallback position of the liberal view in noncorporate private practice remains the presumption of disaffiliation wherever differing interests are perceived. This presumption is explicit in the doctrine on joint representation. The *Code of Professional Responsibility* discourages and sometimes prohibits joint representation in situations involving "differing interests,"[31] and commentators have interpreted the "common interest" requirement for class representation of Rule 23 of the Federal Rules of Civil Procedure to mandate disaffiliation (subclassing or denial of certification) where differing intraclass interests are identified. But this presumption is unjustified. Most opportunities for collective practice involve interests that differ in some respects (and that coincide in others). There is no reason to believe that the risks or sacrifices of collective practice tend to outweigh the benefits. . . .

There is a further problem with the liberal understanding of the lawyer-client relation. Not only are the client's interests indeterminate at any given moment, but the client's understanding of her interests may change in the course of representation. Here is an account by Gary Bellow of an episode from practice that illustrates this phenomenon.

> In Tulare County, I was involved in a law suit on behalf of a Tenants' Union attempting to improve conditions in a farm labor camp by withholding rent. I took a deposition from the head of the Housing Authority which ran the camp—at a place where the tenants could come and watch. I inisted that the deposition be taken in front of those tenants so they could see me challenge him, question him, and get information from him that they had previously been unable to obtain. They left with the sense that he was not invulnerable and that they were not totally without leverage or protection. It helped them, I think, continue the fight. It didn't matter that the case went on for two years, that the Supreme Court denied certiorari on it and that we in fact lost the legal issue. By the time the Supreme Court did rule, new housing was being built for the residents of the camp, over $5,000 in money had been returned to them in back rent, and a set of rules and procedures had been agreed upon that would bar any kind of retaliatory evictions in the future.[36]

It is difficult to make sense of this episode in terms of the professional notion of practice as instrumental to the client's articulated, preexisting interests. Of course, the ultimate gains—new housing, damages, procedural protections—probably corresponded to some of the initially articulated interests of the clients. But those interests were qualified by the clients' initial notions about other interests—in job security, in peaceful relations with their employer, in avoiding demands on their time—that would have affected their willingness to take collective action and the vigor and aggressiveness with which they might undertake it. The ultimate gains appear to have depended on a change these latter notions underwent as a consequence of the way the lawyer structured the deposition. The deposition does not appear to have been instrumental to any initially articulated goal. It does not appear to have produced valuable information or to have had any strategic impact on the adversary. Its importance lies in the way it affected the clients. One interpretation of what happened is this: The experience of confronting their adversary together in circumstances where he was obliged to acknowledge them as a group and as other than subordinates and to account to them in some minimal way increased their sense of solidarity with each other and reduced their sense of vulnerability to their adversary. It intensified the sense of each of them of a common interest in collective practice, a sense which both made them more willing to become vulnerable to each other and empowered them in relation to the adversary.

From the perspective of the professional vision, it is troubling that the lawyer contributed to this change in the client's understanding of their interests through the way he structured the representation. The lawyer consulted his own understanding of the clients' interest, an understanding that they had not articulated and probably did not share initially. Yet, the professional view cannot plausibly condemn this practice as paternalistic or exploitative, for the clients ultimately did come to share the lawyer's interpretation. In order to condemn the practice as unwarranted by the client's interest, the professional would have to look only at the clients at the beginning of the representation and ignore them later. But nothing in the professional conception of interests provides any basis for suggesting that the clients' earlier understanding of their interests is more authentic or reliable than their later one.

Thus, both versions of the professional understanding of the client have common problems. Neither has a satisfactory basis for deciding between relatively individual and relatively collective practice. The conservative approach relies on presumptions that turn solely on an implausible distinction between manifest disputes and intact social relations; the liberal approach, in the frequent situations where asking does not yield unambiguous answers, falls back on an equally implausible presumption of disaffiliation. And neither approach adequately confronts the way the client's understanding of his interests is influenced by the experience of representation. The conservative approach recognizes the problem but responds only by trying ineffectually to confine it; the liberal approach does not recognize it at all.

C. The Critical View

The literature from which I derive these criticisms suggests that the response to the problems of representation should involve not only efforts to devise new procedures or get more information about clients, but also reexamination of the basic premise of the professional culture that representation is instrumental to preexisting subjective ends. It suggests an alternative vision that dispenses with that premise.

The Critical vision resembles the conservative professional approach in seeing social relationships as an integral part of individual identity, rather than as merely instrumental to subjective individual interests, and in acknowledging that representation is potentially constitutive of the client's identity. But unlike the conservative view, it does not presume that intact relations are valuable or that the constitutive tendency of representation is to alienate the client from social

relationships. Moreover, it sees the constitutive tendency of representation not as a danger to be guarded against, but as an opportunity to
be embraced.

The Critical view is animated by an ideal of practice as a process of
constituting or reconstituting nonhierarchical communities of interest. Like the liberal view, the Critical one is open to both individual
and collective practice. But instead of appealing to ostensibly preexisting subjective interests as governing norms, it appeals to the ideal of
nonhierarchical community. Thus, the Critical view is compatible with
aggressive lawyering in situations where the interests of the client or
client community involve a challenge to external hierarchy. Its most
ambitious projects of this kind envision the two mutually reinforcing
processes exemplified in the example recounted by Bellow, one in
which the client is encouraged to enter into nonhierarchical relationships by the experience of solidarity and another in which she is
empowered to withdraw from or challenge hierarchical ones.

But the Critical view is also compatible with fully collective and
conciliatory approaches in situations involving disputes within an
actual or potential nonhierarchical communal relation. Subject to the
important qualification regarding hierarchy, the Critical view supports the challenge to the professional vision developed in the recent
literature of mediation and informal dispute resolution. And it is
consistent with Brandeis's notion of "counsel to the situation" in which
the lawyer attempts to reconcile disputing family members or business associates conventionally held to have interests that conflict too
severely to permit joint representation. Such practice is not designed
to serve the clients' preexisting interests, but to reconstitute them as a
community defined by common interests.

The Critical view does not claim that the ideal of constituting or
reconstituting nonhierarchical communities of interest is more determinate than the professional ideal of loyalty to subjective interests.
Although there have been efforts to develop a theoretical account of
the notion of nonhierarchical community, the Critical view of practice
does not rely on or hope for a determinate explication. It is not
reluctant for the lawyer to make controversial, intuitive judgments in
interpreting and applying the ideal of nonhierarchical community.
Although it recognizes that such judgments are often unverifiable, it
aspires to a distinctive kind of verification. The precept that the
lawyer further the client's interests, as she understands them, is
qualified by the precept that she also try to enhance the client's
capacity to express her own interests. The authoritative test of the
lawyer's judgment is that the client come to share it under conditions
in which the lawyer believes that the client's understanding is not
affected by conditions of hierarchy.

I do not want to exaggerate either the novelty or the distinctiveness
of the Critical view. The problems of the professional vision have

been discussed by a broad range of writers in recent years. And the Critical understanding of practice does not eliminate the problems of cost and communication. It too relies on both asking and presumptions. Nevertheless, the Critical vision understands asking and presumptions differently from the professional one.

The professional notion of asking connotes either a series of discrete communications between lawyer and individual clients or a communication between lawyer and a previously constituted organization of clients. In either event, it connotes a largely passive role for the client; his participation is limited to telling the lawyer what the lawyer wants. Since organization merely serves as a conduit for individual preferences, and representation is merely instrumental to such preferences, neither communication among clients nor direct client participation is valued. By contrast, the Critical notion that a community of interest is something to be created in the course of representation, rather than a premise of representation, suggests the importance of communication among clients and direct participation. Communication among clients and direct participation are valued for their potential to increase understanding and solidarity and to safeguard against hierarchy. Bellow's noninstrumental use of the deposition in the Tulare County litigation, which appears at best anomalous in the professional vision, exemplifies the theme of participation. So does, his program of "focused case pressure" in poverty law—small-scale claim aggregation that sacrifices prospects of broad remedies and rule change in order to increase client involvement and control.[43] And from the perspective of participation, the most promising developments in recent class action doctrine might seem not the notice and intervention provisions on which conflicts doctrine has focused, but the remedial provisions that give class members a direct role in monitoring the decree.[44]

In the professional vision, presumptions are empirical summaries of information about the preferences of people who share the characteristics of the client. Although not expected to be certain or precise, they are understood to be derived from the uncontroversial method of generalization from observed behavior and to be independent of the lawyer's own moral and political commitments. On the other hand, the Critical vision is more insistent about the ambiguity of behavior, and it is willing to consider that people might have interests of which they are not aware. It therefore does not understand judgments about people's interests as empirical or as generalizations from behavior. It suggests that such judgments implicate controversial moral and political commitments.

The Critical notion of interest bears some resemblance to doctrines such as the Marxist notion of objective interests, which asserts that groups sharing certain social circumstances are classes regardless of how the individual members understand their interests at any given

moment,[45] and the notion expressed in recent public law jurisprudence that certain disadvantaged groups constitute "natural classes"
for the purposes of equal protection or standing doctrine.[46] The
Critical view shares with these doctrines the belief that social circumstances create and limit possibilities of affiliation (though within broad
and as yet undetermined limits) and the notion that our normative
judgments explicitly or implicitly classify people by, for example,
distinguishing advantaged from disadvantaged, or powerful from
powerless. On the other hand, the Critical view differs from these
notions to the extent that they suggest that the affiliation of these
groups has been decreed by history or that their definition can be
derived from science or legal doctrine. The basic test of the lawyer's
judgment of the client's interests is that the client come to share that
judgment under conditions which lawyer and client agree are nonhierarchical. The expectation that the client will do so is as much a
hope as a prediction, and it can be fully vindicated only where the
client has had an opportunity to disappoint and refute it.

The Critical notions of asking and of presumptions imply a further
contrast with the professional vision. While the professional vision
sees the lawyer as the servant of the client's interests, the Critical
vision sees the lawyer as an actual or potential member of the same
community of interest as the client. The lawyer's understanding of
the client's interests is derived in substantial part from the lawyer's
own moral and political commitments. Since the lawyer's presumptions should be tentative and rebuttable, she has to remain open to
persuasion by the clients; she as well as the client is vulnerable to
change in the process of representation.

Despite this vulnerability, the lawyer often will be in a position of
power in relation to the client. The Critical vision substitutes for the
professional fiction that the lawyer is always accountable to the client
the prescription that the lawyer seek to create a client capable of
holding her accountable. The check on the lawyer's power lies in the
possibility that she will succeed in creating a community in which
members are capable of calling each other to account. Short of such
success, the Critical vision suggests that the responsibility for making
at least partially unverifiable judgments, and the risk of being wrong,
are inescapable.

The Critical vision raises without answering a host of practical
questions and problems. It also seems to impose formidable responsibilities and risks on the lawyer—responsibilities for changing the
client; risks of being changed herself. But it would be a mistake to
complain that this vision is more utopian than the professional one.
To some extent, the Critical vision merely acknowledges a basic fact of
contemporary law practice—that lawyers commonly make, and have
to make, judgments in terms of their own moral and political commitments about what their clients' interests are. Its most basic difference

from the professional vision is that it sees this fact not as something to be regretted and minimized, but as the source of the most rewarding and exhilarating potential of practice.

NOTES

5. See Bates v. State Bar, 433 U.S. 350, 372-77 (1977); see also In re Primus, 436 U.S. 412 (1978).

23. See, e.g., Derrick A. Bell, Jr. "Serving Two Masters: Integration Ideals and Client Interests in School Desegregation Litigation," *Yale Law Journal* 85 (1976): 470, 471–72.

24. See, e.g., David L. Engel, "An Approach to Corporate Social Responsibility," *Stanford Law Review* 32 (1979); Symposium, *Stanford Law Review* 35 (1982):1.

31. See *Model Code of Professional Responsibility Dr* 5–105 (1980).

36. Comment, "The New Public Interest Lawyers," *Yale Law Journal* 79 (1970): 1069, 1088, quoting G. Bellow.

43. See Gary Bellow, "Turning Solutions Into Problems," *N.L.A.D.A. Briefcase* 34, (1977): 119.

44. See, e.g., Morgan v. Kerrigan, 530 F. 2d 401, 429 (1st Cir. 1976).

45. See, e.g., I. Balbus, "The Concept of Interest in Pluralist and Marxian Analysis," in 1 *Politics and Society* (1971): 151, 167–68.

46. See Owen Fiss, "Groups and the Equal Protection Clause," *Philosophy and Public Affairs* 5 (1976): 107, 126.

18

Building Power and Breaking Images: Critical Legal Theory and the Practice of Law

Peter Gabel and Paul Harris

INTRODUCTION

In this essay we present [an] optimistic approach to radical law practice that is based on a view of the legal system different from . . . both the orthodox Marxist view that the law is simply a "tool of the ruling class" and the liberal-legalist view that powerless groups in society can gradually improve their position by getting more rights. Instead we argue that the legal system is an important public arena through which the State attempts—through manipulation of symbols, images, and ideas—to legitimize a social order that most people find alienating and inhumane. Our objective is to show the way that the legal system works at many different levels to shape popular consciousness toward accepting the political legitimacy of the status quo, and to outline the ways that lawyers can effectively resist these efforts in building a movement for fundamental social change. Our basic claim is that the very public and political character of the legal arena gives lawyers, acting together with clients and fellow legal workers, an important opportunity to reshape the way that people understand the existing social order and their place within it. . . .

I. A POWER-ORIENTED APPROACH TO LAW PRACTICE

A first principle of a "counter-hegemonic" legal practice must be to subordinate the goal of getting people their rights to the goal of

Excerpted from its original publication in *NYU Review of Law and Social Change* 11, 1983, by permission of the authors and NYU Review of Law and Social Change.

building an authentic or unalienated political consciousness. This obviously does not mean that one should not try to win one's cases; nor does it necessarily mean that we should not continue to organize groups by appealing to rights. But the great weakness of a rights-oriented legal practice is that it does not address itself to a central precondition for building a sustained political movement—that of overcoming the psychological conditions upon which both the power of the legal system and the power of social hierarchy in general rest. In fact an excessive preoccupation with "rights-consciousness" tends in the long run to reinforce alienation and powerlessness, because the appeal to rights inherently affirms that the source of social power resides in the State rather than in the people themselves. . . .

A legal strategy that goes beyond rights-consciousness is one that focuses upon expanding political consciousness through using the legal system to increase people's sense of personal and political power. This can mean many different things depending upon the political visibility of any given case and the specific social and legal context within which a case arises. But in any context, a "power" rather than a "rights" approach to law practice should be guided by three general objectives that are as applicable to minor personal injury cases as to major cases involving important social issues. First, the lawyer should seek to develop a relationship of genuine equality and mutual respect with her client. Second, the lawyer should conduct herself in a way that demystifies the symbolic authority of the State as this authority is embodied in, for example, the flag, the robed judge, and the ritual-ized professional technicality of the legal proceeding. Third, the lawyer should always attempt to reshape the way legal conflicts are represented in the law, revealing the limiting character of legal ideology and bringing out the true socioeconomic and political foun-dations of legal disputes. Reaching these objectives may have a transformative impact not only upon the lawyer and client working in concert, but also upon others who come into contact with the case, including the client's friends and family, courtroom participants such as jurors, stenographers, and public observers, and, in some cases, thousands or even millions of people who follow high-visibility politi-cal cases through the media. Of course, any particular lawyer's actions in a single case cannot lead to the development of an anti-hierarchical social movement; we believe, however, that if lawyers as a group begin to organize themselves around the realization of these goals, their impact on the culture as a whole can be much greater than they currently believe is possible. . . .

If one looks at the institutions of the legal system from a power-oriented rather than a rights-oriented perspective, the very nature of these institutions takes on a different appearance from that portrayed in the conventional model. Instead of seeing the judiciary, for exam-ple, as an integrated hierarchy of trial and appellate courts organized for the purpose of establishing the proper scope of procedural and substantive rights, one sees diverse locuses of state power that are organized for the purpose of maintaining alienation and powerlessness. In this perspective the lower state courts, for example, are designed primarily to provide administrative control over the minor disturbances of everyday life in local communities in order to maintain social order at the local level. It is for this reason that lower court judges are often indifferent to the intricacies of legal doctrine and are more concerned with the efficient management of high-volume court calendars through plea-bargaining and the informal mediation of civil disputes. One might say that at this level the manifestation of restrained force and symbolic authority is much more important than legal ideology as such, and an excessive concern by judges with "the law" would actually interfere with the rapid processing and control of street crime, evictions, and small business matters. Conversely, the United States Supreme Court is primarily concerned with reinforcing the legitimacy of the dominant national culture through the publication of *ideas*. Its justices write their opinions not so much to guide the lower courts as to educate the population as a whole in the proper legal way to think about the institutional hierarchies that comprise the socioeconomic and political systems. And in so doing they help to constitute and sustain these hierarchies, by interpreting social conflict according to a form of thought ("constitutional" interpretation) which presupposes their legitimacy.

It is only by reconceptualizing the legal system in terms of these distinct ideological levels or locations that lawyers can struggle effectively to build the power of popular movements within any one of them. Only such an analysis could help to resolve such strategic political issues as, for example, whether tenant lawyers in a local community should focus on organizing with tenants to obstruct the processing of evictions through local housing courts, or engage in collective bargaining over lease contracts with big landlords, or press for more rights through individual appeals and reform litigation. The setting of a priority on an issue like this requires discussion among groups of lawyers and tenants in particular communities about whether one approach will generate more political consciousness and power among tenants as a whole than would another. Similarly, it is doubtful that criminal lawyers can have much impact on the [Supreme] Court's shaping of the popular perception of the causes of crime as long as they unreflectively limit their actions to arguing an endless series of search-and-seizure motions in empty courtrooms and filing invisible amicus briefs for the benefit of the Court majority. If the [Supreme] Court is aiming the rhetoric of its opinions at mass consciousness, left lawyers must theorize about how to use their cases as opportunities to contest the Court's world view in the media and other public contexts. . . .

II. COUNTERPRESSURE IN HIGH-VISIBILITY POLITICAL CASES

Although a central objective of this article is to argue that all legal cases are potentially empowering, the classic political case remains one that receives widespread public attention because it emerges from a social conflict that has already achieved high visibility in the public consciousness. Examples of such cases in recent years include the political trials that arose out of the student and antiwar movements, and the many Supreme Court cases that have emerged from the civil rights and women's movements. Such cases contain unique possibilities and also difficulties for the lawyers and clients involved in them, because the aim is not only to win on the legal issues raised by the case, but to speak for the movement itself. Precisely because the State's objective is in part to defuse the political energy that has given rise to the case, the legal issue is often one that deflects attention from and even denies the political nature of the conflict.

A. The Chicago Eight Trial

Perhaps the clearest example of this "deflection" was the so-called "conspiracy" trial of the Chicago Eight, in which the issue as defined by the prosecutor was whether the defendants who had helped to organize the antiwar demonstrations outside the Democratic National Convention in 1968 had conspired to cross state lines with the intent to incite a riot.[16] The political meaning of the demonstrations was to challenge the morality of the Vietnam War and the political process that served to justify it, but this meaning was, of course, legally irrelevant to the determination of whether the alleged conspiracy had taken place.

Using a case like this to increase the power of an existing political movement requires a systematic refusal to accept the limiting boundaries which the State seeks to impose on the conflict. Had the lawyers and clients in the Chicago Eight trial presented a legal defense in a normal professional way, they would have deferred to the authority of Judge Hoffman and politely tried to show, perhaps with success, that the defendants did not "intend" to incite a riot or did not "conspire" to cross state lines to do so. But the lawyers and clients understood very well that even a legal victory on these terms would have meant a political defeat for their movement. They understood that the prosecutor's real purpose was to channel the political struggle in the streets into an official public chamber, to recharacterize the protestors as hooligans, and to substitute a narrow and depoliticized legal description of the meaning of the Chicago events for their true meaning. In this context State power consists not so much in the use of direct force, but in the use of the sanctity of the legal process to recast the meaning of the disruption that took place.

In concert with their courageous clients, William Kunstler and Leonard Weinglass were able to reverse the government's strategy and cause it to backfire, seizing upon the media's coverage of the trial to strengthen the resistance that had begun in the streets. By openly flaunting the hierarchical norms of the courtroom and ridiculing the judge, the prosecutor, and the nature of the charges themselves, they successfully rejected the very forms of authority upon which the legitimacy of the war itself depended. As Judge Hoffman gradually lost the capacity to control "his" room, he was transformed on national television from a learned figure worthy of great respect into a vindictive old man wearing a funny black tunic. In the absence of an underlying popular movement, the tactic of showing continuous contempt for the proceedings might simply have been an unproductive form of "acting out." But within its concrete historical context, this tactic was the most effective way to affirm to millions of supporters following the trial that their version of the meaning of the Chicago protests was right and could not be eroded by the State's appeal to a mass belief in authoritarian imagery.

B. The Inez Garcia Trial

The importance of this kind of symbolic resistance was demonstrated in a somewhat different, although equally powerful, way in the two murder trials of Inez Garcia, which took place almost ten years later during an intense period in the rise of the women's movement. While the Chicago Eight defense reveals the way that a total refusal to recognize the legitimacy of legal authority can in some circumstances be politically effective, the Inez Garcia trials show that it is sometimes possible to infuse an existing "nonpolitical" legal defense with unique and powerful political meaning.[19]

Inez Garcia shot and killed one of the men who helped to rape her. Twenty minutes after the rape she looked for and found the two men; as one pulled out a knife she killed him and shot at the other as he was running away. At her first trial facing a first-degree murder charge, she was represented by an excellent male criminal lawyer. He defended her on the grounds of "impaired consciousness," a psychiatric defense which argued that Garcia was suffering from a temporary loss of conscious control over her behavior. If successful, such an approach provided a complete defense to murder. The trial strategy was secondarily aimed at achieving a conviction on a lesser included offense, such as second-degree murder or manslaughter. This strategy was somewhat successful from a legal point of view, as Garcia was found guilty of second-degree murder and given a sentence less severe than the one she would have received for a first-degree conviction.

Politically, however, the defense was a failure: it contradicted the defendant's belief in the rightness of her own act, and it failed to place

Garcia's conduct in the context of a rising women's movement that was demanding recognition of the violent effect of rape and sexual harassment upon women. In her defensive and apologetic posture, Garcia was humiliated by psychiatric testimony that exposed her personal life in a denigrating way, and offended by the argument, made in her defense, that she was "sleepwalking" and unconscious of what she was doing. The contradiction between this legal charcteriza-tion of her conduct and her true feelings erupted on the stand when she testified: "I took my gun, I loaded it, and I went out after them. . . . I am not sorry that I did it. The only thing I am sorry about is that I missed Luis."[20] Earlier in the trial, Garcia had reacted violently to the judge's decision to disallow testimony about the emotional trauma of rape. She leaped up from the counsel table and said: "Why don't you just find me guilty? Just send me to jail. . . . I killed the fucking guy because he raped me!"[21] Obviously, after that, the jury could not accept the attempted portrayal of Garcia as a demure and innocent woman who was so overcome that she could not be held responsible for her acts.

Garcia's conviction was reversed on appeal because of an improper jury instruction.[22] In the retrial she was represented by radical-feminist attorney Susan Jordan. The defense was a creative combina-tion of the traditional rules of self-defense and the historical reality of the victimization of women by men.[23] The task Jordan faced was to translate the male-oriented rule of self-defense into a form that would capture the real experience of a woman facing possible attack by a man. She also had to combat, within the confines of the courtroom, the sexist myths that would influence the jurors.

The rule of self-defense is based on one's right to use reasonable force if, and only if, one reasonably perceives that there will be an imminent attack. The heart of the defense is the defendant's state of mind—it is necessary to convince a jury that the defendant acted in a reasonable manner given the circumstances.

In Garcia's situation, the juror's understanding of whether Garcia acted "reasonably" would almost certainly be influenced by cultural myths about the act of rape. The rape myths are that women invite it, that they encourage it, and they like it, and that ultimately the rape is their own fault. Jordan directly confronted these stereotypes by the creative use of voir dire. The jurors were questioned individually, one by one in the judge's chambers. Each juror was asked questions which were designed to bring out any underlying sexist stereotypes. Al-though this was a painful process, initially opposed by the judge, and irritating to some jurors, the process paid off. The final jury of ten men and two women was able to view the rape not as a sexual act caused by male-female flirting, but rather as a violent assault. This view of rape as an act of violence was key to the acceptance of the self-defense theory.

Jordan also faced the problem of Garcia's obvious anger at the men who raped her. If this anger was viewed by the jury as the motive for her shooting, then it would negate self-defense and lead to a verdict of manslaughter. The defense, therefore, attempted to show that the anger was a justified and reasonable response to her rape. Expert witnesses testified to the psychological effects of rape, especially a rape committed on a latina, Catholic woman. Instead of the traditional tactic of trying to hide the woman's anger, the defense affirmed this anger and explained it in human terms which broke through the male prejudices embodied in the law's traditional view of the reasonable person. The result was a complete acquittal.[24]

The two trials of Inez Garcia demonstrate that in the right circumstances it is possible to win a case with a political approach when a more conventional legal approach would fail. Inez Garcia took the action that she did at a time when the women's movement was actively challenging the forms of patriarchal domination characteristic of man-woman relations throughout the social structure, and the central symbol of this domination was the act of forcible rape itself. With a male attorney in her first trial in effect apologizing for her action and the anger that produced it, Garcia was separated from the movement supporting her, and indeed from her own self. In pleading "impaired consciousness" she was forced to deny the legitimacy of her own action and simultaneously the legitimacy of the "unreasonable" rage that women throughout the country were expressing in response to their social powerlessness in relation to men. The form of the first trial turned Garcia into an isolated object of the legal system, a mere "defendant" requesting mercy from a "masculine" legal structure. Even a victory in the first trial would have had negative political consequences because it would have affirmed the wrongness of both her action and the feeling that provoked it, while legitimizing the authority of a benevolent State.

The most important feature of the second trial was that it reversed the power relations upon which the first trial was premised. The defense both affirmed the validity of Garcia's action, and allowed Jordan to join Garcia as co-advocate for a vast popular movement, to speak to the jury not as a State-licensed technician "representing" an abstract "defendant," but as a woman standing together with another woman. Together, the two women were able to put the act of rape itself on trial and to address the jurors, not as "jurors" but as human beings, about the meaning of being a woman in contemporary society. The effect of this was to transform the courtroom into a popular tribunal and to divest the prosecutor and the judge (who, as men, could not abstract themselves entirely from the evident signs of their own gender) of some of the symbolic authority upon which the legitimacy of the "legal form" of the proceeding depended. This shift in the vectors of power within the room also allowed the jurors to escape their own reification, to discover themselves as politically responsible for making a human, rather than a merely formal, decision based on an application of existing law. Thus the conduct of the second trial, coupled with the widespread publicity attendant to it, served to expand the power of the movement from which the political basis of the case derived, and to delegitimate the apparent necessity of existing legal consciousness. This last point deserves special emphasis, for breaking through the sedimented authoritarian forms of a legal proceeding in an overtly political case has radical implications beyond those of the particular case itself: it signifies that the existing order is *merely possible*, and that people have the freedom and power to act upon it. In the special context of a public trial, such action demonstrates the living disintegration of symbolic State power in a heavily ritualized setting, one that is normally a principal medium for the transmission of authoritarian imagery.

III. COUNTERPRESSURE IN LOW-VISIBILITY POLITICAL CASES

In 1971 the Latin community in San Francisco's Mission District was experiencing "brown power" and intense organizing by radical and liberal groups. The most effective radical organization was called "Los Siete" ("The Seven"), named after seven young men who had been acquitted of murdering a policeman after a long, contested trial. Los Siete ran a community clinic, organized a formidable labor caucus, pushed for community control of police, and published a community newspaper.

Los Siete's members were often harassed by police who operated out of the then infamous Mission police station. On a busy shopping day, two of Los Siete's most active members, a latin man and a black woman, were selling their newspaper *Basta Ya* on the sidewalk in front of the largest department store in the Mission. The store manager called the police. When the police arrived they berated the young man, called him "wetback" and told him to go back to Mexico. The police confiscated the papers and arrested both the man and the woman for trespass, obstructing the sidewalk, and resisting arrest.

There was no publicity of the arrest. The store owners saw the arrest as a vindication of their right of private property. The police viewed it as a demonstration of their power in the Mission district and a warning to community groups. The district attorney's office treated the case as a routine misdemeanor. The defendants felt the arrests had been an act of intimidation and racism. The woman was treated as a prostitute at the City Jail, examined for venereal disease and put in quarantine for two days while awaiting the results of the test. The excuse given for such treatment was that she had been charged with obstructing the sidewalk, an offense associated with prostitution.

Los Siete asked the Community Law Collective, a local law office which acted as "house counsel" to many community organizations, to defend their members and to help them develop a legal-political analysis of the case. The attorneys explained that although there was a First Amendment issue present, it was doubtful that such a right could be vindicated at the lower court level. At trial, it would be the defendants' testimony against the testimony of two policemen, a security guard, and possibly the store manager. Even though the defendants had sold their newspapers on the sidewalk without harassing store customers, the State's witnesses would place them on store property obstructing customers, and the police would swear the latin man had pushed them and refused arrest. The jury would be almost all white and predisposed toward the State's witnesses. If the trial was before one of the few liberal municipal court judges, the defendants might receive thirty days in jail if convicted; if before one of the many conservatives, the sentence would probably be six months in jail. If, on the other hand, the defendants were to plead guilty, the district attorney would drop all the charges except trespass, and would offer a sixty-day suspended sentence.

If the lawyers had acted as apolitical professionals in this situation, they almost certainly would have advised their clients to plea bargain. First, it makes sense to accept probation in the face of a likely jail sentence. Second, preparation and trial would be quite time-consuming and remuneration would be small. But for the lawyers to have given such "normal" advice in this context would have made them mere extensions of the system. It is not in the interests of the State in this situation to send defendants to jail and risk an increase of organized anger in the community. Rather, the State's strategy is to break the spirit and limit the options of the community movement. It is the plea bargain which best accomplishes this purpose, by simultaneously vindicating the police, legitimating the store owner's property rights, and making community activists feel powerless and humiliated. Moreover, in offering defendants a six-month suspended sentence, the State is also offering them a two-year probation period, the obvious effect of which is to inhibit any future activism. In this context the plea bargain becomes the iron fist in the velvet glove, and the defense lawyer who passively participates in arranging such an outcome becomes partly responsible for its consequences.

Understanding the dangers of "copping a plea," the lawyers and clients attempted to define what was really at issue and to explore a radical approach to the case. The issue was the exercise of political power, in the form of selling *Basta Ya* on the streets of the Mission community. Selling the newspaper served three purposes. First, the person-to-person contact was an effective organizing tool for Los Siete, helping them to build support for their community programs. Second, the street-corner sales were the primary means of distributing the paper and therefore of getting the information in the paper out to the community. Third, the very act of selling their paper in the streets of the Mission district made the activists feel some power in the face of overwhelming police authority, and the sight of young latinos passing out their radical newspaper helped to create a vague but important sense of indigenous power in the community residents as well. To maintain this sense of power it seemed necessary to reject the psychological defeat inherent in the plea bargain, and to risk a trial.

The tasks facing the lawyers in this case were, first, to empower their clients and Los Siete as an organization and, second, to win the trial. Both goals would be furthered by an overtly political defense, the first because a political defense would insist that the defendants were right to be reaching out to the community; the second because this particular trial could be won only by challenging the narrow "legal" definition of their action as criminal obstruction and trespass.

The lawyers' first tactic was to go on the offensive by filing a motion to suppress the seized newspapers on the grounds that the arrest and seizure violated the First Amendment. This tactic was no different from one that any good defense lawyer would use once plea bargaining had been rejected, but here the purpose was not so much to vindicate a legal right as such, but rather to force the State to *defend* its actions. Surprisingly, the municipal court granted the motion, much to the irritation of the district attorney, who was then forced into the defensive posture of filing an appeal. The defense lawyers asked a young corporate attorney interested in "pro bono" work to prepare the appeal. The coalition of community lawyers and corporate lawyer increased the ideological pressure on the district attorney's office. Although the corporate attorney wrote an excellent brief and argued the case, the municipal court decision was reversed.

Next came the trial plan. The first strategic issue was whether to try to pack the courtroom with community people. Traditional lawyers are wary of this tactic for fear that the presence of third world and "radical" people will frighten the jury and create subconscious hostility. However, lawyers can often use crowded courtrooms to their advantage by dealing with the jury's anxiety and hostility toward the community presence in voir dire, and by openly discussing any negative preconceptions the jurors might have in opening and/or closing arguments. Due to a lack of publicity it was not possible in this case to fill the courtroom with community supporters, but enough were present to prevent the defendants from feeling isolated.

The second issue related to the clients' participation in the preparation and conduct of the trial. In the traditional view of the lawyer-client relationship, the lawyer is defined as the professional who "handles" all legal aspects of the case without client participation. By treating the client as someone who cannot understand the conduct of her own trial, the traditional approach increases the client's sense of powerlessness in the face of the intimidating spectacle going on in the courtroom. In this case the lawyers took the opposite approach, asking the clients to take an active part in all aspects of the case where prior legal training was not absolutely required. Thus the defendants wrote voir dire questions and assisted in the selection of jurors. The lawyers discussed each aspect of the case, explaining their tactics and incorporating many of the suggestions of the clients. In this manner the clients began to feel some control over the process which the State had forced them into.

As for the trial itself, a traditional approach would have been to argue the client's version of the facts against the State's version, relying on a reasonable-doubt defense and keeping the content of the newspaper itself out of evidence. A more liberal approach would have been to focus on the First Amendment aspects of the case, emphasizing the abstract right of dissenters to freedom of speech. The radical approach was to stress the political realities involved; to admit and defend the true nature of *Basta Ya,* and to expose the police department's racism and its attempts to harass and intimidate members of Los Siete.

The trial ended successfully for the defendants despite the judge's persistent attempts to ridicule the attorneys and to prohibit their making any mention of the First Amendment. Instead of feeling that they had won by disguising their politics through either the traditional or liberal approaches, the defendants felt a sense of power and truth because the political meaning of their actions had been presented and vindicated. After the trial the defendants went back with other members of Los Siete to distribute newspapers in the same location, while the police and storeowner looked on. "Basta Ya" means "Enough Already." The case delivered to the arresting officers, the local police station, and the conservative merchants a clear message: if you mess with Los Siete, they have the spirit and resources to hit back.

Low-visibility cases that contain political elements, such as *Basta Ya,* are presented in courtrooms throughout the country on a frequent basis. What is critical to understand is that one can transform a "solely criminal" case into a political case by making a few simple changes in approach and technique. This is possible because the courtroom is a small, closed, intensified experience for the jury and for the participants. Everything that takes place is magnified. Since the district attorney and judge will almost always define the case as nonpolitical, and will attempt to create an atmosphere of neutral application of objective laws, any injection of political and social reality will have a powerful impact. Using the *Basta Ya* trial, we can look at voir dire, opening statement and cross examination to illuminate this analysis.

The two young lawyers in the *Basta Ya* trial had a combined experience of less than four trials. They could not carry off a weeklong antiracist voir dire as Charles Garry did in many of the Black

Panther cases; their clients faced only misdemeanors and there was very little visible community support in the courtroom itself. An extensive voir dire in this context may have been viewed as overkill. However, it was simple to ask a few questions that had the effect of setting a political tone to the trial. For example, the first juror was asked the following: "The community newspaper that was being passed out was called *Basta Ya,* which means 'Enough Already!' Have you ever heard of it?" Since the juror's answer was no, the next question, spoken with enough clarity and strength to grab the attention of all the jurors, was, *"Basta Ya* has articles very critical of the police for harassing latinos and Mission residents. Would that prejudice you against Raul Flores?" By the fourth or fifth juror, this question became shortened to, "Would the articles criticizing police brutality make it hard for you to evaluate the evidence with an open mind?" One of the jurors, an older Italian man, was asked the following series of questions: "Mr. Flores speaks both English and Spanish. Are you familiar with people who have the ability to speak two languages?" Answer: "Of course; in my family, my wife and I, and son do." Question: "Do you take pride in your heritage, your culture?" Answer: "Very much. It's important." Question: "Would you think badly of Mr. Flores if, when he testifies, he speaks with a heavy Spanish accent?" Answer: "No, not if I can understand him." These types of questions give jurors some understanding of the racial and political issues behind the formal charges.

In opening statement, one need not give a political lecture to the jury, nor are most judges likely to allow such an approach. However, a few sentences can inform both the jury and the judge as to the actual nature of the case. For example, the following was one of two or three political comments in the *Basta Ya* opening statement: "Raul Flores will take the stand and testify. You will see that he is 23-years old, married, with one small child. He has been active for many years in community groups, militantly organizing against police abuse and brutality in the Mission district." At the very least, this type of statement puts the jury on notice as to the political context of the trial.

Cross-examination is the most overrated aspect of the trial. In a low-visibility case it is quite difficult for a lawyer to be able to expose the racism and bias of police officers. Consequently, one must try to shed light on that bias rather than attempt to tear the mask off.

Question: "Officer, you are assigned to the Mission police station, correct?" Answer: "Yes." Question: "For two years you have worked out of the Mission station, right?" Answer: "That's right." Question: "You've seen people selling *Basta Ya* up and down the streets of the Mission, haven't you?" Answer: "Yes, I have." Question: "And you have seen *Basta Ya* in the little newsboxes on the corners?" Answer: "I've noticed them occasionally." Question: "Before you arrested Mr. Flores and confiscated his papers, you were aware that the front page photo and headline were about police brutality in the Mission, weren't you?" Answer: "No, I don't think I was aware of that." These questions gave the jury some insight into the political motivations of the police, even though they did not fit the romanticized notion of a great political cross-examination.

One does not have to be defending the Chicago Eight, or Inez Garcia, to bring political reality into the courtroom. One does not have to be a William Kunstler or a Susan Jordan to use the above examples in trial. If we remember that behind each case there is a social reality that the law is trying to hide and suppress, we can find acceptable and practical methods to politicize our cases.

IV. COUNTERPRESSURE IN "NONPOLITICAL" CASES

The advantage of overtly political cases is that they provide opportunities to dramatize the real basis of existing social conflicts and to challenge the State's efforts to control the way that these conflicts are portrayed within existing legal categories. . . . The vast majority of legal cases do not, however, have this immediate potential for public impact. Ordinary divorce, personal injury cases, or unemployment hearings are political in that they involve the influence of large social forces upon individual lives, but they are not normally experienced as such. . . .

We propose three principal approaches to politicizing nonpolitical cases, which we believe will enable both lawyers and clients to begin to overcome this alienation. They are: (a) the disruption of the State's attempt to individualize and isolate such cases by discovering the inherent political content of common types of cases and using this political content to build community organization; (b) the politicization of local courtrooms and other "legal" public spaces that are currently colonized by government officials; and (c) the de-professionalization of the lawyer-client relationship at a widespread level. The unifying objective of all these approaches is to utilize legal conflict as a tool to increase the experienced power of all those affected by the conflict, including lawyers themselves, their clients, and the communities to which they are naturally linked.

A. Discovering the Common Thread

Here are some examples of potential alternative practices that would have as their objective the politicization of non-political cases:

1. A family law practice might be organized with the aim of politicizing issues the State currently characterizes as purely private or personal in nature. Such a practice could include any or all of the following elements: (a) creating new legal forms to support nontraditional relationships that challenge the idea that lasting love and intimacy are available only within isolated "family units" (this is

perhaps the most political aspect of the gay-rights movement); (b) developing a holistic multi-service center providing medical and psychological assistance to families breaking down under the strain of such social forces as stress at the workplace, unemployment, and the privatization of personal life; (c) developing new approaches to traditional divorce and child-custody cases to make the process of separation as educational and empowering as possible (including, for example, the use of face-to-face mediation instead of lawyer-to-lawyer adversary proceedings, and group-forming strategies like the pro se divorce clinic in which women and/or men can discover their common experience of being imprisoned within traditional family roles while working together to change their status).

2. A low-level criminal defense practice might concentrate on breaking the routinization of "criminal control" in a particular section of an urban area. The aim would be to link certain types of crime that repeatedly occur in a given area, e.g., small drug sales by addicts, with their socioeconomic roots, and working with existing neighborhood groups to build consciousness about the way that the defendant's problem is actually the community's problem as an oppressed area within the socioeconomic structure. The guiding principle here would be to penetrate the right wing's appeal for law and order and crime control by seeking to reduce crime through increased community solidarity and resistance to the socioeconomic destruction of the area. One aspect of such a practice might be the development of progessive community arbitration projects that would be designed to educate both "criminals" and the group to which they belong about the social causes of their own activity. . . .

4. In a landlord-tenant practice that primarily consists of fighting evictions on a case-by-case basis, lawyers can politicize cases by encouraging organizing efforts among tenants and by simply suggesting that people discuss their common difficulties *as tenants*. Such a suggestion helps reveal that the political issue at the root of landlord-tenant conflicts is not whether tenants "need more rights," but rather what the destructive effects of the housing market itself are on people's communities and home lives. . . .

Obviously, these examples are both simplistic and overly utopian if conceived as isolated attempts by individual lawyers. But if hundreds of lawyers begin to form networks that make the development of this kind of practice their self-conscious aim, they will have a real impact, not so much from the instrumental gains that they will make in individual cases, but from their contribution to the development of an authentic politics. If *every* dispute is founded ultimately upon conflicts and contradictions within the system as a whole, every such dispute raises the potential for thematizing in both reflection and collective action the relationship between private life and public totality. The activity of engaging in this politicization of legal practice is the activity of realizing the liberating politics of a future, more humane society in the present. It is the experience of engaging in this form of politics that is the true source of its transformative power.

B. The Politicization of the Courtroom

It is not an exaggeration to say that the single most powerful collective image of political authority is that of the courtroom. The robed judge who sits elevated from the gathering, the official and hushed character of the legal proceeding, the architecture of the room, the complex procedural technicalities—all of these and many other features of the courtroom ritual serve to reinculcate the political authority of the State, and through it the legitimacy of the socioeconomic order as a whole. Because the social power of hierarchies in the private sphere depends upon the continuing acceptance of the political authority that the courtroom encodes and symbolizes, a conscious effort to undermine the sanctity of the courtroom can become an important strategy for throwing the entire social order into question. . . .

[It is not] necessary or even desirable for such a strategy to take the form of overt "contempt of court." The strategy proposed here is a more widespread practice of much longer duration, through which a great many lawyers in every kind of case make it a part of their political work to "gently" deconstruct the courtrooms in their local communities, and in so doing contribute to eroding the symbolic power of the State's authority from the bottom up. The following two examples illustrate what is meant by such "gentle" deconstruction.

1. Several years ago Stephanie Kline, a radical healthworker, was falsely charged with murder and possession of explosives. Bail was set at $75,000, and her lawyer moved to have it reduced. In the Oakland Municipal Courts there is a "prisoner's dock" adjoining the holding cell, located to the right or left of the judge's elevated bench. At a bail hearing crowded with Kline's supporters, the bailiff escorted Kline to her dock to the right of the judge. Several yards away to the front-left of the judge sat her defense lawyer. Between them was the district attorney's table, located to the front-right of the judge. The defense lawyer asked the judge to allow the defendant to come over and sit with him. The judge refused. Defense counsel then got up and walked between the D.A. and the judge to the prisoner's dock. Neither the bailiff nor the judge stopped him. He argued for reduction of bail standing next to his client, a location which required the judge to turn to her right to hear the plea. The D.A. argued from his table.

2. Two codefendants in San Francisco pleaded guilty to marijuana smuggling. One was represented by a young National Lawyers Guild attorney, the other by a prestigious New York dope lawyer. At the sentencing hearing, the young lawyer arrived with his client's wife

and children, aged seven and ten. When they walked into the courtroom, the bailiff ordered the children to leave, stating that it was a standing rule of the judge that children were not allowed in the courtroom. This would be the children's last opportunity to see their father before he began serving his sentence. The lawyer explained to the bailiff that the children were not babies and argued that they had a right to be there based upon constitutional guarantees to privacy of family relationship and to a public trial. The bailiff replied that they were dealing with a standing rule. The lawyer told the wife and children to stay and asked the bailiff to inform the judge of his position, which the bailiff did. The judge then entered without ever raising the issue. No motion had to be made to allow the children to stay and the children were not forcibly removed. The other defendant's children remained in the outside hall, never seeing their father because his lawyer obeyed the standing rule.

If we understand the courtroom as a symbolically organized public space that is designed to reproduce, through repeated visible rituals, a collective obedience to political authority, both of these examples show the seizure and transformation of this space through the most ordinary human actions. The lawyers neither produced flashy legal stratagems, nor affirmed the authority of the proceeding by contemptuously railing against it. Rather, they refused to recognize the legitimacy of the official and authoritative façade by acting in accordance with an authentic human morality against which this façade, because it is constructed upon images, is always powerless. In forcing the actors in their false drama to recognize them as actual and ordinary persons, the lawyers were able, however briefly, to transform the courtroom with all of its choreographed style and pretense into a mere room inhabited only by other ordinary people. . . .

The gentle deconstruction of the courtroom cannot be limited to a few isolated instances that become inspiring anecdotes ("Only Kunstler could do that"); the potential for developing a concerted strategy exists every day on a widespread level. The development of such a strategy must occur in working groups of lawyers who are in the best position to understand the available space for action, but there are certain general principles relevant to the conduct of any trial.

The most basic principle refers not to a particular course of action but to a way of being. In conducting a trial the lawyer must resist the pressure to identify her being with the role that is allocated to her. This does not preclude acting like a lawyer in the making of motions or in the conduct of cross-examination; it means maintaining and living out an emotional distance between her true self and her "performance," so that she always expresses herself as merely "acting like" a lawyer and not *being* one. . . .

In adhering to this position of simultaneous detachment and involvment, the lawyer will discover her greatest opportunity for honest and human interventions in her direct and indirect communication with the jury. . . . The greatest possibility for reaching the jury occurs in those moments, often quite extended, when the lawyer has an opportunity to talk to the jury directly without significant interference from the judge or opposing counsel. This extended communication typically takes place in opening and closing statements. At these times the lawyer can break the false reality of the courtroom spectacle by telling the truth to the jurors, speaking not like a courtroom orator but like an ordinary person who is serious about what she has to say. The "truth," as we are using the term, is the sociopolitical truth which the court normally considers to be irrelevant to the legal resolution of the dispute. This truth must therefore be "gotten in," through the invention of an innovative approach as in the Inez Garcia trial, or even more often by speaking to jurors in a way that relates the "case" to experiences in society with which they can empathize. . . .

Many lawyers assume that it is dangerous to be political in the courtroom because it will reduce their chances of winning. This is incorrect as a general principle, particularly if "political" is understood to mean demonstrating the underlying social reality of the case. Although there are undoubtedly many instances when a traditional legalistic approach is the most appropriate course of action, it is also true that, as a general rule, judges, prosecutors, and lawyers feel a loss of power when the roles within which they exercise control are revealed to be artificial and manipulative. The greater the extent to which conditioned images of the courtroom are undermined by honest spontaneity and moral authenticity in speech and action, the more likely it is that the jury will react to the totality of the event with a free and human response.

C. The Deprofessionalization of the Lawyer-Client Relationship

The split between the motivation of progressive lawyers to change society and the content of their daily legal work is extremely debilitating over the long term. As political people they don't feel they can do anything directly to transform society because this must await a mass movement, and they don't experience themselves as a part of such a movement. As lawyers they don't feel they can do anything because they see the legal system as a fixed environment in which they are under more-or-less-constant pressure because they are almost always on the defensive, and must play the game by a set of rules that severely limits their options. Furthermore, they often find legal work to be both boring and deeply alienating after a few years of practice, because in their capacity as lawyers they are intellectually and emotionally starved. For this reason many eventually drop out, either by leaving law practice altogether or by making compromises in the kinds of cases they take. Whatever idealistic feelings led them to go to law school cannot withstand forever the degradation of their spirit that seems to be the inevitable consequence of legal work.

In order to overcome this destructive and depoliticizing process, lawyers must come to see that this split fundamentally derives from their own false consciousness, from their failure to understand the true nature of the legal system and the possibilities that are open to them to assert themselves as political people within the legal arena. . . .

If a political lawyer can recoup her being from the role into which she has fallen and see the system as it really is, her practice can become a source of political strength for herself and her clients, and a source of opportunity to further the development of a true political or class consciousness. If the legal system is understood as nothing more than people in rooms who deploy their power through authoritarian symbols and imaginary laws, every social conflict that is channeled into such a room becomes an opportunity to challenge the dominant consciousness in a public setting. . . . The issue for a client is not initially a legal one that can be addressed by informing him of his abstract legal rights; the issue is a political one that requires that he assert his human needs in relation to others with whom he is in conflict. The lawyer is therefore in a crucial position—not "as a lawyer," but as an ordinary person with special experience—to empathically comprehend these needs and help the client to articulate them in the most effective and meaningful way possible.

In order to do this the lawyer must completely divest herself of the sense that she is merely a neutral and objective figure. This depends on perceiving every social conflict that gives rise to a legal proceeding as an opportunity for both her client and herself to develop a sense of interpersonal power through overcoming the alienation and powerlessness that normally envelop them both in their daily routines as private citizens. Of course, a critical aspect to the lawyer's job will be to provide the client with legal assistance, but this division of labor need not define the lawyer's *way of being* in relation to the client. . . .

The most important political message a client may receive arises from the fact that a legal conflict *forces* the client to come into contact with the public sphere, a sphere which in his imagination is controlled by government officials endowed with virtually magical authoritarian powers. . . . The client's discovery that he is capable of taking a public action on his own behalf is therefore extremely important psychologically, because this action *of itself* can make the "public sphere" vanish. By acting on his situation instead of being a function of it, the client may see "the State" dissolve before his eyes into a mere group of other persons who are trying to silence him. Such an experience can have a powerful politicizing impact on the client's view of his entire life, even if the legal outcome of the specific case is unfavorable.

For the lawyer, the experience of deprofessionalization can be equally significant, because it requires giving up the pseudo-power that the State has bestowed upon her in exchange for the actual power of discovering a way of working that is expressive of her true political being. The notions held by many lawyers that one should feel guilty about being a professional, that political change must be brought about by others, that lawyers "can't do anything"—all of these are merely expressions of a false consciousness resulting from a sense of powerlessness. To transcend this image is to transcend the split between one's authentic being and one's social self that is the universal basis of alienation, and to side with the power of desire against the forces that perpetually attempt to contain it.

V. CONCLUSION

Everything that we have said in this essay depends for its effectiveness on the development of a *movement* of lawyers who meet regularly to further develop the ideas that we have begun to present here, and who give one another the strength to take the risks that a truly politicized law practice requires. The possibility of utilizing social conflict to transform the legal arena from its current moribund state into an arena where a struggle for consciousness is waged obviously cannot be realized through the efforts of isolated practitioners. . . .

Any transformative movement of lawyers must thus begin with the formation of small working groups, where lawyers who already know each other can begin to discuss what possibilities exist in their local communities for delegitimating legal work, and how they can develop a sense of collective support for one another's efforts. The general objective of such groups should be to break through the privatization of ordinary legal work, so that an alternative form of law practice like the one that we have begun to describe begins to achieve a degree of public legitimacy—so that, for example, a small group of lawyers that forms in Norman, Oklahoma, can know that there are other groups of lawyers in Ann Arbor or San Francisco who are trying to realize the same or similar objectives.

Such an initial strategy follows from the theory of law and legal processes described above: that the role of the State in its legal or ideological capacity is to maintain the legitimacy of collective powerlessness through the authoritarian control of popular consciousness. The State's strategy affects lawyers as much as anyone, and a measure of the State's success is the cynicism and sense of hopelessness that many progressive lawyers currently feel. The irony of this position is that it derives as much from our own false consciousness as it does from any actual powerlessness that is imposed upon us from the outside. And with regard to the powerlessness that we impose upon ourselves, the way out remains through the door.

NOTES

16. United States v. Dellinger, 472 F.2d 340 (7th Cir. 1972), *cert. denied*, 410 U.S. 970 (1973).

19. Most of the details concerning the second *Garcia* trial come from conversations between Paul Harris and Susan Jordan. For a discussion of Inez Garcia's first trial and appeal, see generally C. Garry and A. Goldsberg, *Streetfighter in the Courtroom* 217–41 (1977).

20. Ibid., p. 236.

21. Ibid., p. 231.

22. People v. Garcia, 54 Cal. App. 3d 61, 126 Cal. Rptr. 275, *cert. denied*, 426 U.S. 911 (1975).

23. See Elizabeth M. Schneider and Susan Jordan, "Representation of Women Who Defend Themselves in Response to Physical or Sexual Assault," *Women's Rights Law Report* 4 (1978): 149; Elizabeth M. Schneider, "Equal Rights to Trial for Women: Sex Bias in the Law of Self-Defense," *Harvard Civil Rights–Civil Liberties Law Review* 15 (1980): 623; Dolores A. Donovan and Stephanie M. Wildman, "Is the Reasonable Man Obsolete? A Critical Perspective on Self-Defense and Provocation," *Loyola—Los Angeles Law Review* 14 (1980–81): 435.

24. People v. Garcia, Cr. No. 4259 (Super. Ct. Monterey Cty. Cal., 1977).

19

The Critical Legal Studies Movement

Roberto Mangabeira Unger

Critical legal studies arose from the leftist tradition in modern legal thought and practice. Two overriding concerns have marked this tradition.

The first concern has been the critique of formalism and objectivism. . . . Formalism in this context is a commitment to, and therefore also a belief in the possibility of, a method of legal justification that contrasts with open-ended disputes about the basic terms of social life, disputes that people call ideological, philosophical, or visionary. Such conflicts fall far short of the closely guarded canon of inference and argument that the formalist claims for legal analysis. Formalism holds impersonal purposes, policies, and principles to be indispensable components of legal reasoning. Formalism in the conventional sense—the search for a method of deduction from a gapless system of rules—is merely the anomalous, limiting case of this jurisprudence.

A second distinctive formalist thesis is that only through such a restrained, relatively apolitical method of analysis is legal doctrine possible. Legal doctrine or legal analysis is a conceptual practice that combines two characteristics: the willingness to work from the institutionally defined materials of a given collective tradition, and the claim to speak authoritatively within this tradition, to elaborate it from within in a way that is meant, at least ultimately, to affect the application of state power. Doctrine can exist, according to the formalist view, because of a contrast between the more determinate

An earlier version of this chapter appeared in *The Critical Legal Studies Movement* (Cambridge: Harvard University Press, 1986). Reprinted by permission of author and publisher.

rationality of legal analysis and the less determinate rationality of ideological contests. . . .

Objectivism is the belief that the authoritative legal materials—the system of statutes, cases, and accepted legal ideas—embody and sustain a defensible scheme of human association. They display, though always imperfectly, an intelligible moral order. Alternatively they show the results of practical constraints upon social life—constraints such as those of economic efficiency—that, taken together with constant human desires, have a normative force. The laws are not merely the outcome of contingent power struggles nor of practical pressures lacking in rightful authority.

The modern lawyer may wish to keep his formalism while avoiding objectivist assumptions. He may feel happy to switch from talk about interest group politics in a legislative setting to invocations of impersonal purpose, policy, and principle in an adjudicative or professional one. He is plainly mistaken; formalism presupposes at least a qualified objectivism. For if the impersonal purposes, policies, and principles on which all but the most mechanical versions of the formalist thesis must rely do not come, as objectivism suggests, from a moral or practical order exhibited, however partially and ambiguously, by the legal materials themselves, where could they come from? They would have to be supplied by some normative theory extrinsic to the law. Even if such a theory could be convincingly established on its own ground, it would be miraculous if its implications coincided with a large portion of the received doctrinal understandings. At least it would be miraculous unless you had already assumed the truth of objectivism. But if the results of this alien theory failed to overlap with the greater part of received understandings of the law, you would need to reject broad areas of established law and legal doctrine as "mistaken." You would then have trouble maintaining the contrast of doctrine to ideology and political prophecy that represents an essential part of the formalist creed: you would have become a practitioner of the free-wheeling criticism of established arrangements and received ideas. . . .

If the criticism of formalism and objectivism is the first characteristic theme of leftist movements in modern legal thought, the purely instrumental use of legal practice and legal doctrine to advance leftist aims is the second. The connection between skeptical criticism and strategic militancy seems both negative and sporadic. It is negative because it remains almost entirely limited to the claim that nothing in the nature of law or in the conceptual structure of legal thought— neither objectivist nor formalist assumptions—constitutes a true obstacle to the advancement of leftist aims. It is sporadic because short-run leftist goals might occasionally be served by the transmutation of political commitments into delusive conceptual necessities. . . .

THE CRITICISM OF LEGAL THOUGHT

The Critique of Objectivism

In refining the attack upon objectivism, we have reinterpreted contemporary law and legal doctrine as the ever more advanced dissolution of the project of the classical nineteenth-century lawyers. Because both the original project and the signs of its progressive breakdown remain misunderstood, the dissolution has not yet been complete and decisive. The nineteenth-century jurists were engaged in a search for the built-in legal structure of the democracy and the market. The nation, at the Lycurgan moment of its history, had opted for a particular type of society: a commitment to a democratic republic and to a market system as a necessary part of that republic. The people might have chosen some other type of social organization. But in choosing this one, in choosing it for example over an aristocratic and corporatist polity on the old-European model, they also chose the legally defined institutional structure that went along with it. This structure provided legal science with its topic and generated the purposes, policies, and principles to which legal argument might legitimately appeal. Two ideas played a central role in this enterprise. One was the distinction between the foundational politics, responsible for choosing the social type, and the ordinary politics, including the ordinary legislation, operating within the framework established at the foundational moment. The other idea was that an inherent and distinct legal structure existed for each type of social organization. . . .

Successive failures to find the universal legal language of democracy and the market suggest that no such langauge exists. An increasing part of doctrinal analysis and legal theory has been devoted to containing the subversive implications of this discovery.

The general theory of contract and property provided the core domain for the objectivist attempt to disclose the built-in legal content of the market, just as the theory of protected constitutional interests and of the legitimate ends of state action was designed to reveal the intrinsic legal structure of a democratic republic. But the execution kept belying the intention. As the property concept was generalized and decorporealized, it faded into the generic conception of right, which in turn proved to be systematically ambiguous (Hohfeld's insight) if not entirely indeterminate. Contract, the dynamic counterpart to property, could do no better. The generalization of contract theory revealed, alongside the dominant principles of freedom to choose the partner and the terms, the counterprinciples: that freedom to contract would not be allowed to undermine the communal aspects of social life, and that grossly unfair bargains would not be enforced. Though the counterprinciples might be pressed to the corner, they could be neither driven out completely nor subjected to some system of metaprinciples that would settle, once and for all, their relation to the dominant principles. In the most contested areas of contract law, two different views of the sources of obligation still contend. One, which sees the counterprinciples as mere ad hoc qualifications to the dominant principles, identifies the fully articulated act of will and the unilateral imposition of a duty by the state as the two exhaustive sources of obligation. The other view, which treats the counterprinciples as possible generative norms of the entire body of law and doctrine, finds the standard source of obligations in the only partially deliberate ties of mutual dependence and redefines the two conventional sources as extreme, limiting cases. Which of these clashing conceptions provides the real theory of contract? Which describes the institutional structure inherent in the very nature of a market? . . .

The convergent result of these two modes of attack upon objectivism—the legal-historical and the legal-doctrinal—is to discredit, once and for all, the conception of a system of social types with a built-in institutional structure. The very attempt to work this conception into technical legal detail ends up showing its falsehood. Thus, a cadre of seemingly harmless and even toadying jurists partly authored the insight required to launch the attack against objectivism—the discovery of the indeterminate content of abstract institutional categories like democracy or the market—with its far-reaching subversive implications. Those who live in the temple may delight in the thought that the priests occasionally outdo the prophets.

The Critique of Formalism

The starting point of our argument is the idea that every branch of doctrine must rely tacitly if not explicitly upon some picture of the forms of human association that are right and realistic in the areas of social life with which it deals. For example, a constitutional lawyer needs a theory of the democratic republic that would describe the proper relation between state and society or the essential features of social organization and individual entitlement that government must protect, come what may.

Without such a guiding vision, legal reasoning seems condemned to a game of easy analogies. It will always be possible to find, retrospectively, more or less convincing ways to make a set of distinctions, or failures to distinguish, look credible. . . . Because everything can be defended, nothing can; the analogy-mongering must be brought to a halt. It must be possible to reject some of the received understandings and decisions as mistaken and to do so by appealing to some background normative theory of the branch of law in question or of the realm of social practice governed by that part of the law.

Suppose that you could determine on limited grounds of institutional propriety how much a style of doctrinal practice may regularly reject as mistaken. With too little rejection, the lawyer fails to avoid the suspect quality of endless analogizing. With too much, he forfeits his claim to be doing doctrine as opposed to ideology, philosophy, or prophecy. For any given level of revisionary power, however, different portions of the received understandings in any extended field of law may be repudiated.

To determine which part of established opinion about the meaning and applicability of legal rules you should reject, you need a background prescriptive theory of the relevant area of social practice, a theory that does for the branch of law in question what a doctrine of the republic or of the political process does for constitutional argument. This is where the trouble arises. No matter what the content of this background theory, it is, if taken seriously and pursued to its ultimate conclusions, unlikely to prove compatible with a broad range of the received understandings. Yet just such a compatibility seems to be required by a doctrinal practice that defines itself by contrast to open-ended ideology. For it would be strange if the results of a coherent, richly developed normative theory were to coincide with a major portion of any extended branch of law. The many conflicts of interest and vision that lawmaking involves, fought out by countless minds and wills working at cross-purposes, would have to be the vehicle of an immanent moral rationality whose message could be articulated by a single cohesive theory. The dominant legal theories in fact undertake this daring and implausible sanctification of the actual and the unreflective common sense of orthodox lawyers tacitly presupposes it. Most often, the sanctification takes the form of treating the legal order as a repository of intelligible purposes, policies, and principles, in abrupt contrast to the standard disenchanted view of legislative politics. . . .

Having recognized this problem with doctrine, modern legal analysis tries to circumvent it in a number of ways. It may, for example, present an entire field of law as the expression of certain underlying theoretical approaches to the subject. These implicit models, it is suggested, fit into some coherent scheme or, at least, point toward a synthesis. In this way it seems possible to reconcile the recognition that legal analysis requires an appeal to an underlying theory of right and social practice with the inability to show that the actual content of law and doctrine in any given area coincides, over an appreciable area of law, with a particular theory. But this recourse merely pushes the problem to another level. No extended body of law in fact coincides with such a metascheme, just as no broad range of historical experience coincides with the implications of one of the evolutionary views that claim to provide a science of history. . . . It is always possible to find in actual legal materials radically inconsistent clues about the range of application of each of the models, and indeed about the identity of the models themselves.

Once the lawyer abandons these methods of compensation and containment, he returns to a cruder and more cynical device. He merely imposes upon his background conceptions—his theories of right and social practice—an endless series of ad hoc adjustments. The looseness of the theories and the resulting difficulty of distinguishing the ad hoc from the theoretically required make this escape all the easier. Thus, there emerges the characteristic figure of the modern jurist who wants—and needs—to combine the cachet of theoretical refinement, the modernist posture of seeing through everything, with the reliability of the technician whose results remain close to the mainstream of professional and social consensus. Determined not to miss out on anything, he has chosen to be an outsider and an insider at the same time. To the achievement of this objective he has determined to sacrifice the momentum of his ideas. We have denounced him wherever we have found him, and we have found him everywhere. . . .

The implication of our attack upon formalism is to undermine the attempt to rescue doctrine through these several stratagems. It is to demonstrate that a doctrinal practice that puts its hope in the contrast of legal reasoning to ideology, philosophy, and political prophecy ends up as a collection of makeshift apologies.

The Critiques of Objectivism and Formalism Related: Their Significance for Current Legal Theories

As long as the project of the nineteenth-century jurists retained its credibility, the problem of doctrine did not emerge. The miracle required and promised by objectivism could take place: the coincidence of the greater part of substantive law and doctrine with a coherent theory, capable of systematic articulation and relentless application. The only theory capable of performing the miracle would have been one that described the inner conceptual and institutional structure of the type of social and governmental organization to which the nation had committed itself at its foundational moment. Such a theory would not have needed to be imported from outside. It would not have been just somebody's favorite system. It would have translated into legal categories the abiding structure of ordinary political and economic activity. Once the objectivist project underlying the claim to reveal the inherent content of a type of social organization ceased to be believable, doctrine in its received form was condemned to the self-subversion that our critique of formalism has elucidated. But because the nature and defects of the project appeared only gradually, so did the permanent disequilibrium of doctrine.

This view of the flaws in objectivism and formalism and of the close link between the two sets of ideas and the two critiques explains our approach to the most influential and symptomatic legal theories in

America today: the law and economics and the rights and principles schools. Each of these theories is advanced by a group that stands at the margin of high power, despairs of seeing its aims triumph through the normal means of governmental politics, and appeals to some conceptual mechanism designed to show that the advancement of its program is a practical or moral necessity. . . .

The chief instrument of the law and economics school is the equivocal use of the market concept. These analysts give free rein to the very mistake that the increasing formalization of microeconomics was largely meant to avoid: the identification of the abstract market idea or the abstract circumstance of maximizing choice with a particular social and institutional complex. As a result, an analytic apparatus intended, when rigorous, to be entirely free of restrictive assumptions about the workings of society and entirely subsidiary to an empirical or normative theory that needs independent justification gets mistaken for a particular empirical and normative vision. More particularly, the abstract market idea is identified with a specific version of the market—the one that has prevailed in most of the modern history of most Western countries—with all its surrounding social assumptions, real or imagined. The formal analytic notion of allocational efficiency is identified with a specific theory of economic growth or, quite simply, with the introduction, the development, or the defense of this particular institutional and social order. Such are the sophistries by which the law and economics school pretends to discover both the real basis for the overall evolution of the legal order and the relevant standard by which to criticize occasional departures of that order from its alleged vocation. . . .

The rights and principles school achieves similar results through very different means. It claims to discern in the leading ideas of the different branches of law, especially when illuminated by a scrupulous, benevolent, and well-prepared professional elite, the signs of an underlying moral order that can then serve as the basis for a system of more or less natural rights. This time, the objective order that guides the main line of legal evolution and serves to criticize the numerous though marginal aberrations is a harshly simplified version of moral ideas supposedly expressed in authoritative legal materials. No longer able to appeal to the idea of the built-in institutional structure of a type of social organization, this school alternates confusedly between two options, both of which it finds unacceptable as a basis for legal theory. One option is that moral consensus (if only it could actually be identified) carries weight just because it exists. The alternative view is that the dominant legal principles count as the manifestations of a transcendent moral order whose content can be identified quite apart from the history and substance of a particular body of law. The third and mediating position for which the school grasps—that consensus on the received principles somehow signals a moral order resting mysteriously upon more than consensus—requires several connected intellectual maneuvers. One is a drastic minimization of the extent to which the law already incorporates conflict over the desirable forms of human association. Another is the presentation of the dominant legal ideas as expressions of higher moral insight, an insight duly contained and corrected by a fidelity to the proprieties of established institutional roles, a fidelity that must itself be mandated by the moral order. Yet another is the deployment of a specific method to reveal the content and implications of this order: generalize from particular doctrines and intuitions, then hypostasize the generalizations into moral truth, and finally use the hypostasis to justify and correct the original material. The intended result of all this hocus-pocus is far clearer than the means used to achieve it. The result is to generate a system of principles and rights that overlaps to just the appropriate extent with the positive content of the laws. Such a system has the suitable degree of revisionary power, the degree necessary to prove that you are neither an all-out and therefore ineffective apologist nor an irresponsible revolutionary.

The law and economics and the rights and principles schools supply a watered-down version of the enterprise of nineteenth-century legal science. The endeavor of the classical nineteenth-century jurists in turn represented a diluted version of the more common, conservative social doctrines that preceded the emergence of modern social theory. These doctrines pretended to discover a canonical form of social life and personality that could never be fundamentally remade and reimagined even though it might undergo corruption or regeneration. At each succeeding stage of the history of these ideas, the initial conception of a natural form of society becomes weaker: the categories more abstract and indeterminate, the champions more acutely aware of the contentious character of their own claims. Self-consciousness poisons their protestations. Witnessing this latest turn in the history of modern legal thought, no one could be blamed for recalling hopefully Novalis's remark that "when we dream that we dream we are about to awake."

A large part of this history consists in the attempt to deflect the critique of formalism and objectivism by accepting some of its points while saving increasingly less of the original view. The single most striking example in twentieth-century American legal thought has been the development of a theory of legal process, institutional roles, and purposive legal reasoning as a response to legal realism. Perhaps the most creditable pretext for these endless moves of confession and avoidance has been the fear that, carried to the extreme, the critique of objectivism and formalism would leave nothing standing. The very possibility of legal doctrine, and perhaps even of normative argument generally, might be destroyed. Thus, ramshackle and plausible compromises have been easily mistaken for theoretical insight. For many of us, the turning point came when we decided, at the risk of confusion, paralysis, and marginality, to pursue the critical attack *à outrance*. When we took the negative ideas relentlessly to their final conclusions, we were rewarded by seeing these ideas turn into the starting points of a constructive program.

FROM CRITIQUE TO CONSTRUCTION

The Constructive Outcome of the Critique of Formalism: Deviationist Doctrine

The defense of the received forms of doctrine has always rested on an implicit challenge: either accept the ruling style, with its aggressive contrast to controversy over the basic terms of social life, as the true form of doctrine, or find yourself reduced to the inconclusive contest of political visions. This dilemma is merely one of the many specific conceptual counterparts to the general choice: either resign yourself to some established version of social order, or face the war of all against all. The implication of our critique of formalism is to turn the dilemma of doctrine upside down. It is to say that, if any conceptual practice similar to what lawyers now call doctrine can be justified, the class of legitimate doctrinal activities must be sharply enlarged. The received style of doctrine must be redefined as an arbitrarily restricted subset of this larger class. We agree neither on whether this expanded or deviationist doctrine can in fact be constructed nor on what exactly its methods and boundaries should be. But we know that only such an expansion could generate a conceptual practice that maintains the minimal characteristics of doctrine—the willingness to take the extant authoritative materials as starting points and the claim to normative authority—while avoiding the arbitrary juxtaposition of easy analogy and truncated theorizing that characterizes the most ambitious and coherent examples of legal analysis today. . . .

Expanded doctrine—the genre of legal writing that our movement has begun to develop—may be defined by several complementary or substantially equivalent criteria. On one description its central feature is the attempt to cross both an empirical and a normative frontier: the boundaries that separate doctrine from empirical social theory and from argument over the proper organization of society—that is, from ideological conflict. Enlarged doctrine crosses the normative boundary by deploying a method that differs in no essential way from the loose form of criticism, justification, and discovery that is possible within ideological controversy itself. Deviationist doctrine moves across the empirical boundary in two different ways. One way is familiar and straightforward: to explore the relations of cause and effect that lawyers dogmatically assume rather than explicitly investigate when they claim to interpret rules and precedents in the light of imputed purpose. . . . The other way the empirical element counts is more subtle and systematic: it opens up the petrified relations between abstract ideals or categories, like freedom of contract or political equality, and the legally regulated social practices that are supposed to exemplify them. The method is to show, as a matter of truth about history and society, that these abstractions can receive—and almost invariably have received—alternative institutional embodiments, each of which gives a different cast to their guiding intentions.

On another description the crucial feature of deviationist doctrine is the willingness to recognize and develop the disharmonies of the law: the conflicts between principles and counterprinciples that can be found in any body of law. Critical doctrine does this by finding in these disharmonies the elements of broader contests among prescriptive conceptions of society.

Yet another description of expanded doctrine is presupposed by the previous two and makes explicit what they have in common. The revised style of doctrine commits itself to integrate into standard doctrinal argument the explicit controversy over the right and feasible structure of society, over what the relations among people should be like in the different areas of social activity. In the rich North Atlantic countries of the present day, the imaginative vision of the ways in which people can have a life in common appeals to a particular ideal of democracy for the state and citizenship, to a picture of private community in the domain of family and friendship, and to an amalgam of contract and impersonal technical hierarchy in the everyday realm of work and exchange. This social vision helps make the entire body of law look intelligible and even justifiable. Above all, it serves to resolve what would otherwise be incorrigible indeterminacy in the law. Just as the ambiguities of rules and precedents require recourse to imputed purposes or underlying policies and principles, so the ambiguities of these policies and principles can be avoided only by appealing to some background scheme of association of the sort just described. Yet the conflicting tendencies within law constantly suggest alternative schemes of human association. The focused disputes of legal doctrine repeatedly threaten to escalate into struggles over the basic imaginative structure of social existence. . . .

The rationality for which this expanded version of legal doctrine can hope is nothing other than the minimal but perhaps still significant potential rationality of the normal modes of moral and political controversy. You start from the conflicts between the available ideals of social life in your own social world or legal tradition and their flawed actualizations in present society. You imagine the actualizations transformed, or you transform them in fact, if only by extending an ideal to some area of social life from which it had previously been excluded. Then you revise the ideal conceptions in the light of their new practical embodiments. Call this process internal development. To engage in it self-reflectively you need make only two crucial assumptions: that no one scheme of association has conclusive authority, and that the mutual correction of abstract ideals and their institutional realizations represents the last best hope of the standard forms of normative controversy. The weakness of such a method is obviously its dependence upon the starting points provided by a particular tradition; its strength, the richness of reference to a concrete collective history of ideas and institutions. Legal doctrine rightly understood and practiced is the conduct of internal development through legal materials. . . .

The program of expanded legal analysis—the constructive outcome of our critique of formalism—solves the problem of doctrine only by redefining its terms. The received forms of doctrine and the legal theories that try to justify them seek a method guaranteed both to possess just the right degree of revisionary power and to reaffirm the contrast between legal analysis and ideological conflict. The actual result of this search, however, is to reduce all legal reasoning to a tenacious exercise in sophistry, compelled in its most serious and systematic moments to invoke background theories of right and social practice whose implications it must also contain. Deviationist doctrine employs a method, internal development, whose revisionary reach can in the end be limited solely by institutional considerations lacking any higher authority. It lays claim to no privileged status capable of distinguishing it clearly from ideological dispute. Thus, when pushed beyond a certain point, it ceases to look like what we now call doctrine or to serve the narrow purposes of professional argument, especially when such argument takes place in an adjudicative context. Yet at every point it promises only what it can deliver: its looser and more contestable rationality requires no mixture of bold theoretical claims and saving ad hoc adjustments. . . .

The Constructive Outcome of the Critique of Objectivism: Redefining the Institutional Forms of the Democracy and the Market

The constructive outcome of our critique of objectivism is to turn us toward the search for alternative institutional forms of the available institutional ideals, most especially the market and the democracy. The chief medium in which we pursue this quest is deviationist doctrine itself, including the historical and analytic criticism of received legal conceptions. For its full development, such a search requires three bodies of supporting and animating ideas. The first is a credible theory of social transformation. Without such a theory, we would lack standards by which to distinguish more or less realistic programmatic ideals. Programmatic debate would then fall back into its characteristic modern dilemma. The proposals that depart sharply from existing realities end up looking like utopian fantasies that merely invert a social reality they do not seriously imagine transformed. The proposals that stay close to established reality represent marginal adjustments that hardly seem worth fighting for. The programmatic mind alternates between the two converse and complementary dangers of effortless redefinition and blind capitulation. The second supporting set of ideas is a conception of the ideal that should guide the reconstruction of the institutional forms. . . . A third set of ideas is a conception of the proper relation of law to society. The alternative institutional forms, like the arrangements they replace, must be worked out in legal categories and by the method of deviationist doctrine.

One way to clarify the origin and character if not the justification of the ideal that inspires our programmatic institutional ideas is to say that our program arises from the generalization of aims more or less shared by the great secular doctrines of emancipation of the recent past—liberalism, socialism, and communism—and by the social theories that supported them. At the heart of each of these doctrines lay the belief that the weakening of social divisions and hierarchies would reveal deeper individual and collective identities and liberate productive and creative powers. The theoretical and practical consequences of this belief were drastically constricted by dogmatic assumptions about the possible forms of social transformation and their possible institutional results. We have attacked the second set of constraints and therefore, by implication, the first. The result is a more generalized or radicalized version of the social ideal.

This version may be stated in three equivalent forms. The first form is the cumulative loosening of the fixed order of society—its plan of social division and hierarchy, its enacted scheme of the possible and desirable modes of human association. The sense of this progressive dissolution is that to every aspect of the social order there should correspond some practical or imaginative activity that makes it vulnerable to collective conflict and deliberation. (Expanded doctrine itself exemplifies such an activity.) In this way no part of the social world can lie secluded from destabilizing struggle. A second version of the ideal that guides the elaboration of alternative institutional forms is that the life chances and life experiences of the individual should be increasingly freed from the tyranny of abstract social categories. He should not remain the puppet of his place in the contrast of classes, sexes, and nations. The opportunities, experiences, and values conventionally associated with these contrasting categories should be deliberately jumbled. A third, equivalent version of the ideal, is that the contrast between what a social world incorporates and what it excludes, between routine and revolution, should be broken down as much as possible; the active power to remake and reimagine the structure of social life should enter into the character of everyday existence. . . .

From a Social Ideal to an Institutional Program

POLITICAL AND CULTURAL REVOLUTION

The ultimate stakes in politics are always the direct practical or passionate dealings among people. The institutional order constrains, when it does not actively shape, this microstructure of social life. A vision of transformed personal relations may serve in turn to inspire major institutional change. . . .

The guiding and unifying aim of the cultural-revolutionary practice I have in mind lies perhaps in the systematic remaking of all direct personal connections—like those between superiors and subordinates or between men and women—through their progressive emancipation from a background plan of social division and hierarchy. Such a plan provides these dealings with a prewritten script. It makes the opportunities of practical exchange or passionate attachment respect the limits imposed by some established power order. It assigns fixed roles to people according to the position that they hold within a predetermined set of social or gender contrasts.

Thus described, the cultural-revolutionary program may seem entirely negative. It can nevertheless be restated in the affirmative mode. It wants the opportunities and experiences available to different categories of people to be more freely recombined. This facility of recombination matters both as a good in itself and as an occasion to improve the character of social life. It is easy enough to understand how such a facility might respond to practical concerns: productive capabilities may develop as the forms of production and exchange become more independent of any given, rigid organizational or social context. The hope of improvement also extends, though more obscurely and controversially, to the domain of community and passion. For example, people may be enabled and encouraged to combine in a single character qualities that ruling stereotypes assign separately to men and women. . . .

The program outlined here may be justified directly as an interpretation of what a particular social ideal and its corresponding image of personality require for our historical circumstances. . . .

CRITICIZING AND REINVENTING DEMOCRACY

Modern conceptions of democracy range from the cynical to the idealistic. At the idealistic pole lies the confident notion of popular sovereignty, qualified in its own interest by the requirements of partisan rotation in office, and able to survive intact the transition from direct to representative democracy. At the cynical pole stand the versions of the democratic ideal that claim to be satisfied with an ongoing competition among elites as long as the competitors occasionally need to enlist mass support. All contemporary versions of the democratic ideal, however, share a minimal core: the government must not fall permanently hostage to a faction, however broadly the term faction may be defined so as to include social classes, segments of the workforce, parties of opinion, or any other stable collective category. . . .

To imagine and establish a state that had more truly ceased to be hostage to a faction, in a society that had more truly rid itself of a background scheme of inadequately vulnerable division and hierarchy, we might need to transform every aspect of the existing institutional order. The transformed arrangements might then suggest a revision of the democratic ideal with which we had begun. From the idea of a state not hostage to a faction, existing in a society freed from a rigid and determinate order of division and hierarchy, we might move to the conception of an institutional structure, itself self-revising, that would provide constant occasions to disrupt any fixed structure of power and coordination in social life. Any such emergent structure would be broken up before having a chance to shield itself from the risks of ordinary conflict.

One way to develop this conception of an empowered democracy into a set of more concrete institutional principles is to define the more precise obstacles to its realization in each major sphere of institutional change: the organization of the state, the organization of the economy (or of the market), and the organization of rights. This procedure will have the advantage of distinguishing the program from a timeless, utopian blueprint. No matter how radical the proposed rearrangements may appear, they represent the adjustment of an historically specific institutional system in the light of a series of historically given, though possibly self-correcting, ideals.

THE ORGANIZATION OF GOVERNMENT

Take first the shaping of government and of the contest over the possession and uses of governmental power. The main problem lies in the fact that the very devices for restraining state power also tend to deadlock it. They establish a rough equivalence between the transformative reach of a political project and the obstacles that the structure of the state and party politics imposes upon its execution. This structure helps form, and reinforces once formed, the interests and preconceptions that crystallize around any stabilized social situation. As a result, the struggles of official politics fail to provide sufficient occasion to disrupt further the background structure of division and hierarchy in social life, and thus give rise to the facts emphasized by the earlier, internal objections to the established

versions of democracy. Yet—and this is the heart of the problem—
every attempt to revise the institutional arrangements that exercise
this structure-preserving influence seems to undermine the restraints
upon governmental power that are needed to secure freedom. A
successful resolution of this dilemma must provide ways to restrain
the state without effectively paralyzing its transformative activities.

Such a resolution might include the following elements. First, the
branches of government should be multiplied. To every crucial feature of the social order there should correspond some form and
arena of potentially destabilizing and broadly based conflict over the
uses of state power. . . . Different branches of government might be
designed to be accountable to popular sovereignty and party-political
rivalry in different ways. Second, the conflicts among these more
numerous branches of government should be settled by principles of
priority among branches and of devolution to the electorate. These
principles must resolve impasses cleanly and quickly. They should
replace the multiple devices of distancing and dispersal (including the
traditional focus on "checks and balances") that seek to restrain power
through the deliberate perpetuation of impasse. Third, the programmatic center of government—the party in office—should have a real
chance to try out its programs. . . .

THE ORGANIZATION OF THE ECONOMY

The prevailing institutional form of the market in the rich Western
countries works through the assignment of more or less absolute
claims to divisible portions of social capital, claims that can be trans-
mitted in unbroken temporal succession, including inheritance. To a
significant degree, specific markets are organized by large-scale business enterprises surrounded by an abundance of smaller ventures.
Workers are allowed to unionize. Both the segmentation of the
economy into large and small enterprises and the softening of the
confrontation between capital and labor through public and private
deals have helped fragment the workforce. The workers stand divided into groups entrenched in relatively fixed places in the division
of labor and widely disparate in their access to the advantages of
collective self-organization. This way of maintaining a market order
creates two kinds of obstacles for the program of empowered democracy: problems of freedom and problems of economic convenience.

This style of market organization threatens democratic freedom on
both the large and the small scale. It does so on a small scale by giving
the occupants of some fixed social stations the power to reduce the
occupants of other social stations to dependence. Individual or collective contract rights cannot fully counterbalance this dependence.
Practical imperatives of organizational efficiency cannot fully justify
it. This mode of market organization also poses a large-scale threat to

democracy. It does so by allowing relatively small groups, in control of investment decisions, to have a decisive say over the conditions of collective prosperity or impoverishment.

At the same time that it jeopardizes freedom, the dominant form of market organization restrains economic progress through a series of superimposed effects. All show how the existing market order acts as a deadweight upon practical ingenuity and economic progress by subordinating the opportunities for innovation to the interest of privilege and by thwarting plasticity, the secret of worldly success.

The first such damaging effect of the current market system is the constraint that it imposes upon the absolute degree of decentralization in the economy. . . . A second effect goes to what might be called economic plasticity: the encouragement of economic experimentation or, more precisely, the power to recombine and renew not merely factors of production but also the components of the institutional context of production and exchange. The style of the market order I have described makes initiatives for the revision of this context depend overwhelmingly upon the factional interests of those who, in the name of the property norm and impersonal technical requirements, take the lead in organizing work and supervising economic accumulation. . . .

A system of market organization capable of dealing with these multiple dangers to freedom and prosperity must not reduce the generative principle of economic decentralization to the mere assignment of absolute claims to divisible portions of social capital in a context of huge disparities of scale, influence, and advantage. An alternative principle that conforms to the aims of empowered democracy, to its constitutional organization and its system of rights, might be described as either an economic or a legal idea.

The central economic principle would be the establishment of a rotating capital fund. Capital would be made temporarily available to teams of workers or technicians under certain general conditions fixed by the central agencies of government. These conditions might, for example, set the outer limits to disparities of income or authority within the organization, to the accumulation of capital, and to the distribution of profit as income. The rates of interest charged for the use of capital in the different sectors of the economy would constitute the basic source of governmental finance, and the differentials among these rates the chief means with which to encourage risk-oriented or socially responsible investment. The fund would presumably be administered to maintain a constant flow of new entrants into markets. Enterprises would not be allowed to consolidate market-organizing positions or to make use of the devices that enable them today to seclude themselves against market instabilities. Rewards to particular individuals and teams would be distinguished from the imperial expansion of the organizations to which they temporarily belong.

Such a system might hope to become both more decentralized and more plastic than the existing market order. The institutional provisions for decentralized production and exchange would be subject to ongoing political controversy. The relative immunity of these arrangements to serious conflict and frequent revision in the existing democracies and market orders suggests that the arrangements cannot be freely transformed by economic actors. Basic economic structures are fixed by a system of legal entitlements and de facto power relations that governments seem able to change only marginally and that common prejudice dogmatically identifies with the inherent nature of a market system. One of the points of contention in the reformed system might be expected to become precisely the extent to which the range of permissible variation in the institutional forms of production and exchange should be expanded, in the economy as a whole or in particular sectors of it, for the sake of experiment and innovation.

The legal counterpart to the rotating capital fund is the disaggregation of the consolidated property right. As any civilian or common lawyer should have known from the start, what we call property is merely a collection of heterogeneous faculties. These faculties can be broken up and assigned to different entities. Thus, under the revised market system, some of the faculties that now constitute property might be attributed to the democratic agencies that set the terms of capital-taking, while others would be exercised by the capital-takers themselves.

THE SYSTEM OF RIGHTS

Alongside the organization of government and the economy, the system of rights constitutes yet another domain for institutional reconstruction. In its present form, this system causes two main problems for the program of empowered democracy. Individual safeguards rest on two supports: the system of property rights, which threatens to reduce some individuals to direct dependence upon others, and the set of political and civic rights and welfare entitlements, which poses no such threat. Yet any alternative economic order seems to aggravate the danger to freedom. . . .

The established system of rights presents another, less familiar obstacle to the aims of this institutional program: the absence of legal principles and entitlements capable of informing communal life—those areas of social existence where people stand in a relationship of heightened mutual vulnerability and responsibility toward each other. For one thing, our dominant conception of right imagines the right as a zone of discretion of the rightholder, a zone whose boundaries are more or less rigidly fixed at the time of the initial definition of the right. The right is a loaded gun that the rightholder may shoot at will in his corner of town. Outside that corner the other licensed gunmen may shoot him down. But the give-and-take of communal life and its characteristic concern for the actual effect of any decision upon the other person are incompatible with this view of right and therefore, if this is the only possible view, with any regime of rights. . . .

It may not at first seem self-evident either what the question of rights and community has to do with the program of empowered democracy or how it connects with the problem of immunity and domination. Remember that these proposals for institutional reconstruction matter not only for their own sake, but also for their encouragement to a systematic shift in the character of direct personal relations and, above all, in the available forms of community. This is the other element in the translation of the social ideal into concrete social practice: . . . the cumulative emancipation of personal relations from the constraints of some background plan of social division and hierarchy, as the recombination of qualities and experiences associated with different social roles, and as the development of an ideal of community no longer reduced to merely the obsessional and stifling counterimage to the quality of practical social life. These reformed varieties of communal experience need to be thought out in legal categories and protected by legal rights: not to give these reconstructed forms of solidarity and subjectivity institutional support would be—as current experience shows—merely to abandon them to entrenched forms of human connection at war with our ideals. . . .

To deal effectively with the two overlapping problems I have discussed—the problem of immunity and domination and the problem of rights and community—the law might have to distinguish four kinds of rights. The concept of right is subsidiary to that of a system of rights. A system of rights describes the relative positions of individuals or groups within a legally defined set of institutional arrangements. These arrangements must be basic and comprehensive enough to define a social world that encourages certain instrumental or passionate dealings among people and disfavors others. One kind of right gives the individual a zone of unchecked discretionary action that others, whether private citizens or governmental officials, may not invade. But we must not mistake the species for the genus nor claim to have stated how we understand even this species of right until we have made clear the institutional context of its operation. Fully developed, the system of rights described and justified here would presuppose and be presupposed by the principles of governmental and economic organization outlined earlier. The four types of right that constitute this system would carry different senses; the tyranny of consolidated property over our thinking about entitlements would at last be overthrown. All of these categories of right nevertheless share certain fundamental attributes. Each establishes a specific form of human connection that contributes to a scheme of collective self-government and resists the influence of social division and hierarchy.

The first category consists of immunity rights. These rights establish the nearly absolute claim of the individual to security against the state, other organizations, and other individuals. As much as is compatible with the risks of politics, they constitute the fixed Archimedean point in this system. As political and civic rights (organization, expression, and participation), as welfare entitlements, and as options to withdraw functionally and even territorially from the established social order, they give the individual the fundamental sense of safety that enables him to accept a broadened practice of collective conflict without feeling his vital security endangered. The system of immunity rights in the empowered democracy differs from current individual safeguards both by the vastly increased opportunities to exercise these rights and by its scrupulous avoidance of the guarantees of security that, like consolidated property, help defend power orders against democratic politics. . . .

Destabilization rights compose a second class of entitlements. They represent claims to disrupt esablished institutions and forms of social practice that have achieved the insulation and have encouraged the entrenchment of social hierarchy and division that the entire constitution wants to avoid.

Market rights constitute a third species of entitlement. They represent conditional and provisional claims to divisible portions of social capital. The form and substance of these rights, as successors to the absolute, consolidated property right, are suggested by the proposed alternative way of organizing a market. How provisional and conditional they should be, in any given sector or in the economy as a whole, poses one of the key questions to be answered by conscious collective decision. Whatever their fixity, however, they must be treated as a subcategory of right rather than as the exemplary type of entitlement to which all other types must be assimilated.

Solidarity rights make up a fourth category: the legal entitlements of communal life. Solidarity rights give legal force to many of the expectations that arise from the relations of mutual reliance and vulnerability that have neither been fully articulated by the will nor unilaterally constructed by the state. Each solidarity right has a two-stage career. The initial moment of the right is an incomplete definition that incorporates standards of good-faith loyalty or responsibility. The second moment is the completing definition through which the rightholders themselves (or the judges if the rightholders fail) set in context the concrete boundaries to the exercise of the right according to the actual effect that the threatened exercise seems likely to have upon the parties to the relationship. . . .

The program I have described is neither just another variant of the mythic, antiliberal republic nor much less some preposterous synthesis of the established democracies with their imaginary opposite. Instead, it represents a superliberalism. It pushes the liberal premises about state and society, about freedom from dependence and governance of social relations by the will, to the point at which they merge into a larger ambition: the building of a social world less alien to a self that can always violate the generative rules of its own mental or social constructs and put other rules and other constructs in their place. . . .

CONCLUSION: THE LESSONS OF INCONGRUITY

The chief objection to this view of the critical legal studies movement may be simply the formidable gap it suggests between the reach of our intellectual and political commitments and the many severe constraints upon our situation. We must still decide what to make of this gap.

First, there is the disproportion between our transformative goals and the established social peace. We have not sought, in the deceptions of a social and legal theory that claims to trump politics, consolation for our political disappointments. Surrounded by people who implicitly deny the transformability of arrangements whose contingency they also assert, we have refused to mistake the ramshackle settlements of this postwar age for the dispensations of moral providence or historical fate.

Then we face the contrast between the scope of our theoretical concerns and the relatively limited domain in which we pursue them. But every truly radical movement, radical both as leftist and as deep-cutting, must reject the antithesis of the technical and the philosophical. It must insist upon seeing its theoretical program realized in particular disciplines and practices if that program is to be realized at all.

Finally, there is the disparity between our intentions and the archaic social form that they assume: a joint endeavor undertaken by discontented, factious intellectuals in the high style of nineteenth-century bourgeois radicalism. For all who participate in such an undertaking, the disharmony between intent and presence must be a cause of rage. We neither suppress this rage nor allow it the last word, because we do not give the last word to the historical world we inhabit. We build with what we have and willingly pay the price for the inconformity of vision to circumstance.

The legal academy that we entered dallied in one more variant of the perennial effort to restate power and preconception as right. In and outside the law schools, most jurists looked with indifference and even disdain upon the legal theorists who, like the rights and principles or the law and economics schools, had volunteered to salvage and recreate the traditions of objectivism and formalism. These same unanxious skeptics, however, also rejected any alternative to the formalist and objectivist view. Having failed to persuade themselves of all but the most equivocal versions of the inherited creed, they nevertheless clung to its implications and brazenly advertised their own failure as the triumph of worldly wisdom over intellectual and political enthusiasm. History they degraded into the retrospective rationalization of events. Philosophy they abased into an inexhaustible compendium of excuses for the truncation of legal analysis. The social sciences they perverted into the source of argumentative ploys with which to give arbitrary though stylized policy discussions the blessing of a specious authority.

When we came, they were like a priesthood that had lost their faith and kept their jobs. They stood in tedious embarrassment before cold altars. But we turned away from those altars and found the mind's opportunity in the heart's revenge.

Index